OXFORD LEGAL HISTORY SERIES

General Editors

PAUL BRAND
JOSHUA GETZLER
AND
DANIEL HULSEBOSCH

Law's Machinery

OXFORD LEGAL HISTORY SERIES

General Editors

Paul Brand, Joshua Getzler, and Daniel Hulsebosch

This series presents original work in legal history from all periods. Contributions to the series analyze diverse legal traditions, including common law; *ius commune*, civilian, and canon law; colonial, imperial, and international law; and customary, religious, and non-Western cultures of law. The series embraces methods ranging from doctrinal and juristic analysis through to every variety of historical, social scientific, and philosophical enquiry. A leading purpose of the series is to investigate how legal ideas and practices operated in larger historical contexts. Our authors trace changes in legal thought and practice and the interactions of law with political and constitutional institutions and wider movements in social, economic, cultural, and intellectual life.

OTHER TITLES IN THIS SERIES

Capitalism Before Corporations
The Morality of Business Associations and the Roots of Commercial Equity and Law
Andreas Televantos

Federal Ground
Governing Property and Violence in the First U.S. Territories
Gregory Ablavsky

The King's Felons
Church, State and Criminal Confinement in Early Tudor England
Margaret McGlynn

Contract Before the Enlightenment
The Ideas of James Dalrymple, Viscount Stair, 1619–1695
Stephen Bogle

English Administrative Law from 1550
Continuity and Change
Paul Craig

Arbitrating Empire
United States Expansion and the Transformation of International Law
Allison Powers

Law's Machinery

Reforming the Craft of Lawyering in America's Industrial Age

KELLEN R. FUNK

Michael E. Patterson Professor of Law, Columbia Law School, USA

OXFORD
UNIVERSITY PRESS

OXFORD
UNIVERSITY PRESS

Oxford University Press is a department of the University of Oxford.
It furthers the University's objective of excellence in research, scholarship,
and education by publishing worldwide. Oxford is a registered trade mark of
Oxford University Press in the UK and in certain other countries.

Published in the United States of America by Oxford University Press
198 Madison Avenue, New York, NY 10016, United States of America.

Library of Congress Cataloging-in-Publication Data
Names: Funk, Kellen R, author.
Title: Law's machinery: reforming the craft of lawyering in America's industrial age / Kellen R. Funk
Description: New York : Oxford University Press, 2025. |
Series: Oxford legal history series | Includes bibliographical references and index.
Identifiers: LCCN 2024032035 (print) | LCCN 2024032036 (ebook) |
ISBN 9780197543931 (hardback) | ISBN 9780197543955 (epub) |
ISBN 9780197543948 (updf) | ISBN 9780197543962 (online)
Subjects: LCSH: Practice of law—United States—History. |
Practice of law—United States—Philosophy. | Lawyers—United States—History. |
Jurisprudence—United States—Methodology.
Classification: LCC KF300 .F87 2025 (print) | LCC KF300 (ebook) |
DDC 347.73/5—dc23/eng/20240716
LC record available at https://lccn.loc.gov/2024032035
LC ebook record available at https://lccn.loc.gov/2024032036

DOI: 10.1093/9780197543962.001.0001

Note to Readers

This publication is designed to provide accurate and authoritative information in regard to the
subject matter covered. It is based upon sources believed to be accurate and reliable and is intended
to be current as of the time it was written. It is sold with the understanding that the publisher is not
engaged in rendering legal, accounting, or other professional services. If legal advice or other expert
assistance is required, the services of a competent professional person should be sought. Also, to
confirm that the information has not been affected or changed by recent developments, traditional
legal research techniques should be used, including checking primary sources where appropriate.

*(Based on the Declaration of Principles jointly adopted by a Committee of the
American Bar Association and a Committee of Publishers and Associations.)*

You may order this or any other Oxford University Press publication
by visiting the Oxford University Press website at www.oup.com.

The manufacturer's authorised representative in the EU for product safety is
Oxford University Press España S.A. of El Parque Empresarial San Fernando
de Henares, Avenida de Castilla, 2 - 28830 Madrid (www.oup.es/en or
product.safety@oup.com). OUP España S.A. also acts as importer into Spain
of products made by the manufacturer.

To John A. Matzko,
for law, and equity

Contents

List of Figures

Guide to the Principal Versions
of the Field Code

Reference	Citation	Description
First Report	*First Report of the Commissioners on Practice and Pleadings: Code of Procedure* (Feb. 29, 1848)	The initial draft code of 391 sections that abolished the forms of action and attorney fee regulations, fused law and equity, and instituted a qualified form of party testimony. The drafters supplied an introduction and commentary interspersed throughout.
Original Code	1848 N.Y. Laws 497–565 (in effect July 1, 1848)	New York's enactment of the regulations of the First Report without commentary and with a few trivial amendments. A code of 391 sections, broadly referred to as "the" Field Code.
Second Report	*Second Report of the Commissioners on Practice and Pleadings: Code of Procedure* (Jan. 29, 1849)	A brief report recommending forty-seven amendments to the Original Code, with commentary supplied by the commissioners.
Amended Code	1849 N.Y. Laws 613–705 (in effect April 11, 1849)	New York's reenactment of a code of 473 sections—the Original Code with most of the recommended amendments of the Second Report incorporated. A highly influential draft in northern and midwestern states.
Third Report	*Third Report of the Commissioners on Practice and Pleadings: Code of Procedure* (Jan. 30, 1849)	A proposed code supplement of 395 sections providing for "special proceedings"—largely former equitable or prerogative writ actions that preserved regulations from New York's 1829 Revised Statutes.
Final Report / Final Draft	*Final Report of the Commissioners on Practice and Pleadings: The Code of Civil Procedure,* in *Documents of the Assembly of the State of New York,* 73d sess., No. 16 (1850), vol. 2.	A complete draft code of 1,884 sections incorporating the Amended Code, the proposed code of the Third Report, and a code of evidence, with extensive commentary by the drafters. Never enacted in New York, the code was reprinted without commentary in *Documents of the Assembly of the State of New York,* 76th sess., No. 55 (1853), vol. 3. The draft was highly influential in states of the Far West.

Acknowledgments

A work about the craft practices of the law would hardly have been possible without those who introduced me to the practices of law and history and their peculiar alchemy in legal history. I especially thank John A. Matzko for directing my undergraduate wanderings into legal history, and for opening his lectures with the fascinating distinction between law and equity and their attempted fusion in the Field Code. To him I gladly dedicate this volume.

Dirk Hartog was a peerless mentor at Princeton, one who I have often said makes his students better versions of themselves rather than just an imitation of himself. He supervised the dissertation study from which this book grew with characteristic insight and grace. Sean Wilentz's seminar on writing political history gave me a first chapter for this study, and then a second, then a third, until it permeated the whole work. Daniel T. Rodgers has never let my frolics and detours into legal technicality blunt his incisive questioning or gracious enthusiasm for probing the corners of these lost worlds of common law and codified practice.

At Yale Law School, John Langbein taught me the deeper nuances of the common law and equitable traditions—including the ways to talk about cases "at" law and "in" equity. He supervised my first writing on the Field Code, and to the extent this research has achieved any precision and clarity, I owe it to the harsh mercy of his red pen. Judith Resnik has been a sympathetic reader and a keen interlocutor, and John Fabian Witt gave this project much material support by hosting weekly lunches to talk about the craft and profession of legal history.

The trial court at the Southern District of Texas will always feel like my home in the law, and Judge Lee H. Rosenthal will always be "my" judge. Although my clerkship with her commenced late in the progress of this study, it transformed and clarified my thinking about legal and equitable remedies, reasoning from wrongs to rights, and carefully threading the procedural needle to make repairs in the fabric of public justice.

Columbia has been a marvelous home for studying New York legal history. Irina Kandarashiva opened the vault of law student and professor notebooks when I arrived and has offered unwavering support for my research into the instruction of code procedure. My legal history colleagues Maeve Glass, Jeremy Kessler, Stephanie McCurry, Christina Duffy Ponsa-Kraus, and Sarah Seo have indulged and celebrated this project along the way, and I have benefited countless times from the questions and comments of Philip Genty, Jamal Greene, Philip Hamburger, Olati Johnson, Kate Judge, Avery Katz, Jim Liebman, Gillian Metzger, Henry Monaghan, Dave Pozen, Dan Richman, Colleen Shanahan, Susan Sturm, and Eric Talley. Sherwin Nam and Sean Kwon rendered exemplary research assistance, and their many colleagues in civil procedure courses patiently endured Field's harangues on pleading at law and in equity.

Daniel Hulsebosch has long been a kindred spirit writing on the history of procedure and practice. It is a delight to now call him editor. His perceptive questions have

improved every part of the book and continue to challenge my thinking about prac-
tical law and its history. Jane C. Manners, Abby Mullen, Justin D. Patrick, and Emily
Prifogle read through significant swaths of the manuscript. John Matzko, Lincoln
Mullen, and Craig Green read the whole thing and patiently edited line by line. I have
enjoyed and tremendously benefited from discussing this project as well as American
cultural and legal history more broadly with them and with Greg Ablavsky, José
Argueta-Funes, Rabia Belt, Maggie Blackhawk, Bob Bone, Kevin Clermont, Kristin
Collins, Andrew Edwards, Laura F. Edwards, Michael Formicelli, Michael Gaffney,
Abbe Gluck, Sally Gordon, Sam Issacharoff, Ben Johnson, Amalia Kessler, Alexandra
Lahav, Naomi Lamoreaux, John Leubsdorf, Troy McKenzie, Bill Nelson, David Noll,
Bill Novak, Farah Peterson, Leslie Ribovich, Brenda Schoolfield, and Sean Vanatta.
Special thanks go to friends, family, and former students who visited their local state
archives and helped retrieve code reports.

Princeton's Program in American Studies and its Center for the Study of Religion
provided support and opportunities to present my work as it developed. Two summers of research into Western codification were funded by the Charles Redd Center
for Western Studies. Additional grants from the American Historical Society and the
Institute for Political History covered the costs of digital text analysis that ran behind
so many of the chapters. Archivists at the Chautauqua County Historical Society,
Alabama State Archives, New York State Archives, Nevada State Library, Wisconsin
State Archives, New York County Clerk's Office, New York City Municipal Archives,
Yale University Archives, and the Church History Library of the Church of Latter-
Day Saints helped to track down obscure legal materials and often assisted with their
digitization.

The American Society for Legal History (ASLH) does an outstanding job orienting
graduate students to the craft of legal history. I benefited tremendously from having a
collegial and welcoming venue to present my work, both at the annual meetings and
at the legal history boot camp known as the Hurst Institute, where Barbara Young
Welke and a cadre of lifelong comrades helped me figure out the organization of this
study. The ASLH's Cromwell research fellowship supplied significant funding at the
earliest stages. Likewise, the Civil Procedure Workshop, just in its infancy when this
project began, has become one of the most welcoming venues for bringing together
senior scholars and young colleagues eager to try out new ideas in the study of civil
procedure. The reception of the early chapters of this study at the workshop gave fresh
life to the project.

Lincoln Mullen did brilliant work guiding me through the literature on digital text
analysis and constructing elegant software to analyze the Field Code. More than that,
Lincoln was the gravitational force that drew me from law into history during our undergraduate days. He is in every way except blood an older brother whom I can never
surpass but hope to impress.

My mother, Vickie Offner, is the consummate professional. She raised three children on her own in rural New Mexico while becoming the first in our family to graduate from college and grad school, and she recently concluded her long career as an
educator. It is her I thank and blame for giving me the aspiration to become a professional in my own field. Her dining room table has been my writing desk through law

school, clerkships, the commencement of my teaching career, and now the completion of this manuscript.

My deepest gratitude goes to Anna Beth Funk. We married six months before I applied to law school, having no idea where these roads would lead. That they have led to happiness is truly thanks to her. It is difficult to even remember a time when Nellie, Kory, and Augie weren't toddling around during this project, but the records say that it was so. I have learned to write better and edit more quickly with them here, and above all to truly enjoy the time not writing.

Introduction

"You'll have to get a lawyer, and I expect there'll be smart of fuss about it
before it's over.... I've no doubt the old man will get tired of it before you
do; but, after all, law is the most uncertain thing in the world."
— Albion Tourgée, *Bricks Without Straw* (1880)

I

In the wake of the Civil War, the young New York-educated lawyer Albion Tourgée
traveled to the South with his wife and settled in Greensboro, North Carolina. The
Tourgées were quintessential "carpetbaggers"—staunchly abolitionist northerners
migrating to the war-torn South to improve their health and fortunes while educating
freedmen and white southerners alike about the operations of free labor. Tourgée had
been seriously wounded in the opening battle of the war, and at the time of their relocation, the Tourgées' wealth may indeed have fit into a carpetbag. Nevertheless, in the
depressed economy of North Carolina the two quickly secured the loans necessary to
establish their homestead.[1]

As a lawyer, legislator, and judge in North Carolina, Tourgée developed a reputation as a fierce opponent of the Ku Klux Klan in an especially Klan-infested district, and he would go on to great eminence as an early civil rights lawyer. At the end
of the century, Tourgée represented Homer Plessy at the U.S. Supreme Court in the
unavailing challenge to the separate-but-equal doctrine. Swaying only John Marshall
Harlan's dissent at the time, Tourgée's advocacy eventually became a cornerstone in
modern civil rights doctrine.[2] But in his own lifetime, Tourgée's most widely recognized contribution to civil and racial equality stemmed from his bestselling com-
panion novels *A Fool's Errand* and *Bricks Without Straw*.[3]

---

[1] Among early biographies of Tourgée, Otto Olsen's is particularly helpful on Tourgée's career as a legislator before his more famous turn as a judge and novelist. Otto Olsen, *Carpetbagger's Crusade: The Life
of Albion Winegar Tourgée* (Johns Hopkins University Press, 1965). Interest in Tourgée's career has been
reviving among scholars of Reconstruction. See, for instance, David W. Blight, *Race and Reunion: The Civil
War in American Memory* (Belknap Press, 2001), 85–97, 217–21; Mark Elliott, *Color-Blind Justice: Albion
Tourgée and the Quest for Racial Equality from the Civil War to* Plessy v. Ferguson (Oxford University
Press, 2006).

[2] See Elliott, *Color-Blind Justice*, 231–95.

[3] Albion W. Tourgée, *A Fool's Errand: By One of the Fools* (1879); Albion W. Tourgée, *Bricks Without
Straw* (1880). For modern critical editions, see John Hope Franklin, ed., *A Fool's Errand*, by Albion
W. Tourgée (Belknap Press, 1961); Carolyn L. Karcher, ed., *Bricks Without Straw*, by Albion W. Tourgée
(Duke University Press, 2009).

Law's Machinery. Kellen R. Funk, Oxford University Press. © Kellen R. Funk 2025. DOI: 10.1093/9780197543962.003.0001

Less well-known today, Tourgée's novels in the 1880s were viewed as postbellum sequels of sorts to Harriet Beecher Stowe's *Uncle Tom's Cabin*, circulating as widely and generating nearly as much controversy. The novels provided a semi-autobiographical account of Tourgée's sojourn in the Reconstruction South, chronicling southern resistance to federal authority and the struggle of freedmen to turn the paper promises of the Reconstruction Amendments into actual rights. The novels featured Klan violence, of course, but they also documented ways in which white southerners used fully legal processes to make freedmen feel the weight of their second-class citizenship in the postbellum order.

In *Bricks Without Straw*, just after freedmen Nimbus and Eliab Hill acquire their own land and hire their fellow freedmen as workers, a white former master sues them for $1,000 for enticing away his workers. Translating the formal language of the summons, the sheriff explains to Nimbus that he is called to court by "a civil action—an action under the code, as they call it, since you Radicals tinkered over the law." Under this civil action, Nimbus will have "to come and answer old man Granville's complaint, and after that you will have a trial." Nimbus, recognizing the civil action as of a piece with Klan violence, vows to resist both: "I ain't ter be druv off wid lawsuits ner Ku Kluckers. I'se jest a gwine ter git a lawyer an' fight it out, dat I am." The sheriff doubts that former master Granville can get a real remedy, and "no doubt the old man will get tired of it before you do," but the final legal remedy here is not the point: "You'll have to get a lawyer, and I expect there'll be smart of fuss about it before it's over." Hiring a lawyer, the sheriff indicates, will turn Nimbus's act of resistance into Granville's means of oppression. The freedman will have to spend scarce capital on legal representation, defending a meritless suit that may yet turn against him, for "after all, law is the most uncertain thing in the world."[4]

Tourgée placed in the sheriff's mouth words that had often been directed at him, for he was the chief Radical who had "tinkered over the law" with a code that introduced this new legal device known as the civil action. In the early days of Radical Republicanism in North Carolina, Tourgée had joined a commission to draft a new code of laws for the state that would modernize the state's civil institutions, or at least would conform them to the self-proclaimed modernity of Tourgée's native New York. Tourgée's opponents recognized the code of practice as a centerpiece of Radical rule. "The grandest mistake in our existing Constitution, and that which, of itself, would warrant the call of a Convention to remedy it, is the change it has made in our Judicial system," two Democratic senators wrote in a local paper, mourning that the "splendid temple in which such men as Gaston and Ruffin ministered as high priests, is in ruins. The people remember and long for it again, like the captive Jews longed for their ruined sanctuary. Shall it not be rebuilt?"[5]

---

[4] Tourgée, *Bricks Without Straw*, 266–73.
[5] *Wilmington Journal*, Feb. 19, 1870. The senators were referring to Thomas Ruffin and William Gaston, two Supreme Court Justices who dominated the North Carolina bench during their long tenure (1829–1858). Between them, they wrote two of the most influential opinions on the law of slavery, Ruffin on the absolute power of slaveholders in State v. Mann, 13 N.C. 263 (1829), Gaston on preserving criminal liability for masters and overseers who mistreated slaves in State v. Will, 18 N.C. 121 (1834). See Alfred L. Brophy, "The Nat Turner Trials," 91 *North Carolina Law Review* 1817 (2013).

Joining Tourgée on the commission was Victor Barringer, scion of a Democratic planter family in Concord. Barringer, too, had been wounded in the first battle of the Civil War—but fighting on the opposite side of Tourgée. The son of a German immigrant who preferred railroad construction to slaveholding, Barringer had a mildly reformist disposition that kept him from clashing with Tourgée as much as might be expected, but few of Barringer's party tolerated the northern interloper so well. In a biography of Victor, Barringer's granddaughter Anna repeated charges against Tourgée that were common in newspapers of the 1870s. "Since the Carpet-baggers controlled" the commission, "there was a radical departure from the North Carolina Law as it had been written in the wisdom of its judges and the lives of its people, since the American Revolution. The laws of New York were a major influence." But what exactly was exchanged when the civil procedure of New York was foisted on North Carolina? Anna Barringer had little to offer concretely, generalizing that "many of the best features of the old were omitted and much of the new utterly foreign to the customs and ideas of the State." She concluded weakly that "in the light of today, much does not seem so radical."[6]

This study seeks to recapture what it was about a New York procedure code that originally seemed so radical, so politically and socially disruptive, in the mid-nineteenth-century United States. A staple first-year course in modern legal education, civil procedure is, by definition, one of the more technical departments of the law. For procedure prescribes technique itself: the processes whereby courts gain jurisdiction over a dispute, lawyers access the bar, litigants summon one another to court and demand a remedy, juries weigh the proofs, and sheriffs execute a judgment. One might be excused for thinking of procedure as a dry subject of interest only to specialists, but as we can discern from these hints from Tourgée's southern career, civil procedure once occupied a significant part of the public square. In the United States, procedure was headline news, the subject of bestselling novels, daily editorials, and constitutional conventions. Within its rules, lawyers and laymen alike believed that important policies of the day would be advanced or hindered. Freedmen might find deliverance or reenslavement in the rules of procedure; depressed economies might recover or collapse; civilization itself, some said, might rise or fall.

II

For civil procedure to accomplish any of these things, it first had to be invented as a field. As Amalia Kessler has recently noted, "That the category of procedure did not exist in any meaningful way before the mid-nineteenth century is difficult to conceive—and perhaps for this reason has received no scholarly attention."[7] While academic proceduralists like to argue that "process" and "law" form a spectrum rather

---

[6] Anna Barringer, "The First American Judge in Egypt," 198 (manuscript biography of Victor C. Barringer), Barringer Family Papers, University of Virginia Library Special Collections.

[7] Amalia D. Kessler, *Inventing American Exceptionalism: The Origins of Adversarial Legal Culture, 1800–1877* (Yale University Press, 2017), 11.

than a dichotomy, the distinction between procedure and "real" law is so deeply ingrained in modern legal thought that it appears too natural to seriously question.[8] Yet, as Kessler argues, that distinction is surprisingly recent. Procedure was an "unknown entity" until the New York code "recognized and gave content to the conception."[9] Before then, lawyers spoke not of procedure but of "pleading," not of legal rights but of legal writs courts used to award remedies.[10]

This book tells a story of legal practice in the United States as it underwent this transformation from "pleading" to "procedure," from an all-encompassing law of practice to a segmented law of substantive right and procedural remedy that remains familiar in American courts and law schools today. Its central focus is the New York Code of Procedure, known colloquially as the Field Code after its chief drafter, the Manhattan trial lawyer David Dudley Field II. "The" Field Code was not a single statute but rather a series of drafts—some enacted in New York, some not—that went on to influence or be directly copied by some thirty other jurisdictions in the nineteenth-century United States.[11]

What Field and his imitators achieved was the creation of a distinctively lawyerly code, written and enacted by lawyers and written for and addressed to the trial bar. It was a lawyer's code not only in the way it addressed professional interests but in the way it assumed them. As a code, it was geared toward easing the burden of practicing lawyers by giving them a single volume to consult rather than the "vast irregular mass" of case law on pleading.[12] It advanced professional interests most notably by eliminating the public regulation of fees and thereby ushering lawyers into an age of market capitalism. In addition to control over their compensation, the code effectively gave lawyers control over a host of proceedings, from the mode of trial to the investigation of facts to the election of remedies and the speed of their enforcement. But most of all, the code was a lawyer's code for what it did not say. Despite its attempt at comprehensiveness, the massive code neglected to define the key terms of its most fundamental requirements for legal practice, leaving it to the lawyers to fill the gaps with inherited habits of thought and practice. Quite contrary to Field's intentions, the lawyers' code preserved much of the common law tradition even as it spurred the gradual transformation of the law from practice into a novel field known as "procedure."[13]

---

[8] See, e.g., John Hart Ely, "The Irrepressible Myth of Erie," 87 *Harvard Law Review* 693 (1974). See also Jay Tidmarsh, "Procedure, Substance, and *Erie*," 64 *Vanderbilt Law Review* 877 (2011) (reviewing the post-Ely literature).

[9] Kessler, *Inventing American Exceptionalism*, 10.

[10] See Daniel J. Hulsebosch, "Writs to Rights: 'Navigability' and the Transformation of the Common Law in the Nineteenth Century," 23 *Cardozo Law Review* 1049 (2002), 1050–55.

[11] For a guide to the chronology of the multiple drafts and reports that made up "the" Field Code, see Mildred V. Coe & Lewis W. Morse, "Chronology of the Development of the David Dudley Field Code," 27 *Cornell Law Review* 238 (1942).

[12] David Dudley Field, *Legal Reform: An Address to the Graduating Class of the Law School of the University of Albany* (1855), 21.

[13] To be sure, a conceptual distinction between substantive and procedural law had some life before the Field Code. French law arguably distinguished a domain of procedural law as early as 1667, but as the leading study of continental procedure asserts, "it is not too bold a statement to say that . . . civil procedure in Continental Europe starts with the 1806 French Code of Civil Procedure." C.H. van Rhee, "Introduction," in C.H. van Rhee, ed., *European Traditions in Civil Procedure* (Intersentia, 2005), 5. In America, Napoleon's codes, including the procedure code, supplied the basis for codifications in Louisiana in 1808 and 1825. See

At the time Napoleon promulgated a *code de procédure civile* in France, the Anglo-American common law had no word for procedure, though it had much to say about "practice and pleading."[14] By learning practice and pleading, a law student became acquainted with the medieval writ system, and through the writs he learned what rights could be vindicated and in what manner. As one classic explanation of the early forms of action put it, "substantive law" was "secreted in the interstices of procedure," so much so that one blended seamlessly into the other.[15] A wrong required a remedy; a remedy was obtained by a writ; each writ had a distinct set of processes to follow and requests to make. But wrong, remedy, and writ were tightly bound up in a practical legal logic that did not neatly divide into an abstract proposition about "rights" and the merely "technical" processes for complaining about a violation of one's rights.

Trying to describe English common law scientifically, William Blackstone in his famed *Commentaries* attempted to use a continental structure, but instead of expounding the law of Persons, Things, and Actions, the closest analogs Blackstone could come up with were Persons, Things, and Wrongs (Private and Public). It was left to Blackstone's antagonist, Jeremy Bentham, to develop a vocabulary of "substantive" law as distinguished from "adjective," or procedural, law.[16]

But it was one thing to claim a distinction between a law of private rights and a law of procedure and quite another to demonstrate it. That work of division is what the Field Code and its imitators set out to do for law in the United States. By taking apart the common law writ system and redescribing Anglo-American practice in terms of "a civil action" consisting of complaints and answers, trials and remedies, the codes created legal procedure by drawing lines between substance and form among their thousands of detailed regulations.[17]

If that project sounds rather mundane and mechanical, that was precisely the codifiers' aim. Over and over again, in commentary justifying codification or explaining the codes, in treatises gathering judicial interpretations of the codes, in educational literature training a new generation in the code system, codifiers repeatedly returned to one central metaphor for their reforms, the figure of the *machine*. Procedure, codifiers insisted, was the "mere machinery" of the law, as separable and independent from the "real law" as the artisan's tools were from the natural materials on which he worked.

In the age of American industrialization, interest in and talk about machines were everywhere. Leo Marx's classic study *The Machine in the Garden* traced through American literature themes of novel industrial technologies crashing up against

---

John W. Cairns, *Codification, Transplants and History: Law Reform in Louisiana (1808) and Quebec (1866)* (Talbot, 2015).

[14] See, e.g., Joseph R. Swan, *The Practice in Civil Actions and Proceedings at Law and Precedents in Pleading* (I.N. Whiting, 1845); Robert Edmund Daniell, *Pleading and Practice of the High Court of Chancery* (Little Brown, 1st American ed., 1846); Henry Whittaker, *Practice and Pleading under the Codes* (E.O. Jenkins, 1852).

[15] Sir Henry Summer Maine, *On Early Law and Custom* (London, 1890), 389.

[16] See Michael Lobban, *The Common Law and English Jurisprudence 1760–1850* (Clarendon Press, 1991), 33–46; David Lieberman, *The Province of Legislation Determined: Legal Theory in Eighteenth-century Britain* (Cambridge University Press, 1989), 219–40.

[17] For the key drafts of the code defining a civil action in New York, see the Guide at the beginning of this volume.

pastoral ideals of accommodation to nature in the quest to build up national wealth and prosperity. While, in time, "contempt for the machine became a stock literary attitude," American writers at first greeted the new age of mechanized technology with exhilaration.[18] So did the code-writing lawyers. The depiction of procedure as law's machinery gave codifiers a useful two-sided argument they deployed constantly in the latter half of the nineteenth century. As a neutral, mechanical supplement to the real, or "substantive" law, procedure was both inoffensive enough for legislative reform yet technical enough that lawyerly experts had to control it. On the one hand, procedure was a field open to experimentation and wide-ranging reform precisely because it could not affect the underlying law of substantive rights and relations between property and people. And yet, on the other hand, the experiment could not be performed by just any amateur legislator. Law's machinery was too delicate to trust to the hands of the inexperienced, making lawyers the ideal, indeed the only available, machinists. The first five chapters of this volume offer a chronological narrative of how these arguments succeeded—or were contested—as lawyers pressed for codification both in Field's home state of New York and around the growing nation.

As Leo Marx observed generally of the *belle lettres* in America, the machine did not have an easy entrance into the garden. Lines between the artificial and the natural, the mechanical and the organic, were often difficult to maintain. Technical procedure was to be a field only lawyers could love. But because American procedure codes classified remedies as procedural, the domain of procedure continued to expand into substantive domains and threatened to swallow the law itself. That classification was defensible as a matter of common law tradition since the writs of pleading had been so closely bound to the remedies courts could grant. But it made the lawyers' code distinctive, and distinctively difficult to fit with their theory of procedure's relative superficiality and unimportance. Tourgée's experiences in North Carolina and the many other political squabbles recounted in this study belied the codifiers' pretensions that a "mere" procedure code of remedial law could be insulated from matters of substantive policy.

The political volatility of procedure becomes especially clear when one breaks down the machine to examine the five key areas of practice that codifiers from New York to the Carolinas identified as the foundation of the "reformed American procedure": the abolition of the common law forms of action and their replacement with "fact pleading"; the authorization to allow parties to take the oath and testify in their own cases; the empowerment of lawyers to investigate the facts of a case before trial; the fusion of the formerly separate institutions and traditions of law and equity; and the privatization of lawyer fees. None of these reforms were viewed as superficial or merely procedural at the time, either inside or outside the legal profession. Each of these foundational reforms, and the political and legal contests that swirled around them, is the subject of a separate chapter in the second half of this volume. Because these reforms were passed in the form of a code, central to all these reforms were questions about the nature of law and legislation and whether nature itself imposed

---

[18] Leo Marx, *The Machine in the Garden: Technology and the Pastoral Ideal in America* (Oxford University Press, 1964), 146–50; see also John Lardas Modern, *Secularism in Antebellum America: With Reference to Ghosts, Protestant Subcultures, Machines, and Their Metaphors* (Chicago University Press, 2011).

boundaries on the machine the lawyers had constructed. Whereas Part I offers a political and intellectual history of the machine, Part II takes a thematic approach, studying discrete legal practices as law's machinery ran up against barriers claimed to be
natural, practices that had been long-cultivated and inherited, like a garden.

III

Codification is, as Lawrence Friedman has written, "one of the set pieces of American
legal history." [19] Law reformers advocated for codification of the common law from
the earliest days of the Republic through the Gilded Age, from Massachusetts to South
Carolina. Efforts ranged from mere compilations of existing statutes to attempts at
writing a full European-style code meant to be an entirely comprehensive and systematic statement of the law. At a basic level, codification proposed that legislation
ought to be the sole source of law. Law was to be made by democratically responsible
legislators in terse, unambiguous statements, not discovered through application and
analogy in particular cases by judges. Debates over codification thus ranged from the
metaphysics of law to political theories of institutional competency and the separation of powers. [20]

At an even more basic level, codification was itself a technology, one deployed to
organize knowledge and authority in an era of legal practice that was becoming increasingly complex as it became increasingly mechanized. Publication of case reports
exploded in the early nineteenth century as printers used modern methods to send
transcriptions of judicial opinions around the globe. By the 1840s, enterprising practitioners had collated case law and oral traditions of practice into dozens of market-
able treatises, but these remained works of private opinion—no court was bound to
agree with the treatise writers as to the weight, relevance, or proper interpretation
of a legal statement. [21] The common law was accordingly known as "unwritten law,"
despite the proliferation of published texts, because the common law was not precisely determined until a particular case demanded resolution. Statutes, on the other
hand, were "written law," prescribing or reforming the rules even before a case put
the precise question in issue. Within the realm of written law, codes were the ultimate
statutes. [22]

The pure form of codification as a complete repudiation of the unwritten common
law and as a total restraint on the reasoned decision-making of judges came to
America in the proposals of Jeremy Bentham and especially in the advocacy of the
Irish exile and renowned litigator William Sampson. Field admired both Bentham
and Sampson, but held more modest hopes for codification. Field expected judges to
continue to issue reasoned opinions that analogized to and built up legal precedents

---

[19] Lawrence M. Friedman, *A History of American Law* (Simon & Schuster, 3d ed., 2005), 302.

[20] Perry Miller, ed., *The Legal Mind in America: From Independence to the Civil War* (Doubleday, 1962).

[21] For the rise of treatises in America generally, see Angela Fernandez & Markus D. Dubber, *Law Books in Action: Essays on the Anglo-American Legal Treatise* (Hart, 2012).

[22] Or, to use a term from contemporary analysis, "super statutes." William N. Eskridge Jr. & John Ferejohn, *A Republic of Statutes: The New American Constitution* (Yale University Press, 2010). See also Lieberman, *The Province of Legislation Determined.*

by accretion, but as a practitioner who believed his craft was being inundated by ever more hopelessly unorganized precedents, Field's aim for codification was to gather all the law on a subject into one authoritative volume and thus ease the research burdens of lawyers. That codification would have to be periodically repeated seemed no short-coming to Field.

Thus, not only was "the" Field Code a set of multiple drafts in New York, then a set of multiple codes enacted across the nation, it was also a set of reenactments and recodifications, usually about once per decade in every state that adopted the code. A major source for this study is, of course, the code itself, including its iterations that migrated to thirty different jurisdictions and were instantiated in multiple drafts and reenactments. The magnitude of that corpus presents a unique historical challenge, one that rewards an unconventional approach. The Field Code was the longest pro-posed statute of its time in American history, and its imitators were usually the longest regulations on the books of their respective jurisdictions until the legislation of the Progressive Era. The shortest version of the New York code was nearly 400 sections; the final draft was 1,885 sections spanning 800 pages. Derivative procedure codes averaged nearly 750 sections in 200 pages. Reenactments across the thirty code juris-dictions, as well as comparisons to non-Fieldian codes from other states, brings an adequately analytic project up to about 180,000 distinct rules and regulations spread across 50,000 pages.

As codes were a new technology to manage ever-increasing lines of published prec-edent, so this study relies on new technologies to track the history of the American procedure codes. Techniques from the digital humanities have empowered a variety of approaches to the "distant reading" of large networks of texts and authors.[23] This study makes use of several of those techniques, from citation detection and network analysis to stylometry and algorithmic clustering. So as not to clutter the narrative or sidetrack readers more interested in the history than the digital, discussion of meth-odology is generally left to the notes or online guides.[24] Suffice it to say here that from the start of this study, digital analysis directed much of the archival research that even-tually spanned thousands of newspapers, novels, cases, treatises, tracts, and legislative materials housed in dozens of state archives. This introduction itself is one product of this reciprocal interpretive method. Digital analysis of the codes highlighted Reconstruction North Carolina as a promising site for future study, a study that then brought me to Albion Tourgée, his novels, and Anna Barringer's biography of her cod-ifier grandfather.

---

[23] See Lisa Samuels & Jerome McGann, *Deformance and Interpretation*, 30 *New Literary History* 25 (1999); Stephen Ramsay, *Reading Machines: Toward an Algorithmic Criticism* (University of Illinois Press, 2011), ch. 3. Gathering the corpus of codes was also aided by digitization efforts that have made the contents of academic libraries—which hold most of the session laws for most of the fifty states—publicly available in Google Books or the Hathi Trust. Since the commencement of this project, the subscription database HeinOnline has also made significant strides toward a comprehensive digital collection of state legislative materials. These digitization efforts are not without their own political valence. See Lara Putnam, "The Transnational and the Text-Searchable: Digitized Sources and the Shadows They Cast," 121 *American Historical Review* 377 (2016), 399–400. The American South, in particular, is extremely underrepresented in digital archives.

[24] Kellen Funk & Lincoln A. Mullen, "The Spine of American Law: Digital Text Analysis and U.S. Legal Practice," 123 *American Historical Review* 132 (2018), https://legalmodernism.org.

IV

It bears repeating that this study is about a code and legal practices before and after it. It is not primarily a study of the man who wrote the code, even if he necessarily appears everywhere throughout it. The numerous works on the Field Code tend to fall into one of two tracks. The first is quasi-biography, in which studies of the code seek to illuminate its reforms, especially the concept of "fact pleading," from the life and psychology of David Dudley Field.[25] In the second track, works seek to excavate the practices and theories surrounding one or another aspect of codified practice on its own, say fact pleading,[26] or cost shifting,[27] or witness examinations.[28]

The trouble with both tracks is that neither provides the right scale to understand practice as such. The biographies treat the procedure code as one constellation in the broader galaxy of Field's work. But the other literature takes one segment of the code and treats it as a whole universe. We commonly speak of "the legal system." Yet it is increasingly rare for legal historians these days to treat legal practice as a system, self-contained yet constantly invaded by external forces, and with many internal moving and interlocking parts. Without that sense of system, we can easily miss how changes to one practice were, in fact, guided by or made in response to another seemingly unrelated practice elsewhere in the system.[29] As it turns out, fact pleading and fee-shifting were not discrete practices under the Field Code. Both were centrally concerned with a lawyer's daily work, how that work should be valued and monetized,

---

[25] E.g., Stephen N. Subrin, "David Dudley Field and the Field Code: A Historical Analysis of an Earlier Procedural Vision," 6 *Law & History Review* 311 (1988); J. Newton Fiero, "David Dudley Field and His Work," 51 *Albany Law Journal* 39 (1895). In some works of this kind the procedure code can at most take up a chapter or two since Field's life and legal practice spanned so many other codifications and reform (or anti-reform) efforts. See, e.g., Daun Van Ee, *David Dudley Field and the Reconstruction of the Law* (Garland Press, 1986); Michael Joseph Hobor, The Form of the Law: David Dudley Field and the Codification Movement in New York, 1839–1888 (Ph.D. dissertation, University of Chicago, 1975).

[26] William P. LaPiana, "Just the Facts: The Field Code and the Case Method," 36 *New York Law School Law Review* 287 (1991); Robert G. Bone, "Mapping the Boundaries of a Dispute: Conceptions of Ideal Lawsuit Structure from the Field Code to the Federal Rules," 89 *Columbia Law Review* 1 (1989).

[27] John Leubsdorf, "Toward a History of the American Rule on Attorney Fee Recovery," 47 *Law & Contemporary Problems* 9 (1984); Peter Karsten, "Enabling the Poor to Have Their Day in Court: The Sanctioning of Contingency Fee Contracts, a History to 1940," 47 *DePaul Law Review* 231 (1998).

[28] Amalia D. Kessler, "Our Inquisitorial Tradition: Equity Procedure, Due Process, and the Search for an Alternative to the Adversarial," 90 *Cornell Law Review* 1181 (2005).

[29] I don't mean by this statement to resolve the debate between "internalist" and "externalist" approaches to legal history. See the discussion in Kessler, *Inventing American Exceptionalism*, 8–13. For the most part, this account agrees with the critique that internalists—those who see legal history as primarily driven forward by the unfolding of legal logics, for legal institutional reasons—have a hard time of explaining why a certain legal logic unfolds at the precise time and place that it does historically. See, e.g., James Q. Whitman, "The Transition to Modernity," in Markus D. Dubber & Tatjana Hörnle, eds., *The Oxford Handbook of Criminal Law* (Oxford University Press, 2014), 91–94. But it does not go as far as Lawrence Friedman's claim that law is entirely "relative and molded by economy and society," with no "kingdom unto itself, not as a set of rules and concepts, not as the province of lawyers alone, but a mirror of society." Lawrence M. Friedman, *A History of American Law* (Simon & Schuster, 1st ed., 1973), 15–16. Instead, and despite its almost oxymoronic quality, Sally Falk Moore's concept of law as a "semi-autonomous" domain is this project's polestar, with law neither a fully autonomous totalizing discourse (despite its ambitions and pretensions to be such) nor a total mirror reflecting only external forces. Sally Falk Moore, "Law and Social Change: The Semi-Autonomous Social Field as an Appropriate Subject of Study," 7 *Law & Society Review* 719 (1973).

and what parts of that work the public had a right to regulate. The two practices have to be understood together before either can really make sense on its own.

That said, because he was one of the leading thinkers writing on the question of the lawyer's value and the lawyer's craft, it is useful to get some sense of who the archetypal codifier of procedure was up front. Though generally unknown today, the man who drafted much of the New York code was a fascinating figure of American history. The life of David Dudley Field spanned nearly the entire nineteenth century and intersected with a number of its more famous events. The Fields rivaled the Adams family in number of talented members and public servants across the generations. David's younger brother Cyrus laid the transatlantic cable that first allowed instantaneous communication between continents. Another brother, Stephen, became one of the more transformative justices of the U.S. Supreme Court. Field's sister became one of the first American missionaries to Turkey. Her son, David Brewer, joined his uncle Stephen on the Supreme Court. Among David Dudley's other siblings (eight total) were prominent lawyers, engineers, and clergymen.[30]

No one person in America—or in the world, perhaps—produced as much original legislation in his lifetime as David Dudley Field. By the time of his death in 1894, Field had drafted a penal code, civil code, and political (constitutional) code, as well as codes of criminal and civil procedure, of evidence, and even of international law (in two volumes). For such a prolific legislator, the striking feature of Field's career is that he never won a regular election to legislative office. He ran unsuccessfully for the New York Assembly in 1841 and for the state constitutional convention in 1846. He briefly served in the nation's Forty-Fourth Congress, but only as a vacancy appointment.[31]

In his biography of his brother, Henry Martyn Field explained David Dudley's lack of success at the polls as resulting from his never having precisely the right political convictions at the right time and place. An ardent Democrat in a Democratic ward, Field nevertheless alienated many Catholics by opposing state funding for parochial schools on the (very Protestant) ground of "separation of church and state." An antislavery man, Field joined a vocal minority of New York Democrats in opposing war with Mexico on the ground that it would expand the territory of slave states. The party of Polk thus denied Field election to the state convention in 1846. Over the next three decades, Field switched parties four times in the search for a political home that best supported his free market and free labor principles. He joined the Free Soil revolt from the Democratic Party in 1848, became a Republican in the 1850s and a Liberal Republican in the 1870s, and finally rejoined the Democracy after the end of Reconstruction.[32]

---

[30] Field's personal papers, such as they are (most were burned), are found in the collection of Field's son-in-law, Sir Anthony Musgrave, Duke University Library Special Collections. On Field's family, see the biography by his layman (in the legal sense) brother, Henry M. Field, *The Life of David Dudley Field* (Charles Scribner's Sons, 1898).

[31] The congressional vacancy was caused by Smith Ely Jr.'s resignation to become the mayor of New York. As a formality, the vacancy was filled by popular vote, Field winning 5,000 votes of the nearly 6,500 cast, but most newspapers announced Field's appointment as soon as he had been nominated as the choice of Samuel Tilden and the assembly Democrats. *New York Herald*, Dec. 31, 1876; *New York Tribune*, Jan. 3, 1877.

[32] Field, *Life of David Dudley Field*, 46, 110–13.

While his forays into electoral politics proved ineffectual, Field thrived as a lawyer—both in the office and in the courtroom. Field may have been the first American lawyer to make a million dollars from a single representation. Saying he "earned" it might put it too strongly, for it is not clear that Field's forensic skills were any sharper than the average lawyer's. A survey of Field's reported cases found that he lost more than he won, and most accounts portray Field as a humorless and in-temperate oral advocate, easily lured into counterproductive outbursts when he felt his honor impugned.[33] Instead, Field's genius seems to have been of the out-of-court tactical sort. Field excelled at moving through New York's high society, connecting the right people to broker deals or settlements and to foster relationships. Herman Melville's introduction to Nathaniel Hawthorne, Cyrus's financial backing from Peter Cooper, and John C. Frémont's offloading of troublesome land litigation before his presidential nomination—all these lines ran through David Dudley Field's drawing room.[34]

Indeed, Field's chief political influence was not as a public legislator but as a back-room mediator. Field was one of the New Yorkers who helped to swing the 1860 Republican nomination to Abraham Lincoln against William Seward, a prominent New York Whig and one of Field's arch-rivals from his Democratic days. Sixteen years later, after bitterly fighting to take down Field's client William "Boss" Tweed in New York, the Democratic reformer Samuel Tilden also hired Field as his own counsel to broker the deal that resolved the disputed presidential election of 1876 between Tilden and Rutherford B. Hayes. Historians still do not know the exact negotiated compromises through which Lincoln and Hayes became presidents while Seward and Tilden did not. But we do know that, like a famous New York lawyer before him, Field was in the room where it happened.[35]

For some, Field's "switching sides" to represent Tilden proved the mercenary quality of his lawyering—after voting for Hayes, Field happily followed a paycheck to try to deprive Hayes of the presidency. But for others, Field's representation of Tilden enhanced his reputation and ennobled him—here was a man who voted for Hayes but followed his principles against his political interests when he saw that Tilden had the stronger legal right. The same debate swirled around Field's Gilded Age represen-tations when Jim Fisk, Jay Gould, and Boss Tweed became his clients. Again, Field's oral arguments often proved unavailing—the robber barons "lost" most of the claims litigated by Field. But the time and expense consumed in litigation and the many pro-cedural roadblocks Field threw in the path of his opponents touched off a major phase in America's long-running debate about the dual role of the lawyer as both a public servant and a private zealot for his client.[36]

---

[33] See Van Ee, *David Dudley Field*, 57–112, 156–61.

[34] Bernard A. Drew, *Literary Luminaries of the Berkshires: From Herman Melville to Patricia Highsmith* (Arcadia, 2015), 41–44; John Steele Gordon, *A Thread Across the Ocean: The Heroic Story of the Transatlantic Cable* (Bloomsbury, 2002), 40–42; Van Ee, *David Dudley Field*, 156–58.

[35] Philip J. Bergan, "David Dudley Field: A Lawyer's Life," in *The Fields and the Law* (Federal Bar Council, 1986), 34–35. Lin-Manuel Miranda, *Hamilton: An American Musical* (2015).

[36] Michael Schudson, "Public, Private, and Professional Lives: The Correspondence of David Dudley Field and Samuel Bowles," 21 *American Journal of Legal History* 191 (1977).

The modern American bar association traces its origins to this debate. Originally formed to censure Field and reign in his mercenary lawyering, the Association of the Bar of the City of New York ended up excusing him and adopting the zealous-advocate model as their professional ideal. The organization of the ABCNY then became a model for the national American Bar Association founded in New York in 1878.[37] By the ABA's tenth anniversary, Field had been elected its president. Still, the dual view of Field as grasping soldier of fortune and consummate professional would dog him to the end of his life, and biographers since have rarely succeeded at holding the two sides of the mercenary and the statesman together.[38]

Perhaps the best way to get a handle on Field's multifaceted career, personality, and politics is to think of him as a quintessential nineteenth-century American liberal. Field adamantly opposed slavery in principle and the Slave Power in politics, but he was almost equally opposed to the growth of statist institutions and especially of federal power.[39] After helping to found the Republican Party on an explicitly antislavery platform, Field became one of the most effective opponents of Republican rule in Reconstruction. Field argued several of the signature Reconstruction cases before the Supreme Court, including *Cruikshank*, the case limiting the reach of the Reconstruction Amendments to "state action" only. This time, Field succeeded in every argument he made before the high Court, occasionally seeing his brief copied into majority opinions written or joined by his brother Stephen.[40] After striking significant blows against federal power in his Supreme Court advocacy, Field turned his attention to fighting the "agrarian" impulses of a rising populism. Free Labor and Free Men—but not Free Land—was the core ideology of Field.[41]

In this liberal legal orientation, Field was typical of the American codifiers. Political affiliations spanned the spectrum, but nearly all were antislavery unionists in the early or midpoint of their legal careers. Judges were plentiful, but by far the most common experience of code commissioners was trial lawyering. Often that experience came through some kind of federal appointment to the territories, meaning the codifiers

---

[37] See George Martin, *Causes and Conflicts: The Centennial History of the Association of the Bar of the City of New York, 1870–1970* (Fordham University Press, 1997); John A. Matzko, "'The Best Men of the Bar': The Founding of the American Bar Association," in Gerald W. Gawalt, ed., *The New High Priests: Lawyers in Post-Civil War America* (Greenwood Press, 1984), 75–96.

[38] Henry M. Field, for instance, never even mentions his brother's corporate clients in his *Life of David Dudley Field*. Other biographical works that focus on Field's jurisprudence apart from his practice include Stephen Subrin, "David Dudley Field and the Field Code: A Historical Analysis of an Earlier Procedural Vision," 6 *Law & History Review* 311 (1988); LaPiana, "Just the Facts."

[39] Field's ideology was quite similar to that of the antislavery democrats described in Sean Wilentz, "Slavery, Antislavery, and Jacksonian Democracy," in Melvyn Stokes & Stephen Conway, eds., *The Market Revolution in America: Social, Political, and Religious Expressions, 1800–1880* (University of Virginia Press, 1996), 202–23.

[40] Among Field's successful Supreme Court arguments were *Ex parte* Milligan, 71 U.S. (4 Wall.) 2 (1866) (holding the trial of civilians by military commission unconstitutional); Cummings v. Missouri, 71 U.S. (4 Wall.) 277 (1867) (striking a loyalty oath as unconstitutional); *Ex parte* McCardle, 74 U.S. (7 Wall.) 506 (1869) (affirming the power of Congress to "strip" the Court of habeas jurisdiction); and United States v. Cruikshank, 92 U.S. 542 (1875) (enforcing the Fourteenth Amendment only against "state action").

[41] For Field's attack on "agrarian" populism, see David Dudley Field, "Corruption in Politics," (1877), in A.P. Sprague, ed., *Speeches, Arguments, and Miscellaneous Papers of David Dudley Field* (D. Appleton, 1884), 2:494. Eric Foner, *Free Soil, Free Labor, Free Men: The Ideology of the Republican Party Before the Civil War* (Oxford University Press, 1995).

were well connected enough to draw the attention of a presidential cabinet member. Indeed, a significant number were the sons, brothers, or law partners of Supreme Court justices, presidents and vice presidents, governors, and attorneys general. With few exceptions, the codifiers were every bit as elite and "orthodox" as their common law opponents who have drawn most of the attention of historians of the nineteenth century.[42] And at their center, in most relevant ways the mean and median codifier, was David Dudley Field.

V

Field's biography is surveyed at some length here both to introduce the man but also to relieve subsequent chapters of the burden of biography. What follows is decidedly not a biography of Field. In a way, Field's life was too colorful, complicated, and contradictory for one study to track while simultaneously explicating the civil justice system he attempted to craft. From another perspective, Field's life was much smaller than the life of his code. Field was not, after all, a lone genius laboring in isolation. The original code was produced by a commission of three lawyers which included the equally talented and prolific David Graham, who might have received more credit for the code if he had not died in 1852. Field traveled the world to promote his code, but he did comparatively little traveling in the United States, and it took a host of other codifiers to copy, adapt, promote, and enact the code in other states. While Field moved on in his codification efforts, others like his law partner Thomas G. Shearman were left to write the treatises that would guide lawyers in the actual practice of the reformed system.[43]

A study that stuck too closely to Field's life would thus be overburdened with detail yet remain analytically incomplete. What follows then is not a biography of Field but a biography of a legal text, or more precisely, of a set of legal practices. In this I take inspiration from the great English legal historian Frederic Maitland, who preferred organic metaphors in his history of civil practice over the codifiers' mechanistic ones. In a memorable passage on the early modern forms of action, Maitland wrote, "They are—we say without scruple—living things. Each of them lives its own life, has its own adventures, enjoys a longer or shorter day of vigour, usefulness and popularity, and then sinks perhaps into a decrepit and friendless old age. A few are still-born, some are sterile, others live to see their children and children's children in high places."[44]

---

[42] Cf. Morton J. Horwitz, *The Transformation of American Law: The Crisis of Legal Orthodoxy, 1870–1960* (Oxford University Press, 1992), 117–21; David M. Rabban, *Law's History: American Legal Thought and the Transatlantic Turn to History* (Cambridge University Press, 2013), 322–77; Kunal M. Parker, *Common Law, History, and Democracy in America, 1790–1900: Legal Thought Before Modernism* (Cambridge University Press, 2011), 230–41; Lewis A. Grossman, "James Coolidge Carter and Mugwump Jurisprudence," *Law & History Review* 20 (2002). For a complete list of code commissioners in the nineteenth-century United States and sources of their biographies, see http://kellenfunk.org/field-code/the-american-codifiers.

[43] See John L. Tillinghast & Thomas G. Shearman, *Practice, Pleadings, and Forms in Civil Actions in Courts of Record in the State of New York* (Lewis Brothers, 2d ed., 1865).

[44] Frederick Pollock & Frederic W. Maitland, *The History of English Law Before the Time of Edward I* (Cambridge University Press, 2d ed., 1898), 559.

Maitland might have added that if Field had had his way, all would have been eutha-nized in a drafting room in Gramercy Park in 1848.

Field did not have his way, though, not entirely. And while his code would live to see its children seated in high places—most notably in the major federal codification of 1938—the codifiers of the twentieth century commonly looked on Field's efforts as quixotic.[45] That is one of the peculiarities of historiography on the code. The literature simultaneously treats the Field Code as an inevitable modernization and "rationali-zation" of obviously obsolete common law practices, yet also recognizes that for all its inevitability, the code's modernizing aims were not achieved if at all until the mid-twentieth century.[46] Lawyers and jurists continued to analogize cases to the forms of action the code had abolished, continued to recognize a distinction between law and equity the code said did not exist, and continued to appeal to oaths the code had stripped of sacred significance. As Maitland summarized it in 1909, "The forms of ac-tion we have buried, but they still rule us from their graves."[47]

Codifiers at the time believed their political battles simply had not yet ended. What common law lawyers had lost in the legislature the codifiers believed they were trying to usurp from the bench. Codifiers attributed resistance to their reforms to the jurists' old age, the natural reluctance of the elites to change, and the years of training in common law writs that had closed their minds to reform.[48] What they should have done, this volume argues, is look to themselves. Their own codes trafficked so much in inherited modes of thought purportedly abolished on the page that legal practice could not have but persisted in a somewhat altered but largely stable form. Despite the codifiers' aim at comprehension, the codes left enormous undefined gaps in the law of procedure and practice, incorporating by assumption a whole world of unarticu-lated legal practices to keep the codified system running. The difficulty is, as with craft practices generally, those practices with the most staying power were the ones whose logic and effects the lawyers could least articulate at the time.

If that sounds rather mystical, perhaps it is one indication that scholars of religion have done a much better job of thinking deeply about the interpretation of craft prac-tices and embodied ritual performances than legal historians have.[49] One particularly challenging source from that other realm is Charles Taylor's gloss on Pierre Bourdieu. What does it mean for practice to have a logic, Taylor asks? Practice is itself a form of understanding, a way of knowing, but one that is essentially unarticulated, a logic that is always in the background. Once explicate the logic of practice, and the practice

---

[45] See, for instance, Charles E. Clark, "Addresses on the Proposed Rules of Civil Procedure," 22 *ABA Journal* 787 (1936), 787.

[46] See Friedman, *A History of American Law*, 296–97 and 299–301.

[47] F. W. Maitland, *Equity and the Forms of Action at Common Law: Two Courses of Lectures*, ed. A. H. Chaytor & W. J. Whittaker (Cambridge University Press, 1910), 296.

[48] See especially *Third Report of the Commissioners on Pleading and Practice* (New York, 1849), 4.

[49] There are, of course, exceptions. For an outstanding reading of courtroom rituals in the Revolutionary Era, see Richard Lyman Bushman, "Farmers in Court: Orange County, North Carolina, 1750–1776," in Christopher L. Tomlins & Bruce H. Mann, eds., *The Many Legalities of Early America* (University of North Carolina Press, 2012), 388–413. Works on spatial legal history share a promising kinship with ritual studies. See especially Judith Resnik & Dennis E. Curtis, *Representing Justice: Invention, Controversy, and Rights in City-States and Democratic Courtrooms* (Yale University Press, 2011); Nicholas Blomley et al., *The Legal Geographies Reader: Law, Power and Space* (Wiley-Blackwell, 2001).

ceases to be as such. Instead it becomes a rule purporting to represent practice. Taylor concludes that articulated rules represent practice only in the way a map represents a place. It can be a kind of guide, even an "accurate" one, but reading a map is almost nothing like traversing real terrain. "The practical ability exists only in its exercise, which unfolds in time and space." Fundamentally, practice can only ever be "embodied, not represented"—a real challenge for a book seeking to convey something of the realities of legal practice.[50]

Ronald Grimes's *The Craft of Ritual Studies* is particularly helpful for addressing Taylor's challenge.[51] Perhaps it is inevitable, as Bourdieu and Taylor contend, that "distortion arises from the fact that we are taking a situated, embodied sense and providing an express depiction of it."[52] Nevertheless, Grimes offers his handbook as a guide to interpretive labor that "is most productive when it circles a ritual, approaching it from multiple vectors," such as various modes of formal, production, and reception criticism. Representation cannot offer the same kind of understanding that practice does, but it can at least "'triangulate' a ritual [practice] by crosscutting it in several ways to develop a critical interpretive edge."[53] One aim of this study is to triangulate the rituals and practices of mid-nineteenth-century law in the United States by crosscutting many different types of legal and lay literature from the era. But the primary aim is to show that this kind of triangulation was also in fact the activity that many lawyers of the time were engaged in.

One lawyer who struggled to put into words the practices he knew from experience was a West Virginian common law lawyer named Connor Hall. In a 1926 editorial, Hall wrote that "legislatures have, from time immemorial, enacted statutes that causes should be decided according to the very substance of the right without regard to technical defects." What made such admonitions futile in practice, Hall observed, was practice itself. It was all well and good to speak of the substance of rights, but in vindicating a right some sequence had to be followed, some time had to be taken to determine the worthiness of the claim, and so technique remained the indispensable gatekeeper to substance. Hall expressed what for most common law lawyers never had to be articulated:

> Practice is a mere tool, but in any system of government having anything like a guaranty of private rights and a judiciary of integrity and consistency, there must be a way to bring causes to the attention of the court; to adduce proof; to hear argument; to conclude the cause; to give the proper judgment; to take the proper steps for enforcing it; to seize the property which, perhaps, really belongs to the debtor and not to somebody else, yet at the same time not permit him to hide what he really owes; to

[50] Charles Taylor, "To Follow a Rule . . .," in Richard Shusterman, ed., *Bourdieu: A Critical Reader* (Blackwell, 1999), 29–44, 31–32, 37–39.

[51] Ronald L. Grimes, *The Craft of Ritual Studies* (Oxford University Press, 2014). See also Robert Wuthnow, *What Happens When We Practice Religion?: Textures of Devotion in Everyday Life* (Princeton University Press, 2020); Lorraine Daston, *Rules: A Short History of What We Live By* (Princeton University Press, 2022).

[52] Taylor, "To Follow a Rule," 39.

[53] Grimes, *The Craft of Ritual Studies*, 73–75.

grant certain exemptions for the relief or self respect of himself and family and yet not permit these to be abused.[54]

A guaranty of private rights, a consistent judiciary, power over property, and judgment over fraud, these and so many other notions served as a bedrock so foundational it need not be named in a procedure code or in any code.

And on this bedrock rested the whole structure of "practice," which as Hall described it was a "mere tool" that nevertheless contained worlds within itself. Hall concluded his editorial by denouncing "the present scheme" of procedural codification for being too "typically American in its faith in machinery."[55] The problem the codifiers faced was where to draw the line between the machine and the ghost within. The more they treated "procedure" as a synonym for "practice," the more their codes threatened to swallow the whole of the law and belie their claims that procedure was a narrow and unimportant subdepartment of the law. The more they narrowed, the more they tore open the gaps through which uncodified practices poured past the texts that supposedly abolished them. The Field Code became the lawyers' code not just because lawyers controlled the code's political fortunes and benefited professionally from its enactment, but also because its silences and inconsistencies could be filled only by the American bar's inherited practices.

That lesson was quickly lost to history. When Frederic Maitland opened a series of lectures on the writ system in 1909, he parodied the typical response of his students: "Substantive law should come first—adjective law, procedural law, afterwards. The former may perhaps be studied in a university, the latter must be studied in chambers. As to obsolete procedure, a knowledge of it can be profitable to no man."[56] Already by the early twentieth century, the codifiers had largely won their battles. "Procedure" had taken up its place in both lay and professional understandings as an apolitical, boring, and technical subdepartment of the law, useful enough for actual practitioners, but unworthy of serious scrutiny. The chapters that follow take inspiration from Maitland in retracing procedure's steps, showing the politics of procedure's creation in their contemporary vibrancy, and recounting the consequences for American legal practice after a technical field of procedure became the peculiar preserve of the lawyers.

Whether the invention of the lawyers' code and its machinery should be viewed overall as a triumph of modernity brings us back to Albion Tourgée's puzzling indictment of his own codified system in *Bricks Without Straw*. The novel left uncontradicted the final bit of advice to Nimbus and Eliab, that the "law is the most uncertain thing in the world." Tourgée placed the words in the mouth of an antagonistic sheriff— a layman, technically, but one endowed with official power. The sheriff's claim that Radicals had "tinkered over the law" with the new code was certainly true and a way

---

[54] As one indication of how out of step Hall's common law defense was in a world of increasingly codified law, the editorial was refused by the American Bar Association's journal of record multiple times. It can be found in the papers of Senator Thomas J. Walsh, Library of Congress Manuscript Division. Connor Hall, "Uniform Law Procedure in Federal Courts," unpublished editorial sent to the *ABA Journal*, dated Oct. 15, 1926, p. 5.

[55] *Ibid.*, 6.

[56] Maitland, *Equity and the Forms of Action at Common Law*, 295.

for Tourgée to compliment himself. As a state district judge, Tourgée was no doubt aware that the sheriff's description of former masters using civil litigation to harass their freed workers was also true. What then of the claim of the law's uncertainty?

In a study of early modern codification, Roger Berkowitz argues that, rather than addressing the problem of legal uncertainty, codification is the original progenitor of that problem. "Lawyers and jurists have been well aware of the impossibility of true and certain interpretations of law since at least the time of ancient Rome," he writes, yet indeterminacy was not equated with injustice until codification redefined the very nature of law. "At the heart of the shift is law's transformation from an insightful knowing of justice into a product of scientific knowledge. As a product of science, law comes to be a justified rule that is knowable in advance and can be applied to particular cases. Only once law becomes a product of science . . . does the indeterminacy of law come to be such a forbidding problem."[57]

Judge Tourgée seems not to have been particularly bothered by the law's uncertainty, and his use of the code pointed forward to the time when judges, rather than lawyers, would become both the political and professional masters of procedure.[58] A curious feature of a procedure code is that, standing alone, it leaves the law's indeterminacy in the air, as it were. That is why European codifiers saved their procedure codes for last, why Bentham argued procedure ought to be the one area of law left uncodified, and why Maitland's students assumed that procedure would be the last thing they should study rather than the first.[59] That is why major studies of codification debates in the nineteenth century have concluded that America lacked any real codification effort to speak of.[60] A procedure code on its own could not tell you how a case would come out on the merits; it lacked all the certainty that was supposed to be a leading virtue of codification. Perhaps that was its appeal to Judge Tourgée. Planters could not get far in their litigiousness under Tourgée's watchful procedural eye. The writs issued out one day to annoy the freedmen might be reissued another day to enjoin the nascent Klan. So also in a later century the injunctions that once restrained striking workers might then again integrate their children's schools.[61]

When it came to a code of legal practice, one never quite knew what one would get.

[57] Roger Berkowitz, *The Gift of Science: Leibniz and the Modern Legal Tradition* (Fordham University Press, 2010), xv.

[58] See Judith Resnik, "Managerial Judges," 96 *Harvard Law Review* 374 (1982); Steven S. Gensler, "Judicial Case Management: Caught in the Crossfire," 60 *Duke Law Journal* 669 (2010).

[59] See generally Rhee, *European Traditions in Civil Procedure*; Jeremy Bentham, *Principles of Judicial Procedure With the Outline of a Procedure Code*, in John Bowring, ed., *Works of Jeremy Bentham* (William Tait, 2d ed., 1843), preface; Lobban, *The Common Law and English Jurisprudence*, 127–31; Maitland, *Equity and the Forms of Action at Common Law*, 295.

[60] E.g., R. C. Van Caenegem, *Judges, Legislators and Professors: Chapters in European Legal History* (Cambridge University Press, 1987).

[61] See Olsen, *Carpetbagger's Crusade*, 141–42, 180; Peter Charles Hoffer, *The Law's Conscience: Equitable Constitutionalism in America* (University of North Carolina Press, 1990); Owen Fiss, *The Civil Rights Injunction* (Indiana University Press, 1978).

I

THE MACHINE

"I came near losing a case on a policy of insurance, by filing in assumpsit," the elderly New York City lawyer David Dudley Field recalled in 1891. Reminiscing on his early days in the practice of law, he continued: "When the policy was produced at the trial, the defendant's counsel insisted that it had a seal and so the action should have been covenant." However, the faint lighting of the courtroom saved Field's case because "the judge looking at it without his glasses said he could see no seal and denied the motion for non-suit." While Field chuckled about his misfiling in the courts of common law, the prominent abolitionist Henry Brewster Stanton spun his own anecdotes about New York's court of chancery. He claimed to know of a case in which "one witness, coming from Troy, was sworn in." During the length of the protracted trial, the witness "became acquainted with a young lady, married her, and was a father before he left the stand."[1]

Such reminiscences were common in late nineteenth-century New York as a passing generation of lawyers looked back and congratulated themselves on reforming the practice of law in the United States. Losing a suit for filing in assumpsit instead of covenant, gathering written testimony for years, bringing suits either "at common law" or "in chancery"—these notions seemed hardly thinkable anymore. Practice had changed in 1848 when New York enacted a code of civil procedure drafted in large part by Field. The code abolished pleading in assumpsit or covenant altogether, fused the systems of common law and chancery, and required oral testimony in open court to keep proceedings brief. By the time these lawyers set down their recollections, procedure systems imitating New York's had been adopted in thirty other states and territories, including every jurisdiction west of the Mississippi.

Scholars have rightly identified the New York Code of Procedure, known since the 1870s as the Field Code, as a major force in modern American litigation and statutory law, but their accounts skip over the focus of lawyers' recorded memories: the politics of law reform. In their less lighthearted moments, the reminiscences of Field and his colleagues about codification almost entirely concerned politics—running for office, currying favor with news media, lobbying lawmakers, and compromising over legislation.[2] Indeed, the code and its imitators were enacted in some of the most politically

---

[1] David Dudley Field, "Law Reform in the United States and Its Influence Abroad," 25 *American Law Review* 515 (1891), 518; Henry B. Stanton, *Random Recollections* (Harper & Brothers, 1887), 142.

[2] Major secondary sources on the code include Lawrence M. Friedman, *A History of American Law* (Simon & Schuster, 3d ed., 2005), 293–308; Charles M. Cook, *The American Codification Movement: A Study in Antebellum Legal Reform* (Greenwood Press, 1983), 185–200; John H. Langbein et al., *History*

divided times and places in the country, among legislatures wrangling with vastly different priorities. The same state legislatures that spurred the Compromise of 1850, that first opened the franchise to women in the West, and that first installed mixed-race governments in the South were also the legislatures that adopted Field's code from New York.[3] By prescribing the design of the civil courts and the remedies judges could administer, and by delineating who could be an officer, a lawyer, a litigant, or a witness, the code dealt with both mundane procedures but also with fundamental issues of constitutionalism and legal philosophy. Accordingly, its reforms were politically controversial and frequently contested by shifting party alliances in an era where those alliances were shifting dramatically.

Given the political volatility of the code and its reforms, it might be surprising just how closely so many jurisdictions adhered to the text of a code originally written to address the idiosyncrasies of law practice in New York. Most states did not have a byzantine array of courts and officers to reorganize as New York did, nor did the pressures of metropolitan industrialization stress their credit systems as they had New York City's. Many of the code's reforms could have been adopted piecemeal, allowing states to experiment with, say, pleading reform before moving on to witness testimony or coercive remedies. Nevertheless, the further the codes got from New York, the more closely they copied the code of the Empire State.[4]

What aided the code's transmission, both among the rancorous legislatures and a skeptical bar, was a powerful image first deployed to support the original draft in New York: the idea that procedure was merely "law's machinery." Like an artisan's tool that worked upon but could not essentially alter material nature, procedure was described as a set of practices that could aid or inhibit the application of the law without fundamentally transforming it. As the mere machinery of the law, procedure invited legislative experiment. Whereas the protection of private property and liberty might be a sacred task best left to the courts, changing mere process could be trusted to the policy judgments of legislators. At the same time, the machinery image warned legislators not to get too close. In an age of rising industrialization, machines could be complicated, dangerous devices even when handled skillfully. While the idea of procedure as law's machinery opened the door to legislative reform, the code-writers insisted that only expert lawyers like themselves were competent to tinker with the invention they had made.

---

of the Common Law: The Development of Anglo-American Institutions (Aspen, 2009), 382–83; Stephen N. Subrin, "David Dudley Field and the Field Code: A Historical Analysis of an Earlier Procedural Vision," 6 *Law & History Rev.* 311 (1988); Robert G. Bone, "Mapping the Boundaries of a Dispute: Conceptions of Ideal Lawsuit Structure from the Field Code to the Federal Rules," 89 *Columbia Law Review* 1 (1989). For lawyers' reminiscences, see David Dudley Field, *A Third of a Century Given to Law Reform* (1873); Arphaxad Loomis, *Historic Sketch of the New York System of Law Reform in Practice and Pleadings* (1879); William Allen Butler, *The Revision of the Statutes of the State of New York and the Revisers: An Address Delivered Before the Association of the Bar of the City of New York* (1889).

[3] See 1850 California Laws 428; 1870 Wyoming Laws 508; The Code of Civil Procedure of North Carolina (N. Paige, 1868); 1870 South Carolina Laws 2:433.

[4] For a detailed analysis of the text families of the Field Code and their adherence to the original New York drafts, see Kellen Funk & Lincoln A. Mullen, "The Spine of American Law: Digital Text Analysis and U.S. Legal Practice," 123 *American Historical Review* 132 (2018).

Metaphors can go only so far. In the end, many of the codifiers had to admit that their machine was best deployed toward some ends and not others. At different times and in different jurisdictions, codifiers argued that their machine was better calibrated than the common law had been to arrive at truth and to protect civil rights with legal remedies. In New York, that meant valorizing the forensic examinations in the code-reformed trial. In the West, code lawyers advertised the efficient debt collection procedures that would draw out capital from the metropoles back east. In the South, the codes used procedure to safeguard access for freedmen to the witness stand and the jury box. Lawyers eagerly joined issue over the wisdom of these policies, but the fact that lawyers would get to make these ultimate policy decisions went almost unquestioned.

Almost. Occasionally, elite lawyers challenged the codifiers on their own terms. Procedure, they pointed out, could not be so cleanly marked off from the "substantive" law as codifiers supposed. After all, an accelerated debt collection changed an essential feature about the debt itself. How soon the violence of the state would be visited against a private debtor, and what form that violence would take, could hardly be described as "ancillary" or "adjectival" issues, at least from the perspective of the indebted.[5] Moreover, the rush to codify *just* procedure seemed to always slip its bounds. Field's final draft included the jurisdiction of the courts as well as the full law of remedies, of evidence, and even of attorney compensation and ethics. More seemed to be smuggled under a procedure code than the "mere machinery" image advertised, and defenders of traditional practice kept up a steady opposition against the very idea of codes to the end of the century. For the most part, their resistance proved to be a rearguard action. Finding success in the legislatures, code procedure eventually won its way into the university curriculum and then into federal policy in the twentieth century. Down to today it features heavily in America's "Litigation State," the US reliance on civil litigation as a mode of governance and as an alternative to regulatory bureaucracy.[6]

The chapters that follow tell the political story of the Field Code, from its advent in New York to its migration across the states and its eventual retrenchment in national legal institutions. Chapter 1 surveys the early debates around codification in the United States and introduces Field's practitioner-focused approach to codification as a response to technological change in the lawyer's daily work. Chapter 2 provides an overview of the procedural system of 1820s New York, culminating in the blend of procedural reform and codification undertaken in the Revised Statutes of 1829. Chapter 3 addresses the advent of both the Field Code and the field of civil procedure as they simultaneously came into being, sustained by the political imagery of process as the mere machinery of the law. Chapter 4 traces the migration of the code first to the Midwest then to the states and territories of the Reconstruction South and West. Chapter 5 concludes the story with the institutionalization of the code in treatise literature, legal education, and federal court practice.

---

[5] Cf. Robert Cover, "Violence and the Word," 95 *Yale Law Journal* 1601 (1986).

[6] Sean Farhang, *The Litigation State: Public Regulation and Private Lawsuits in the U.S.* (Princeton University Press, 2010); Louis L. Jaffe, "The Citizen as Litigant in Public Actions: The Non-Hohfeldian or Ideological Plaintiff," 116 *University of Pennsylvania Law Review* 1033 (1968); Abram Chayes, "The Role of the Judge in Public Law Litigation," 89 *Harvard Law Review* 1281 (1976).

1

Sampson Against the Philistines

The Allure of an American Code

I

President James Madison received a strange message in the spring of 1812, as the United States drew closer to trans-Atlantic war. English philosopher Jeremy Bentham had written to Madison with an offer of help—not with diplomacy, but with something Bentham considered much more significant. A cover letter from the law reformer Henry Brougham tried to forewarn Madison that Bentham's "style is somewhat peculiar" because of its "excessive subdivisions" and tendency "of coining new terms." True to form, Bentham's first paragraph was one endlessly tangled sentence of dashes, underlines, and false starts that eventually ended with a grand but indecipherable offer from Bentham to produce an American "*Pannomion*."[1]

The letter hurried to explain that Bentham was writing "not to the person" of Madison, "but to the Office," and all Bentham wanted in return was for any governmental functionary to authorize his work. But just what was the work being proposed? Bentham at last clarified that "Pannomion" meant "a body of Statute law," a "*complete* body," that would turn "*Unwritten* law" into its opposite. The philosopher was offering the United States the service of "codification"—to use another term of Bentham's coining.[2]

No mere technical exercise, codification was pressed in Bentham's note as an emergency at least as great as the imminent war between Britain and the United States. Whether or not the two nations met on a battlefield, Bentham imagined a militant English common law already arrayed against American popular sovereignty. The common law had for "its authors—not the people themselves, nor any persons chosen by the people, but the creatures . . . of the King alone." Bentham contended that the precedents of the royal judges in England were entirely unsuited for the young republic. The common law "had of course for its main object—not the good of the people, but . . . the sinister & confederated interests of the creator," a despotic monarch.[3]

Although the Revolution had sundered the Crown's authority over the United States, Bentham explained that importing England's judge-made system of law would have as pernicious effects as it had in the motherland. The law announced case-by-case by judges was "law, blundered out by a set of men, who in their course of

---

[1] Jeremy Bentham to James Madison, October 30, 1811, in *The Papers of James Madison, Presidential Series, 3 November 1810–4 November 1811*, J. C. A. Stagg et al., eds. (University of Virginia Press, 1996), 3:505–35.

[2] The idea of codification had a longer history than Bentham's terminology. See Barbara Shapiro, "Codification of the Laws in Seventeenth Century England," 1974 *Wisconsin Law Review* 428 (1974).

[3] Bentham to Madison, 517.

Law's Machinery. Kellen R. Funk, Oxford University Press. © Kellen R. Funk 2025. DOI: 10.1093/9780197543962.003.0002

operation [were] not at their own command, but at the command of plaintiffs in the several causes." In some ways, the control of judges by artful lawyers was even worse than control by the King. Lawyers litigating particular cases had no concern for general principles, the public good, or systemic coherence in the law. Worse yet, judges used their pronouncements in particular cases to spring new rules of property and contract on unsuspecting litigants. The retroactive effect of judicial opinions meant that litigants were expected to conduct their affairs according to unwritten rules they could not possibly foreknow. In all, Bentham viewed "*unwritten* alias *common* law" as an "impostrous law" whose "perpetual fruits" were "*uncertainty, uncognoscibility, particular disappointments* without end, [and a] *general sense of insecurity* against similar disappointment and loss."[4]

Madison politely declined Bentham's offer. In a terse, straightforward style that achieved what Bentham promised for his code but failed to deliver in his letter, Madison assured the philosopher that the Revolution had sufficiently "lopped off" enough of England's common law that the crisis of unwritten law was less severe in the United States than Bentham imagined. And while "a digest of our laws on sound principles" might be worthwhile, Madison feared that a code would complicate matters with "complex technical terms," which in the end would only demand more case law to explicate. The irony of the law was that statutes aiming to displace judicial opinions only ended up calling forth more opinions.[5]

So ended what may have been the first attempt at a US code, but it was certainly not the last.[6] Codification remained of intense interest to the American bar and was often a significant reform demanded by those who, like Bentham, were not lawyers. Codification is, as Lawrence Friedman has written, "one of the set pieces of American legal history," and historians have found in the codification debates a microcosm for the story of American political economy more generally.[7] Like Madison's rebuff of Bentham, American codification is usually told as a story of failure and disappointment, the triumph of a conservative judiciary and vested property rights over legislative democracy and distributive justice.[8] The following account differs by telling a success story of codification, albeit one whose ends were not what radicals like Bentham expected they would be. As it turned out, American codes written by and for lawyers struggled to imagine institutions for sound governance beyond litigation in courts. That America retained the structure of a liberal "Litigation State" through the course of the nineteenth century was not the failure of codification but a sign of its striking success.[9] A product

---

[4] *Ibid*, 517–18.

[5] James Madison to Jeremy Bentham, May 8, 1816, in *The Papers of James Madison*, 11:12–14.

[6] At least, post-Founding. New England Puritans had been crafting codes from the earliest days of settlement. See Daniel R. Coquillette, "Radical Lawmakers in Colonial Massachusetts: The 'Countenance of Authoritie' and the Lawes and Libertyes," 67 *New England Quarterly* 179, 187 (1994); Yu-yeh Wang, "The Codification Movement in the Massachusetts Bay Colony, 1630–1650," 19 *American Studies* 73 (1989).

[7] Lawrence M. Friedman, *A History of American Law* (Simon & Schuster, 3d ed., 2005), 302.

[8] See especially Morton J. Horwitz, *The Transformation of American Law: The Crisis of Legal Orthodoxy, 1870–1960* (Oxford University Press, 1992), 117–21; Robert W. Gordon, "The American Codification Movement," 36 *Vanderbilt Law Review* 431 (1983).

[9] On litigation as a mode of governance, one that often substitutes for or displaces a regulatory bureaucracy, see Sean Farhang, *The Litigation State: Public Regulation and Private Lawsuits in the U.S.* (Princeton University Press, 2010); Martha Minow, "Public and Private Partnerships: Accounting for the New

of legislation that nevertheless limited the reach and power of a legislature—for many lawyers, that was the allure of an American code.

II

Despite the pervasive influence of judge-made common law, codification is virtually unavoidable in American legal history. When the intellectual historian Perry Miller published a reader surveying *The Legal Mind in America*, Miller treated codification as the only intellectual topic that could attract lawyers away from their practices for debate.[10] Slaveholding aristocrats like Thomas Jefferson in Virginia urged codification of the common law, as did evangelical abolitionists like Thomas Smith Grimké in South Carolina. Codification was a standard theme of law school commencement addresses in the early nineteenth century and bar association keynotes at the end of the century.[11] The topic was of pressing interest outside of the American bar as well. Napoleonic France promulgated a series of codes in the early nineteenth century; Germans debated the wisdom of codification after Napoleon's fall; and in the 1860s, the British imposed codes on their colonies in India and Singapore.[12] Lawyers in the United States followed the international development of these codes with interest, many regarding codification as the leading edge of modern legal science.[13]

Religion," 116 *Harvard Law Review* 1229 (2003); Trevor W. Morrison, "Private Attorneys General and the First Amendment," 103 *Michigan Law Review* 589 (2005); Louis L. Jaffe, "The Citizen as Litigant in Public Actions: The Non-Hohfeldian or Ideological Plaintiff," 116 *University of Pennsylvania Law Review* 1033 (1968); Abram Chayes, "The Role of the Judge in Public Law Litigation," 89 *Harvard Law Review* 1281 (1976).

[10] Perry Miller, ed., *The Legal Mind in America: From Independence to the Civil War* (Doubleday, 1962), 11.

[11] See Christopher Michael Curtis, *Jefferson's Freeholders and the Politics of Ownership in the Old Dominion* (Cambridge University Press, 2012), 69–70; Thomas Smith Grimké, *An Oration on the Practicability and Expediency of Reducing the Whole Body of the Law to the Simplicity and Order of a Code* (1827); James Coolidge Carter, *The Proposed Codification of Our Common Law: A Paper Prepared at the Request of the Committee of the Bar Association of the City of New York* (1884), George Hoadly, *Codification in the United States: An Address Delivered Before the Graduating Classes at the Sixtieth Anniversary of the Yale Law School* (1884); Robert Ludlow Fowler, *Codification in the State of New York* (1884); R. Floyd Clarke, *The Science of Lawmaking: Being an Introduction to Law, a General View of Its Forms and Substance, and a Discussion of the Question of Codification* (1898).

[12] See James Q. Whitman, *The Legacy of Roman Law in the German Romantic Era: Historical Vision and Legal Change* (Princeton University Press, 1990); Jean-Louis Halperin, *The French Civil Code* (University of Texas Press, 2006); Robert B. Holtman, *The Napoleonic Revolution* (Louisiana State University Press, 1981); R. H. Kilbourne, *A History of the Louisiana Civil Code* (Paul M. Herbert Law Center, 1987); Brian Young, *The Politics of Codification: The Lower Canadian Civil Code of 1866* (Osgoode Society, 1994); John W. Cairns, *Codification, Transplants, and History: Law Reform in Louisiana (1808) and Quebec (1866)* (Talbot, 2015). On common theories of codification that transcended jurisdictional boundaries, see Csaba Varga, *Codification as a Socio-Historical Phenomenon* (Szent István Társulat, 2d ed., 2011 [1991]); Roger Berkowitz, *The Gift of Science: Leibniz and the Modern Legal Tradition* (Fordham University Press, 2010).

[13] See Charles M. Cook, *The American Codification Movement: A Study in Antebellum Legal Reform* (Greenwood Press, 1983); Gunther A. Weiss, "The Enchantment of Codification in the Common-Law World," 25 *Yale Journal of International Law* 435 (2000); Maurice Eugen Lang, *Codification in the British Empire and America* (Lawbook Exchange, 1924); Roscoe Pound, "The French Civil Code and the Spirit of Nineteenth Century Law," 35 *Boston Law Review* 79 (1955).

Across these varied contexts, lawyers used a broad range of meanings for "codifi-cation." In its simplest version, a code collected a jurisdiction's generally applicable statutory laws currently in force. Yet even such a mere compilation of a state's oper-ative legislation could be daunting to arrange. From their earliest days, state legis-latures chronologically published all the bills enacted during an annual session in a single volume, usually known as "sessions laws." But session laws were impractical for day-to-day use because statutes regulating the same subject might be separated by hundreds of pages and dozens of volumes. Furthermore, the vast bulk of sessions laws were irrelevant to most readers because they were so-called private bills—laws that had no general application but rather incorporated only a single company, granted a divorce to a particular couple, or altered the unique boundaries of a municipality. Thus, the task of a statutory compilation was to cull the private legislation from the sessions laws and put the remaining "public" or "general" law in order, even if it was simply alphabetical order by keyword or topic. Such compilations were often called "revised statutes," if not codes. In theory, they ensured that amendments and retrac-tions made by the legislature over time were faithfully represented in the consolidated texts. Yet even modest compilations could occasion a high degree of editorial discre-tion and provoke political contests over the nature of legislative authority.[14]

A proper code of the kind recommended by Bentham and his American admirers intensified these controversies by aiming to compile and arrange not just all of the operative statutes but also all of the rules that judges used to decide cases in court. "Revised Statutes," as the Massachusetts legislator Robert Rantoul Jr. noted, "still cover but a small part of the ground. We are governed, principally, by the Common Law," which, Rantoul advised, "ought to be reduced, forthwith, to a uniform written Code." Rantoul contrasted the "positive and unbending text" of statutory law with the judge's "arbitrary power, or *discretion*" to bend the common law's malleable rules and effectively legislate new law for every case. Rantoul argued that only the duly consti-tuted legislature "must act on general views, and prescribe at once, for a whole class of cases." In contrast, if a conniving judge "wishes to decide the next case differently, he has only to *distinguish* and thereby make a new law."[15]

In modern parlance, "codify" implies that a policy or practice will be enshrined and hardened into place. But as Rantoul's argument illustrates, the codifiers often intended not just to collect and articulate existing legal rules, but to reform those rules as well as the very process of rulemaking itself. The articulation of the law was to be an exclusive prerogative of the democratically elected legislature. Above all, codification of this sort aimed to cut off further manipulation of rules and the creation of new exceptions by judges who might favor special interests. Mere statutory compilers insisted (however truthfully) that they never substantively altered the laws they collated, but for jurists like Rantoul, the point of codifying the common law was to change it.

Not all codifiers followed Rantoul's program for radical law reform. The Harvard professor and Supreme Court Justice Joseph Story, for example, chided the "visionary

---

[14] See especially Farah Peterson, "Interpretation as Statecraft: Chancellor Kent and the Collaborative Era of Statutory Interpretation," 77 *University of Maryland Law Review* 712 (2018).

[15] Robert Rantoul Jr., *An Oration Delivered Before the Democrats and Antimasons, of the County of Plymouth; at Scituate* (1836).

statesmen" who pretended "that the legislature can do no wrong" and "that popular opinion is the voice of unerring wisdom." Rejecting Rantoul's premise that only the democratic legislature gave due regard to the public interest, Story nevertheless endorsed codification insofar as it could produce "a gradual digest under legislative authority of those portions of our jurisprudence, which under the forming hand of the judiciary shall from time to time acquire scientific accuracy."[16] Story's biographers have tended to see his moderate support for codification as an attempt to forestall or co-opt the process of codifying the common law before it took on more radical dimensions. Still, as Jane C. Manners argues, "In codification, Story saw the possibility not just of stasis, but of progress."[17]

Scientific improvement of law remained Story's guiding principle. A good code could provide "the true rule [of a line of cases], instead of leaving it open to conjecture and inference by feeble minds." A code offered clarity, much like the treatises Story was famous for writing, and indeed, Story praised the Code Napoleon for being "the most finished and methodical treatise of law that the world ever saw." The advantage of a code was that it took the best of legal learning and paired it with the authoritative force of the legislature. Story looked forward to "the future jurists of our country" who could "accomplish for the common law" what Napoleon had for France. Story even agreed with Rantoul, the firebrand codifier from his state, that "a code furnishes the only safe means of incorporating qualifications upon a general principle." Codification restrained the discretion of judges on the bench while allowing expert jurists room to advise the codifying legislature on the best rule statements to adopt.[18]

Story's hopes for codification rested on two conditions. First, those tasked with producing the code must be jurists "of high standing in the profession" who would approach their task "with a cautious and skillful hand, and with a deep sense of the delicacy of intermeddling with established principles." When Story accepted appointment to the Massachusetts Codification Commission, he illustrated just what kind of careful jurist he had in mind: a judge like himself.[19] Story's second condition was that any resulting code confine itself to "the general principles" of the common law and thus leave judges some freedom to maneuver within the rules. For examples, Story directed legislators to look to "elementary treatises"—several of which Story had now written—"which approach very near to scientific accuracy."[20] But treatises, however much they might guide judicial reasoning, never compelled a particular outcome, and judges were accustomed to massaging the rule statements of treatises or finding

---

[16] Joseph Story, "An Address Delivered Before the Members of the Suffolk Bar on the 4th of September, 1821," 1 *American Jurist and Law Magazine* 1 (1829), 25, 31–32.

[17] Miller, *Life of the Mind*, 250–51; R. Kent Newmyer, *Supreme Court Justice Joseph Story: Statesman of the Old Republic* (University of North Carolina Press, 1985), 278. Jane C. Manners, Congress and the Problem of Legislative Discretion, 1790–1870 (Ph.D. dissertation, Princeton University, 2018), 211.

[18] "Law Legislation, Codes," 7 *Encyclopedia Americana* (Francis Lieber ed., 1831), 576. Special thanks to Jane C. Manners and Daniel J. Hulsebosch for identifying Joseph Story's authorship of this anonymous encyclopedia entry (citing William Wetmore Story, *Life and Letters of Joseph Story* [1819–1895] (2013), 2:27).

[19] "Story's Report," reprinted in David Dudley Field, ed., *Codification of the Common Law* (1882), 41, 61–62.

[20] *Ibid.*, 42. Story's Massachusetts Commission recommended that the law of bailments, agency, bails of exchange, promissory notes, and partnership were all ripe for codification. Story had written and published treatises on all these topics. See Manners, Congress and the Problem of Legislative Discretion, 219.

new exceptions as new cases arose.[21] Story expected the same play in the joints to continue under a code. Codes, like treatises, could further the progress of legal science, but that progress would not end with codification. Judges would continue to extend and refine the law, and the codes would always have to catch up.

Legal historians have discerned a pattern in the exchanges between Bentham and Madison, Rantoul and Story. Radical calls to reshape the law based on democratic principles and legislative supremacy ended with a milquetoast endorsement of statutory consolidation and a limited borrowing of treatise literature for the statute books, mainly under the control of judicial advisors.[22] Story's code commission in Massachusetts, for example, produced little more than a new edition of the commonwealth's revised statutes. Early on, most other states followed the model of Story's Massachusetts or Jefferson's Virginia, both of which pronounced the excellence of the codification ideal but then settled for organizing and re-printing colonial statutes while declaring that English common law would continue in force in the courts.[23] Judged by Bentham's or the Napoleonic commissioners' standards, American efforts at codification did not amount to much.

But not everyone judged by those standards, not even the most ardent American codifiers. While Benthamite arguments about the superiority of a democratically enacted Pannomion and envy of the French were never entirely absent from the American codification debates, they were not entirely at the center either. Rather, codification in the United States more often resounded with overtones of anti-English political and religious dissent—dissent that could speak in a democratic voice, to be sure, but usually did not, favoring the interests of lawyers more than legislators. These resonances are less familiar in our modern world of statutes and were often missed by the critical historians of codification. By attending to them, we can better grasp what American codifiers were aiming for and what, over time, they believed they achieved. That story of a distinctively lawyerly, distinctively American approach to codification begins, appropriately enough, on Independence Day, 1806, when the fiery Irish exile William Sampson first arrived in America with a firm conviction of what was wrong with its laws.

III

If Joseph Story's measured support for gradual codification represented the views of a high-minded jurist, William Sampson most forcefully pressed the workaday interests of the practicing lawyer. Born in Londonderry in 1764, the son of a Protestant

---

[21] See Angela Fernandez & Markus D. Dubber, eds., *Law Books in Action: Essays on the Anglo-American Legal Treatise* (Cambridge University Press, 2012).

[22] See Lawrence M. Friedman, "Law Reform in Historical Perspective," 13 *St. Louis University Law Journal* 351 (1969); Horwitz, *The Crisis of Legal Orthodoxy*, 117–21; Cook, *The American Codification Movement*; Gordon, "The American Codification Movement," 439.

[23] On New York's "reception" of the common law, see New York Constitution of 1777, art. 35; William B. Stoebuck, "Reception of English Common Law in the American Colonies," 10 *William and Mary Law Review* 393 (1968). Several states followed New Jersey in adopting the English common law but forbidding citation to English cases decided after July 1, 1776. See Anton-Hermann Chroust, *Rise of the Legal Profession in America* (University of Oklahoma Press, 1965), 2:54.

minister, Sampson gained notoriety as a barrister who pleaded the causes of persecuted Catholics and working-class Irishmen. The failed Irish Revolution of 1798 and resultant British prosecutions instilled in Sampson a fierce hatred of English legal institutions.[24] Sampson broadly dismissed any suggestion that the English jury system protected liberty, because jurors had "to hear with the *law's ear*, see with the *law's eye*, speak with the *law's voice*, of which law the court are alone to judge."[25] As was the case for Sampson's fellow codifiers, the unwritten law of the judges haunted Sampson's philosophy.

Sojourning in France when Napoleon promulgated the French Civil Code, Sampson witnessed the radical possibilities of a codification built atop the rubble of the old order. Sampson met several of Napoleon's commissioners and staff who worked on the code, and some of them eventually followed Sampson to New York with advice for constructing an American code.[26] Sampson thought it auspicious that he arrived in New York Harbor on July 4. Compared to the Old World, the United States appeared to be the land of liberty that American enthusiasts had advertised. With appreciative levity, he told Irish allies that "the government here makes no sensation. It is round about you like the air, and you cannot even feel it."[27]

Sampson gained national renown as one of Manhattan's leading attorneys even as he undertook unpopular litigation for working-class Catholic immigrants and labor radicals. Today, Sampson is remembered for arguing the first reported case establishing the religious freedom of a priest to refuse to testify against a penitent.[28] One of his biographers refers to the success of Sampson and his small circle of Irish lawyer-exiles as representative of a distinctive "Orangeism in America."[29] Respectable and orthodox but never quite as elite as jurists like Story or New York's Chancellor James Kent, the Orangeists escaped social condemnation for representing disreputable clients because their grounds of defense resounded so strongly with developing ideals of American liberalism. Their fierce advocacy of liberty and toleration with explicit contrasts to Old World tyranny won them both begrudging respect and the occasional victory in court. Thus, when the New-York Historical Society approached its twentieth anniversary in 1823, the Society's selection of Sampson to deliver the keynote address seemed a natural choice. At least, the organizers had no reason to expect the coming fury.

Sampson's announced topic was "The Origin, Progress, Antiquities, Curiosities, and Nature of the Common Law," but that benign title thinly cloaked Sampson's polemical intent. After condemning English jurisprudence for its "disingenuous mystery, its language a barbarous jargon, its root in savage antiquity," Sampson's lecture

---

[24] See Maxwell Bloomfield, "William Sampson and the Codifiers: The Roots of American Legal Reform," 11 *American Journal of Legal History* 234 (1967); William Sampson, *Memoirs* (Samuel B.T. Caldwell, 2d ed., 1817); Charles Currier Beale, *William Sampson: Lawyer and Stenographer* (1907).

[25] William Sampson, *A Faithful Report of the Trial of Hurdy Gurdy* (1807), 10.

[26] See Count Pierre François Réal to William Sampson, October 27, 1824, in Pishey Thompson, ed., *Sampson's Discourse and Correspondence with Various Learned Jurists Upon the History of the Law* (E. Bliss and E. White, 1826), 191.

[27] Quoted in Beale, *William Sampson*, 13.

[28] Steven T. Collis, *Deep Conviction* (Shadow Mountain, 2019), pt. 1. On Sampson's defense of labor radicals in New York, see Sean Wilentz, *Chants Democratic: New York City and the American Working Class, 1788–1850* (Oxford University Press, 2d ed., 2004), 97–99.

[29] Walter J. Walsh, "William Sampson, a Republican Constitution, and the Conundrum of Orangeism on American Soil, 1824–1831," 5/7 *Radharc* 1 (2006).

demanded that American law start fresh. "It is time we should assert our own independent judgment, and act and think for ourselves." To Sampson, thinking "for ourselves" meant creating a code and then binding judges to it.[30]

To be sure, many of Sampson's remarks gave voice to Benthamite or European ideals
for codification. Sampson denounced English common law for having "obliged judges
to legislation *pro re nata* [as each case arises], upon every new point." With codification, lawmaking power would properly rest with legislators as agents of the sovereign
populace, breaking the spell of common law authority when "the People know that
their law is the creature of their power; the work of their own hands; and that, if it is not
good, it is to their own shame." Under a codified system, sober political deliberation
would change the law without relying on the "mummery" of common law development.[31] Sampson also believed legal institutions would have to change for codification
to work. Favoring a French model, Sampson suggested that judges must cite only to the
code and avoid producing long, reasoned decisions. If judges encountered a novel or
ambiguous issue, they would have to certify the question to the legislature to create a
new general law covering future cases.[32] Bentham had proposed similar measures, as
well as novel institutions such as a Public Opinion Tribunal and a Legislation Minister
who would periodically audit the laws for "clearness" to the lay reader.[33]

Yet the draw of *Sampson's Discourse*, as it became known, arose not from the transatlantic debates it rehashed but rather from two themes that stood out for their novelty and lasting resonance in the American codification debates: one of technology
and one of faith. In Sampson's account, a code was primarily a tool, a practical device
for daily use, even daily rituals, not a historical artifact of democratic will. To go by
some jurists, a code's significance culminated with its production. To Sampson, that
was only the beginning—a code then had to be used and put into practice, especially
by lawyers. These imagined uses of a code tapped Sampson's convictions of religious
dissent. In his telling, codes broke the spell of common law "mummery," not in a fig-
urative sense, but in the same real ways the Protestant Reformation had destroyed the
power of the parish priest. Codification offered a rebalance of power, not just of political power contested by judges and legislators, but of the oracular, quasi-divine power
to declare just what the law was. Both the theme of codification as a tool of lawyerly
control and the theme of quasi-religious reformation were echoed across *Sampson's
Discourse* and the debates it spawned up and down the eastern seaboard.[34]

Both were also taken immediately to heart by an eighteen-year-old journeyman in
the law named David Dudley Field. Like Sampson, Field was the son of a latitudinarian

---

[30] William Sampson, "Anniversary Discourse on the Origin, Progress, Antiquities, Curiosities, and
Nature of the Common Law, Delivered Before the Historical Society of New York, December 6, 1823," in
Sampson's Discourse, 5.

[31] *Ibid.* 10–12; 37–38.

[32] See William Sampson to Thomas Cooper, President of Columbia College, August 1823, in *Sampson's
Discourse*, 61–62.

[33] See David Lieberman, "Bentham's Jurisprudence and Democratic Theory: An Alternative to Hart's
Approach," in Xiaobo Zhai, ed., *Bentham's Theory of Law and Public Opinion* (Cambridge University Press,
2014), 136–39.

[34] *Sampson's Discourse* attracted widespread attention. Lawyers from Massachusetts to South Carolina
wrote Sampson to express both praise and criticism. Their letters and Sampson's lengthy responses were
published a few years after his address. See *Sampson's Discourse*, 41–202.

minister with ambitions of becoming an elite New York lawyer. Never one to give credit where he did not have to, Field long remembered *Sampson's Discourse* as a touchstone in his legal education. Born in 1805, forty years Sampson's junior, Field was a second-generation American codifier. After haphazard studies at Williams College, Field joined a group of writers and politicos calling themselves "Young America." Adherents like Nathaniel Hawthorne dreamed of a distinctive American literature, while editor John O'Sullivan prophesied a "manifest destiny" of continental conquest. Field declared his own role would be to supply the "Code American" to the national enterprise. Field had just begun his apprenticeship in the Manhattan law office of Henry Sedgwick when *Sampson's Discourse* fell like fire from heaven. His master wrote an admiring review for O'Sullivan's newspaper, possibly some of it ghostwritten by Field. In time, Field's name would become synonymous with American codification. At the beginning of Field's career, however, the arguments and complaints about New York law—its technological deficiencies and its religious distortions—sounded with the voice of Sampson.[35]

IV

Sampson's treatment of codes as a technology for handling legal argument surmised that worthwhile judicial precedents "require little more than regulation and systematic order." A code could provide that order, settling "all doubts that hang upon them." Instead of "overwhelming showers" of precedents to sift, practitioners need consult only a passage or two from a code.[36]

Sampson understood very well the mass of precedents that were swamping New York lawyers with seemingly endless rules and exceptions. Shortly after his arrival, Sampson supplemented his legal practice with income as a case stenographer, demonstrating impressive facility and output. New York case decisions remained almost entirely unpublished at that time, leaving practitioners to cite either published English reports or oral traditions learned over a course of practice before local judges. Publishers occasionally produced pamphlets about high-profile cases, including Sampson's (which often were "his" proceedings in the double sense that he served as both lawyer and case reporter).[37] A few editors attempted to publish an entire run of decisional law from especially important tribunals, such as opinions of the US Supreme Court. But even through 1815, many of these works appeared only at the whim of private initiative.[38]

---

[35] David Dudley Field, *A Third of a Century Given to Law Reform* (1873), 1. See Edward L. Widmer, *Young America: The Flowering of Democracy in New York City* (Oxford University Press, rev. ed., 2000); Yonatan Eyal, *The Young America Movement and the Transformation of the Democratic Party 1828–1861* (Cambridge University Press, 2007). For Sedgwick's anonymous review, see "Review of An Anniversary Discourse by William Sampson," 19 *North American Review* 429 (1824).

[36] Sampson, "Anniversary Discourse," 33, 38.

[37] See Beale, *William Sampson*, 8–9.

[38] On the oral culture of the common law system, see Michael Lobban, *The Common Law and English Jurisprudence, 1760–1850* (Clarendon Press, 1991), 17. On the early history of case reporting in America, see Craig Joyce, "The Rise of the Supreme Court Reporter: An Institutional Perspective on Marshall Court Ascendency," 83 *Michigan Law Review* 1291 (1985), 1332–48.

New York was among the first states to publicly subsidize the professional publishing of notable decisions rendered by its higher courts. The state's official reporting system began in 1804, likely instigated by the famous Chancellor James Kent. The many published opinions from Kent's tenure aimed to instruct lawyers on how to cite and argue from written precedent as Kent did, by drawing upon a whole library of legal literature from around the world to support reasoned decision-making.[39] But under Kent's methods, lawyers soon complained not that they had too little literature but too much.

The problem was that although states had been slow to start publishing case reports, an industrial revolution in printing swiftly accelerated the pace of reporting, even as the addition of new states to the Union produced more courts writing more decisions. In England, Bentham had complained that the so-called unwritten common law filled far more printed volumes than statutory law, but the diversity of US jurisdictions made the English scale look puny. An effort to compile all the published case law of the English royal courts from the time of Henry III to 1866 yielded just over 120,000 published decisions. By that same year, only five decades of American law reporting had rendered at least twice as many published reports. Lawyers keenly felt the struggle to keep up. By 1836, the Philadelphia lawyer David Hoffman groaned that "the increase of this portion of our legal literature within the last thirty years, has no parallel in the juridical history of any other country. More than four hundred and fifty volumes of American law reports now load our shelves!"[40]

The multiplicity of jurisdictions need not have occasioned so much alarm if each state had simply stuck to its own case reports as authoritative statements of the law. But most states, led again by New York, were not so discriminating. Although only New York judgments had formal precedential authority within the state, judges might be informed and persuaded by recent decisions reported anywhere else in the common law world. From the mid-1830s to the mid-1840s, New York judges based their decisions on rules and arguments cited from Pennsylvania and Massachusetts over three hundred times each; from South Carolina, Kentucky, Virginia, and Connecticut more than one hundred times each; and from every other state in the Union at least a couple times.[41] Lawyers swiftly learned that any reported case was fair game for a legal argument, and some excelled at ferreting out obscure cases from distant jurisdictions that might be sprung on an adversary or used to overawe a susceptible judge. Others despaired at keeping up with such a hunt, and they dreaded

[39] See John H. Langbein, "Chancellor Kent and the History of Legal Literature," 93 *Columbia Law Review* 547 (1993). On Kent's sources for adjudication, see Daniel J. Hulsebosch, *Constituting Empire: New York and the Transformation of Constitutionalism in the Atlantic World, 1664–1830* (University of North Carolina Press, 2005), 283–87.

[40] David Hoffman, *A Course of Legal Study* (2d ed., 1836), 657. W.T.S. Daniel, *History of the Origin of the Law Reports* (W. Clowes, 1884). For a comparison of English and American case reporting rates, see Kellen Funk & Lincoln Mullen, Making Law Modern: Discovering the Restructuring of Law through Legal Citations in American Treatises,

Working Paper, 2023, https://legalmodernism.org/docs/Funk-Mullen.Making-Law-Modern.pdf.

[41] Counts derived from a partial dataset of citations in published opinions. See https://observablehq.com/@lmullen/legal-citations-across-state-jurisdictions. On Kent's role in having some of the more far-flung reports published in New York, see Daniel J. Hulsebosch, "An Empire of Law: Chancellor Kent and the Revolution in Books in the Early Republic," 60 *Alabama Law Review* 377 (2009), 382–89.

NEW LAW BOOKS.

VOL. 7—Hill's Reports, Supreme Court, New-York.
Vol. 1—Denio's Reports, New York.
Vol. 2—Sandford's Chancery Reports, New York.
Vol. 4—Howard's U. S. Reports, Supreme Court.
Vol. 9—Metcalf's Reports, Massachusetts.
Vol. 50—English Common Law Reports, entire.
Vol. 14—Meeson and Welsby's Exchequer Reports.
Vol. 18—English Chancery Reports, now published verbatim, with notes and references to English and American Decisions, by John A. Dunlap, Counsellor at Law : each American contains two entire English volumes ; vol. 18 contains Mylne and Craig's Chancery Reports, vol. 4, and Craig & Phillip's Chancery Reports, vol. 1.
Vol. 24—Maine Reports, Shepley, vol. 11.
Vol. 1—Johnson's Cases, second edition, much enlarged, with additional cases, and with copious notes and references to the American and English Decisions, by Lorenzo B. Shepard, Counsellor at Law.
Vol. 6—Benj. Munroe's Reports, Kentucky.
Vol. 5—Iredell's Law Reports, North Carolina.
Vol. 3—Iredell's Equity Reports, North Carolina.
Vol. 3—Iredell's Digest of North Carolina Reports, 1846.
Vol. 10—Laws of the United States.
Vol. 2—Richardson's Equity Reports, South Carolina.
Vol. 17—Connecticut Reports.
Vol. 1—Kaufman's Mackeldy's Civil Law.
Vol. 2—Greenleaf's Evidence.
Vol. 3—Story's Circuit Court Reports.
Vol. 6—Humprey's Reports, Tennessee.
Vol. 5—Arkansas Reports, by A. Pike.
Vol. 5—Kinne's Law Compendium.
Wharton's American Law, Criminal.
Barbour's American Criminal Treatise.
Greenleaf's Testimony of the Evangelists.
Wheaton's History of the Law of Nations in Europe and America to 1845.
Wheaton's International Law, third edition, revised and corrected.

Abbott on Shipping, fifth American, from the seventh English edition, with the notes of Judge Story and J. C. Perkins, Esq., 1846.
Saunders' Reports, 3 vols, sixth edition ; much enlarged and improved, by Edward V. Williams, Esq., 1846.
Hilliard on real property, second edition, revised, corrected and enlarged, 2 vols, 1846.
Conklings Treatise on the practice of the Supreme, District and Circuit Courts of the United States, second edition, much enlarged and improved by the author.
American Military Laws and the Practice of Courts Martial, by John O'Brien, Lieutenant in the United States' Army.
Barbour's Chancery Practice, 2 vols, with a collection of precedents.
Humphrey's Precedents, 2 vols. A collection of Practical Forms in Suits at Law ; also, Precedents of Contracts, Conveyances, Wills, etc., and Precedents under the Pension, Patent and Naturalization Laws of the United States, with Annotations and References, by Charles Humphrey, Counsellor at Law.
Vol. 1—Kelley's Reports, Supreme Court, Georgia.
Vol. 7—Robinson's Reports, Louisiana.
Vol. 1—Graham's Practice, third edition, Supreme Court of New York.
Dunlap's Paley's Agency, American Notes.
English Common Law index, vol. 1 to 47 inclusive.
Gilchrist's Digest of New Hampshire Reports, vol. 1 to 12 inclusive.
Debates in the N. York Convention, Atlas and Argus editions.
Vol. 3—Green's Chancery Reports, New Jersey.
Dayton's Law of Surrogates, Executors, etc.
Revised Statutes of New Jersey, 1847.
Splendid Supreme Court Licences, on parchment from Copper Plate Engravings. Also, Solicitors and Counsellors Licenses in Chancery.
The above, with a general assortment of Law Books, and all the new State Reports, as soon as published ; Law Libraries, and the Profession, supplied on the best terms, by BANKS, GOULD & CO.
Law Booksellers and Publishers,
No. 144 Nassau street.

Figure 1.1 This advertisement ran through the summer of 1847. It shows that even young states on the American periphery, like Arkansas, had produced a half dozen volumes of precedents that New York jurists were citing and consulting.
National Police Gazette (New York, N.Y.), June 5, 1847, p. 6.

the newspaper advertisements like the one in Figure 1.1, which announced the never-ending importation of new books of precedents. "Who can guess what he may have to meet in a law suit," one practitioner despondently wrote, "as no lawyer can afford to buy or read all the books in the world?"[42]

For lawyers attempting to keep up, the solution to overabundant publishing appeared to be only more publishing. In addition to treatises that introduced neophytes to the rules of practice, publishers circulated digests of recent cases and indices of citations to cases discussing related points of law.[43] Over time, the guidebooks to case reports became just another set of volumes filling the shelves. One practitioner in

[42] Hiram P. Hastings, *An Essay on Constitutional Reform* (1846), 27. See also Stuart Banner, *The Decline of Natural Law: How American Lawyers Once Used Natural Law and Why They Stopped* (Oxford University Press, 2021), 119–36.
[43] See Patti Ogden, " 'Mastering the Lawless Science of Our Law': A Story of Legal Citation Indexes," 85 *Law Library Journal* 1 (1993); Thomas A. Woxland, " 'Forever Associated with the Practice of Law': The Early Years of the West Publishing Company," 5 *Legal Reference Services Quarterly* 115 (1985).

1846 observed that a minimally adequate law library should contain eight hundred to one thousand volumes; a good library would have upward of five thousand volumes. In David Dudley Field's experience, "the lawyer's library had become a collection of books from the Old World and the new, reports of all the courts in England and in all our States, and treatises from every legal authority in America or Europe." Sampson denounced digests and indices as so many "clouds of cyphers" which "would not be missed off the shelves of a young attorney" after a code swept them away.[44]

Precedents were not the only legal tools changed by industrialized publishing. The print revolution also transformed the compensation structure of New York attorneys with respect to pleadings and motions filed in court. Like most Anglo-American jurisdictions, New York law required the loser in a legal controversy to pay the winner's costs and attorney's fees. Since the colonial era, New York had precisely regulated the fees a lawyer could collect, usually tagged to the number of pages in court filings—including pleadings, affidavits, deposition transcripts, or appellate briefs.[45] One reformer, Theodore Sedgwick, alleged that clients usually demanded—and lawyers often had to accept—fees at only the prescribed rates that could be shifted to a losing adversary.[46] Sedgwick's self-interested testimony left out of view retainer fees, which could be immense for elite lawyers. However, the general rule that lawyers could collect only what they could win in prescribed fees likely described workaday practice for many of New York's lawyers.[47] What the general public usually considered "law reform," Sedgwick complained, consisted of nothing more than lowering the fees lawyers could charge for their filings. Significant fee reductions were legislated at the turn of the nineteenth century and again in 1828 and 1840.[48]

Such "law reform" galled New York City's lawyers especially, who likened themselves to the city's other artisans who were undergoing what lawyers perceived to be a similar crisis of overabundant labor, falling prices, and degraded working conditions. "A boy is now made an attorney and grows up into a counsellor with habits that would dishonor the profession of a tailor," wrote the *National Advocate* in 1825. "Is not a Lawyer a laborer—a workman?" Sedgwick asked. Yet "no other workman is paid

---

[44] Michael Hoffman, "Letter on Reforms Necessary in the Body of Law, in the Written Pleadings, and in the Practice of the Courts" (Mar. 21, 1846), in Thomas Prentice Kettle, ed., *Constitutional Reform in a Series of Articles Contributed to the Democratic Review* (1846), 63–64; David Dudley Field, *Legal Reform: An Address to the Graduating Class of the Law School of the University of Albany* (1855), 21. Sampson, "Anniversary Discourse," 39.

[45] See, for instance, *Revised Statutes of the State of New York* (1829), 2:630–33, §§ 15 & 18.

[46] Theodore Sedgwick, *How Shall the Lawyers Be Paid?* (1840), 9–10.

[47] An analysis of Daniel Lord's account books found that Lord, one of Manhattan's leading attorneys in the antebellum era, frequently grossed $15,000 a year, largely through retainers. Justin Simard, "The Birth of a Legal Economy: Lawyers and the Development of American Commerce," 64 *Buffalo Law Review* 1059 (2016), 1108–11.

[48] See *Laws of the State of New York* (Kent & Radcliffe 1802), 2:69–70; *Revised Statutes of the State of New York*, 2:630–33, §§ 15 & 18; 1840 N.Y. Laws 327–36, ch. 386. Field estimated from returns filed in 1838 that chancery, in a single year, adjudicated about $9.2 million in claims at a cost of over $920,000. During the same year, common law courts adjudicated $28.8 million in claims at a cost of $1.9 million. The average common law case was for debt and damages in the amount of $996.75, with costs of $35.97. Considering costs were taxed for court personnel, witnesses expenses, and lawyers' fees, a lawyer might expect about $5 per case to be paid by the adverse party. See Appendix: A Letter from D. D. Field, Esq. of New York, on Law Reform, to Representative John O'Sullivan, in *Documents of the Assembly of the State of New York*, 65th Sess., No. 81 (1842), 5:28–29.

according to statute." Even as artisans across the city complained that industrialization and low prices had "bastardized" journeymen, preventing them from earning the competence of a master, Sedgwick and other lawyers complained that the same was happening in the practice of law. Sedgwick groused that the prevalent system of legislatively fixed costs was "degrading to the profession" and turning "lawyers and gentlemen into pettifoggers and knaves."[49]

That use of the word "pettifogger" was especially evocative. In the eighteenth century, the epithet "pettifogger" described people who were untrained in legal advocacy, but nineteenth-century lawyers increasingly applied the term to members of their profession who excelled at degrading forms of legal practice, such as filing frivolous motions and bloated pleadings in order to boost fees that were tethered to page counts. No longer an interloper among a closed guild, the pettifogger was a craftsman who had neither the skill nor the desire to attain the level of master—the perpetual journeyman, content with his own degradation.[50]

In actual practice, virtually all lawyers—including the master practitioners—maintained or at least supplemented their income by increasing the length (and number) of their court filings. Using common counts to restate the same claim and adding in legalistic "aforesaids" and redundancies ("paid out, laid out, and expended by the plaintiff"), even the most straightforward claims could fill a dozen pages or more.[51] For lawyers like Field, the useless multiplication of form and fiction to earn a competence had transformed daily employment into "mere drudgery."[52]

Innovations in legal publishing brought other problems of mass production to the practice of law since, as one New York lawyer wrote, "Books are to a lawyer or a judge what tools are to a mechanic."[53] Seeking convenience in pleading, innovative printers marketed "law blanks." Since common law pleadings were largely fictitious anyway, the same fictions could be used repeatedly while lawyers filled in blank lines with the dates, party names, and the few other necessary details (see Figure 1.2). Printers thus produced reams of common pleadings styled in their lengthiest possible formulations to save lawyers the trouble of reproducing such forms by hand. But for lawyers pursuing a craftsman ideal, these conveniences did nothing to reverse the degradation of the legal profession. One supreme court judge complained that law blanks destroyed the educational value of apprenticeships, teaching students "no more of

---

[49] "Codal Revision of State Laws," *National Advocate* (New York, N.Y.), Apr. 8, 1825. Sedgwick, *How Shall the Lawyers Be Paid*, 7, 9. For the sources of Sedgwick's language of craft dignity and degradation, see Wilentz, *Chants Democratic*, 61–144.

[50] On the older use of "pettifogger" as an interloping amateur, see John E. Douglass, "Between Pettifoggers and Professionals: Pleaders and Practitioners and the Beginnings of the Legal Profession in Colonial Maryland 1634–1731," 39 *American Journal of Legal History* 359 (1995). For examples of pettifoggers as degraded lawyers, see, for instance, the satirical "Natural History of the New York Bar," *New York Herald*, Nov. 29, 1844; *National Advocate* (New York, N.Y.), Apr. 9, 1825.

[51] See Alexander M. Burrill, *A Treatise on the Practice of the Supreme Court of the State of New York* (J.S. Voorhies, 2d ed., 1846), 2:268–72. In chancery, each page of interrogatories and answers had its corresponding court and lawyer's fee—in 1830, twenty-eight cents a folio to the solicitor drawing up the questions and twenty cents a folio for the court examiner recording the answers (in addition, of course, to other costs). *Revised Statutes of the State of New York*, 2:626–30, ch. 10, tit. 3, §§ 9 & 15.

[52] David Dudley Field, "The Study and Practice of the Law," 14 *Democratic Review* 345 (1844), 345–47.

[53] Report of Mr. Elisha Crosby on Civil and Common Law, *Journal of the Senate of the State of California* (1850), 478.

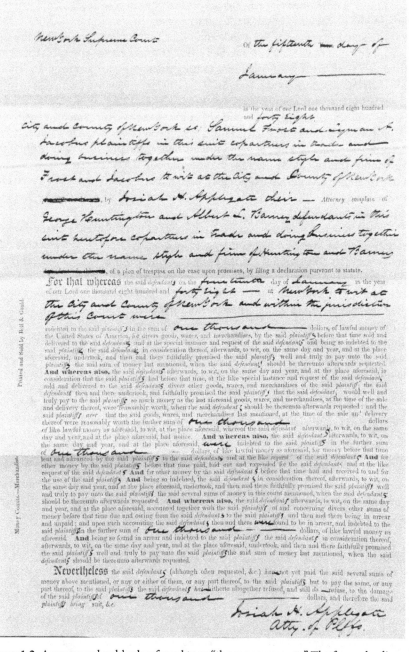

Figure 1.2 A common law blank referred to as "the money counts." The form pleading alleges four different liabilities, or "counts," as four different ways of describing the same dispute. For each count, the lawyer has filled in the round sum of $1,000 in a suit that actually recovered $483.42 in damages, costs, and fees. With the increase in printing, a "folio" for purposes of costs and fees was redefined from an actual folio page to a segment of one hundred words (later reduced to seventy-five). Although this blank is only one sheet, it was charged as ten folios.

actual pleading than how properly to fill out blanks." To Field, blanks promoted "a vicious system of procedure" and made "pecuniary emolument disproportionate to intellectual exertion."[54]

In sum, New York lawyers complained that they had to work both too hard and too little to earn their fees. Thanks to the legislature's fee reduction acts, lawyers felt they had to produce ever more written work product to maintain their incomes, yet the mass production of form filings generated unfulfilling work that undercut their self-image as learned master craftsmen of the law. The proliferation of case reports required a rapid mechanical search for favorable decisions instead of a focused appreciation for the reasoning that produced such rulings. "Those who have the best practice," remarked Field, "are tasked almost beyond endurance. The multiplication of law-books . . . have quadrupled their labors." And for what? Lawyers had to know their precedents to win their cases, but they were rarely compensated for the time and effort expended in research. Instead, a routine drudgery of stuffing pleadings and examinations supplied a lawyer's income. Another practitioner complained that instead of spending his time "in the study of the law as a most extensive, enlightened and liberal science," pressure to collect fees meant he was "compelled to spend one half of the best seventeen years of my life" hunting through forms and precedents.[55]

Sampson promised that a code could solve the problems of unmanageable precedents and tedious pleadings. Unlike the digests and "cyphers" that only directed lawyers toward sprawling case reports, an authoritative code would limit judges' options in formulating rules. Lawyers need only consult the legislation and not the volumes of decisions. "Particular cases will not then be resorted to, instead of general law," Sampson figured. "The law will govern the decisions of judges, and not the decisions the law." Having eliminated the enormous costs of scrambling after precedents, Sampson expected a code to rescue practitioners from "chicane and pettifogging" in their pleading, as attorneys would "no longer [be] forced into the degrading paths of Norman subtleties, nor to copy from models of Saxon barbarity." A code naturally inclined practitioners "to resolve every argument into principles of natural reason, universal justice, and present convenience."[56]

Echoing the argument that "a code will lessen the labor of Judges and lawyers in the investigation of legal questions," Sampson's young admirer David Dudley Field explained the practitioner's point of view. "Instead of searching, as now, through large libraries . . . it will be sufficient to examine the articles of the Code relating to the subject."[57] Field nonetheless disagreed with Sampson about whether codification should

---

[54] For sample forms and catalog listings of Law Blanks, see M. H. Hoeflich, "Law Blanks and Form Books: A Chapter in the Early History of Document Production," 11 *Green Bag 2d* 189 (2008). John W. Edmonds, *An Address on the Constitution and the Code of Procedure* (1848), 16; Field, "Study and Practice of the Law," 347.

[55] Field, "Study and Practice of the Law," 345; R.W. Wells, *Law of the State of Missouri Regulating Pleadings and Practice* (1849), 112–14 (It was as though a lawyer "is almost compelled by the system, to degenerate into a pettifogging caviler about words and phrases and forms, which diminish his intelligence and usefulness; and by the injustice of which he is the instrument, *he* becomes odious and his *profession* disreputable.").

[56] Sampson, "Anniversary Discourse," 32, 38.

[57] David Dudley Field, "Reasons for the Adoption of the Codes" (1873), in A. P. Sprague, ed., *Speeches, Arguments, and Miscellaneous Papers of David Dudley Field* (D. Appleton, 1884), 1:361, 371.

completely displace the common law's precedential system. Field expected that accumulating judicial "glosses and comments" on the code's text might require fresh codifications "at certain intervals." But Field argued that the benefits of consolidation and systematic reform made the effort worthwhile, even if it would have to be periodically repeated. Field agreed with Sampson that commonly "judges, instead of interpreting, are making law," and he believed that a code would substantially restore the "independence of the different departments of government." Yet Field approached the question foremost as a harried practitioner. His chief aim in codification was to see "our libraries superseded by a single work." As much as he decried "judicial legislation," he was prepared to accommodate judicial interpretation and comment as long as judges, in principle, focused their interpretations on a more limited set of sources: the single volume of a slender code.[58] That was at least one major allure of a code for overworked and undercompensated lawyers: by escaping the endless research into case law and the stultifying copying of pleading forms, elite lawyers hoped to restore the law to a "liberal science" worthy of their cultivated minds.

V

Minds, and perhaps also their souls. For Sampson, a code was a technology that did not just organize judicial rules; a code destroyed judicial authority itself by demystifying it, or to put it as harshly as the codifiers did, by desecrating it. In an era when an ascendant liberal Protestantism was challenging old orthodoxies, *Sampson's Discourse* invited its audience to imagine the power codes had to overthrow the old oracles of the law. "Oracles" had been William Blackstone's characterization of common law judges in his massively influential *Commentaries on the Law of England*. Blackstone explained that English law essentially originated from the judges as "the depositaries of the laws; the living oracles," whose "knowledge of that law is derived from experience and study; from the 'viginti annorum lucubrationes' [nighttime labors of many years], . . . and from being long personally accustomed to the judicial decisions of their predecessors."[59] Sampson retorted that that precisely was the common law's problem: It treated judges as actual oracles, a mystical community whose rulings went unquestioned by "superstitious votaries."[60] Treatises and other learned literature reverenced judicial decisions and further reinforced the oracular quality of the common law. Codes, on the other hand, could break the spell.

References to oracular devotion and mystical spells were more than incidental. Sampson's legal history was at least as much a religious history, and his prescriptions conflated a legal reformation with the capital-R Protestant Reformation of the previous centuries. Describing the legal profession, Sampson regretted that young apprentices "cannot enter the vestibule without paying constrained devotion to idols" of common law writs. The "history and antiquities" part of Sampson's lecture located the common law's origins in pagan Britain, where an "abundance of gods

---

[58] Field, *Legal Reform*, 28–30.
[59] William Blackstone, *Commentaries on the Law of England* (1765), 1:68–70.
[60] Sampson, "Anniversary Discourse," 5.

and goddesses" enclosed the law within "the veil of mystery." The Norman Conquest only further "imported the whole farrago of superstitious novelties, engendered in the blindness and superstition" of medieval Catholic Europe. Scholasticism rendered "the administration of both the prayers of the church and the law of the land, in a foreign and unknown language; the frittering both law and divinity, into . . . a science of the greatest intricacy."[61]

As a Protestant who famously defended Catholic toleration, Sampson took some care to avoid anti-Catholic polemic when he could, often selecting derogatory imagery that cast the common law as pagan Celtic (comparing judges to "druids"), Arabic ("prostrate ourselves before the offended genii of the common law"), Semitic ("mystical and cabalistic name of Common Law"), or pre-Columbian ("the practices of the Gentoos, the Mexicans, and the children of the Sun") by turns. Nevertheless, Sampson's prescriptions for purging "bad faith . . . from the temple of justice," insisted that "we have but to put our hands to the good work of reformation," using the Protestant revolt against Rome as a model for American codification. Just as the "ministers of the Gospel long worshipped in the temples and vestments of the heathens" in the days of Catholic syncretism, Sampson described American lawyers as people who "had reduced the practice of religion to its purest principles" yet nevertheless retained "one pagan idol to which they daily offered up much smoky incense": the common law. But like the Reformers opening the Bible to the people, the code-writers could dispel "the air of occult magic" surrounding the judges and their case law.[62]

Sampson's imagining of the common law as the one area of English culture untouched by the Protestant Reformation had a broad and deep influence among American codifiers. For instance, the southern codifier Thomas Grimké thought that "the Reformation shut for ever the dark book of despotism, in religion, politics, and science," but as yet had no influence over the common law. David Dudley Field likewise described New York's legal system as one "conceived in the midnight of the dark ages, . . . when chancellors were ecclesiastics and logic was taught by monks." Field expected that a New York code would contribute to the overthrow of medieval scholasticism and superstition begun by the Protestant Reformation. "There is no magic in forms," one of his early reports concluded. The forms of action were merely "old jingles of words, invented somewhere about the times of the Edwards."[63]

After the publication of *Sampson's Discourse*, many readers rediscovered an anonymous pamphlet from 1805 titled *Sampson Against the Philistines, or the Reformation of Lawsuits*. Some supposed by the misspelled name in the title that the author was Sampson himself, but the publication preceded Sampson's arrival in America, and the evidence points toward an obscure Delaware law reformer named Jesse Higgins as the author.[64] Higgins's pamphlet clarified that "Reformation" was not a general reference to law reform but a specific invocation of the Protestant faith. Like Sampson, Higgins

---

[61] *Ibid.*, 6–7.
[62] *Ibid.*, 8, 11, 32, 37–38.
[63] Grimké, *Oration*, 5; *First Report* (New York, 1848), 141; David Dudley Field, *Legal Reform: An Address to the Graduating Class at the University of Albany* (1855), 20; Field, "Study and Practice of the Law," 349.
[64] See G. S. Rowe, "Jesse Higgins and the Failure of Legal Reform in Delaware, 1800–1810," 3 *Journal of the Early Republic* 17 (1983).

identified the history of the common law with "the invention of the same times and same men" who crafted the papal indulgence system "to make sale the *mercy of God* [and] the *justice of man*." If anything, Higgins drew even more explicit links between Protestant theology and law reform through codification, and his tract offers a compact guide to the ways early nineteenth-century codifiers in the United States assumed and argued from Protestant principles to support their notions of legal authority and textual interpretation.[65]

Following Sampson and *Sampson*, codifiers compared the authority of common law judges to "the Romish priesthood when that imperious hierarchy was most ambitious and intolerant; . . . *they* were learned, and *laymen* ignorant."[66] Historian Lawrence Friedman writes that codifiers like Higgins hoped to make litigation "so simple and rational that the average citizen could do it on her own." As within liberal Protestantism, however, that theory was more complex in practice.[67] Though often caricatured by their opponents as democratic levelers, the codifiers displayed significant internal divisions over whether their movement claimed interpretive authority for all readers, for all insiders (i.e., the lawyers), or only for all educated insiders (academic jurists). Some, like Higgins, hoped codes would indeed eliminate the legal profession entirely. But most codifiers agreed that "such hopes will never be realized this side of utopia," as one law journal put it. More representative of his profession, David Dudley Field declared that "justice is attainable only through lawyers," because "only a few men, set apart for that particular calling, and devoting to it the best part of their lives" could master the law even in a codified jurisdiction.[68]

Whatever their disagreements on the exact level of interpretive authority, codifiers agreed that law did not need to be mediated through judicial authority. Field wrote that in monarchies and aristocracies, "it would not be so much to be wondered at that a class should arrogate to itself the knowledge and interpretation of laws; but that this should happen in a republic, where all the citizens both legislate and obey, is . . . incredible." Codifiers compared judges' purported authority to declare and apply the law as similar to the claim that priests had special powers to absolve sin—an explicit comparison codifiers often made with the epithet "priestcraft." Field's mentor, Henry

---

[65] *Sampson Against the Philistines, or, The Reformation of Lawsuits* (1805), 33. American codifiers were not alone in their conflation of legal and religious reform. Codification efforts in British India also comprised explicitly Protestant efforts to "disenchant" Hindu law, converting otherwise magical utterances into mundane charges and counter-charges. Robert A. Yelle, *The Language of Disenchantment: Protestant Literalism and Colonial Discourse in British India* (Oxford University Press, 2012).

[66] *Sampson Against the Philistines*, 16.

[67] Generalizations across Protestant denominations risk oversimplification. By "liberal," this account refers to the variety of Christian denominations that could be said to have moved beyond the communal and deterministic Calvinist orthodoxy of the Puritans to emphasize the importance and authority of individual actors and self-determination. See especially Peter J. Thuesen, "Agency, Voluntarism, and Predestination in American Religion," in *Oxford Research Encyclopedia of Religion* (Oxford University Press, 2017); Leo Hirrel, *Children of Wrath: New School Calvinism and Antebellum Reform* (University of Kentucky Press, 2014); Daniel Walker Howe, "The Decline of Calvinism: An Approach to its Study," 14 *Comparative Studies in Society and History* 306 (1972).

[68] Friedman, *History of American Law*, 297; "Nature and Method of Legal Studies," 3 *United States Monthly Law Magazine* 380 (1851), 380; David Dudley Field, "Reform in the Legal Profession and the Laws," in *Speeches of Field*, 1:509–10. On the parallel Protestant ambiguities on the locus of interpretive authority, see Nathan O. Hatch, *The Democratization of American Christianity* (Yale University Press, 1991), 179–83.

Sedgwick, condemned "the veneration and obedience paid to authority and precedent" in both law and religion and drew on anti-Catholic polemic to criticize the mysterious, quasi-private reasoning judges used in formulating their decisions.[69]

Obliterate the mediated authority of the judges, Sampson's circle of codifiers believed, and the legal texts left behind would be readily *perspicuous*, a Protestant term that American lawyers used frequently. When applied to scripture, the doctrine of perspicuity held that important truths (those about salvation especially) were immediately apparent from the text without external aids or magisterial interpreters. "No creed but the Bible" was a typical American formulation of perspicuity.[70] Advocates of codification believed legal texts had achieved similar perspicuity. And since texts sufficiently spoke for themselves, the codifiers figured the time had come to discard oral traditions of practice. Whatever oral traditions or courtroom practices persisted in particular locales, the written case reports were sufficient to communicate the general law. A contemporary treatise writer described the process of codification working off of case reports: "The report of a case sets forth, at length, all the facts which it involves, the arguments of counsel, and the opinion, with all its reasons and illustrations of the Court, while the principle recognized or decided may be concisely but clearly expressed in a few marginal lines." Simply extract those lines, case by case, and one had a compendium of the rules.[71]

At this point, codification efforts could seriously fracture, at least when they came to put pen to page. Codifiers disagreed about whether legal texts were perspicuous to ordinary readers or only to what Grimké called "the *inquiring* reader"—meaning a trained lawyer. They further disagreed about the level of generality with which rules could be stated or described. "Some one has estimated the whole number of rules laid down in the reports at two million," Field wrote, but "no man would dream of collecting and arranging all these in a code." Instead, "the province of a code is not to give all the rules of law, general and particular, but only such as are general and fundamental." However, where to draw those lines was far from clear, and each expert codifier seemed to come up with different general rules for his draft code. Typical reviews, even among the supporters of codification, declared one another's drafts "grossly incomplete in some branches, absurdly minute in others."[72] Opponents of codification delighted in pointing out the endlessly fracturing "sectarianism" of the codifiers and the ever-increasingly glosses interpreting their codes. One drew a comparison to Protestantism, which had by that time splintered into twenty thousand American

---

[69] Field, "Reform in the Legal Profession," 510; "Review of An Anniversary Discourse," 421. See *Sampson Against the Philistines*, 16.

[70] See Mark Noll, *America's God: From Jonathan Edwards to Abraham Lincoln* (Oxford University Press, 2002), 231, 367–84; Keith D. Stanglin, "The Rise and Fall of Biblical Perspicuity: Remonstrants and the Transition toward Modern Exegesis," 83 *Church History* 38 (2014).

[71] Grimké, *Oration*, 15. David Dudley Field, "Final Report of the Code Commission" (1865), in *Speeches of Field*, 1:326. See also *ibid.*, 322 ("Whatever is known to the judge or to the lawyer can be written, and whatever has been written in the treatises of lawyers or the opinions of judges, can be written in a systematic Code."); Francis Hilliard, *The Elements of Law: Being a Comprehensive Summary of American Jurisprudence* (John S. Voorhies, 2d ed., 1848), v.

[72] Grimké, *Oration*, 16; David Dudley Field, "Reasons for the Adoption of the Codes by New York, Address Before the Judiciary Committees of the Two Houses of the Legislature" (1873), in *Speeches of Field*, 1:367; William B. Hornblower, *Is Codification of the Law Expedient? An Address Delivered Before the American Social Science Association* (New York, n.p., 1888), 3.

denominations. Protestantism vaunted perspicuity, yet "how various have been the opinions and dogmas of its professors upon what would seem to be the most plain and intelligible portions of its text," the common law lawyer John Pickering tittered. If Protestants divided in their interpretation of divine law, "how vain, then, is the hope of attaining to perfect exactness in the formation of any laws which are the work of man?"[73]

But codifiers did not think they worked in vain, no matter how much the common law lawyers jeered. In this, too, they expressed a kind of liberal Protestant optimism that once the cobwebs of the past were cleared away, truth and common sense would easily prevail. Legal judgment itself would become a simple task. While "subtleties, quibbles, refinements, and false analogies have been introduced into it," Sedgwick wrote, "nothing is . . . more simple than the ownership of real property." Freed from the scholastic tradition, even the most arcane law of property would be easy to understand and apply under a code. "When the whole facts (or truth) are known," the *Sampson* tract summarized, "the decision agreeable to law is easy; the law properly being agreeable to the simplest dictates of nature and reason."[74]

Common-sense philosophy, an offshoot of nineteenth-century liberal Protestantism, encouraged the codifiers that their search for general principles in the lawbooks would ultimately yield universal legal truths. Grimké confidently affirmed that "the common sense of the people, becoming every day more enlightened" could not "suffer the indefinite continuance of the Laws, in their present condition." Others declared that practices variously labeled Catholic, feudal, or European would appear absurd if they were separated from the authority of tradition. While a few lawyers may have learned Scottish philosophy from its source, most adopted the American pairing of common-sense realism with religious ideas of natural or biblical revelation. For instance, Francis Hilliard's *Elements of Law* reasoned that legal "rules are founded upon the basis of equity, reason, and right. If this be so, then obscurity no more belongs to the former than to the latter; upon which the instinct of conscience, the conclusions of the understanding, and the teachings of revelation, pour their mingled light."[75]

If the texts of the law were so perspicuous, and general legal truths so easy to discern, why hadn't the authority of the common law judges already collapsed? Sedgwick explained the common law's persistence in terms of a Catholic upbringing. Noting that many otherwise brilliant men adhered to Catholicism, a religion "equally at variance with right reason and divine revelation," he surmised that they did so only because they "had been *brought up* to be catholics. . . . Had these men been born in a protestant country," they would have been "champions of a purer faith." So, too, the

---

[73] John Pickering, "A Lecture on the Alleged Uncertainty of the Law," 12 *American Jurist* 285 (1834), 293–94, 297. See also Carter, *The Proposed Codification of Our Common Law*, 85–86; Orestes Brownson, "Authority in Matters of Faith," 14 *Catholic World* 155 (1871).

[74] "Review of an Anniversary Discourse," 424; *Sampson Against the Philistines*, 26.

[75] Grimké, *Oration*, 21; Hilliard, *Elements of Law*, vi. See also, for instance, Sedgwick, *English Practice*, 6; Parker, *Common Law, History, Democracy*, 68. In sum, the immediate target of American common sense rationalism was not the skepticism of David Hume but the crippling depravity propounded by John Calvin. See Noll, *America's God*, 93–113. On the pervasive influence of common-sense rationalism on antebellum legal doctrine, see especially Susanna L. Blumenthal, *Law and the Modern Mind: Consciousness and Responsibility in American Legal Culture* (Harvard University Press, 2016), ch. 1.

common law lawyer: "He is brought up to think with the highest reverence of the wisdom of our ancestors, and especially the wisest of them, the ancient sages of the law. These are to him the holy fathers, whose creed he thinks it almost impious to doubt." But faith went beyond creeds, Sedgwick recognized. It shaped and was shaped by the practices and rituals of both law and piety. "The particular forms, modes, and principles" lawyers used in practice gave rise to habits that then insulated belief from criticism, "in the same way in which many pious Christians sincerely believe the particular rites and dogmas of their own sect to be the very body and soul of religion, and that whatever affects the one must endanger the other." Practice instilled and then protected belief; belief interpreted and then legitimated practice. In all, Sedgwick concluded "the *faith* of the lawyer is much akin to that of the theologian," and in both cases, Sedgwick lamented that some Americans grew up too habituated to the authority of tradition and hierarchy.[76]

This Protestant framework made codification efforts in the United States notably distinct from similar efforts elsewhere. The leading proponents of positivism and codification in England and France—Comte, Mill, Bentham, Austin, Cambacérès, Thibaut—all adhered to varieties of irreligion, dismissive of Catholic and Protestant modes of argument alike.[77] That is not to say that all American codifiers were orthodox Protestants. Most engaged in varying levels of adherence to liberal or rationalistic Protestant denominations like Unitarianism. However, as the sons and brothers of some of America's leading ministers, the codifiers inherited a facility with theological modes of arguments about textual authority and the links between ritual practices and belief.[78] Bentham once sarcastically asked when a Martin Luther would arise for the common law.[79] Whatever their intensity of religious devotion, American codifiers like Field sincerely believed they were answering that call.

VI

"All that we know of the law, we know from written records," Field announced in commentary to one of his draft codes. The writtenness of the law was for Field not just the root but the sum of his codification philosophy. "Whatever is known to the judge or to the lawyer can be written," he surmised, "and whatever has been written in the

---

[76] [Henry Dwight Sedgwick], *The English Practice: A Statement Showing Some of the Evils and Absurdities of the Practice of the English Courts* (1822), 6. See also David Dudley Field, *A Short Response to a Long Discourse* (1884), 8.

[77] See Young, *The Politics of Codification*, 117–20; Whitman, *The Legacy of the Roman Law in the German Romantic Era*, 3–40.

[78] One historian of religion in America has recently argued that the Protestant Bible was "primarily a medium through which public discourse happened" in the nineteenth-century United States, "rather than primarily a substantive source for that discourse." That is, "people said what they had to say in the language of the Bible." Lincoln A. Mullen, *America's Public Bible: A Commentary* (Stanford University Press, 2022), https://americaspublicbible.supdigital.org/essay/introduction/. One could conclude much the same about the codification debates—not that a particular theology dictated a stance or method on codification, but that when lawyers argued about the law, they did so using discursive tools supplied by their religious context.

[79] Jeremy Bentham, *Rationale of Judicial Evidence*, in John Bowring, ed., *The Works of Jeremy Bentham* (William Tait, 2d ed., 1843), 7:270 n.10.

treatises of lawyers or the opinions of judges, can be written in a systematic Code." Field's reduction of the law to its writings became the lasting response to William Sampson's call for a distinctively American approach to codification. Admirers like Henry Sedgwick had retained a sense of the ways unwritten practice could bolster or reformulate written doctrine, but that was not the sense of the arch-codifier David Dudley Field. For him, in the beginning was the word, and only the word.[80]

Field's religiously inflected epistemology made the written word not just the chief but sole technology for knowing and mastering law, and in a way, that orientation lessened the importance of a code overall while sharpening its utility for lawyers like Field. Blackstone—whose *Commentaries* were first delivered orally until market-driven publishers wrote them down—reverenced common law judges as "the living oracles" of the law, whose status and power were derived from their technological access to the law. Judges contained within themselves special judicial knowledge of their precedents, which they gained only through years of monastic devotion.[81] Where Sampson believed a code was necessary to cast down the oracular judges, Field's generation of codifiers believed that case reporting had already done that. As Gutenberg's press had done for Martin Luther, industrial American publishers transmitted the oracular word beyond the chambers of law's priesthood. Broad access to opinions that announced rules and rendered judgments meant anyone could undertake the "nighttime labors" that Blackstone associated with legal knowledge. "It may be safely asserted that the whole body of the Common Law has ceased to be *lex non scripta*, and actually is now a part of the *lex scripta*," one codifier wrote, years before any code had been attempted.[82]

On this account, it was not a code that destroyed the idols of common law judging—that was simply the work of law itself in the age of its mechanical reproduction.[83] Instead, a code collected the fragments of the law and set them in order, especially for lawyers. The written word was a gift, but its reproduction at industrial scales threatened to overwhelm its recipients. "To make a Code of the known law," however, was "but to make a complete, analytical, and authoritative compilation from these records," Field concluded. With the compilation in hand, the lawyers, more than judges or the populace at large, stood to gain from codification's mastery of the law.[84]

Field's emphasis on the lawyerly users of codes helps to dispel the myth that American codification necessarily went hand-in-hand with a politics of distributive democracy in the Age of Jackson. Theorists have supposed that if codifiers could

---

[80] Field, "Final Report of the Code Commission," 1:322. On the similar primacy of word over ritual in American Protestantism at the time, see Candy Gunther Brown, *The Word in the World: Evangelical Writing, Publishing, and Reading in America, 1789–1880* (University of North Carolina Press, 2004); David Paul Nord, *Faith in Reading: Religious Publishing and the Birth of Mass Media in America* (Oxford University Press, 2004); Monica L. Mercado, "'Have You Ever Read?': Imagining Women, Bibles, and Religious Print in Nineteenth-Century America," 31 *U.S. Catholic Historian* 1 (2013).

[81] See Kunal M. Parker, "Historicizing Blackstone's *Commentaries on the Laws of England*: Differences and Sameness in Historical Time," in *Law Books in Action*, 22–42.

[82] Grimké, *Oration*, 15.

[83] Cf. Walter Benjamin, "The Work of Art in the Age of Mechanical Reproduction," in Hannah Arendt, *Illuminations*, trans. Harry Zorn (Schocken Books, 1969 [1939]), 211–44; Miriam Bratu Hansen, "Benjamin's Aura," 34 *Critical Inquiry* 336 (2008).

[84] Field, "Final Report of the Code Commission," 1:326.

consolidate the rules of property and reduce judges' power to announce new rules or exceptions protecting property, then transformative regimes of equal rights to and re-distribution of property would be as simple as a legislative enactment, an enactment that would necessarily reflect the rising democratic majorities of working-class voters. Thus legal historians asking why there was no codification in the United States have tended to adopt the same polemical tone and import of Werner Sombart's *Why Is There No Socialism In the United States?*[85]

But paradoxically, it was the codifiers, and not their common law-defending oppo-nents, who most vehemently defended absolute property rights and the limited role of a legislature in the liberal state.[86] For many, American Protestantism again provided the model, as leading codifiers grounded their views about liberty and the American state upon their understanding of religious toleration during the era of American dis-establishment. The aggressive codifier Robert Rantoul argued that "the principles of civil and religious freedom" represented "the only sure foundation" for codifica-tion. In Rantoul's telling, the liberal individual "may rove free as the free air which he breathes, calling no man his master, acknowledging no power above him but in heaven" when it came to religious toleration. The common law itself thus needed to be reframed on the understanding that "the whole object of government is negative. It is to remove, and keep out of his way all obstacles to his natural freedom of action."[87] Religious and legal freedom were two sides of the same coin.

Field also counted "the separation of church and state"—a phrase he cherished—to be the greatest achievement of American government. No antagonist to religion, Field valued disestablishment for the ways it sapped the legislature's authority over "pri-vate" life and property. Interested in extending codification globally, Field conceded that any international code would be limited to a "public law of Christendom" only, as the nations of the East entangled religion, property, and communalism in ways incompatible with Western law.[88] In contrast to the Benthamites in England, Field routinely denounced "agrarian measure[s] to divide property among those who have not earned it," and he frequently contributed to John O'Sullivan's *Democratic Review*,

[85] Werner Sombart, *Why Is There No Socialism in the United States?* (M. E. Sharpe, 1979 [1906]). See especially Morton J. Horwitz, *The Transformation of American Law, 1780–1850* (Oxford University Press, 1977), 160–201, 265–66. Gordon, "The American Codification Movement"; Charles Sellers, *The Market Revolution: Jacksonian America, 1815–1846* (Oxford University Press, 1991), 48–61

[86] For defenses of the anti-codification common law lawyers as economic and political progressives of their day, see David M. Rabban, *Law's History: American Legal Thought and the Transatlantic Turn to History* (Cambridge University Press, 2013), 322–77; Kunal M. Parker, *Common Law, History, and Democracy in America, 1790–1900: Legal Thought Before Modernism* (Cambridge University Press, 2011), 230–41; Lewis A. Grossman, "James Coolidge Carter and Mugwump Jurisprudence," *Law & History Review* 20 (2002).

[87] Rantoul, *An Oration Delivered Before the Democrats and Antimasons*, 41–42. On the Protestant sources of disestablishment, and indeed the Protestant framework of secularization itself, see Brad S. Gregory, *The Unintended Reformation: How a Religious Revolution Secularized Society* (Harvard University Press, 2012); John Lardas Modern, *Secularism in Antebellum America* (Chicago University Press, 2011); Tracy Fessenden, *Culture and Redemption: Religion, the Secular, and American Literature* (Princeton University Press, 2007).

[88] David Dudley Field, "On a Project for an International Code," 22 *Law Magazine & Law Review Quarterly* (3d Series, 1867), 151. See also David Dudley Field, *Applicability of International Law to Oriental Nations: Address Before the Institute of International Law at the Hague* (1875), 447, 450.

whose masthead announced "The best government is that which governs least."[89] In short, the autonomous liberal individual—Western, male, and Protestant (but not fanatically so)—was the basic actor in Field's legal imagination, as it was for many of his code-writing associates.[90]

A codification movement that devalued legislatures and was indifferent to mass politics might sound too contradictory to have possibly gained adherents. But for lawyers like Field, codification was a tool for managing judges and judicial precedent without sacrificing the property protections those precedents secured. Paired with short, biennial legislative sessions restricted to passing only "general laws"—institutional reforms many codifiers like Field favored—the legislative supremacy implied by codification was a power to be left unused.[91] Ultimately, the authoritative individual readers of the perspicuous codes were not to be found in the populace at large but among the professional bar. As disestablishment had withdrawn religion from the state, codification would further sap the state of centralized power, leaving the lawyers to their negotiations over the rights of property. That was its allure, at least to Field and his generation of codifiers. In their hands, codified laws would render a government as William Sampson had idealized it: Insensible, like the air.

[89] David Dudley Field, "Corruption in Politics" (1877), in *Speeches of Field*, 2:494. A series of Field's travelogues, his first published writings, appear in the *United States Democratic Review* under the title "Sketches over the Sea" from October to May, 1839–1840. On the association of Field and O'Sullivan within the broader "Young America" movement, see Widmer, *Young America*, 155–84.

[90] See Barbara Young Welke, *Law and the Borders of Belonging in the Long Nineteenth-Century United States* (Cambridge University Press, 2010). Claims of representativeness among lawyers can be just as fraught as generalizations about Protestants, but for one attempt at a comprehensive survey of codifiers that closely aligned with Field's ideology, see Appendix A to Kellen Richard Funk, The Lawyer's Code: The Transformation of American Legal Practice, 1828–1938 (Ph.D. dissertation, Princeton University, 2018), 446–69.

[91] See, e.g., "The Progress of Constitutional Reform in the United States," 18 *Democratic Review* 243 (April 1846). On the growing movement for "general laws" in the nineteenth century, see Naomi R. Lamoreaux & John Joseph Wallis, "Economic Crisis, General Laws, and the Mid-Nineteenth-Century Transformation of American Political Economy," 41 *Journal of the Early Republic* 403 (2021).

2

The Rule of Writs

Civil Justice Before the Code

I

In an 1854 essay, Charles Dickens compiled his favorite "legal and equitable jokes," which, to his relish, were "all of a practical nature"—the pun uniting practical jokes with the practices of the law. In the guise of an English barrister, Dickens lamented that "the leveling spirit of the times has destroyed some of the finest practical jokes connected with the profession." But despite mid-nineteenth-century reforms to legal practice, the narrator still found many "practical" jokes remained in the law:

> A sea-captain ejected from his ship a noisy and drunken man, who misconducted himself; and at the same time turned out certain pot-companions of the drunken man, who were as troublesome as he. Bibo (so to call the drunken man) bringeth an action against the captain for assault and battery; to which the captain pleadeth in justification that he removed the plaintiff 'and certain persons unknown,' from his ship, for that they did misbehave themselves. 'Aye,' quoth the learned counsel for Bibo, at the trial, 'but there be seventeen objections to that plea, whereof the main one is that it appeareth that the certain persons are *known* and not *unknown* as by thee set forth.' 'Marry,' crieth the court, 'but that is fatal, Gentlemen of the Jury!' Verdict accordingly.

Dickens admitted that "with great delay and expense" the sea captain eventually "got judgment in his favour. But, no man to this hour hath been able to make him comprehend how he got it, or why; or wherefore the suit was not decided on the merits when first tried." The joke, commented the narrator, put "the density, obstinacy, and confusion of the sea-captain in a richly absurd light." But of course, the real professional target of Dicken's joke was not the mariner but the lawyer, the bitter irony being that Dickens described an actual case at common law.[1]

Dickens's joke conveyed the central concerns of mid-nineteenth-century law reform both in England and America. Suits, reformers complained, were too often determined on "technicalities"—like the wording of an immaterial part of the pleadings—instead of on "the merits." Even when ordinary litigants like the sea captain obtained justice, they could not understand the language of the courts that

---

[1] Charles Dickens, "Legal and Equitable Jokes" (1854), in *The Works of Charles Dickens: Miscellaneous Papers* (Chapman & Hall, 1911), 14:477, 480–81. Dickens embellished the details of a case reported by Graham Willmore, the counsel for the steamer captain. See *First Report of the Commissioners Appointed to Inquire into the State of the County Courts and the Course of Practice Therein*, No. 1914, *House of Commons Sessional Papers* (1855), 18:162.

Law's Machinery. Kellen R. Funk, Oxford University Press. © Kellen R. Funk 2025. DOI: 10.1093/9780197543962.003.0003

provided it. Such, at least, were the complaints about the courts of common law. The court of chancery inspired its own "equitable" jokes that often focused on the extreme costs and delays of equity suits. Dickens offered one that repeated the plot of his 1853 novel *Bleak House*: Creditors brought suit against a decedent's estate and won their decree. "But, the property realizing seven hundred pounds, and the suit costing seven hundred and fifty, these creditors brought their pigs to a fine market, and made much amusement for the Chancery Bar."[2] Similar jokes—whether purporting to relate actual cases or rhetorical exaggerations—also abounded among the American bar.[3]

While such humor at the expense of the legal system may reveal something about the perceptions of contemporaries, American legal historians have tended to take the jokes too seriously. They often tell the story of the practice and profession of law as one of relatively smooth and inevitable modernization. Inherited technical rules were obviously absurd, but they remained entrenched within a professional bar that could deny access to any who refused to play the game by its medieval rules. The rules changed only when they encountered equal and opposite forces of commerce. Business demanded certainty, it is said. The "slow ritual dance" of common law practice thus had to give way to a system where the law was clearly and systematically codified and where remedies would not be snared in technical traps.[4]

The following account offers a different perspective. It takes the jokes literally without taking them too seriously. By the nineteenth century, the practice of law had created a complex system of civil justice that was constantly evolving. Small changes in one department could create unexpected chaos across the system, and lawyer jokes often highlighted those unforeseen turns. But, as it had for centuries, Anglo-American civil practice found ways to work, as even critics at the time had to admit. One of New York's most elite lawyers, Charles O'Conor, roundly criticized technicalities and fictions in the common law, in which "almost throughout, the allegations in [a legal] declaration are false to every common and ordinary intent." Nevertheless, he conceded, "the relation between the fiction in the pleadings, and the truth it represented, was well understood by lawyers and judges; and between them, they could instruct the jury to bring in such a verdict as worked out the ends of justice."[5] Many shared O'Conor's professional understanding that the common law was working well enough as well as his growing anxiety that the system was starting to show signs of failure in need of serious reform.

At the end of the nineteenth century, the English legal historian Frederic Maitland offered a sympathetic account of the early "technicality" of legal practice. Maitland

[2] Dickens, "Legal and Equitable Jokes," 478.

[3] For two particularly rich sources of anecdotes and jokes about the New York bar, see Henry B. Stanton, *Random Recollections* (Harper & Brothers, 1887); Charles Edwards, *Pleasantries About Courts and Lawyers of the State of New York* (Richardson, 1867).

[4] Lawrence M. Friedman, *A History of American Law* (Simon & Schuster, 3d ed., 2005), 294–97; Alison Reppy, "The Field Codification Concept," in Alison Reppy, ed., *David Dudley Field Centenary Essays* (New York University Press, 1949), 17, 34–36; Charles M. Cook, *The American Codification Movement: A Study in Antebellum Legal Reform* (Greenwood Press, 1983), 187–88. On constructing a pre-modern legal order out of the anxieties of modern theorists, see Steven Wilf, "The Invention of Legal Primitivism," 10 *Theoretical Inquiries in Law* 485 (2009).

[5] William G. Bishop & William H. Attree, eds., *Report of the Debates and Proceedings of the Convention for the Revision of the Constitution of the State of New York* (Evening Atlas, 1846), 562 (O'Conor).

cautioned modern lawyers inclined to sneer at the rigid adherence to common law forms that "formalism is the twin-born sister of liberty." The technical limitations of pleading according to common law writs had checked royal judges from making law according to their sense of fairness, a sense that Maitland reasonably believed was often opposed to the interests of ordinary litigants. Over time, as it became clear that more discretionary authority could be "safely entrusted to judges whose impartiality is above suspicion and whose every act is exposed to public and professional criticism," the writs could be "made to do work for which they were not originally intended, and that work they can only do by means of fiction." Together, technical form and legal fiction struck a balance between arbitrary judicial discretion and rule-bound jurisprudence. "We shall do well to remember," Maitland concluded, "that the rule of law was the rule of writs."[6]

The 1820s and 1830s were decades of feverish law reform in New York under the rule of writs. Subtle changes in the practice of law coupled with industrialization and an expanding economy brought unprecedented strains on the daily work of practitioners. At the same time, jurists continued to pursue a century-long project to reformulate the common law as a system of principles and rules rather than a set of ad hoc practices and modes of reasoning about legal remedies—a movement, in Maitland's phrasing, from a rule of writs to a rule of law. New York's first experiment with codification in the late 1820s failed to end the rule of writs, but it sharpened ideas about legislative supremacy and practical reform. It also provided a legislative strategy that legal reformers would use again and again to navigate the politics of law reform, a strategy that enduringly combined codification and the reform of legal procedure in an unusual but unalterable alchemy.

II

In 1847, a young law professor named David Graham Jr. anticipated "alterations of a very extensive character in the body of practice itself." Nevertheless, he decided to move forward with publishing the third edition of his popular treatise on common law practice in New York. Graham felt "much embarrassed" about advertising a treatise that might soon become obsolete, but he reasoned "that whatever may be the character of that system, it will not so wholly remove the ancient landmarks of the practice, as to render a work based upon the existing system wholly valueless." After the first volume was published, the legislature appointed Graham along with David Dudley Field and one other lawyer to a commission to revise New York's pleading and practice. Their efforts removed more ancient landmarks than Graham had anticipated, and the second volume never appeared.[7] Still, Graham's partial treatise,

---

[6] Frederick Pollock & Frederic William Maitland, *The History of English Law Before the Time of Edward I* (Cambridge University Press, 2d ed., 1898), 561–62.

[7] David Graham, *A Treatise on the Practice of the Supreme Court of the State of New York* (Banks & Gould, 3d ed., 1847), v–vii. For a more concise introductory account of Graham's views on the common law, see David Graham Jr., "The Practice of the Law, As Illustrated in the Study of Pleading and Practice," in *Inaugural Addresses Delivered by the Professors of Law in the University of the City of New York at the Opening of the Law School of That Institution* (E.B. Clayton, 1838), 51.

covering ordinary proceedings from pleading to judgment, provides an invaluable examination of New York practice on the very eve of the Field Code reforms.

The New York legal system described in the treatise closely mimicked English legal institutions, especially in the division between two separate and sophisticated court systems known as common law and equity. The distinctive feature of the common law courts, at least in theory, was their reliance on trial by jury to resolve disputed "facts," while judges ruled on questions of "law." A jury might be charged to say whether a party had, in fact, expressed certain promises, but a judge would rule on what legal rights and remedies arose from such a promise.[8] Many hailed jury trial as an essential right, but some lawyers—like Charles O'Conor—complained that common law practice had become burdensome because of the jury requirement. "Jurors were originally very ignorant," O'Conor explained, and many of the rules accommodating their ignorance remained fundamental features of practice. Common jurors were not expected to answer complex questions of intent, so the text of an agreement alone was binding at common law. Jurors might be easily misled by the self-interested (and probably false) testimony of personally interested litigants, so all parties to litigation were forbidden from testifying. Cases had to be simplified for juries, and ideally this meant that only a single issue of fact should be presented to the jury, who could then weigh the proofs on one precise question and render a yes-or-no answer.[9]

Yet even before the revolutions of codification, the system Graham described had been one of continual change and innovation. From the 1820s to the 1840s, New York had undertaken significant reforms to the practice of law nearly every year. Equity courts had begun experimenting with jury trials, while the courts of common law were borrowing informal proceedings and investigative practices from equity. Only in 1845 had the state even begun to standardize admissions to the bar.[10] Nevertheless, Graham began his treatise where practice treatises commonly began, in the thirteenth-century reign of King Edward I. Despite how much common law practice was changing in the nineteenth century, practical jurists like Graham continued to organize the subject around the medieval writ system.[11]

---

[8] The leading treatises on common law practice in pre-code New York include Alexander M. Burrill, *A Treatise on the Practice of the Supreme Court of the State of New York* (J.S. Voorhies, 2d ed., 1846); David Graham, *A Treatise on the Practice of the Supreme Court of the State of New York* (Gould & Banks, 2d ed., 1836). Scholars have shown that well into the antebellum era, many jurors believed it was their right to decide questions of law as well, a view that drew some support from elite lawyers. See Alexandra D. Lahav & R. Kent Newmyer, "The Law Wars in Massachusetts, 1830–1860," 68 *American Journal of Legal History* 326 (2018), 349–50; William E. Nelson, *Americanization of the Common Law: The Impact of Legal Change on Massachusetts Society, 1760–1830* (University of Georgia Press, 1994 [1975]).

[9] Bishop & Attree, *Report of the Debates*, 562–64 (O'Conor). See also Alexis de Tocqueville, *Democracy in America*, ed. J.P. Mayer, trans. George Lawrence (Fontana, 1969 [1839]), 276 ("The jury system arose in the infancy of society, at a time when only simple questions of fact were submitted to the courts; and it is no easy task to adapt it to the needs of a highly civilized nation, where the relations between men have multiplied exceedingly and have been thoughtfully elaborated in a learned manner."). On the ambivalent attitude of nineteenth-century lawyers toward the jury, see especially Renée Lettow Lerner, "The Failure of Originalism in Preserving Constitutional Rights to Civil Jury Trial," 22 *William & Mary Bill of Rights Journal* 811 (2014).

[10] Graham, *A Treatise on the Practice of the Supreme Court*, 149–52, 408. See also David Graham, *A Treatise on the Organization and Jurisdiction of the Courts of Law and Equity in the State of New York* (Halsted and Voorhies, 1839), 364, 490–91, 556–75..

[11] See, for instance, Burrill, *A Treatise on the Practice of the Supreme Court*, 1:20; John Wentworth, *A Complete System of Pleading* (J. Moore, Dublin ed., 1791 [1677]); William Bohun, *The English Lawyer*

As Graham explained, the writ system developed from the king's prerogative to grant remedies to his injured subjects. "When any one had received an injury... he made application or petition to the king himself, as the fountain of justice," and the king's chancellor "framed or selected a writ" to remedy the harm. The writ, Graham explained, "was nothing more than a letter" to a local sheriff explaining a plaintiff's injury and requiring the sheriff to exact a remedy from the defendant or else summon the defendant to explain himself before the king's officers, the royal judges sitting at the courts of common law. Over time the form of the writs became standardized. Rather than draft a new writ for each case, the chancellor's staff relied on previous writs as precedents to redress similar injuries and compel similar remedies. "But now," Graham wrote, the writs "had assumed a new character;—they were invested with the authority of precedents;—were considered as evidences of the law;—their form could not be changed;—and no *new* one could be framed but by the aid of parliament." Instead of a guide to practice, the standard writs had become the law of practice. "The *register of writs*," Graham summarized, had become "a *compendium of legal remedies.*"[12]

The number and nature of writs that made up this fixed compendium varied over time; some fell out of use while others took on new significance when fictions stretched their reach over more cases. Graham counted fifty-one writs by the reign of Edward I, but only fourteen were in use in contemporary New York (others said ten).[13] Each sought a particular remedy to a different type of harm. Covenant granted a plaintiff money damages for an unpaid contract, while assumpsit provided money damages for an unperformed contract. Replevin recovered personal goods, while trover recovered money damages for the value of those goods. Following form and guided by precedent, much of the writ might be fictional. For trover, a plaintiff claimed to have possessed goods, lost them, and then discovered that the defendant found the goods and converted them to his own use. "The conversion is the gist of the action, the remainder being a mere fiction," Graham explained. So, in cases where a defendant manufactured defective goods, stole personal property, or misdelivered on a contract, the plaintiff used the same fictional story of losing and finding to plead for the desired remedy: monetary damages for the value of the (damaged, missing, or stolen) property.[14]

With this background, one can appreciate the argument of the English legal historian Michael Lobban that common law lawyers were much less inclined than their

---

(E. and R. Nutt, and R. Gosling, 1732); George Crompton, *Practice Common-Placed* (Eliz. Lynch, 1780). For an excellent overview of "premodern" procedure, see David Noll, "A Reader's Guide to Pre-Modern Procedure," 64 *Journal of Legal Education* 414 (2015).

[12] Graham, *A Treatise on the Practice of the Supreme Court*, 401–03.

[13] *Ibid.*, 402. David Dudley Field numbered the forms at ten, down from a high of fifty-nine. See *First Report* (New York, 1848), 139. See also George van Santvoord, *A Treatise on the Principles of Pleading in Civil Actions Under the New York Code of Procedure* (Little & Co., 2d ed., 1855), 24.

[14] The quoted language comes from Graham's second edition (1836), p. 172. The later edition used more technical language. Graham, *A Treatise on the Practice of the Supreme Court*, 451 ("It is founded on the supposition, that the chattel came into the defendant's possession by finding, and that he afterwards converted it to his own use; but the allegation of finding is, in general, a mere fiction, and the conversion is the only thing material or traversable.").

modern counterparts to speak of "rights," and much more likely to speak of "wrongs" and their "remedies."[15] The sources of this remedial reasoning could be quite varied. At the turn of the seventeenth century, Lord Edward Coke listed twenty such sources, ranging from moral theology to the formulaic precedents in the register of writs.[16] On this account, trover was not a clumsy device for protecting a coherent legal right. Rather, trover was a remedy—the payment of money for the value of goods. Over time, judges and lawyers had reasoned their way toward a set of wrongs in which a defendant's blame could be clearly proved, goods could be easily valued, and thus a whole category of harms could be remedied by transferring payment for those goods. The fiction of finding and losing operated as an analogy: The harm of a particular case was *like* the harm suffered when a defendant failed to return lost goods, and thus it deserved the same remedy.[17]

By the turn of the nineteenth century, several English and American jurists had become dissatisfied with the haphazard remedial basis of the common law and sought to reformulate the law as a rule-based system of rights. William Blackstone's *Commentaries* (published between 1765 and 1769) marked the first significant attempt to present the common law as a set of principles derived from a science of jurisprudence rather than ad hoc remedial reasoning drawn from the variety of sources Lord Coke had cataloged. While practitioners appreciated Blackstone's organization for an elementary study of the law, Professor Lobban shows that they found his jurisprudence nearly worthless as a description of how common law cases were decided in practice. After Blackstone, treatise literature tended to divide between works of theory, which, like Blackstone, tried to discern the principles and rules operative in the common law, and works more suitable for actual practice, which tended to follow the outline of the writ system and advised on the proper framing of the pleadings.[18]

Those who sought to redescribe the common law as a system of rules faced a long-standing challenge, one that had certainly troubled Counselor Sampson and the early codifiers: the problem of the oracular judge. Blackstone divided the sources of common law rules into the "written" statutory law of Parliament and "unwritten" customs that judges decreed as "the living oracles" of English law and custom, but several eighteenth-century constitutionalists disputed the authority of judges to promulgate law. Critics of the royal judges argued that they lacked the representative capacity to create general legislation, and without a definite and certain set of rules, their oracular decrees could quickly turn into arbitrary despotism.[19] After the age of Blackstone,

---

[15] Michael Lobban, *The Common Law and English Jurisprudence 1760–1850* (Clarendon Press, 1991), 6–9, 53–55.

[16] See *The First Part of the Institutes of the Laws of England; Or a Commentary on Littleton*, ed. Francis Hargrave & Charles Butler (Clarke & Sons, 17th ed., 1817), 1:11. See also Thomas Reeve, *Lord Chief Justice Reeve's Instructions to His Nephew Concerning the Study of Law* (London, 1791); Frederick Ritso, *An Introduction to the Science of Law* (W. Clarke & Sons, 1815).

[17] See Michael Lobban, "Legal Fictions Before the Age of Reform," in *Legal Fictions in Theory and Practice* (Springer, 2015), 199–223.

[18] Lobban, *The Common Law and English Jurisprudence*, 26–46.

[19] See *Ibid.*, 123–51. At the turn of the nineteenth century, Jeremy Bentham had become one of the most trenchant critics of "judicial legislation." See Jeremy Bentham, *Of Laws in General*, ed. H. L. A. Hart (Athlone Press, 1970 [1782]), 158–68; David Lieberman, *The Province of Legislation Determined: Legal Theory in Eighteenth-century Britain* (Cambridge University Press, 1989), 219–40.

common law theorists struggled to describe what judges did in a way that legitimized their apparent role as lawmakers who at times followed their own discretion.[20]

The English serjeant Henry John Stephen took a novel approach to the problem by theorizing about the least theoretical department of the law, the law of pleadings. Stephen claimed his 1824 treatise was the first to be "intended for the use rather of those who are exploring the principles, than of those who are engaged in the practice" of pleading, and the manual became especially popular among American lawyers and codifiers, a staple required coursebook at basically all American law schools to the end of the century. Rather than summarizing the case law on pleading writ by writ, as practical treatises did, Stephen presented a systematic set of "rules" for pleading, such as "a pleading which is bad in part, is bad altogether."[21] Most of Stephen's rules focused on "singleness of issue," which he thought solved, or at least dodged, the problem of judicial lawmaking. In the theory of single-issue pleading, the goal was for parties to agree among themselves upon one and only one question that divided them. This single question could then be resolved by the judge if the question turned on a point of law, or by the jury if it turned on the facts. Stephen argued that this process created a "public adjustment" of "the precise question for decision," and against this "public adjustment" Stephen posed the "private discretion" of oracular judges.[22]

Alone among the world's legal systems, Stephen argued, the common law pleading gave judges no real discretion in framing a dispute and thereby prejudging a case or creating openings for their own legal innovations. "In almost every plan of judicature," he wrote, pleadings were made "at large." Each party told his own story at length and "indulge[d] in such amplification . . . to propound the facts in such form as may be thought most impressive or convenient, though at the expense of clearness or precision." The problem with such narrative pleadings was that each could follow a different organization centering on different theories of right. Defendants' answers did not necessarily mirror plaintiffs' allegations, and so "it will always be in some measure doubtful . . . in what exact sense, the allegations on one side, are disputed on the other." A judge in such a system necessarily had to exercise his own discretion to say precisely what a dispute was about, which points should be proved at trial, and whether new rules of law were required. The common law, on the other hand, aimed "to preclude the exercise of any discretion, in extracting from [the parties] the true question in controversy." Fictional pleadings aided this enterprise. Parties could not organize

---

[20] Blackstone supposed common law cases acted as precedents to create definite and certain rules, but as Lobban notes, his "discussion of the role of judges and judicial precedents was confusing and allusive . . . largely because he placed this discussion in the context of a treatise seeking to define law as a system of rules, and because he therefore spent very little time discussing the process of legal reasoning by judges." Lobban, *The Common Law and English Jurisprudence*, 33.

[21] Henry John Stephen, *A Treatise on the Principles of Pleading in Civil Actions* (2d ed., 1827 [1824]), vi, 448. Francis J. Troubat edited and produced an American edition of Stephen on pleading approximately every five years from 1831 to 1857, and American editions continued to appear until the end of the nineteenth century. The Field Commission cited Stephen as "one of the ablest commentators" on pleading, and other commissions spoke just as highly of Stephen's authority. *First Report* (New York, 1848), 81–82; *The First Report of the Commissioners to Revise the Rules of Practice and Pleadings* (Maryland, 1855), 79; *Report of the Commissioners on Practice and Pleadings* (Ohio, 1853), 3, 50–53; Report of W. F. Cooper, in *Journal of the Senate of the State of Tennessee* (1857), 189. Regarding the required readings noted in law school catalogs, refer to the discussion in chapter 5.

[22] Stephen, *A Treatise on the Principles of Pleading*, 498.

their pleadings to tell a good tale or shade the facts if all they could plead was the traditional story of casually losing their goods. The half-fictional forms of action thus comprised a limited set of propositions with which an adversary could take issue, and a party took issue by precisely denying one of those propositions. Stephen analogized such pleading to "that analytical process, by which the mind, even in the private consideration of any controversy, arrives at the development of the question in dispute." Thinking through a case in one's own mind was not unlike jotting down a personal pro's and con's list: "It is always necessary to distribute the mass of matter into detached contending propositions, and to set them consecutively in array against each other, till, by this logical conflict, the state of the question is ultimately ascertained." The difference was that the common law required this process to be performed on the record, in writing, thus creating a "public adjustment" of the dispute. European procedure purportedly allowed this process to unfold privately in the mind of the judge.[23]

In practice, maneuvering a case toward a single issue could be one of the most technical and cumbersome aspects of the law. In almost every dispute, parties had multiple disagreements about the facts or the legal theories that supported their claims. If a party believed he had multiple defenses—say, that the statute of limitations had run on a contract claim, and that the contract was illegal and void—he had to choose one defense on which to stake his case. That, however, was the virtue of the system to Stephen. The parties, and not the judge, chose the dispositive issue. Whether that issue was a trivial argument about the pleadings themselves or a material disagreement about possession of goods, the parties consented to a trial on that single ground, the judge convened the trial on the parties' terms, and the parties had to live with the consequences of their own choices.[24] To Stephen, this was the rule of writs. It granted that oracular judges might make law, but it minimized their reach. Judicial officers had to decide a limited question within a particular case, and adjustments to the rules had to be demanded by litigants in properly pleaded arguments that left no room for judges to make law from their own discretion.

Coming from a seasoned practitioner with a bent toward theory, Stephen's *Treatise* helpfully articulated what most practicing lawyers took for granted. The oracular judge was mainly a problem for those who sought to describe the common law in the abstract, as a set of rules apart from the practices that produced those rules. When David Graham wrote his practitioner's treatises in New York a decade later, he, like most practitioners, ignored questions about the sources of law entirely and instead provided the exacting details for proper pleading. He did, however, add one refinement to Stephen's account. Graham believed the development of the writ system "completed an entire revolution," not just because it constrained the judges but because it turned the system over to the lawyers. Once the writ system had hardened into place, "the selection [of the proper writ] in practice, had become the science, if such it could be called, of the attorneys."[25] To speak more precisely than Stephen had, it was not the parties who crafted single issues or consented to trial, it was their counsel. In common law practice, the rule of writs was the rule of lawyers. Attorneys

---

[23] *Ibid.*, 86 n.29, 498–502.
[24] *Ibid.*, 78–87.
[25] Graham, *A Treatise on the Practice of the Supreme Court*, 404.

became the agents of legal change as they bent and amended the forms to provide a remedy in a case that did not quite fit the precedents. Only after lawyers for both sides had adequately framed the dispute and offered plausible arguments was a judge called upon to accede to or deny the remedy.[26]

III

In both England and New York, a separate court of chancery administered an equity jurisdiction that was supposed to ameliorate the jury-based limitations of common law practice and "do equity" between the litigants. A single judge—the chancellor or his representative—presided over equity cases and, unlike a jury, could rule on complicated questions of intent, fraud, and abuse of common law procedures that resulted in injustice. In time, chancery gained exclusive jurisdiction over bodies of law deemed too complex for jury trial, such as the law of mortgages, trusts, and guardianships. Although parties were still barred from directly testifying, a procedure known as discovery could put a party under oath to provide factual information through the written pleadings.[27]

As at common law, the high-level descriptions of equity underemphasized the role of lawyers, especially in antebellum New York. When the New York merchant Philip Hone "passed a couple hours . . . in the Chancellor's Court" purely for amusement, the number and activity of the solicitors impressed him. Although the court was held "in a small office in a wing" of Chancellor Reuben Walworth's home, Hone counted "about twenty lawyers, seated without order, some at a green table, but the greater number on chairs with their backs against the wall, and their legs cocked up." He likened the scene to an unruly classroom with the chancellor as a nominal schoolmaster. Lawyers from around the room intervened in the discussion "on points as they arise in the case" and freely cracked jokes at the parties' expense (the case that day sought an injunction "to prevent a man named Lance from selling a famous nostrum called 'Brandreth's Pills'"). Although Hone complimented Chancery as "this great court of little form," he unwittingly described the very forms that constrained Chancellor Walworth. As with common law, lawyers pushed and pulled at the margins of the rules, agreeing on expansions here and checking one another there.[28]

Still, the rules of equity were understood to be qualitatively different from common law, and equity too had a substantial literature of both practical and theoretical treatments. In 1843, the prominent New York case reporter Oliver Barbour produced

[26] See Lobban, *The Common Law and English Jurisprudence*, 53–54.
[27] The leading treatises on chancery practice in pre-code New York include Joseph W. Moulton, *The Chancery Practice of the State of New York* (O. Halsted, 1829); Joseph Parkes, *The Statutes and Orders of the Court of Chancery and the State Law of Real Property of the State of New York* (Maxwell & Stevens, 1830); John Sidney Smith, *A Treatise on the Practice of the Court of Chancery: With an Appendix of Forms and Precedents*, ed. David Graham Jr. (T. & J. W. Johnson, 2d American ed., 1842); Oliver Barbour, *A Treatise on the Practice of the Court of Chancery* (W. & A. Gould, 1843).
[28] Philip Hone, *The Diary of Philip Hone, 1828–1851* (1889), July 23, 1840, 2:36–38. On the gradual insertion of lawyers into New York equity proceedings on a more "adversarial" model, see Amalia D. Kessler, *Inventing American Exceptionalism: The Origins of American Adversarial Legal Culture, 1800–1877* (Yale University Press, 2017).

yet another practical treatise on equity. He observed that unlike common law treatises, which were almost universally organized according to the writ system, "no two [equity treatises] are alike, or even similar, in the general plan or the arrangement." Barbour attempted to organize the field according to the chronology of a case, from pleading to decree, followed by enforcement. Still, he admitted the third section of the work had to be "a sort of omnium gatherum" of topics that did not fit easily in the first two sections. The organization illustrates what struck many practitioners as the distinctive feature of equity: its abandonment of the writ system. As Charles O'Conor summarized equity, "There was literally no form about it. The party stated his case, and asked the relief he desired, and the court, if he proved his case, gave him the relief."[29] Like Hone, O'Conor's observation that equity had no forms of proceeding nicely described just what equity's forms of proceeding were: the narrative pleadings and discretionary judgments that had horrified Serjeant Stephen.

O'Conor meant that equity did not have forms of action in the same way that common law did. Equity did, however, have a standard structure to its pleading, and Barbour devoted hundreds of pages of commentary to these forms. Equity did not generally allow fictions in pleading, but in the same way that fictions illustrated the historical development of a common law writ (like the origin of trover in cases of losing and finding property), the typical equity plea recapitulated the development of chancery as an ancillary jurisdiction to the courts of common law.

As a matter of course, a litigant at chancery pleaded that "your orator is remediless in the premises at and by the strict rules of the common law." An equity court, that is, was asked to intervene when strict adherence to common law practices caused a failure of remedy, perhaps because money damages were an insufficient remedy or perhaps because only the defendant had knowledge of the relevant facts but could not be called to testify. It also implied that if common law processes and remedies were sufficient, no claim could be supported in equity.[30] Whereas common law courts awarded money damages or title to land, equity petitions frequently prayed for a remedy against a defendant "personally." Chancery could order a party to give evidence under oath, turn over property, or refrain from acting on penalty of imprisonment of the defendant's person (a procedure known as contempt). Pleadings routinely concluded with a request for a decree "as shall be agreeable to equity and good conscience." That concluding prayer made a virtue of the type of judicial discretion the common law writ system sought to avoid. Instead of precluding a judge from framing the case and constructing new rules of law at his own initiative, the equity petition specifically invited such behavior.[31]

Therefore, the problem of the oracular judge was more acute in the chancery system, and when critics attacked judicial lawmaking, the chancellor was often a

---

[29] Barbour, *A Treatise on the Practice of the Court of Chancery*, iv–vi; Bishop & Attree, *Report of the Debates*, 562 (O'Conor).

[30] See, e.g., Barbour, *A Treatise on the Practice of the Court of Chancery*, 567.

[31] See, e.g., *ibid.*, 37. On the maxim that equity acts in personam, or "on the person," see Joseph Story, *Commentaries on Equity Pleadings and the Incidents Thereto* (Little and Brown, 1838), 315; William Wait, *A Treatise Upon Some of the General Principles of the Law* (W. Gould, Jr., & Co., 1885), 1:20–21; Walter Ashburner, *Principles of Equity* (Butterworth Law Publishers, 1902), 59–97.

primary target.[32] The most well-known American theorist to answer the challenge was the Harvard professor and Supreme Court justice Joseph Story. In his 1834 *Commentaries on Equity Jurisprudence*, Story, by his very title, joined the enterprise of Blackstone and Stephen in describing the law in terms of rules rather than practices. If equity followed a jurisprudence, it was not the creature of "discretion" and "conscience" that so many previous commentators had described. Story lamented that "many persons are misled into the false notion" that equity's "real and peculiar duty" was "correcting, mitigating, or interpreting the law." His treatise was dedicated to the opposite proposition, the maxim "that Equity follows the law." Story purposely chose to make that ambiguous maxim central to his treatise. By it, he meant not just the practitioner's explanation that equitable remedies were available only after common law remedies had failed—that a successful suit in chancery had to follow an unsuccessful one at common law—but also that chancery "seeks out and guides itself by the analogies of the law." By adhering to precedent, statute, and even form, Story insisted that equity was as restrained and law-bound as the common law was.[33]

Story began his treatise by surveying what he believed were false notions of equity that continued to be perpetuated by commentators. "In the most general sense, we are accustomed to call that Equity, which, in human transactions, is founded in natural justice, in honesty and right," but, Story cautioned, "it would be a great mistake to suppose that Equity, as administered in England and America, embraced a jurisdiction so wide and extensive, as that." Various jurists were making that exact mistake, Story contended. They wrote of equity "in contradistinction to strict law" as though chancery were concerned only with just outcomes and not with rules and process. He observed that such commentators frequently cited Aristotle's definition of equity as "the correction of law, wherein it is defective by reason of its universality." On this view, prescriptive human laws—whether those prescriptions sprang from legislation or forms of proceeding—inevitably failed to render justice in particular, unforeseen cases. An equitable jurisdiction, grounded in natural justice or right conscience, could set aside the law's unjust rigors to fix a more appropriate outcome.[34]

That was precisely what equity did not do, Story argued.[35] Courts were not to be legislatures, willfully prescribing rules according to their own policies. They were to be legal institutions, following legal rules and processes in their decision-making. In a central passage, Story summarized the legal processes that equity followed:

> Every system of laws must necessarily be defective; and cases must occur, to which the antecedent rules cannot be applied without injustice.... It is the office, therefore, of a judge to consider, whether the antecedent rule does apply, or ought, according to

---

[32] Critics were fond of repeating the complaint of John Selden that rulings according to "conscience" in Chancery could be as variable as the size of "a Chancellor's foot." *Table Talk of John Selden*, ed. Frederick Pollock (Quaritch, 1927), 43.

[33] Joseph Story, *Commentaries on Equity Jurisprudence as Administered in England and America* (Hilliard, Gray & Co., 1836), 1:10, 11–12, 22.

[34] *Ibid.*, 1:1–2, 4–7 (citing Aristotle, *Nicomachean Ethics*, bk. 5 ch. 10). Story was particularly aggrieved by the supposed maxim that equity construed statutes "not according to the letter, but to the reason and spirit of them."

[35] *Ibid.*, 1:22 (quoting 3 *Blackstone's Commentaries* 433, 440–42); 15–16 (quoting Cowper v. Cowper, 2 P. Will. 753 (1735)).

the intention of the lawgiver, to apply to a given case; ... and if there exists no rule, applicable to all the circumstances, whether the party should be remediless, or whether the rule furnishing the closest analogy ought to be followed.[36]

Story thus agreed with the Aristotelian premise that human foresight could not legislate for every eventuality. However, he disagreed with the conclusion that an extraordinary jurisdiction automatically vested upon judges to remedy the shortcomings of the law. Notably, leaving a party "remediless" appeared a legitimate alternative to Story. Just as the common law writ system gave no satisfactory resolution in some cases, neither would chancery. Story thought illustrations "may be found in every state of the Union." By the common law, a husband, for instance, might be enriched through his wife's dowry but then "by his own act, or will, strip her of every farthing, and leave her a beggar." The injustice of the rule was supposed to be obvious to Story's audience, yet no court of equity would use its personal remedies to enjoin a husband from acting against "natural justice" in this situation.[37]

The occasional unjust outcome, even in equity, was tolerable to Story because it proved equity was, in fact, rule-bound. As much as commentators might speak of equity searching out "the spirit of the law," Story insisted that chancellors did not have the power to rewrite an unforgiving statute and were "often compelled to stop, where the letter of the law stops." The eighteenth-century jurist Richard Francis had opined, "Equity is so extensive and various, that every particular case in Equity may be truly said to stand upon its own particular circumstances; and ... I apprehend precedents not of that great use in Equity." Story condemned such ideas as a danger to legal stability. "It would literally place the whole rights and property of the community under the arbitrary will of the Judge," he concluded.[38] Although equitable remedies "are flexible, and may be suited to the different postures of cases," Story insisted that equity cases too "have prescribed forms of proceeding." Even in equity, the rule of law was the rule of writs. Although equity did not use particular forms of action like trover and covenant, Story surmised that equitable remedies were granted only where common law writs already recognized a right but were themselves "not sufficient to afford a complete remedy." By this theory, equity never made its own rules; it never legislated. It provided a particular set of remedies where "a plain, adequate, and complete remedy does not exist in any other Court," but the rights were already "acknowledged in the Municipal Jurisprudence." Equity followed the law, the law followed the writs, and the oracular judge was constrained to provide remedies only where statutes or common law had previously identified a remediable harm.[39]

If common law and chancery followed the same rules while granting different remedies, could they be integrated into a unitary system of courts and remedies? Story thought so, but he hedged his answer. "The union of Equity and Law in the same Court," Story wrote, "must be a mixed question of public policy and private

---

[36] *Ibid.,* 1:8.
[37] *Ibid.,* 1:15.
[38] *Ibid.,* 1:16, 11–12 (quoting Richard Francis, *Maxims of Equity* (E. and R. Nutt, and R. Gosling, 1728), 5–6), 21, 32–33 n.3.
[39] *Ibid.,* 1:27, 31, 53, 60, 94.

convenience; and never can be susceptible of any universal solution, applicable to all times, and all nations, and all changes in jurisprudence." Nothing inherent in the nature of jurisprudence demanded their institutional separation, but Story reasoned there might be political reasons for preserving the traditional distinction. Story noted that many features of the law might be "accidental," but still, not every "arbitrary" or "irrational" rule needed to be purged. The legal system was large and complex, with rules interweaving with one another in multiple and sometimes unexpected places. Jurists might be unwise to remove even a clear "deformity in the general system," because often such deformities "cannot be removed, without endangering the existence of other portions of the fabric, or interfering with the proportions of other principles, which have been moulded and adjusted with reference to them." Remedies were tricky things, and remedies to a remedial system were even trickier. "The new remedy, to be applied, may otherwise be as mischievous, as the wrong to be redressed," Story warned.[40]

Story the reluctant fusionist was thus the twin side of Story the reluctant codifier. Just as Story believed codification might be valuable if pursued cautiously, gradually, and above all by competent jurists like himself, he also allowed that the somewhat arbitrary and accidental division between common law and equity might eventually be sewn up. Story did not draw any connections between his writings on codification and those on law and equity, though. Until late in the 1820s, the codification of practice and the reform of practice were wholly separate concerns. Their union would come about, itself quite accidentally, in New York's first attempt to respond to William Sampson's call for an American code.

IV

If they wanted to follow Sampson's advice, New York legislators had two models of promulgation from which to draw. The first came from the French. Napoleon had appointed four- or five-member commissions to codify and reform the law of revolutionary France under several headings, including civil law, criminal law, civil procedure, and commercial law. When Sampson delivered his discourse, one of the members of the French civil procedure commission, Count Pierre François Réal, was living in exile in upstate New York and wrote enthusiastically to Sampson to advise him on the mechanics of codification: "Do as we did, but do it better, profiting by our mistakes. Let four or five good heads be united in a commission, to frame in silence the project of a code. It is not so difficult a task. It is only to consult together, and to select. Do so with your best authors as we did with ours, and principally with Pothier's treatise on Obligations, which we simply converted into articles of our code." Tellingly, Count Réal assumed a commission's code would automatically be promulgated as law, as the French codes had been.[41]

---

[40] *Ibid.*, 1:35, 61.
[41] Count Pierre François Réal to William Sampson, October 27, 1824, in Pishey Thompson, ed., *Sampson's Discourse and Correspondence with Various Learned Jurists Upon the History of the Law* (E. Bliss and E. White, 1826), 191.

At the same time as this correspondence, a commission in Louisiana was preparing codes of civil law and civil procedure. The lead commissioners, Moreau Lislet and the New York-trained Edward Livingston, admired French law and adapted as much of the French codes as they could while engrafting in common law novelties like the jury trial.[42] In 1825, the Louisiana legislature decreed that the code would become law when the commissioners published it. Although the commissioners reported to the legislature, they did not submit the actual text of the code in their reports, and the legislature had no opportunity to amend or revise the text until after promulgation.[43]

The other model came from England. Royal commissions had been employed since before the Revolution of 1688 to advise on various matters. After the Revolution, royal commissions became disfavored while Parliament undertook many of the same functions through "committees of inquiry" to which only members of Parliament were appointed. By the nineteenth century, royal commissions were revived. Unlike committees of inquiry, royal commissioners usually were not legislators. That was both a virtue and a deficiency. Commissioners were not bound to the rhythms of Parliament's schedule—they could continue their focused work even as Parliament adjourned or turned its attention to other matters—but without authority to make law, their advised legislation had to pass through the normal politicking, drafting, and revising processes of Parliament.[44]

The three previous times New York had compiled its statutory law, it had imperfectly adhered to the English model of royal commissioners. New York's Revolutionary legislature, like those of most former colonies, decreed that "such parts of the common law of England, and of the statute law of England" that were not overwritten by the new constitution would continue as the law of the state. Even if one looked only at the "statute law" side of the equation, that included an immense amount of material from diverse sources dating back over a century. The 1786 legislature thus commissioned two lawyers "to collect and reduce into proper form . . . all the said statutes and lay the same bills before the legislature of this State from time to time as they shall prepare the same." The task amounted to a glorified printer's commission. The lawyers were to

---

[42] In addition to *Sampson's Discourse*, Field cited Livingston's codes as a chief influence in his early career. Field, *A Third of a Century Given to Law Reform* (1873), 1.

[43] See generally George Dargo, *Jefferson's Louisiana: Politics and the Clash of Legal Traditions* (Harvard University Press, 1975). On Livingston's contributions to Louisiana procedure in particular, see Kent A. Lambert, "An Abridged History of the Absorption of American Civil Procedure and Evidence in Louisiana," in Vernon Valentine Palmer, ed., *Louisiana: Microcosm of a Mixed Jurisdiction* (University of North Carolina Press, 1999), 105–15. This mode of promulgation in 1825 differed somewhat from that of Louisiana's 1808 Digest, drafts of which were submitted to the legislature for enactment. For an argument that the Digest should still be considered a modern code, see John W. Cairns, *Codification, Transplants and History: Law Reform in Louisiana (1808) and Quebec (1866)* (Talbot, 2015), 427–76.

[44] See Thomas J. Lockwood, "A History of Royal Commissions," 5 *Osgoode Hall Law Journal* 172 (1967); Barbara Lauriat, " 'The Examination of Everything': Royal Commissions in British Legal History," 31 *Statute Law Review* 24 (2010); Joanna Innes, *Inferior Politics: Social Problems and Social Policies in Eighteenth-century Britain* (Oxford University Press, 2009). English proposals to consolidate and modernize the nation's body of statute law received significant support from Francis Bacon, who insisted "that parliamentary participation was essential; commissioners should be appointed by both houses to prepare the necessary legislation," but "the newly modeled body of laws then required confirmation by the legislative body, 'lest, under pretence of digesting old laws, new laws, be secretly imposed.' " Barbara Shapiro, "Codification of the Laws in Seventeenth Century England," 1974 *Wisconsin Law Review* 428 (1974), 443, 447; see also Lieberman, *The Province of Legislation Determined*, ch. 9.

compile previously enacted statutes, update the spelling and typescript, and give the collected statutes some logical order "under certain heads or titles of bills." Like royal commissioners, the lawyers were commissioned to work even when the legislature was not in session, and they presented their final drafts to a different legislature than the one that had appointed them.[45]

A dozen years later, New York's statutory law had grown by as many volumes, and a new commission was created to recompile the state's statutes into two manageable volumes. That commission included the young James Kent, who would go on to a celebrated career in the state's court of chancery. This time, the legislature requested that Kent note "contradictions, omissions, or imperfections" of the law in his reports so the legislature could correct them. Kent often proposed such corrections in the margins of his reported bills, but he also changed the text itself as he saw fit, usually with a note to the legislature that he had done so. As Farah Peterson notes, "What Kent did when he revised the statutes was quintessentially legislative, and he did it with the legislature's permission and gratitude." Legislators reviewed the drafts and, on rare occasions, overruled Kent's suggestion, but clear lines of legislative prerogative were neither drawn nor guarded in these statutory revisions. What bound the lawmaking powers of the commissioners was the subject matter itself: The commissioners were revising previously enacted legislation; they were not venturing into a codification of the "rules" of the common law. However, within the domain of prior legislation, they followed their practical sense of which laws worked and which needed to be updated to conform to republican theory and practical utility.[46]

By the mid-1820s, another twelve years had passed since the last compilation, and New Yorkers had enacted a new constitution in 1821 that restructured the court system and made several prior legislative acts unenforceable. Though a new commission was created in 1824, after Sampson's acerbic demand for codification, the nature of the commission's work changed. In his opening message to the legislature, Governor DeWitt Clinton called for "a complete code" that would "utterly destroy judicial legislation, which is fundamentally at war with the genius of representative government."[47] Like Sampson, Clinton hoped to replace the foundations of law with the positive decrees of a democratic legislature.

The 1820s revision of New York statutes thus became much more politically charged than previous revisions. While codifiers promoted their theories as most compatible with democratically representative government, opponents decried codification on

---

[45] "An Act for revising and digesting the laws of this State," passed April 15, 1786, reprinted in *Laws of the State of New York Passed at the Sessions of the Legislature Held in the Years 1785, 1786, 1787, 1788, Inclusive* (1886), 2:247–48. See generally "Statute Law in New York from 1609 to 1901," in *Report of the Joint Committee on Statutory Revision*, in *Documents of the Assembly of the State of New York*, 124th Sess., No. 72 (1901), 25:45–116.

[46] "An Act making provision for the revision of the laws of this State," passed March 28, 1800, reprinted in *Laws of the State of New York Passed at the Sessions of the Legislature Held in the Years 1797, 1798, 1799 and 1800, Inclusive* (1887), 4:519–20; Farah Peterson, "Interpretation as Statecraft: Chancellor Kent and the Collaborative Era of American Statutory Interpretation," 77 *Maryland Law Review* 712 (2018), 729. Another twelve years saw yet another compilation, carried out in the same manner as Kent had done. See Michael Joseph Hobor, The Form of the Law: David Dudley Field and the Codification Movement in New York, 1839–1888 (Ph.D. dissertation, University of Chicago, 1975), 9–11.

[47] "Governor Clinton's Message," *National Advocate* (New York, N.Y.), Jan. 8, 1825.

the same grounds. "The leveling principles of Counselor Sampson," one paper wrote, took democracy to a dangerous extreme. The reason for representative government, the *Evening Post* explained, was that most people were not capable legislators, and even many representatives lacked the requisite skill. Judicial lawmaking often arose because the existing statutes were poorly drafted, contradictory, and vague. A desultory statutory system was unsurprising, the *Post* added, given that legislatures were "subject to caprice, to the power of eloquence, to party feeling, and even to worse influences." Of the branches of government, only the judiciary had proven to have sufficient "dignity and responsibility" to be entrusted with the "discretionary power" to declare the law.[48] Defenders of the common law pressed the new commission not to go beyond the bounds of previous revisers, and in making this appeal, critics retold the history of New York's statutory revisions with much more precise lines drawn between legislating and compiling than had actually been the case. Kent's revision, one article wrote, "did not profess to be more than a collection of general laws, with such modifications as they had received from legislative acts." Gone from this account were Kent's many alterations to the law made at his discretion and reflecting his sense of sound policy.[49]

The legislature and the revising commission attempted to navigate between the two positions on codification. The legislature permitted the revisers to "complete the said revision in such manner as to them shall seem most useful and proper." However, one important limitation was placed on this discretion. The revisers were not to alter "any statute that has been the subject of judicial decision." Legislation that had been judicially interpreted had to maintain its same "phraseology" so as not to disturb judicial precedents, including precedents of statutory construction.[50] The legislature then appointed three revisers who balanced the state's partisan divisions: the Clintonian John C. Spencer, the Van Burenite Democrat Benjamin F. Butler, and the nonpartisan marine lawyer John Duer.[51] When the revisers set to work, they modeled their efforts on the commissions of France and Louisiana, providing the legislature a "project" of their proposed revision. The project loosely tracked Blackstone's division of the law into four parts: statutes regarding public institutions and jurisdiction, the law of property and domestic relations (Blackstone's persons and things), civil proceedings (private wrongs), and penal law (public wrongs).[52] Unlike the French-style

---

[48] *Commercial Advertiser* (New York, N.Y.), May 22, 1826; *New York Evening Post*, Aug. 28, 1824.

[49] *Chautauqua Phoenix* (Westfield, N.Y.), Jan. 14, 1829.

[50] 1825 New York Laws 446–47.

[51] The original appointments included the old federalist James Kent and the agrarian Democrat Erastus Root. Both declined the commission implying an unwillingness to work with Butler. They were replaced by Duer and Henry Wheaton, a well-known Supreme Court reporter. Wheaton left the project in 1827 with a diplomatic appointment to Denmark and was then replaced by Spencer. See "Statute Law in New York," 76–79; William Allen Butler, *The Revision of the Statutes of the State of New York and the Revisers* (1889). On the partisan affiliation of the commissioners, see Thomas D. Morris, *Free Men All: The Personal Liberty Laws of the North, 1780–1861* (Lawbook Exchange, 2001), 54–55.

[52] For the project, see *Journal of the Assembly of the State of New York* (1825), Appendix D, elaborated again the next year at *Assembly Journal* (New York, 1826), 885–94; *American* (New York, N.Y.), Mar. 27, 1826; *American* (New York, N.Y.), May 5, 1827. Other reports to the legislature can be found at *Assembly Journal* (New York, 1826), 912; *Journal of the Senate of the State of New York* (1827), 31–33, 49, 105–06, 123, 157–58, 356, 517–19; *Assembly Journal* (New York, 1827), 125–26, 476, 641–42, 692–93, 803; *Assembly Journal, Special Session* (New York, 1827), 4–5, 23–24, 63–65, 98, 108.

commissions, though, they submitted reports to the legislature, inviting that body to omit any proposed sections "at their pleasure."[53]

After the approval of their project, the revisers' first major report detailed their working arrangement. Agreeing at least in part with the critics of democracy, they found New York's statutes a mess. "Many of these statutes have not only been drawn up carelessly and immethodically," they reported, "but in all of them, numerous propositions are crowded together in the same section, and words multiplied without motive or necessity." Instead, they proposed "to adopt the most simple arrangement; to confine the sections to short propositions; to omit unnecessary words; and to avoid, as far as practicable, all ambiguities of expression." They admitted that such an effort went beyond a mere compilation of statutory law and "carried to their full extent, the powers given us by the legislature." They defended the move only by appealing to their expertise and careful procedures. They promised to make "no changes or additions" to the law, but then qualified the statement by adding "if there did not appear sufficient reasons to our minds."

Although it would have been more efficient, the commissioners did not think it "consistent with the great importance of the trust confided to us, to leave to any one of our number exclusively, the completion of any part of the work." Rather, after each had drawn up his allotted portion, the three committed "the drafts prepared by each to the separate and critical revisal of the others; and then [subjected] them to the joint examination of all." Expertise and process were all that were offered. Unlike Kent's revision, subsequent reports provided minimal commentary justifying new or altered rules, the commissioners explaining that they "supposed that the propriety of such alterations would best be explained and understood, by an actual exhibition of the text, as it would stand, after the proposed changes had been made."[54] The revisers thus supplied a new oracle: the very text of the statute would speak for itself.

The work of revision lasted three years, and during that period, the commissioners continually directed attention to the unclear boundary between compilation, revision, and codification. In compiling and systematizing New York's statutes, they were "surprised" at how many legislative gaps were uncovered. There was a dearth of "necessary details to carry out a principle, or to provide for its enforcement, which we had never suspected until the effort was made to arrange the statutes upon the plan prescribed." In such cases, a coherent revision required new legislation to supply the details. At times, they pushed against the boundaries of their commission, complaining that they "have not been able to understand why the language of the written law should defy all attempt at improvement" merely because judges had happened to construe a particular statute.[55]

The revisers' mandate also shifted as petitions were forwarded from the legislature.[56] An 1826 petition to the senate complained "that our present system of law,

---

[53] *Assembly Journal* (New York, 1826), 891.

[54] *Ibid.*, 889–92.

[55] *Assembly Journal, Second Session* (New York, 1827), 63.

[56] When the Senate Judiciary Committee referred a petition to reform the penal system so that it could be "adapted to the genius of our government, and the enlightened policy of the age," the revisers refused to act on it "until the intentions of the legislature shall have been more distinctly and fully expressed." At least on criminal reform, the revisers were not prepared to substitute their own policies for those of actual legislators. *Assembly Journal* (New York, 1826), 892.

together with the rules and regulations of our courts of record, have been copied from the English practice" and argued that it should be replaced by a system "formed on the plain and simple principles of common sense." The Senate Judiciary Committee derived two questions from this petition: "1. Whether the whole body of our laws may not be reduced to a written code or text, and comprised within a moderate compass? and 2. Whether the existing practice of our courts of law, (which is substantially the English practice with some amendments,) ought not to be reformed and simplified?" The revisers dodged the first question as beyond the scope of their mandate, but they reasoned the second "comes more properly within the range of our inquiries; many parts of the practice being regulated by statutory provisions." They agreed that practice deserved serious reform, and they promised when they reached that part of their project they "would extend the statutes already passed" to address complaints over civil proceedings.[57]

First, however, they had to address the law of property and obligations in their Blackstonian division of the law. The regulation of contracts posed particular problems. "Almost every statute embraced" under that heading had been the subject of judicial interpretation, yet these statutes were just as poorly drawn up as any they had encountered. "Parts of sections have been repealed or qualified, and an amendment has again been amended. . . . In other cases it became necessary to break up sections containing provisions on distinct subjects, or containing complicated and voluminous details and provisos." In such conditions, they explained, "this unavoidably produced a change in the language" of the revision. They assured the legislature, however, that "in expressing the supposed meaning of various statutes, we have been guided by the decisions of the chancellors and judges of our state." Ultimately, they proposed a true Sampsonite codification for the law of contracts: the transformation of judicial practices and understandings into legislative rules.[58] The legislature, however, rejected the proposed report. Only after the revisers replaced their attempted codification with a compilation that left the "complicated and voluminous" statutes intact did the legislature give its approval. Defenders of the common law cheered that the revisers had been kept from taking "the broad-axe and cleaver" to the legal system.[59]

Thus, when the revisers reached Part III on civil proceedings, they adhered closely to the idea that they had delivered in response to the earlier petition, that in this area at least, they were "extending" statutes without attempting to codify the unwritten law. The report included many sections that were purportedly "new" but defended as "necessary to carry out" statutes already in force. As the revisers had noted, the state had enacted many statutes over the decades making minor adjustments to civil practice, and many of the more detailed regulations had not become subject to extensive judicial commentary the way statutes regulating property and contracts had. Moreover, by the time the revisers submitted their work on Part III, Butler had been elected to the state assembly and Spencer to the state senate, providing the commissioners

---

[57] *Ibid.*
[58] *Assembly Journal, Second Session* (New York 1827), 63–64.
[59] *Spectator* (New York, N.Y.), Nov. 23, 1827.

actual legislative authority to defend their more striking innovations as sound policies worthy of enactment whether or not they reflected prior practice or statutory regulation. Butler, for instance, took up multiple daily sessions in the assembly fending off objections to the revisers' proposal to extend powers of documentary discovery and witness examination from chancery to courts of common law.[60] With the commissioners debating and voting within their numbers, legislators defeated fewer of the proposed changes to legal practices. But if the line between compilation, revision, and outright legislation had been blurry from the start, it became impossible to discern as the revisers entered the later stages of their work.[61]

When the *North American Review* studied the resulting "Revised Statutes," it misinterpreted politics as principle. The author approvingly observed that the revisers had taken a different approach to statutes regulating "modes of public proceeding, [from] those which concern private rights more nearly, regulating the distribution of property and the domestic relations. With the former, they have felt themselves at greater liberty to fill up what was wholly unprovided for by the existing letter of the Statute Book." Modes of proceeding seemed more amenable to legislative change and even experimentation. The settled law of property, however, could at best be arranged, not revised, lest "too much of substance may be sacrificed to mere method; . . . lest systematizing should degenerate into absolute codification." Modes of public proceedings, however, could aim more directly at "practical convenience." In this domain, it was appropriate that the revisers had produced "not merely a consolidation" but "provisions wholly new, to supply and remedy what are in their judgment palpable omissions and imperfections."[62] The *Review* thus extracted a legal philosophy from circumstances primarily produced by political happenstance. The revisers had altered legal practice not because they saw it as jurisprudentially severable from the law of property but because, in that area, they already had more statutory texts with which to work, and because, as a matter of timing, they were better able to influence the legislative reception of the later stages of their work after they themselves had become legislators. From a certain distance, however, New York's Revised Statutes of 1829 appeared to demonstrate that matters of procedure and practice were peculiarly suited to legislative modification, an idea that would last long after the political contingencies of the 1820s were forgotten.

---

[60] See *Assembly Journal* (New York, 1826), 892; *Report of the Commissioners Appointed to Revise the Statute Laws of this State* (New York, 1828), passim; "State Legislature," *New York Commercial Advertiser* (New York, N.Y.), Jan. 22, 1828.

[61] The revisers wrote that "exertions have been made, to prevent multiplicity of suits; to avoid fictitious, useless, and protracted forms; and to save unnecessary expense," and it urged the legislature not to reject the material "merely because it is new." *Report of the Commissioners Appointed to Revise the Statute Laws of this State* (New York, 1828), 5.

[62] "Revision of the Laws of New York," 24 *North American Review* 193 (1827), 207–08. A local New York paper came to a similar conclusion. It reasoned that in the law of property "peculiar caution will be requisite in the revision of these statutes" inasmuch "as the consequences, even of partial innovation, are not easily foreseen." It attributed the quotation to the revisers themselves, but no such material appears in the cited report. *American* (New York, N.Y.), May 5, 1827.

V

Although the Revised Statutes of 1829 significantly altered the practice of law in New York, lawyers' complaints about an overwhelming bulk of precedents, uninformative pleadings, and the degrading fee system continued. Graham wrote in his 1847 treatise that in the past decade, "there have been published more than twenty volumes of the reports of the Supreme Court, besides ten volumes of statutes, embracing a greater amount of *practical* law [than] during any portion of the former history of the practice in this state." Volumes of precedent continued to pile up, and treatise writers struggled to digest it all for the profession.[63] Lawyers continued to compare themselves with degraded artisans unable to earn a competence through their work.

One such lawyer was Gulian C. Verplanck, a writer and legislator who held to the old ideal of the lawyer as a leisurely man of letters.[64] In an 1839 address to the state assembly in which he sat, Verplanck complained that "there is an unaccountable reluctance" to compensate "any sort of public labor, on the same scale and with the same object which any large merchant, manufacturer, or any wealthy corporation establishes the salaries of persons whom he or they may employ."[65] Verplanck lamented that even the great jurists of the bench and bar were compensated like journeymen because they were public officers rather than private contractors.

Verplanck accused the Revised Statutes of exacerbating the two problems they were designed to alleviate: the cost and delay of civil suits. The revisers' attempted solution had sought to merge practices of common law and equity, mainly by sharing certain powers of the chancery court with common law judges. Common law courts were empowered to order the "discovery" of documents between parties and the deposition of certain witnesses, a type of pretrial investigation of evidence formerly available only in equity.[66] These reforms were expected to reduce the number of cases filed in both court systems. The most common occasion for double filing—seeking information through equity to support a remedy at common law—could now be handled in one court with only one bill of costs. Further, New York's eight common law circuit judges were invested as vice chancellors, and an additional full-time vice chancellor was appointed to busy New York City.[67] Thus, chancery's investigative processes

---

[63] Graham, *Treatise on the Practice of the Supreme Court*, vii–viii.

[64] On the transition of lawyers from men of letters to professional tradesmen, see especially Michael Grossberg, "Institutionalizing Masculinity: The Bar as a Man's Profession," in Mark Carnes & Clyde Griffen, eds., *Meanings for Manhood: Masculinity in Victorian America* (Chicago University Press, 1990), 133–51. In literary circles, Verplanck was a lesser light among the famed Knickerbocker Group, which included Washington Irving, James Fenimore Cooper, William Cullen Bryant, and Lydia Marie Child.

[65] Gulian C. Verplanck, *Speech When in Committee of the Whole in the Senate of New-York on the Several Bills and Resolutions for the Amendment of the Law and the Reform of the Judiciary System* (1839), 18.

[66] For citation to the relevant statutes as well as explanations of the practical details, see Graham, *Treatise on the Organization and Jurisdiction of the Courts*, 364. Common law judges could also administer equitable remedies for real property such as partition and waste, using equitable petitions and answers rather than the writ system's forms of actions. *Ibid.*, 564–68 (partition), 573–75 (waste), 556–57 (dower), 490–91 (document discovery). On the pre-code merger of examination practices in common law and equity, see Kessler, *Inventing American Exceptionalism*, 96–111.

[67] Graham, *Treatise on the Organization and Jurisdiction*, 348. Two additional vice chancellors were commissioned in the early 1840s. By 1846, the chancery bench included the chancellor, three vice chancellors, and seven circuit judges who exercised chancery jurisdiction. See "Civil Officers," *New York Evening Post*, July 13, 1846.

were shared by common law judges while the workforce of chancery dramatically expanded to resolve controversies under equity's exclusive jurisdiction.

In his address, Verplanck pointed out the problem: on a fair reading of the state's constitution, all "equitable" decisions could still be appealed up "to be decided by a single Chancellor, sitting alone."[68] By expanding the number of officers rendering equitable decisions, the Revised Statutes had only multiplied the occasions for appeal to the chancellor a hundredfold. This problem was exacerbated by New York's abolition of imprisonment for debt in 1831, a novel experiment unforeseen by the statutory revisers. Jurists then and now have celebrated New York for being among the first American states to free insolvent debtors from imprisonment, but few gave serious attention to a problem of civil remedies that followed this humanitarian reform: the concealment of assets.[69] As Bruce Mann demonstrates, conditions at Manhattan's New Gaol where debtors were held until they worked off or refinanced their loans were unwelcoming, to say the least.[70] If debtors could pay to avoid the cramped and squalid Gaol, they usually did. But once the threat of imprisonment had been statutorily abolished, creditors increasingly turned to the investigative powers of chancery to discover whether debtors were truly insolvent or merely hiding assets while avoiding their obligations.

The process worked out by lawyers in the 1830s became known as the "creditor's bill." By the 1820s, chancery had permitted creditors to file a bill to disgorge a debtor's fraudulent transfers of property from a colluding third party. For instance, in the landmark *Hadden v. Spader*, the indebted merchant John Davis made a "confidential debt" to his friend Lot Hadden. Instead of making payments on his original debts, Davis "paid" Hadden his entire stock of goods and accounts, but Hadden permitted Davis to continue to run his business as a trustee. Davis continued his merchant operations but "owned" nothing his creditors could collect. The chancellor, sustained by New York's highest appellate court, ruled that equitable remedies of discovery, injunction, and imprisonment for contempt were available to assist the defrauded creditors as long as those creditors had won a judgment on the debt at common law. (As ever, equity followed the law.)[71]

The state's abolition of imprisonment for debt also applied to chancery proceedings, but the statute made an explicit exception for "fraudulent" debtors. Accordingly, lawyers pressed for the expansion of the creditor's bill to cover not just cases of fraudulent transfer to third parties but cases of concealment as well, and the equity courts obliged. "After the right to coerce the debtor by imprisonment of his body was abolished, something of the kind was necessary," Oliver Barbour's treatise explained.

---

[68] Verplanck, *Speech When in Committee*, 6–7.

[69] See especially Peter J. Coleman, *Debtors and Creditors in America: Insolvency, Imprisonment for Debt, and Bankruptcy, 1607–1900* (Wisconsin University Press, 1974); Edward J. Balleisen, *Navigating Failure: Bankruptcy and Commercial Society in Antebellum America* (University of North Carolina Press, 2001); Bruce H. Mann, *Republic of Debtors: Bankruptcy in the Age of American Independence* (Harvard University Press, 2002). For contemporary figures on the numbers and relative indebtedness of New York prisoners on the eve of abolition, see "Imprisonment for Debt," 32 *North American Review* 490 (1831).

[70] Mann, *Republic of Debtors*, 86–88, 96–102.

[71] Hadden v. Spader, 20 Johns. 554 (1822). The expansion of the remedy to "fraudulent debtors" was affirmed in Gleason v. Gage, 7 Paige 121 (1838). See also Burrill, *A Treatise on the Practice of the Supreme Court*, 2:290–303.

"While it is the policy of the non-imprisonment act, therefore, to relieve the unfortunate debtor from imprisonment, it is the design of . . . creditors' bills, to compel him to surrender all his property and effects" or face imprisonment once again.[72] Creditors could, therefore, put debtors under oath to make admissions about their assets, and imprisonment for contempt could punish evaders.

Verplanck blamed "the imperfections of the law of [1831] *abolishing imprisonment for debt*" for putting the profession in "the habit of collecting commercial debts by what are called creditors' bills." In Verplanck's experience, execution of common law judgments routinely required the supplemental remedies of chancery, including the expensive bill of discovery, whose written question-and-answer format racked up fees by the page count besides costs for the interrogating lawyers and recording examiner.[73] Thus despite the aims of the Revised Statutes, many actions continued to require two lawsuits. By 1838, creditors' bills had so flooded the system that equity courts in the busiest circuits were hearing few other cases. Theodore Sedgwick observed that in New York City's chancery circuit, the number of filed bills had grown from 45 per month in 1831 to 112 per month in 1838 with the rise of creditors' bills. The current docket contained 130 other causes ready for trial, 104 of which had been sitting without a hearing for more than three years. During the first three terms in 1838, Sedgwick tallied, none of these cases had been heard at the January or July terms, and only six had been tried in April. The rest were held over to the following term while new cases continued to accumulate.[74] Graham commented that the delays of chancery and the cumbersome proceedings of creditors' bills led some creditors to seek their remedy through criminal procedure. Since New York still permitted private prosecutions before a grand jury, creditors could resort to criminal indictments of a debtor or a colluding third party. Graham concluded that "the just legislation, which has abolished the imprisonment of the debtor in a civil action, has led to an unexampled number of complaints" within the criminal system.[75] Despite its "abolition," the risk of imprisonment for debt lurked everywhere in 1830s New York.

Legislators considered further reforms in the sessions from 1836 to 1839, but Verplanck thought most suggestions were futile, for "they are all the mere hap-hazard patching up of a system which needs a much more thorough and radical reform." If hasty statutory changes to legal practice had brought on these unforeseen problems, Verplanck wondered, what would further legislative "remedies" do?[76] Inspired by an English royal commission that had sat from 1829 to 1831 and proposed reforms to common law pleading, the 1837 legislature called on the governor to appoint a similar commission of three lawyers.[77] Verplanck was unimpressed with the New York

---

[72] Barbour, *A Treatise on the Practice of the Court of Chancery*, 149, 150–157; Graham, *A Treatise on the Practice of the Supreme Court*, 506–508; 568.

[73] Verplanck, *Speech When in Committee*, 21–22

[74] Theodore Sedgwick, *A Statement of Facts in Relation to the Delays and Arrears of Business in the Court of Chancery of the State of New York* (1838), 30–35.

[75] *Fourth Report of the Commission on Practice and Pleadings* (New York, 1849), xxxvi. (The commission's Fourth Report included a code of criminal procedure that was reputed to be primarily the work of Graham. See, for instance, People v. Willis, 23 N.Y.S. 808, 809 (1898).)

[76] Verplanck, *Speech When in Committee*, 3.

[77] On the English commission, see Lobban, *The Common Law and English Jurisprudence*, 211–15. From 1829 to 1833, the commission produced six volumes of reports that contained extensive interview transcripts and collections of data from across the realm. The New York Legislature authorized the governor

commissioners, most of whom were old Federalist lawyers. He complained that, unlike the English commission that had produced multiple volumes of research and proposed legislation, New York's commissioners "reported very briefly their theory of legal reform, with few reasons for it and little external evidence." Their thirteen-page report concluded that "questions of practice, pleadings and costs" ought to be left "principally to the regulation of the higher courts of the State." The commissioners proposed a constitutional amendment to expand the chancellor's office to include up to six chancellors, but the rest of their legislation limited itself to vesting lawmaking authority among the appellate judges, who "may, in their discretion, prescribe the forms of all process, pleadings, records and proceedings."[78]

Verplanck thought the commission had gotten the English imitation all wrong. It was true, he conceded, that English royal commissions mostly comprised reformist judges, but the primary purpose had not been to employ judges as legislators but rather as examiners. The English commission sat for three years and made inquiries of "Chancellors and Ex-Chancellors, equity and common lawyers, and civilians, attorneys and bankers, money-borrowers and money-lenders, philosophers and brokers, every one who had knowledge or experience, or even ingenious theory to communicate." Rather than legislate, in Verplanck's telling, the English judge-commissioners merely organized the data into "clear and intelligible rules" for Parliament to consider. "This is a very different thing from authorizing the Chancellor and the three Judges to revolutionize the whole system of practice and pleading next August." According to Verplanck, what was needed was not a brief report and a quick delegation of lawmaking power to the judiciary. Instead, law reform required expertise, time, and a set of legislators who could think through the system holistically, ensuring that reforms in one department of remedies did not work against another.[79]

Verplanck's address garnered the admiration of David Dudley Field, now a thirty-five-year-old trial attorney of middling prominence (see Figure 2.1). Field wrote an enthusiastic letter of support that he later published as an anonymous tract. He agreed the recent commission report had "been prepared in haste, upon insufficient information. As unlike as possible the reports of the English Commissioners on the same subject." And he further approved of Verplanck's stance against judicial lawmaking. In addition to breaching the separation of powers, it was unlikely to be effective because judges would be reluctant to admit "any vice inherent in the system in which they were the chief officers."[80]

Most importantly, Field agreed on the need for holistic reform by a legislator with an eye for detailed interconnections. Field likened the legal system of remedies to

to appoint its commissioners. 1837 New York Laws 502. Governor William Marcy appointed Daniel Cady, a former Federalist member of the state assembly; Thomas Oakley, a former Federalist congressman and New York assemblyman; and Jacob Sutherland, a Democratic-Republican delegate to the 1821 state convention and an associate justice of the Supreme Court of Judicature.

[78] Verplanck, *Speech When in Committee*, 3–4; Report of the Commissioners Appointed under the Act of the 15th of May, 1837, in *Documents of the Senate of the State of New York*, 61st Sess., No. 2 (1838), 2:11, 15–19.
[79] Verplanck, *Speech When in Committee*, 3, 19–20.
[80] [David Dudley Field], *A Letter to Gulian C. Verplanck, on the Reform of the Judicial System of this State* (1840), 4–7.

Figure 2.1 Daguerreotype of David Dudley Field, most likely produced in the mid- to late 1840s, around the time Field produced the New York Code of Civil Procedure.
Library of Congress Prints and Photographs Division, Daguerreotype Collection, Film Reproduction No. LC-USZ62–28267.

complicated yet noiseless "machinery"; "and the eye, except of the attentive and prac- ticed observer, fails to perceive how it works, how complicated it is, what delicate ad- justment it requires, what nice adaptation of parts, at once the most complex and the most potent of all the engines by which society is regulated and moved."[81] The con- summate law reformer, therefore, had to be a master craftsman, one who understood complicated machinery so well he could avoid introducing defects among attempted corrections. By elaborating on Verplanck's concern for expertise, Field hinted that he just might be the expert Verplanck was looking for.

In part because of Verplanck's opposition, the proposed constitutional amend- ments failed to pass the legislature.[82] Hoping to provide a more systematic and du- rable reform from within the legislature, Field secured the Democratic nomination for a seat in New York's 1842 assembly. However, he was defeated when the Roman

---

[81] *Ibid.*, 4–7.

[82] The commissioners' recommendations were divided by the assembly into a series of bills and pro- posed constitutional amendments. See Report of the Committee on the Judiciary, Relative to a Judicial and Equity System for the State, in *Documents of the Assembly of the State of New York*, 61st Sess., No. 238 (1838) 5:1. The constitutional amendments failed to pass one or the other chamber over the next couple sessions. The legislature did pass a bill that permitted either party to request a trial by jury or to examine witness tes- timony orally before the fact-finder, but in both cases, the parties' choices were subject to the "discretion" and "judgment" of the chancellor and vice chancellors. 1838 N.Y. Laws 244–45; 1839 N.Y. Laws 292–93.

Catholic Archbishop John Hughes withheld support because of Field's Protestant views on public education.[83] Field nevertheless drafted a proposed reform bill and sent it to the assembly judiciary committee, whose chair, the retired probate judge Arphaxad Loomis, had prepared a reform bill of his own. Though Field's was more extensive—both in length and degree of innovation—the two bills were similar in many respects. Both exhibited a code-like style, taking the form of systematic, multi-provisioned legislation that could be inserted straight into the Revised Statutes, and both replaced lawyers' fee assessments based on page counts with "costs in gross" based on the amount in controversy.[84]

More significantly, the reform bills attempted a fusion of common law and equity practice to fix the significant problems in both systems. Both required common law pleadings to adopt the factual recitations of equitable pleadings, while Field's legislation allowed parties to testify at common law, thus obviating the need for discovery and creditors' bills at equity. These reforms cut to the essence of Field's complaints about legal craftsmanship, eliminating much of the paperwork filed to pursue a case and moving more of the action into the trial courtroom. Neither bill made it to a vote, however, as many assembly delegates thought the 1821 constitution barred such reforms. Outside the chancery court, the constitution required tribunals to "proceed according to the course of the common law," which implied the continuance of pleading the forms of action. All "equity powers," on the other hand, were "subject to the appellate jurisdiction of the chancellor," implicitly, a lone officer able to review any dispute about equitable discovery or execution. Practical reform seemed blocked by the constitution, and a portion of the New York City bar accordingly demanded amendments to the constitutional structure of the courts in an 1840 memorial to the legislature.[85]

Lawyers were not the only ones seeking to amend the constitution in the 1840s. Loomis, the judiciary chairman, and his co-delegate from Herkimer County, Michael Hoffman, had joined together to oppose Whig Party spending on state infrastructure by drafting a "People's Resolution" that would constitutionally require all major public expenditures to be submitted to popular referendum before taking effect. By the legislative session of 1844, the Democrats had proposed not one but five anti-spending amendments. The Whigs, who were seeking their own constitutional amendment expanding the state's eminent domain power, prevented any of them from passing. In the deadlocked debates, no other amendment could be reported out of committee. Law reformers gained an opening in 1845 when a faction of Democrats called for a constitutional convention to break the deadlock. Expecting the Democrats to factionalize further and give them an electoral advantage, the Whigs gambled and joined the call for a convention, a move approved by the state's voters in 1845 and scheduled for the summer of 1846.[86] With the state's fundamental law facing imminent revision,

[83] See Henry Martyn Field, *The Life of David Dudley Field* (Charles Scribner's Sons, 1898), 46.

[84] Report in Part of the Committee of the Judiciary, in Relation to the Administration of Justice, and Appendix: A Letter from D. D. Field, Esq. of New York, on Law Reform, to Representative John O'Sullivan, in *Documents of the Assembly of the State of New York*, 65th Sess., No. 81 (1842), 5:1.

[85] *Ibid.*, 21–22. N.Y. Const. of 1821, art. 5. See "Memorial of the New York Bar for a Reform in the Judicial System of the State," in *Documents of the Senate of the State of New York*, 63d Sess., No. 16 (1840), 1:1.

[86] See Charles Z. Lincoln, *The Constitutional History of New York from the Beginning of the Colonial Period to the Year 1905* (Lawyers' Cooperative, 1905), 2:10–101.

fusionists, codifiers, and reformers of all types now had their opportunity. To take advantage of it, they would need a political coalition and a theory of reform.

Lawyers' experiences in the 1820s and 1830s already set much of the reform agenda. While codification remained alluring, it was becoming increasingly clear that the democratic legislature vaunted by the early positivists was actually a hindrance to successful and far-reaching code reforms. Some critics worried that the Revised Statutes had carried codification too far and gave too much lawmaking authority to legislators who were shortsighted amateurs at best. Still, the resulting work hardly satisfied the codifiers. What codifiers regarded as the largest and most important areas of "unwritten law" remained beyond the scope of New York's statutes (now compiled into three volumes). Only the "modes of proceeding" had received thorough treatment and garnered innovative reforms. Indeed, a purported treatise on "practice in civil actions" in 1830 was little more than a reprinting of the recently published statutes.[87] In the following decades, this peculiarity would become the defining feature of American codification. Seizing the opening where they could, American lawyers would suggest that codification ought to begin with procedure and work out from there.

With all the political attention paid to the New York revisers and their method of working, debates about institutional competence in lawmaking increasingly focused less on the courts and more on commissions. When the District of Columbia contemplated a revision along the lines of New York in 1830, an editorial complained that hiring "some three or four lawyers . . . to make laws for the people" undermined fundamental principles of "REPUBLICANISM."[88] If the oracles of an unelected judge were an illegitimate source of lawmaking, what were the oracles of an unelected commissioner? If they were going to succeed at their task beyond mere "revised statutes," lawyers would have to become legitimate lawmakers apart from or even to the exclusion of actual legislators. Codifiers would have to find a way to justify lawmaking by an extra-legislative commission. For the rule of writs to end, lawyers would have to become supreme even over legislators.

---

[87] See Elijah Paine, *The Practice in Civil Actions and Proceedings at Law in the State of New York* (G. & C. & H. Carville, 1830).

[88] *Daily National Intelligencer* (Washington, D.C.), Mar. 26, 1830.

3

Mere Machinery

The Political Shape of Civil Procedure

I

Not yet forty years old in 1847, David Graham had already proven himself a master practitioner. Besides his well-known work on common law practice appearing in its third edition, Graham had also prepared a volume on civil jurisdiction in New York and had edited for American lawyers John Sidney Smith's two-volume treatise on English equity practice. Graham was the inaugural professor of common law pleading at New York University and also a well-compensated solicitor in the court of chancery. He was thus an ideal choice for appointment to a legislative commission to revise practice and pleadings in the state.[1]

But Graham was not chosen. At a party caucus meeting on the evening of February 4, 1847, Graham received thirty votes to join the commission, while Theodore C. Peters, a farmer from the distant western Genesee County, received thirty-five.[2] Peters sounded like a quintessential Jacksonian agrarian. "I grant you that we farmers are about as great a set of asses as could well be," he wrote in 1846, "for we bear all the burdens of the whole community, but yet have no proportionate share in the law making." Peters had run for the state constitutional convention that year, breaking with customary politeness by openly campaigning in the papers as "a stump candidate . . . in relation to *reform*." He lost, reportedly after having to withdraw to attend to a family illness, but that did not dampen his invectives against the state's system of law and legislative policy. Even when farmers did enter the legislature, he groused, they were "led by the nose by the gentlemen of a certain other trade or profession"—that is, the lawyers.[3]

Yet as much as Peters sounded in the papers like an anti-legalist populist, it turned out he was neither. Peters was, first of all, a stalwart member of the anti-Jacksonian Whig Party, a party known for its class hierarchy and capture by merchant capitalists rather than for populist agrarianism. Nevertheless, it was the Whigs who pressed Peters's nomination and who ultimately championed the reformed code the commission produced. Moreover, Peters was, it turned out, a licensed lawyer—a member of the bar for over a decade before his nomination to the commission.[4] Peters's

---

[1] On Graham's treatises, see chapter 2. Graham was the chief counselor to the municipal corporation of New York City and frequently appeared in chancery on the city's behalf. See, for instance, judgments recorded against the city in Indices of Judgments Docketed in the City and County of New York, 1844–1855 (1857), New York City Municipal Archives.

[2] See *Albany Evening Journal*, Mar. 30, 1847; *New York Evening Post*, Feb. 6, 1847.

[3] T. C. Peters to the Chairman of the Genesee Agricultural Association, July 10, 1846, in 7 *Genesee Farmer* 181 (1846); *New York Daily Tribune*, Mar. 12, 1846.

[4] *Albany Evening Journal*, Mar. 25, 1847; *Albany Evening Journal*, Apr. 3, 1847.

Law's Machinery. Kellen R. Funk, Oxford University Press. © Kellen R. Funk 2025. DOI: 10.1093/9780197543962.003.0004

complaints about access to law and lawmaking thus have to be understood as coming from someone who was not formally blocked from appearing or arguing in court but who nevertheless felt alienated from what legislative chambers and courts of law owed to an honest farmer like himself.

In the end, Peters was not seated on the reform commission, but someone he endorsed was. When the Democrats had to fill a vacancy, they chose among their members a reformer who, by all accounts, shared Peters's program for codification, the New York trial lawyer David Dudley Field. Under the Field Code, access to the bar and court-ordered remedies did become somewhat more direct. For large property holders like Peters, the Field Code accomplished what they wanted out of a legal system. To an extent, that meant opening up access to lawmaking and legal practice beyond the control of learned judges and common law pleaders, at least so far as to make the law legible to elite merchant creditors and their allies like Peters and Field.

But if facilitating merchant credit was an end to which the politics of codification could press, what the codifiers still needed was a means of navigating one of the most politically tumultuous eras of the New York legislature. It would have been obvious to most observers that a coalition of lawyers and professed lawyer-abolitionists, urban creditors and rural landholders was not fated to last long. So during the brief moment of Whig ascendance in New York, reformers developed a practical theory of law that would become a mainstay of American jurisprudence. According to this theory, the Anglo-American tradition of pleading writs and remedies was recast as "civil procedure," a benign field of regulation that left the real, or "substantive," law undisturbed while simply instructing the courts how to administer the law. In a favorite metaphor of the industrial age, procedure provided the "machinery of the law," but only the machinery. Codification could thus tinker with and improve the machine without capturing or interfering with the spirit within.

II

By the mid-1840s, lingering economic hardship from the Panic of 1837, rancorous debates over the annexation of Texas, and a looming war with Mexico put immense strains on the major political parties in New York. Typically a minority in New York, the Whigs continually sought out ways to broaden their coalition, but by the 1840s these efforts had created rifts in the party. Liberal Whigs such as William Seward hoped to appeal to newly arrived Irish immigrants, while others sought electoral success through nativism. The Democrats, meanwhile, engaged in what one historian has called "political fratricide." On the one side, "Hunkers"—those who "hunkered" after the spoils of James K. Polk's victorious presidential campaign—often aligned with the Whigs on matters of state spending. Like Polk, Hunkers favored territorial expansion even at the risk of war with Mexico. "Barnburners," on the other hand, remained committed to rooting out special corporate and banking interests, so much so that they were likened to a farmer who burned down his own barn to destroy the rats. Barnburners counted among their ranks a number of antislavery activists unwilling to see territorial expansion lead to the spread of slavery, who later became the organizers of the Free Soil Party in 1848.[5]

Science talk became the glue that connected these fractured parties to lawyers' professional concerns. "Political science," "legal science," "constitutional science," even the "science of pleading"—nearly every argument in the codification debates entered politics as the professed result of universal and methodologically sound reasoning. Morton Horwitz has written that "every defense of the common law system [against codification] was based on some assertion of the objective, apolitical, and scientific character of common law adjudication."[6] But conservators of the common law tradition were not the only ones deploying the language of legal science. Fusionists, codifiers, and other legal reformers claimed that legal science was precisely why electoral parties and legislative politics had to be engaged rather than avoided.

Lawyers could assert their authority as legal scientists, but they also had to make their concerns sound in political science to build partisan coalitions. Law—like any artisan craft—involved an applied science, an inductive enterprise open to evaluation by outside observers. Wherever one came down on the codification question, most tended to agree with the writer for the *Democratic Review* who surmised that "for the past half century the national mind of this country has been storing up a vast amount of political wisdom, which is sure to make itself heard and felt in our legislation and in the administration of our public affairs, but which has never been formally incorporated into the body of our political science."[7] The nation was now in its fiftieth year of experiment with freedom under law. But what could one scientifically conclude from this experiment?

For Professor Graham, common law practice was, as Lord Coke had written of it, "the perfection of human reason," the cumulative science of a thousand years. It was, in Graham's craft metaphor, "the cornerstone, upon which is built the proudest superstructure which the wisdom or ingenuity of man has devised." In its absence, all other experiments in rendering justice had failed, "the spirit of innovation and reform has been compelled to shrink from the vain and hopeless task of substituting another system in its stead, which should, with any thing like equal efficacy, contribute to the advancement of justice, or to the development of truth and right."[8]

Against this view of the common law as the pinnacle of legal science, codifiers scoffed. Appropriating the craft metaphor, the *Democratic Review* taunted that "he who should predicate the highest skill in the mechanical efforts of the early ages—who

---

[5] See Michael Holt, *The Rise and Fall of the American Whig Party: Jacksonian Politics and the Onset of the Civil War* (Oxford University Press, 1999), 238–43; James Henretta, "The Birth of American Liberalism: New York, 1820–1860," in Jürgen Heideking et al., eds., *Republicanism and Liberalism in America and the German States, 1750–1850* (Cambridge University Press, 2002), 165–86; Jonathan H. Earle, *Jacksonian Antislavery and the Politics of Free Soil, 1824–1854* (University of North Carolina Press, 2004); Herbert Donovan, *The Barnburners* (Porcupine, 1925).

[6] Morton J. Horwitz, *The Transformation of American Law, 1870–1960: The Crisis of Legal Orthodoxy* (Oxford University Press, 1992), 119.

[7] "The Progress of Constitutional Reform in the United States," 18 *Democratic Review* 243 (1846).

[8] David Graham Jr., "The Practice of the Law, as Illustrated in the Study of Pleading and Practice," in *Inaugural Addresses Delivered by the Professors of Law in the University of the City of New York at the Opening of the Law School of That Institution* (1838), 60–62. See also "The Independence of the Judiciary," 57 *North American Review* 400 (1843), 405.

should say that they were the wisest and greatest of human art and science, would be laughed at for his foolish credulity."[9] The long continuity of the common law was in this case proof against its responsiveness to scientific breakthroughs. Critics of New York's legal practice took special aim at the primitive state constitution of 1821. "The present Constitution of the State of New-York was adopted at a time when the subject of Constitutional Science was very imperfectly understood," argued one lawyer. Surveying four other state constitutions written in the early 1840s, the author summed up the scientific principles on which all agreed: "They all limit the official term of the Judiciary. All provide for biennial sessions of the Legislature, and all impose civil disabilities upon the clergy." The first two represented the leading edge of political science, but the lawyer disagreed with the last point, writing it off as an error of "political faith"—faith, not science, had produced that illiberal provision.[10]

The rhetoric of legal and political science helped to link codification to partisan politics. Whig Party political science imagined harmonious class relations in America predicated upon a system of state-sponsored development, or "internal improvement." Whig views on governance generally trusted neither the executive (marred forever by the memory of Andrew Jackson) nor common voters (who had put Jackson in office), but were more at ease with a hierarchical elite expertly deploying resources to maximize commercial production. Democratic Party political science, on the contrary, opposed "class-based" legislation that appeared to favor special interests—especially banks or commercial corporations—or that centralized government administration.[11]

Both Democrats and Whigs found their scientific reasons to support and resist codification. Some Whigs saw codification as one of the major "questions of internal improvement." The codifiers' claims to represent the best modern legal science fitted them, in the eyes of these Whigs, to aid "the immense extension of commerce . . . [and] great public schemes of internal improvement" with "new laws, adapted to the improved condition and modern exigencies of society."[12] And if a new code could shorten the delay and cut the expense of debt collections without the trouble of creditors' bills, it would be favored by the creditor class of bankers, merchants, and cash-crop farmers who made up the bulk of Whig support in New York.[13]

Although they rejected the language of public internal improvement and drew strength from perennially indebted farmers and laborers, the Democrats found their own reasons to favor codification. Simply because the common law originated in feudal England, many Democrats found it an affront to popular sovereignty. Field's mentor,

---

[9] "The Code of Procedure," 29 *Democratic Review* 481 (1851), 482.

[10] "Progress of Constitutional Reform," 253.

[11] The literature on Jacksonian era politics is, of course, vast. For general works that give particular attention to New York, see Holt, *The Rise and Fall of the American Whig Party*; John Lauritz Larson, *Internal Improvement: National Public Works and the Promise of Popular Government in the Early United States* (University of North Carolina Press, 2001); Sean Wilentz, *The Rise of American Democracy: Jefferson to Lincoln* (Norton, 2006); Marvin Meyers, *The Jacksonian Persuasion: Politics and Belief* (Stanford University Press, 1957). For a marvelously detailed analysis of New York's political factions across the 1840s, see Charles McCurdy, *The Anti-Rent Era in New York Law and Politics, 1839–1865* (University of North Carolina Press, 2001).

[12] "Revision of the Laws of New York," 24 *North American Review* 193 (1827), 193–99.

[13] See Holt, *The Rise and Fall of the American Whig Party*, 83–87; Coleman, *Debtors and Creditors in America*, 23–25.

Henry Sedgwick, was adamant on this point. Whereas Blackstone had thought the early common law possessed a "pristine vigor," Sedgwick saw early common law as "a feeble, tottering, unstable thing, till the reason, wisdom, humanity, and experience of more modern times [developed] civilized and settled governments."[14]

Democrats also viewed codification as a way to combat "special legislation" that favored individual corporations or discrete classes of society. "By a very cursory examination of the New-York session laws for the last ten years," observed the *Democratic Review*, "it will appear that the great mass of them concern private and local interests, with which government, properly restricted, would have nothing whatever to do." A code necessarily addressed itself to the general rules governing all society. For this reason, some Democrats who favored biennial meetings of the legislature likewise favored codification, expecting the two to go hand in hand. Codification would set the pattern for general legislation; short and infrequent legislative sessions would hold legislators to that pattern.[15]

Both parties likewise had reasons to resist codification, often stemming from an outspoken distrust of civilian Europe, the heartland of codification. Although equity's juryless proceedings and modes of investigation appeared to draw directly upon civilian traditions or at least operated like them in effect, civilian law was widely unpopular in the Early Republic.[16] Democrats hailed popular sovereignty in the jury system, and Whigs admired the way common law writs like habeas corpus could thwart a despotic executive. Arrayed as these rights were in common imaginations against a European-like tyranny, the threat that codification and law reform might overturn them along with the entire writ system could turn either party ideologically against codification.[17]

As New York's 1846 constitutional convention neared, two other factions became especially important to the development of a New York code: Young America Democrats and Anti-Rent Whigs. More famous as a loose confederation of artists and writers seeking to craft a distinctively American art and literature, the "Young America" movement also formed a distinctive political faction within Democratic politics. The movement's best known adherents typically combined literary pursuits with political activism, including John O'Sullivan, a New York assemblyman and editor of the *Democratic Review*, and Nathaniel Hawthorne, the Romantic novelist and Franklin Pierce's consul to Liverpool.[18] David Dudley Field considered himself among their number. Field contributed travelogues to O'Sullivan's *Review* and first introduced Hawthorne to the aspiring author Herman Melville. When Field's run for

---

[14] [Henry Sedgwick], "The Common Law," 19 *North American Review* 411 (1824), 411–23.

[15] "History of Constitutional Reform in the United States," 18 *Democratic Review* 403 (1846), 408.

[16] See Thomas McSweeney, "English Judges and Roman Jurists: The Civilian Learning Behind England's First Case Law," 84 *Temple Law Review* 827 (2012); Stanley N. Katz, "The Politics of Law in Colonial America: Controversies over Chancery Courts and Equity Law in the Eighteenth Century," in Donald Fleming & Bernard Bailyn, eds., *Perspectives in American History* (Little, Brown & Co., 1971), 5:257–84, 265; see also Daniel J. Hulsebosch, *Constituting Empire: New York and the Transformation of Constitutionalism in the Atlantic World, 1664–1830* (University of North Carolina Press, 2008), 60.

[17] See, e.g., Juvenus Alumnus, *The Crudities of the Code and the Codifiers* (1850), 9–10.

[18] Edward L. Widmer, *Young America: The Flowering of Democracy in New York City* (Oxford University Press, rev. ed., 2000); Yonatan Eyal, *The Young America Movement and the Transformation of the Democratic Party 1828–1861* (Cambridge University Press, 2007).

the assembly failed in 1842, he sent his reform bills not to the judiciary committee's chair but to O'Sullivan, who made sure to print them with the chairman's report.[19]

Politically, Young America adhered to the Jacksonian rhetoric of limited government and general legislation. "The best government is that which governs least," O'Sullivan's *Review* declared on its front page, while Field denounced "agrarian measure[s] to divide property among those who have not earned it."[20] Practically, however, Young America Democrats had made their peace with banks and railroads. New technologies and means of capitalization were necessary to achieve Young America's vision of territorial expansion and national influence on the world stage. It was O'Sullivan's *Review* that had coined the term "Manifest Destiny" as a slogan for US continental aspirations, and many followed O'Sullivan in the belief that Jackson's old feuds with soft money and corporate capital would have to be laid aside to realize those aspirations. Thus one study concludes that in their views of federal power, constitutional interpretation, and the means of commercial growth, "Young America Democrats could claim to be as welcoming of the modern economic world and its possibilities as their Whig opponents."[21]

As much as they favored expansion and nationalism, many Young America Democrats, including O'Sullivan and Field, counted themselves Barnburners who opposed slavery and Polk's seeming capitulation to the "Slave Power." In this regard as well, Young America appeared more Whiggish than Democratic, although their antislavery principles relied less on evangelical religion than did those of leading Whigs and more on the political empowerment of laboring classes.[22] For Young Americans such as Field, codification could unite all these concerns with expansion, nationalism, free labor, and a uniquely American literature. Altogether, Field wrote, the triumph of democratic reform would produce "a CODE AMERICAN" that could "move with every emigration, and make itself a home in the farthest portion of our own continent."[23] Democrats like Field thus turned on its head the criticism of codification as a tool of imperialism. European empires might use their Code Napoleon to exercise arbitrary power, but the Code American would be well-suited for America's empire of liberty.[24]

If Young America Democrats appeared indistinguishable from Whigs, the Anti-Rent Whigs looked more like Democrats. The anti-rent movement arose among

---

[19] For Field's letter, see chapter 2. The Field-Hawthorne-Melville "Berkshire picnic" details are compiled in Bernard A. Drew, *Literary Luminaries of the Berkshires: From Herman Melville to Patricia Highsmith* (Arcadia, 2015), 41–44. Field's travelogues appear in the *United States Democratic Review* under the title "Sketches over the Sea" from October to May, 1839–1840.

[20] "Front Pages," 1 *Democratic Review* 1 (Oct. 1837), i; David Dudley Field, "Corruption in Politics" [1877], in A. P. Sprague, ed., *Speeches, Arguments, and Miscellaneous Papers of David Dudley Field* (D. Appleton, 1884), 2:494.

[21] Eyal, *Young America Movement*, 233.

[22] See Sean Wilentz, "Slavery, Antislavery, and Jacksonian Democracy," in Melvyn Stokes & Stephen Conway, eds., *The Market Revolution in America: Social, Political, and Religious Expressions, 1800–1880* (University of Virginia Press, 1996), 202–23; Eyal, *Young America Movement*, 147.

[23] David Dudley Field, *Legal Reform: An Address to the Graduating Class of the Law School of the University of Albany* (1855), 32.

[24] On the Jeffersonian idea of America as an empire of liberty, see Drew McCoy, *The Elusive Republic: Political Economy in Jeffersonian America* (University of North Carolina Press, 1980), 185–208; Robert W. Tucker & David C. Hendrickson, *Empire of Liberty: The Statecraft of Thomas Jefferson* (Oxford University Press, 1990).

Hudson Valley farmers whose lands remained under feudalistic tenures held over from colonial days. These feudal dues required annual rents paid to the descendants of the van Rensselaers and severely limited farmers' ability to sell their land. A band of laboring farmers too poor to pay dues to a privileged elite ought to have fit naturally into the Democratic coalition, but state Democrats struggled to find a solution that would not violate their stance against class legislation—any reform would have divested a secure right of property from the van Rensselaers and transferred it to a discrete class of agrarians. Moreover, when the anti-renters' ritualized violence caused the death of a sheriff during the tenure of a Democratic governor, the Democrats had to face the quandary of either prosecuting the anti-renters or appearing to sacrifice the rule of law for pet constituents.[25]

By the mid-1840s, William Seward's efforts to expand the Whig Party were reaping gains among the anti-renters, who reasoned that if Democrats would not help them, perhaps the Whigs' looser construction of eminent domain principles in service of commercial development could. The anti-renters had no discernable position on codification or the reform of civil remedies, but it was anti-rent strength in the legislature that deadlocked debates over constitutional amendments. Thus any road toward the reform of chancery practice or common law pleading would have to run through the party of anti-rent.[26] The anti-rent allegiance to the Whigs further defined the late 1840s as a peculiar moment in New York politics. While Democrats divided over Polk's expansionist war, the Whigs gained sweeping majorities from an unusual coalition, the same coalition that would create the New York code: urban merchants and their legal counsel united with rural smallholders seeking particular reforms. The latter became known at the convention not as anti-renters but "anti-lawyers." The anti-lawyers' demands for simplified proceedings in plain language would give the code its Jacksonian reputation, but the votes of pro-creditor Whigs and the draftsmanship of Young America Democrats would give it its structure.

III

In a grand compromise between New York's political factions, the 1845 legislature summoned a constitutional convention to meet the next year. Barnburners hoped to rein in state spending, anti-renters expected to abolish feudal tenures, and fusionists and codifiers anticipated remaking New York's system of civil remedies. During the spring of 1846, around forty-five lawyers won election to the convention, making them the best represented profession except for the forty-seven who called themselves farmers (some of whom were also lawyers). Field ran for a delegate's seat, but his strident opposition to the invasion of Mexico kept from him the Democratic nomination in New York City.[27] The legal profession did not unite behind a single party, but even

---

[25] McCurdy, *Anti-Rent Era*, 128–81.

[26] See *ibid.*, 83–87, 162–63, 200–04.

[27] Field, *Third of a Century*, 2; H. M. Field, *The Life of David Dudley Field* (Charles Scribner's Sons, 1898), 110–13. For occupational identifications, see William G. Bishop & William H. Attree, *Report of the Debates and Proceedings of the Convention for the Revision of the Constitution of the State of New York* (Evening Atlas, 1846), 3–6.

lawyers within the same party rarely advocated the same set of reforms. On the organization of the courts and the reform of legal practice, party lines and party discipline were nonexistent, making the convention both a visionary and chaotic scramble as lawyers brought their professional practices into political conversation.

Two weeks after the delegates convened on June 1, 1846, the first reform proposed for the legal profession was its abolition, or at least its privatization. Enoch Strong, a Whig farmer from Monroe, urged the convention to "inquire into the expediency of reserving to the people their dormant right of freely choosing their counsel and attorneys in all courts of law, with the like freedom from state interference that they now enjoy in the selection of their spiritual advisers." Strong objected to the prerogative of state judges to certify courtroom advocates through bar admissions, and he offered his resolution to break this "close and gainful monopoly."[28] A publication by a fellow Whig accused Strong of betraying his party by declaring "every man a lawyer (even as he is a 'democrat') by right of birth." The writer likened the sentiment to "the vulgar error respecting the non-productiveness of mercantile classes." Just as those of only "common intelligence" raised a cry against merchants for contributing nothing to society, Strong and his associates were missing a basic fact of political economy "as ancient as the practice of law for pay," that lawyers ultimately were the "*makers* of law" through their arguments, decisions, and legislation, and thus they acquired an expertise that deserved to be certified, distinguishing true craftsmen from fraudulent hucksters.[29]

But Enoch Strong was no leveling democrat wearing a Whiggish disguise. Although Strong identified himself in the convention journal as a farmer, he was also, like Peters, a licensed lawyer, and in fact a former legislator. In 1843, Strong had had the delicate task of chairing a committee and reporting on a petition from his county "praying for the repeal of all laws for the collection of debts." Strong rebuked his own constituents, claiming they had "perhaps, unconsciously to themselves" been deluded by the Democratic tactics of class warfare in which "the prejudices of the poor were sought to be excited against the rich." Credit, he argued, "occupied an important position in the machinery of commerce," and in New York, the "poor man" was just as likely to be a creditor as a debtor, and he therefore needed "to collect his honest due." What was needed, Strong said, was enforcement and protection of the law, not its abrogation.[30] Strong's position cautions us not to overread anti-lawyers at the time as anti-*legalists* pursuing a radical politics toward the rights of property and the distribution of wealth. Strong's anti-lawyer proposals arose from a retired lawyer-farmer seeking to make his former profession more accessible to those who did not inherit connections from their fathers or could not afford long training in the technicalities of assumpsit, trover, and the creditor's bill.[31]

[28] Sherman Croswell & R. Sutton, *Debates and Proceedings of the New York State Convention for the Revision of the Constitution* (Albany Argus, 1846), 72–73.
[29] "The Legal Profession, Ancient and Modern," 4 *American Whig Review* 242 (1846).
[30] *Assembly Journal* (New York, 1843), 450–52.
[31] Croswell & Sutton, *Proceedings of the Convention*, 575–77. A quantitative study of "anti-lawyer sentiment" in Massachusetts arrived at a similar conclusion. Lawyers commanded majorities within legislative bodies, and much of the commercial business of chartering, contracting, and collecting of payments required assistance of a licensed counselor. A well-organized bar association restricted licensing to the sons and associates of current members only, provoking the ire of anti-monopoly Jacksonians. In 1835,

Strong withdrew his convention motion the day after he introduced it, to the disgust of his supporters. One of them, a Whig writing in the *Daily Tribune* on behalf of "the millions" interested "in the removal of this odious taxing monopoly," argued that the convention had given up its best chance to simplify legal practice by keeping its reform in the hands of "practicing lawyers." Later in the convention, Strong tried again, proposing a clause that entitled "any citizen . . . of good moral character" to practice law in the state. Barnburner merchant Campbell White sarcastically asked if advocates could at least be required to read and write. Strong countered with a less radical amendment, admitting to practice "any male citizen of the age of 21 years, of good moral character, and who possesses the requisite qualifications of learning and ability." That clause passed, but Strong clumsily appended it to the article specifying the powers of the judiciary, implicitly leaving it to judges to determine who was "of good moral character" and what "requisite qualifications of learning" would be.[32]

Although Strong's anti-lawyer provision failed to open access to the profession through constitutional mandate, anti-lawyers would have other chances to achieve similar aims. Throughout the summer, agreement among lawyers on a package of reforms remained elusive. To the end of the convention, lawyers engaged in widespread pamphleteering, but no two law reform tracts agreed in their essentials. Hiram Hastings, a Barnburner lawyer from New York City, argued for a total reorganization of the courts, complete with a salaried, elective judiciary as the best means of improving civil practice. The elderly Jacksonian Michael Hoffman urged that courts had to be constituted so that judges would travel among the people and sit with juries, but Hoffman refrained from calling for an elective judiciary. Field, meanwhile, continued to advocate the fusing of common law and equity while counseling against an elective judiciary and ignoring the question of codification.[33]

The variety of proposals continued well into August, even after the judiciary committee reported its proposed article. Of the thirteen delegates on the judiciary committee, three filed minority reports, while two others, not wishing to embarrass the committee further, filed no report but nevertheless voiced their dissent against multiple provisions in the majority bill. The majority report abolished the court of chancery but provided no further details as to whether equitable proceedings and jurisdiction would be retained by the common law courts. Charles O'Conor's minority report, following advice from Hoffman, provided that "a code of procedure in civil suits shall be enacted within two years, subject to alteration by law." The majority

---

Massachusetts's Revised Statutes destroyed the power of the bar association over admissions, which were made automatic upon a course of study in any law office in the state or examination by any judge. With that single reform to admissions, anti- lawyering sentiment swiftly faded. Gerard W. Gawalt, "Sources of Anti-Lawyer Sentiment in Massachusetts, 1740–1840," 14 *Journal of American Legal History* 283 (1970), 283–307.

[32] Roger Sherman, "Allow Me to Choose My Lawyer," *New York Daily Tribune*, Sept. 3, 1846. Croswell & Sutton, *Proceedings of the Convention*, 575–77. N.Y. Const. of 1846, art. 4, § 7.
[33] Hiram P. Hastings, *An Essay on Constitutional Reform* (1846); Michael Hoffman, "Letter on Reforms Necessary in the Body of Law, in the Written Pleadings, and in the Practice of the Courts" [Mar. 21, 1846], in Thomas Prentice Kettle, ed., *Constitutional Reform in a Series of Articles Contributed to the Democratic Review* (1846), 63; David Dudley Field, *Re-Organization of the Judiciary: Five Articles Originally Published in the Evening Post on That Subject* (1846).

report remained undecided about judicial elections, offering two alternative texts for the convention to choose between. One minority report pressed for an elective judiciary; another disavowed it.[34]

In the final month of the convention, short-term calculations determined the shape that law reform and codification would take, though the delegates could hardly have suspected how their maneuvers for the sake of partisan expediency would later be interpreted as legal principle. Those in favor of codification feared that the judiciary committee, staffed mostly by older common law lawyers, would prove resistant. They accordingly maneuvered a codification resolution to a select committee headed by Campbell White, a pro-codification merchant from New York City. A separate resolution, concerning an open-ended "reform of practice and pleadings" was shunted off to the judiciary committee, and only O'Conor's minority report suggested reforming through a code.[35]

By the time reformers moved for a constitutional entrenchment of procedural reform, it was mid-August and many delegates had already returned to their farms, businesses, and law practices. Forming an alliance across the political spectrum, the remaining delegates worked out a judiciary article that provided for both the practice commission and a separate commission to inquire into codification (each set at three members).[36] An elective judiciary was the more famous reform to emerge from these debates, but many saw the reform of pleading and practice as closely related. In his judiciary committee report proposing judicial elections, the Hunker Charles Ruggles surmised that popularly elected judges who lacked legal training would help keep lawyers from falling "into the track of technical rules." Hoffman agreed that fusion of law and equity would force judges to simplify equitable proceedings so that they could be understood by lay jurors in the course of a few hours.[37]

It was the Whigs who united these few Democrats with creditor merchants and anti-lawyers under a theory of "independence" in the judiciary. From its inception, the Whig Party had been a stalwart defender of an independent judiciary, especially, as the historic allusion in their name indicated, against the overreaching of a central executive. By the 1840s, some Whigs extended their arguments to defend the

---

[34] Croswell & Sutton, *Proceedings of the Convention*, 369–84. For the list of judiciary committee members, see *Documents of the Convention of the State of New York* (Carroll & Cook, 1846), 1:70.

[35] Bishop & Attree, *Debates and Proceedings of the Convention*, 109–11.

[36] Croswell & Sutton, *Proceedings of the Convention*, 642; Bishop & Attree, *Debates and Proceedings of the Convention*, 838–40. On an amendment linking procedural reform to codification, Whigs voted 12–21 against while Democrats split 23–28. Hunkers overwhelmingly voted against, while Barnburners narrowly supported the provision. Measuring the votes by occupation and geography reveals much more about the politics of practice reform. Only a third of the lawyers and farmers still present at the convention voted in favor of both codifying and reforming civil practice, while three-fourths of the merchants did so. Adding a geographic dimension makes the divide even starker: 100 percent of both New York City merchants and lawyers (of any party) supported both proposals, while lawyers opposed to both provisions came from outlying border counties to the west and north of the state, counties less affected by the booming business of the Erie Canal. Party affiliation derived from Philip L. Merkel, "Party and Constitution Making: An Examination of Selected Role Calls from the New York Constitutional Convention of 1846" (May 2, 1983) (unpublished graduate seminar paper, University of Virginia (on file with author), app. 1, with corrections from the *New York Herald*, Apr. 18, 1846.

[37] Croswell & Sutton, *Proceedings of the Convention*, 371–72. Bishop & Attree, *Debates and Proceedings of the Convention*, 677–82.

independence of the judiciary from partisan politics. One writer argued that the independence of the judiciary was actually more important for partisan America than it was for monarchial England, "to guard the property, the interests, and even the life of a citizen, not against the arbitrary will of a single despot, but against the violence and recklessness of a more formidable enemy, an excited political party." For these Whigs, the chief danger to the rule of law was the direct link between a majority faction that both made the laws and appointed the judges who would apply them.[38]

The Whigs' aversion to partisan politics might seem to contradict their support of an elective judiciary. But in a close study of the debates over judicial elections at the convention, Jed Shugerman demonstrates that Whigs believed partisanship had strong influence in gubernatorial and legislative appointments yet was virtually absent in local elections. An independent judiciary therefore had to be independent of, above all, patronage appointments in Albany.[39] The other reforms of the judiciary article followed a similar logic. As the judiciary became independent of the other branches, so Whigs reasoned the bar ought to be independent of the judiciary to prevent patronage appointments. Making a renewed anti-lawyer effort, Enoch Strong favored a provision that barred judges from exercising "any power of appointment to public office." Democrats like O'Conor and Henry Nicoll pointed out the futility of the clause, noting that attorney admissions and remedial uses of receivers and referees were not considered "appointments to public office" in any conventional sense. Strong's amendment was adopted anyway.[40] And even if the bar could not be made completely independent of the judiciary, some Whigs argued that the simplification of practice could at least make the judiciary independent of the bar by permitting access to court remedies without the payment of fees and costs to lawyer-mediators.[41]

Institutional independence also informed the choice for law reform by commission. The use of legislative commissions might have seemed natural given the precedent of the Revised Statutes commission, but convention Democrats offered numerous alternatives. Lorenzo Shepard, a lawyer from New York County, proposed the "establishment of practice courts ... for the adjudication of all questions of practice, in the first instance, that may arise." O'Conor suggested empowering the state's apex court to draft rules of practice. Writing for the majority of the judiciary committee, Charles Ruggles favored doing nothing and letting the evolution of case law "gradually by the action and practice of the court" reform and unify the disparate systems of law and equity. The anti-rent lawyer Ira Harris proposed that a single chief justice could regulate procedure. All these choices gave effective control over the practice of law to the judiciary. By August, Democratic delegates had come around to reforming legal practice

---

[38] "The Independence of the Judiciary," 419–20.
[39] Jed Handelsman Shugerman, "Economic Crisis and the Rise of Judicial Elections and Judicial Review," 123 *Harvard Law Review* 1061 (2010), 1088–92. Shugerman further argues that some Whigs compromised with Democrats on judicial elections in order to save a clause preserving the right to jury trial. Others pragmatically reasoned that Democrats would soon regain their statewide majority, and election by judicial district would at least allow Whigs to retain certain judicial offices.
[40] Bishop & Attree, *Debates and Proceedings of the Convention*, 575–77. Further stretching the incoherence of the prohibition of judicial appointments, the clause was attached to Strong's other amendment that implicitly assigned attorney admissions to the judiciary. See N.Y. Const. of 1846, art. 4, § 7.
[41] See, for instance, Sherman, "Allow Me to Choose My Lawyer."

by "cautious and gradual legislation" instead of by court rules. Because the Democrats were intent on limiting legislative sessions to ninety days, one argued, "this work if done at all should be done by a commission" which could continue its efforts beyond the short sessions.[42]

New York's Constitution of 1846 thus marked an unusual compromise between Whigs and Barnburner Democrats, formerly two poles of the state's political system. Out of a concern for state credit, Whigs cooperated with Barnburners to pass restrictions on state spending, and the same coalition produced the compromises of the judiciary article, including the elective judiciary, the abolition of chancery, and the establishment of separate commissions to codify the law and to reform legal practice. Whig contributions to these measures and the Whig philosophy that underlay them were swiftly effaced in the partisan press after the convention. Newspapers interpreted the reforms to be mainly the work of Barnburners like Arphaxad Loomis and Michael Hoffman, who had succeeded in transforming their "People's Resolution" from the 1845 legislature into a "People's Constitution" at the 1846 convention.[43] That autumn, New Yorkers voted two-to-one in favor of the new constitution.[44]

IV

Despite his own misgivings about an elected judiciary, Field was pleased with the new constitution, especially the mandate for procedural reform. Early in 1847, he dashed off a pamphlet titled "What Shall Be Done with the Practice of the Courts? Shall It Be Wholly Reformed?" The answer, of course, was yes. "Great changes in legal proceedings are now inevitable," he declared, "and . . . in making them it is as easy to build anew from the foundation, as to add to and repair what is old." Field's plea to his fellow members of the bar to embrace change slipped into vaguely threatening language: "We must either take part in the changes, or set ourselves in opposition, and then, as I think, be overwhelmed by them." Field concluded his tract by reiterating his basic proposal: "nothing less than a uniform course of proceeding, in all cases, legal and equitable."[45]

Turning from the bar to the legislature, Field drafted a memorial urging precise instructions. "Declare," advised Field, "that it shall be their duty to provide for the abolition of the present forms of action and pleadings in cases at common law, for a uniform course of proceeding in all cases, whether of legal or equitable cognizance, and for the abandonment of every form of proceeding not necessary to ascertain or preserve the rights of the parties." Such a mandate had failed on the convention floor but was now offered up for normal legislation. Gracing Field's lobbying effort were the

[42] See Croswell & Sutton, *Proceedings of the Convention*, 74, 372–74, 643; Bishop & Attree, *Debates and Proceedings of the Convention*, 785.

[43] See Shugerman, "Economic Crisis and the Rise of Judicial Elections," 1086; Peter J. Galie, *Ordered Liberty: A Constitutional History of New York* (Fordham University Press, 1996), 110; *Evening Post*, Apr. 25, 1849.

[44] Charles Z. Lincoln, *The Constitutional History of New York* (Lawyer's Co-operative, 1905), 2:213.

[45] David Dudley Field, *What Shall Be Done with the Practice of the Courts? Shall It Be Wholly Reformed?* (1847), 6–7, 37.

signatures of fifty prominent New York lawyers—including those of former vice chancellors, congressional representatives, and leading trial attorneys.[46]

Because the constitution required the establishment of both a commission to reform legal practice and a commission to inquire into codifying the entire common law, the legislature needed to fill six total seats on two commissions. Although one senator "did not wish to make this a party question," the parties appear to have swiftly reached an agreement that a Whig majority would sit on the codification commission and a Democratic majority on the practice commission. The Democrats split their votes on the practice commission between their two leading factions, nominating the Barnburner Arphaxad Loomis and the Hunker Nicholas Hill, a member of the elite appellate bar in Albany. A Whig newspaper complained that the commission "has been drawn into the party vortex." Instead of talent or skill being the leading qualification, "they were selected on party grounds and as party men." But the Whigs too held a caucus, where they formally nominated the anti-lawyering farmer Theodore C. Peters to the practice commission.[47]

The legislative sessions of the next few years that would determine the fate of codification were dominated by Whigs. Whigs had a substantial majority in the 1847 assembly but were outnumbered in the senate. When the Democracy disintegrated with the departure of Free Soilers in 1848, Whigs gained large majorities in both chambers through the 1848 and 1849 sessions.[48] With Whig support, the senate voted to adopt Field's memorial as the mandate to the practice commission. Democrats—and lawyers—split their votes evenly on the matter. So while the constitution vaguely required the revision and simplification of forms of proceeding, the legislature specified the abolition of "the present forms of action" and the fusion of law and equity.[49]

On March 5, Democrats secured the appointment of Hill and Loomis as planned by their caucus. Several Whig senators thought better of nominating Peters, however. William van Schoonhoven, a Whig lawyer, pressed for Whigs to hold the course, arguing that Peters had the best combination of professional experience: he had practiced law but was not "attached to the complicated system of practice now existing." Abraham Gridley, the lone Whig from the Seventh District, retorted that Peters's onetime association with the law made him a poor choice. A novice "layman who knew nothing of the law" was preferable to a dilettante "quack lawyer." Richard Williams, a Democrat, inserted himself into the Whig debate to express his admiration of Peters

[46] "Memorial of Members of the Bar in the City of New York Relative to Legal Reform," in *Documents of the Assembly of the State of New York*, 70th Sess., No. 48 (1847), 2:1.

[47] See, for instance, the statements of Senator Spencer in "Legislative Acts and Proceedings," *Albany Evening Journal*, Mar. 5, 1847; *Commercial Advertiser* (New York, N.Y.), Feb. 8, 1847. See *supra* notes 1–3 and accompanying text.

[48] The Senate and Assembly partisan compositions by years were: 1847 Senate—21 Democrats to 11 Whigs; 1847 Assembly—54 Democrats to 74 Whigs; 1848 Senate—8 Democrats to 24 Whigs; 1848 Assembly—32 Democrats to 96 Whigs; 1849 Senate—15 Democrats to 17 Whigs; 1849 Assembly—21 Democrats to 107 Whigs. Party affiliation derived from *Albany Evening Journal*, Dec. 31, 1846; "Election Returns," *Commercial Advertiser* (New York, N.Y.), Nov. 3, 1847; "Election Returns," *New York Evening Post*, Nov. 3, 1847; "The Whig Victory!" *Albany Evening Journal*, Nov. 4, 1847; *Cabinet* (Schenectady, N.Y.), Nov. 28, 1848; *New York Weekly Herald*, Oct. 28, 1848.

[49] See *Journal of the Senate of the State of New York* (1847), 239–42. A move to strike the instructions was defeated 7–13, with six Democrats and one Whig supporting the motion and six Democrats and seven Whigs opposing it; six lawyers supported the motion and five resisted it.

and to note that what went against the interests of professional lawyers might well lie within the interests of the "People." If Peters was unacceptable as a layman, however, Williams suggested the senate consider David Dudley Field, a lawyer who Williams believed would make the same reforms as Peters. As the Democrats had already filled their seats on the commission, no one took the suggestion seriously at the time. Instead, senate Whigs met behind closed doors after the debate and agreed to replace Peters with the law professor David Graham the next day.[50]

The senate's decision provoked a fierce anti-lawyer debate in the assembly. Herman Blodgett, the Whig representative of Peters's Genesee County, railed against the "mummeries and complications" of legal practice and asserted that Peters's only flaw was "that he was not acceptable to that *professional* [senate] judiciary committee," even though Peters had provided "more substantial benefit to the producing classes than all the speeches of" the Whig lawyers. Blodgett produced letters of recommendation from the bench and bar of Genesee, one judge suggesting that Peters's ability to file a minority report would keep a conservative reform commission honest.[51]

Blodgett was countered by the other Whig from Genesee, Alonzo Upham. Against his colleagues' charges that lawyers sought to control reform for the benefit of their own class, Upham appealed to Whig Party ideology that presumed essentially harmonious class relations in republican society. Law reformers—both from the legal profession and lay society—"wage war against no class of men as such," nor could they "be fooled or blinded by the senseless cry of lawyer or anti lawyer." Upham produced his own correspondence from citizens of Genesee County, "not one of whom is a lawyer." From them, Upham concluded that Peters "has not the talent necessary for the station" and, on that ground alone, had to be rejected. Professional identity was otherwise irrelevant. "I am a mechanic, and am neither proud nor ashamed of it. I am for sound, wholesome, legal reform," Upham declared. "I am opposed to all efforts to set up one class of men against another."[52]

Blodgett predicted that with Graham and Hill, the commission would have "a majority of Old Hunkers in law" and "we are to have no reform whatever." Nevertheless, when debate concluded, the Whigs voted 34–12 to concur with the senate on appointing the undisputed expert Graham to the commission.[53]

Loomis, Hill, and Graham accepted their appointments and met to commence their work over the summer. In the midst of the anti-lawyer debate in the senate, Graham had written to the old Jacksonian Senator Samuel Young, promising that if appointed to the commission, he would give his full effort to simplifying and reforming practice.[54] Representative Blodgett doubted the sincerity of those "who never was heard to lisp a word in favor of reform until their names have been mentioned in connection with this commission," but under Field's specific instructions,

[50] *Albany Evening Journal*, Mar. 10, 1847; *Albany Argus*, Mar. 11, 1847; *Albany Evening Journal*, Mar. 11, 1847.

[51] "Legislative Acts and Proceedings," *Albany Evening Journal*, Mar. 25, 1847. "Speech of Mr. Blodgett," *Albany Evening Journal*, Apr. 3, 1847.

[52] "Speech of Mr. Upham," *Albany Evening Journal*, Apr. 4, 1847.

[53] "Speech of Mr. Blodgett," *Albany Evening Journal*, Apr. 3, 1847; *Assembly Journal* (New York, 1847), 628–30.

[54] See statements of Senator Young, *Albany Evening Journal*, Mar. 10, 1847.

Graham abandoned his popular treatise to obsolescence and joined Loomis in drafting a reform statute.[55] In September, the legislature convened an extra session and requested an update from the commissioners. After reading the others' drafts, Nicolas Hill concluded that the fusion of law and equity and the abolition of the forms of action would be undesirable if not impossible. Instead of filing a minority report, Hill resigned his commission, refusing to participate in "so purely experimental" a project. Loomis later recorded his impression that "a high judicial source" had counseled Hill to keep his name unassociated with whatever reforms came out of the commission.[56]

Hill's resignation pressured Loomis and Graham to defend the legitimacy of their activities. In their report, the two remaining commissioners expressed their regret that they could not come to an agreement with Hill, but they remained adamant that if their proposed procedural system "should incur the reproach of being radical, it should possess the redeeming merit of being neither superficial nor inadequate." In making their defense, Loomis and Graham turned Hill's accusation into a compliment. Of course their system was "experimental"—all sciences were, and once again, craft rhetoric pervaded the arguments of law reformers. Surely, argued the report, legal practice could not be "the only exception to the progressive power of the human mind in the improvement of every art and science upon which its energies are employed."[57]

Although science talk as the basis of reform was common, what ultimately proved persuasive was the mixture of science with craft in a theory that made legal practice and procedure uniquely amenable to political reform. Conceiving of "procedure" as a distinct field, the commissioners reasoned that it possessed an essential difference from the rest of a common law system composed of substantive rules and principles. "The system of procedure by which law is administered, differs from the law itself in this," the commissioners explained: "the latter is a body of elementary rules founded in the immutable principles of justice, drawing their origin from the obligations which divine wisdom has imposed . . . ; while the former consists, in its very nature, but of a body of prescribed rules, having no source but the will of those by whom they are laid down." Substantive law was universal, natural, grounded in divine justice, and therefore politically immutable. But God apparently cared nothing for the "mere prescribed and arbitrary regulation" of the courts which adjudicated the substantive law, the "the mere machinery by which law is to be administered."[58] In this theory, substantive law functioned as the natural materials upon which artisans labored. Carpenters and smiths could not change the fundamental nature of wood or metal, nor could mere legislation redefine the rights of property or contract.

---

[55] "Speech of Mr. Blodgett," *Albany Evening Journal*, Apr. 3, 1847; Arphaxad Loomis, *Historic Sketch of the New York System of Law Reform in Practice and Pleadings* (1879), 15–16. Loomis's reprinted diary shows that by August he had prepared a working bill with eighty sections, while Graham had prepared an additional thirty articles.

[56] See "Report of the Commissioners on Practice and Pleadings," in *Documents of the Assembly of the State of New York*, 70th Sess., No. 202 (1847), 7:3. N. Hill, "Letter to Albert Lester, President of the Senate, Sep. 20, 1847," in *Senate Journal* (New York, 1847), 679. Loomis, *Historic Sketch*, 15.

[57] "Report of the Commissioners," 4–5.

[58] *Ibid.*, 4.

Machinery, however, could be more or less improved to skillfully manipulate natural materials, even as nature itself remained unchanged.

The commissioners' report marked a striking departure in common law thought. The division of law into substance and procedure was not wholly new, but it was largely foreign to common law jurisprudence. Civilian systems made such a distinction, and the French produced a *code de procédure civile* two years after their civil code. The problem was that the common law writ system made no such distinction, and it was rarely clear where the "procedural" aspects of a writ ended and a substantive law of rights began. William Blackstone ran headlong into the difficulty in his attempt to redescribe common law practice using the structure of civil law systems. Since Roman times the civil law had been divided into persons, things, and actions. Blackstone had persons and things, but in place of actions (or procedures) his third book was titled "wrongs" and included what would today be known as the substantive law of contract, torts, and personal property. The "excellence of our English laws," he explained, was that they "adapt their redress exactly to the circumstances of the injury, and do not furnish one and the same action for different wrongs, which are impossible to be brought within one and the same description."[59] By abolishing the forms of action, fusing law and equity, and crafting a code of "procedure," New York law reformers aimed to fundamentally change the definition of law and how it operated in American society. From statutes and precedents the commissioners expected a substantive law of rights and rules would emerge, while a neutral, transubstantive procedure would vindicate those rights with remedies drawn from former common law and equity practice.[60]

The commissioners' "mere machinery" report satisfied the legislature and received acclaim from a Whig convention in Monroe County—home to the anti-lawyer supporters of Enoch Strong.[61] When a senator requested Loomis's advice on Hill's replacement, Loomis recommended Field, his fellow Barnburner Democrat. Field's nomination thus did nothing to disturb the party balance of the commission, and Field moreover solved the Whigs' dilemma that had arisen over Peters's nomination. Field was well regarded as an expert trial attorney and "one of the best lawyers in the State," according to one Whig senator. Field was also popular among the reformist anti-lawyers, who had already signaled their willingness to consider Field if they could not seat a layman on the commission. Field's nomination received unanimous assent in both houses of the legislature.[62]

---

[59] 3 *Blackstone's Commentaries* 266; see Michael Lobban, *The Common Law and English Jurisprudence: 1760–1850* (Clarendon Press, 1991), 31–46.

[60] On other early American efforts to distinguish procedure from substantive categories, see William E. Nelson, *Americanization of the Common Law: The Impact of Legal Change on Massachusetts Society, 1760–1830* (University of Georgia Press, 1994 [1975]), 69–88; John H. Langbein et al., *History of the Common Law: The Development of Anglo-American Legal Institutions* (Aspen, 2009), 148, 248–56; Daniel J. Hulsebosch, "Writs to Rights: 'Navigability' and the Transformation of the Common Law in the Nineteenth Century," 23 *Cardozo Law Review* 1049 (2002).

[61] "The Right Spirit," *Albany Evening Journal*, Oct. 6, 1847.

[62] Remarks of Senator Folsom, "Legislative Acts and Proceedings," *Albany Evening Journal*, Feb. 12, 1847; *Assembly Journal* (New York, 1847), 1551–52; *Senate Journal* (New York, 1847), 713–14.

V

When Field met with the commissioners early in 1848, he came prepared with a draft code that the three lawyers then read through, amending as they went. Even in his later efforts to downplay Field's role, Loomis had to admit that "more of Mr. Field's manuscripts than those of either of the other Commissioners were used as the basis of the action of the board from day to day." Field would propose a chapter, and each commissioner would then recommend amendments and vote on each section, the votes recorded informally in Loomis's diary. By March, the commission had a draft of 391 sections ready for the legislature. The code did not cover the entirety of civil proceedings, and the commissioners emphasized that they were making "but a report in part." It nevertheless included the major reforms dictating the fusion of legal and equitable procedures, simplified common law pleading, and speedier creditor remedies. Finding themselves near the end of the session with a statute the constitution arguably required them to adopt, legislators enacted the code without significant amendment in less than two weeks, the senate voting 23–3, the assembly 74–9. Although some objected to "this hurried mode of disposing of this important subject," most concluded that taking the time fully to read and amend the code might prevent its passage and thus violate the constitution.[63]

The terse, systematically organized sections of the code reworked nearly every touchstone of New York practice. The code "abolished" common law pleading and required all pleas to be factually accurate, verified by oath, and expressed "in such a manner as to enable a person of common understanding to know what is intended." It made jury trials available in all cases, subject to the choice of the litigants. And it required all testimony to be taken orally in court, even, in most cases, the testimony of the parties themselves. With regard to fees, the code flatly declared that "all existing rules . . . restricting or controlling the right of a party to agree with an attorney, solicitor, or counsel, for his compensation, are repealed," ushering the legal profession into the world of free labor.[64]

The commissioners made especially sure to demonstrate how these reforms served commercial credit. Fusion eliminated the possibility of double-filing a suit. "Every bill that is filed in aid or defense of a suit at law, and every creditor's bill is a witness against our legal establishment," a note explained. Instead of summoning debtors to respond with fictitious pleadings in court, the code permitted creditors to file process with court clerks. Debtors had to have a factually based defense verified on oath, or clerks would automatically issue default judgments. The code thus made New York's court terms irrelevant. Under prior practice, a debtor did not have to answer a complaint until the court was in session, and fictitious defenses were allowed to ensure a plaintiff carried his burden of proof. If time was insufficient, the trial might be held over to a subsequent session, and then the process began again in chancery with a creditor's

---

[63] Loomis, *Historic Sketch of the New York System of Law Reform in Practice and Pleadings*, 17–22; *First Report of the Commission on Practice and Pleadings* (New York, 1848), iv; *Senate Journal* (New York, 1848), 457; *Assembly Journal* (New York, 1848), 1019. See the remarks of Assemblymen Walsh, Myers, and Coe, "Legislative Acts and Proceedings," *Albany Evening Journal*, Mar. 31, 1848.

[64] 1848 N.Y. Laws 521, 544. Each of these reforms is taken up in a chapter in Part II.

bill to actually collect judgment.[65] Where collections under prior practice could take from six months to two years—sufficient time for a bumper harvest to allow renegotiation of a debt—the code aimed to allow collection in twenty days, exchanging the rhythms of agriculture for those of merchant finance. As one country lawyer noted, "the cities, and particularly that of New-York, appear to suffer much less from the incongruities of the code, than the country." The commissioners, however, assured their readers that the code "cannot injure the substantial rights of any party. No rule of law, by which rights and wrongs are measured, will be touched."[66]

When the code took effect in the summer of 1848, political opinion sharply divided. Some thought the commissioners' "industry and zeal worthy of the highest commendation"; others reported the code a "great dissatisfaction to the legal profession and to the public generally." The law on the books certainly had an effect on the law in action. New law blanks and form books shrank simple pleadings for the recovery of a debt from fourteen pages to a couple of paragraphs or even a few lines. Several judges reported similar savings to cost and delay in equity cases. One judge wrote to Field, "Under the old mode, several days would have been spent in the Examiner's office, taking testimony in writing, at an expense equal to half the costs of the suit; and the hearing would have occupied quite as long as the trial did before me, which was less than a day."[67]

Nevertheless, the political coalition that had supported the commission began to express misgivings. While the constitution had at first appeared to be the work of a radical Barnburner plurality, the legislative sessions of 1847 and 1848 revealed how fully Whigs were in control, cooperating with Barnburners and advancing the policies of anti-lawyers. At the convention, Whigs had followed a principle of independent institutions in government—the judiciary would be independent of the other branches for its appointments, the bar would be independent of the judiciary for its admissions, and law reform would be carried out by an independent commission. But outside the convention, the elective judiciary, a more open bar, and law reform by legislative commission provoked the complaint that Whigs had debased all legal institutions and subjected them to partisan politics. "I was surprised," wrote a stunned New York City lawyer named Joshua Van Cott, "I blushed for Whiggism;

---

[65] *First Report* (New York, 1848), 146. On the use of fictitious defenses to maintain the burden of proof, see the discussion of Stephen's *Treatise* in chapter 1.

[66] *Albany Evening Journal*, Mar. 27, 1849; *First Report* (New York, 1848), 146. No single section of the code announced its preference for creditors' rights; rather, the acceleration of creditors' remedies resulted from the combined effect of several sections. In the original code, § 107 required a defendant to answer the complaint within twenty days, regardless of whether the court was in session (see § 622 in the final draft); § 202 provided for default judgment as a matter of course, issued by a clerk without a judicial order if no answer was received within the twenty days (final draft § 755); the requirement that answers state true facts verified by a defendant's oath were intended to prevent sham pleadings from requiring the delay of trial for uncontestable obligation (§§ 128–133 in the 1848 Code, §§ 645–52 in the 1850 draft; see also chapter 7 on the verification requirement); finally, the code abolished a traditional thirty-day waiting period between issue of judgment and commencement of execution (see *First Report* (New York, 1848), 197).

[67] "The Code of Procedure," *Albany Evening Journal*, Jan. 8, 1850; "The New Code of Practice," *New York Weekly Herald*, Feb. 3, 1849. Compare, for instance, the form pleading in Alexander M. Burrill, *Treatise on the Practice of the Supreme Court of the State of New York* (J. S. Voorhies, 1846), 2:268–72, with Henry Whittaker, *Practice and Pleading Under the Code, Original and Amended, with Appendix of Forms* (E. O. Jenkins, 2d ed., 1854), 772; Letter of Lewis Sandford to David Dudley Field, in David Dudley Field, *The Completion of the Code* (1850), 6–7.

I blushed for the legal profession; that no voice of Whig or of Lawyer was raised in denunciation of this new and foul political heresy." All the pretentious offense at the political patronage of "Hunker" Democrats was hypocritical, Van Cott argued, for the only thing that really irked Whigs and Barnburners about patronage was that they did not control it. Handing legal institutions over to partisan politics would now grant these "the NEW SHUFFLEITES . . . a new deal of the cards in the game of politics."[68]

Others wrote that opening the judiciary to nonprofessionals and setting the standard of pleading "such . . . as to enable a person of common understanding to know what is intended" would destroy the craft of the law. "With such a bench as we're likely soon to have," wryly commented the lawyer George Templeton Strong in his diary, "this reduction of legal practice to a Hottentot standard of simplicity and dispatch is indispensable." The transcendentalist-turned-conservative intellectual Orestes Brownson pursued a similar line: "The radical movement of the country exerts all its force to destroy the independence of the courts, and to make them, like every thing else, mere agencies for executing whatever may be the popular will, caprice, or prejudice for the moment." Resorting to an artisan analogy, Brownson sarcastically goaded Whigs to take "law reform" further: "Every man should be free to make hats or coats without ever having served an apprenticeship, or learned the mysteries of the craft; and if he cannot do it, then you have no business to have hats or coats."[69]

In his last novel, *The Ways of the Hour*, the ambivalent Jacksonian James Fenimore Cooper likewise argued that the Whigs had left no check on the degrading influences of popular sovereignty. The people who ruled through the legislature were now to rule through the law courts, too, "making the law as well as interpreting it." Cooper's lawyer-protagonist Thomas Dunscomb was "emphatically" a common law lawyer who bragged he had never married because "I fell in love, early in life, with a certain my lord Coke, and have remained true to my first attachment." Dunscomb lamented of the new constitution that "there is no compromise about it; . . . the conquerors took all"—extremist democrats had destabilized law and order with their "constitutions, codes, and elective judges." Although Cooper griped about the code of procedure in nearly every chapter, his solution accorded remarkably with the views of the code commissioners: "Legislators alone can change this system, and men very different from those who are now sent must go to the legislature, before one is found, honest enough, or bold enough, to get up and tell the people they are not all fit to be trusted." Lawyers needed legislation to improve their practice, but proper legislation required convincing the people's representatives that they were too inexpert to make good law and had better defer to master lawyers. The repair of the common law would have to work through partisan politics while simultaneously transcending it.[70]

Among the other subset of the Whig coalition, anti-lawyers were finding that the code failed their expectations for unmediated access to legal remedies. The code's four

---

[68] Joshua Marsden Van Cott, *Strictures on the Judiciary System of the Proposed Constitution* (1848), 7–19.
[69] *Diary of George Templeton Strong*, ed. Allan Nevins (Macmillan, 1952 [Sept. 28, 1848]), 1:301; Orestes Brownson, "Cooper's Ways of the Hour," 5 *Brownson's Quarterly Review* 273 (1851), 285.
[70] James Fenimore Cooper, *The Ways of the Hour: A Tale* (1850), 84. On Cooper's ambivalent Jacksonianism, see Meyers, *Jacksonian Persuasion*, 57–100; Charles Hansford Adams, *The Guardian of the Law: Authority and Identity in James Fenimore Cooper* (Penn State University Press, 1990), 135–48.

hundred regulations with a promise of more to come was not what many anti-lawyers were expecting from the "simplification" of practice. One anti-lawyer, writing under the name Anti Humbug, observed that the code had "*simplified*' with a vengeance." Anti Humbug objected particularly to the code's declaration that it applied not only to the regular civil courts but to justices of the peace as well. Justices' courts typically resolved small, local disputes through informal processes and more than a little neighborly influence. By bringing them under the rules for formal written pleadings, trials, and motions practice, Anti Humbug found practice in the justices' courts "delayed by a thousand new embarrassments never heard of before."[71] Anti-lawyer editorials and calls for extending codification waned after 1848.

Whigs thus faced increasing criticism that they had out-democratized the Democrats and plunged the nation's leading legal system into amateurism and disorder. Although Whigs increased their majority in the 1849 session, only 16 of 107 Whigs returned from the previous session. Several commentators attributed this turnover to the '48 Whigs' inept handling of codification.[72]

VI

The commissioners continued their work through the end of 1848, drafting amendments and codifying specialized procedures in equity and prerogative writs like habeas corpus. Largely under Graham's direction, they also prepared a code of criminal procedure. A brother who lived with Field during this time recalled that Field would work on the civil procedure code two or three hours in the morning (probably meeting his fellow commissioners during this time), counsel clients, and try cases the rest of the workday and then return to the code from after dinner until midnight or later. The commissioners were compensated $2,000 a year—not a trivial sum for a state that had just adopted a constitution to rein in spending, but not enough to replace the annual compensation of a Manhattan attorney.[73]

By February 1849—when their commission was set to expire—the commissioners submitted their reports of "a code of procedure which should comprehend the whole law of the State concerning remedies."[74] This time they encountered stiff political resistance. When one representative moved to extend the practice commission an additional year so the drafters could consolidate the amendments and new material

---

[71] "To the Commissioners on Practice and Pleadings," *Albany Evening Journal*, Feb. 3, 1849. On the general history of justices of the peace (with an emphasis on criminal jurisdiction), see Langbein et al., *History of the Common Law*, 229–38, 578–587, 628–634; on New York practice in justices' courts, see Sung Yup Kim, *Justices of the Peace, Lawyers, and the People: Local Courts and Contested Professionalization of Law in Late Colonial New York* (Ph.D. dissertation, Stony Brook University, 2016).

[72] See, for instance, Statements of Thomas Clark, "Practice and Pleadings," *Albany Evening Journal*, Feb. 1, 1849. Such turnover was extraordinarily high, even by standards of nineteenth-century legislatures. Cf. Rosemarie Zagarri, "The Family Factor: Congressmen, Turnover, and the Burden of Public Service in the Early American Republic," 33 *Journal of the Early Republic* 283 (2013).

[73] H. M. Field, *Life of David Dudley Field*, 50–52; 1847 N.Y. Laws 67–68.

[74] *Second Report* (New York, 1849); *Third Report* (New York, 1849); *Fourth Report of the Commission on Practice and Pleadings: Code of Criminal Procedure* (New York, 1849). "Practice and Pleadings," *Albany Evening Journal*, Jan. 19, 1849.

into one complete volume, the Whigs on the assembly judiciary committee returned a negative report.

Among the myriad objections to the code, the committee raised two constitutional complaints. First, the committee had become uneasy with the idea of legislating by commission. They regarded it a "solemn mockery" that the previous legislature had passed the code "without even reading it." The committee claimed no ill will toward the commissioners personally, but wondered, "Responsible as the Commissioners undoubtedly are, should we place in them a blind and implicit confidence that shall commit to their discretion the peace and property, the personal liberty and the lives of those who sent *us* here to make laws for them?"[75]

Second, committee members were alarmed at how much material the commissioners included in a code of "procedure," and they directly disputed the commissioners' claims that procedure was merely the law's machinery. They wrote that "provisions for rights and for the mode of pursuing remedies, insensibly run into each other," and distinctions between substance and procedure were difficult to draw in practice. In the common law system, "the 'practice, pleadings, forms and proceedings of courts' are the means and include the remedies for vindicating a right and obtaining redress for a wrong." The attempt to codify the law of remedies in a "procedure" code involved a serious effort to codify the law itself. Even the partial code of procedure was found "full of provisions affecting rights," and this showed that "the parts of a system of law are more dependent on each other, and run into and affect each other, infinitely more than any machine of human contrivance." Procedure, at least in the common law tradition, was no mere machinery—it involved the apparatus of the law itself.[76]

Indeed, although New York's was not the world's first code of civil procedure, its inclusion of the "law of remedies" made its scope unique. Neither Jeremy Bentham's ideal codification system nor the French or Louisiana codes included remedies under the heading of procedure. In those systems, remedies appeared self-evidently substantive. Substantive rights were by definition the rules that demanded particular remedies, while civilian "procedure" dealt only with the technical sequence of pleadings and proofs at trial.[77] In the common law tradition, the legitimacy of court-ordered remedies had developed not out of a law of rights but by the evolution of lawyers' procedures. While the inclusion of remedies in a procedure code thus seemed appropriate within a common law context, it was difficult to see where such a code ought to stop. Field's final draft included seemingly substantive issues of contract formation, such as what meaning a seal had when applied to written promises.[78] The assembly committee complained that the code included constitutional regulations concerning "the organization and jurisdiction of [courts of record]" as well as the law of evidence and witness proofs, which it denied ought to be included in a code of "practice and pleadings" only. They suspected the commissioners' forthcoming code of criminal

---

[75] Report of the Committee on the Judiciary on the Bill to Continue in Office the Commissioners on Practice and Pleadings, in *Documents of the Assembly of the State of New York*, 72d Sess., No. 47 (1849), 3:15.

[76] Report of the Committee on the Judiciary ... on Practice and Pleadings, 2.

[77] See *Code de Procédure Civile: Édition Originale et Seule Officielle* (1806); Jeremy Bentham, *Principles of Judicial Procedure with the Outline of a Procedure Code*, in John Bowring, ed., *The Works of Jeremy Bentham* (William Tait, 1843), 2:1–189.

[78] *Final Report* (New York, 1850), 2:740.

procedure would include all of the criminal law as well, "as they seem to understand practice and pleadings to include all the law upon a given subject."[79]

In defense of the commission, James Elwood, the lone Free Soiler on the committee, filed a minority report, trotting out the anti-lawyer line that his colleagues formed "a committee composed entirely of men belonging to the legal profession" who filed a report "so flattering to themselves and their profession, and so derogatory to the intelligence and judgment of others." Elwood claimed the revision of pleadings and practice was the most "eagerly desired" and "imperiously demanded" reform of the "People" represented in the convention, though he had no answer for why pleading and practice involved all the topics the code actually covered. Instead, Elwood counseled that "the work of preparing a plan to regulate the practice of the courts of record is not the task of an hour or a day," and the legislature would have to trust the "high legal attainments and ability" of the commissioners who had been working for two years on the project.[80] The *Albany Evening Journal*, the state's leading Whig organ, sided with Elwood. It criticized the judiciary committee for believing "LAW AND PRACTICE are necessarily united." Law, it argued, "consists of the great principles and rules which govern the morals, the conduct, and the business of the citizen in their infinite variety" while "*Practice or the course of Procedure* embraces only that system of means or contrivances . . . provided by the Legislature to enforce the law." Procedure, that is, was mere machinery, and, continued the *Journal*, "all new machinery works with some friction and jar, when complete, but who can safely condemn what is but half done?"[81]

The legislature was not so accommodating, however. One Whig noted the reports coming in totaled 406 pages of 1,393 additional regulations, and he wondered if there was "time for deliberation; or is it expected that it will be passed through the House on the run, as it was the last year, without receiving even the poor compliment of a perusal?" In the assembly, another Whig asked lay supporters of the code "if there be one of them who pretends to have read this code, or having read it understand it?" The same challenge resounded in the senate, where one Whig declared that, given the code's length and intricacy, "there were not 20 members who knew what they were doing, any more than they did about the language of the Koran or the hieroglyphics of the Chinese." Both representatives argued it would be irresponsible for a legislature to pass a law they did not understand, another senator concluding, "It was not the province of the servants of the people to try experiments on such important matters as this was. They were bound to know and understand how laws would work before they passed them."[82]

Given that the constitution required practice reform, the 1849 legislature reluctantly agreed to adopt the commissioners' short report of amendments, but the reports that would have completed the codification never came to a vote. Whig

---

[79] Report of the Committee on Judiciary . . . on Practice and Pleadings, 12–14.

[80] Minority Report of the Committee on Judiciary, in *Documents of the Assembly of the State of New York*, 72d. sess., No. 51 (1849), 2:7–10.

[81] "The New Code and the Legislature," *Albany Evening Journal*, Feb. 9, 1849.

[82] "Legislative Acts and Proceedings," *Albany Evening Journal*, Jan. 31, 1849; "Practice and Pleadings," *Albany Evening Journal*, Feb. 3, 1849.

lawyers in the senate succeeded in cajoling their colleagues into extending the commission through the end of the year, allowing Field, Loomis, and Graham one more effort to amend their work and lobby for its passage.[83]

Compiling and editing their reports, the commissioners finished their work on the last day of their commission, December 31, 1849. The Final Report included a code of 1,884 sections in addition to a statute repealing all previous legislation and overriding all prior judicial rulings on practice and procedure. Coupled with lengthy explanatory notes, the final work—now christened a "Code of Civil Procedure"—ran to more than eight hundred pages.[84]

The 1850 session went even worse for the commissioners. The Democrats had finally reconciled; Barnburners and Free Soilers returned to the fold, and the Whigs lost their majority. Whereas the bulk of the 1848 code, the constitutional mandate, and a short legislative session had all worked in favor of the first draft's enactment, this time a select committee on the code complacently reported little progress on reading through the lengthy report by the end of the session, and no vote was ever called. Faced with the choice of blindly enacting the entire code, as the 1848 legislature had done, or doing nothing, legislators decided to do nothing.[85]

Even had the 1850 report made it to a vote, passage was by no means assured. David Graham filed a minority report, dissenting against Field's codification of the law of evidence. Although Graham agreed that the law of evidence more properly belonged to "remedies" than to "rights," he pointed out that the constitution and the legislative mandate gave the commissioners authority only to revise practice, not to codify the unwritten law. Most of the reported code, Graham believed, amended the Revised Statutes to some degree, but going out into the case law to define every rule of evidence "would have required at least the time originally allotted to the commission, and...even then, he would hardly have hoped to complete" it. Moreover, Graham, the Whigs' representative on the commission, did not believe the code went far enough to provide opportunities for arbitration without lawyers and without the formal rules of pleading and practice. Finally, he objected to the code's attempt to change the name of habeas corpus to "writ of deliverance from imprisonment." While he was not "disposed to attach much importance, either to the retention or change of name of a particular proceeding," Graham believed habeas corpus was too well known a remedy, and too important, for any interference. Critics widely repeated the three points of Graham's dissent, which also made it into Cooper's novel when one character joked "it was proposed to call the old process of '*ne exeat*' a writ of 'no go.'"[86]

---

[83] By the end of the session, the code commission had finally offered a report on highway regulation that was immensely popular with the Whigs. In order to extend the code commission, however, Senate Whigs insisted that the Assembly also had to extend the practice commission. See *Senate Journal* (New York, 1849), 583, 592, 622–23, 652; *Assembly Journal* (New York, 1849), 1454–55; *New York Herald*, Apr. 14, 1849.

[84] *Final Report* (New York, 1850); David Dudley Field, "Special Acts Reported in Connection with the Codes of Civil and Criminal Procedure," in *Documents of the Assembly of the State of New York*, 73d Sess., No. 19 (1850), 3:28–29.

[85] "Report of the Committee on the Code," in *Documents of the Assembly of the State of New York*, 73d Sess., No. 149 (1850), 6:6.

[86] "Dissent of Mr. Graham from Certain Portions of the Code of Civil Procedure," in *Documents of the Assembly of the State of New York*, 73d Sess., No. 149 (1850), 2:4–6, 23; *A Brief Review of the Latest Production*, 18–20; Alumnus, *Crudities of the Codifiers*, 6–7. Cooper, *Ways of the Hour*, 183.

With the closing of the 1850 legislative session, the last chance to complete procedural codification slipped away, though the commissioners did not know it at the time. Confident that the legislature would resume its reading in 1851, Graham and Field departed for vacations in Europe, the latter to be feted by members of the English bar interested in fusing law and equity for their own practice. *Hunt's Merchant Magazine* enthusiastically reviewed the draft code, writing that "the commercial bearings of this great reform are important." The final draft attempted to shorten creditor collections from twenty days to five, and *Hunt's* judged the provisions "well adapted to the circumstances of an enterprising and commercial State like New York." The Democratic *Weekly Herald* reported that "a number of whig journals and others are coming out in favor of the new code, and are endeavoring to make a great noise about its defeat," but it assured its readers that "all systems of legal practice are the natural growth of time and experience; and it is supreme folly to demolish them for the sake of a few inconsiderable improvements."[87] Actually, time defeated the code. The short legislative sessions that had aided the first partial draft and its amendments doomed the final, completed draft. The Field Code, a signal victory of nineteenth-century positivism, never became positive law in its home state in finished form.

VII

The result of partisan compromise and limited political horizons, the code ended up representing neither a triumph of Jacksonian democracy nor a straightforward modernization of commercial remedies. Although the code obliged its merchant sponsors with a speedier route to debt collection, the summary proceedings of the final code were never enacted. Rather than certainty and predictability, the commercial classes received a partial code with no clear direction as to which of the Revised Statutes or uncodified practices of equity remained in force, nor what pleading "such . . . as to enable a person of common understanding to know what is intended" actually required.[88]

Perhaps the greatest irony is that the code achieved such limited aims not because legislators accepted the lawyers' argument that procedure was the benign "mere machinery" of the law but because they understood the profound scope of procedure in the common law tradition. Critical historians have contended that across the antebellum era, elite lawyers "transmute[d] programs for substantive social change into professionally controlled proposals for technical changes in procedures or forms." On that basis, Robert W. Gordon dismisses the production of the New York procedure code as "nothing that contemporaries would have called a real codification." Although

---

[87] See Patricia I. McMahon, "Field, Fusion, and the 1850s: How an American Law Reformer Influenced the Judicature Act of 1875," in P. G. Turner, ed., *Equity and Administration* (Cambridge University Press, 2016), 424–62; Michael Lobban, "Preparing for Fusion: Reforming the Nineteenth-Century Court of Chancery," 22 *Law & Hist. Rev.* pts. I & II, 389, 565 (2004), 584; H. M. Field, *Life of David Dudley Field*, 53–55. "The Codes of Procedure, Civil and Criminal, in the State of New York," 23 *Hunt's Merchants' Magazine & Commercial Review* 67 (1850), 67–79; "The New Code of Legal Practice," *Weekly Herald* (New York, N.Y.), Apr. 14, 1849.

[88] 1848 N.Y. Laws 521.

reformers emerged within the legal profession, "conservative lawyers easily defeat[ed] anything genuinely innovative in the ideas of their moderately reformist brethren and agree[d] to only unexceptionable technical reform."[89]

Yet the reformers on whom Gordon concentrates were in fact adamant about procedural reform, while staid lawyers and their political allies felt they had suffered a total defeat with the promulgation of Field's code. Whether or not self-proclaimed anti-lawyers expected or desired to change the substantive law of property and obligation, they absolutely demanded the reform of property and contract remedies. And as the common law was hardly anything more than a remedial system, good common law lawyers understood what was at stake in the proposal. Respectable lawyers like Nicolas Hill distanced themselves from "radical" and "experimental" legislation, and when the assembly judiciary committee reviewed the code of procedure, it recognized that procedural reform could extend to any corner of the common law. If the Field Code does not ultimately appear to the critics to be "real codification," it should not be assumed the "anti-legalist" calls for substantive reform were necessarily defeated.[90]

Indeed, the politics of the Field Code helped to create the very concept of "civil procedure" in American law and imbue it with such remarkably "substantive" features. As Amalia Kessler notes, *Bouvier's Law Dictionary* did not even define "civil procedure" until its 1897 edition, describing the term as "rather a modern one." Before 1848, the term was largely restricted to French usage, and American remedial law had carried the typical designation—as it did in both Graham's treatise and his professorial title— of "practice and pleadings," the name likewise given to the reform commission. When the commission designated its final draft a "Code of Civil Procedure," it marked the first American attempt to give content to this category.[91]

Ironically, the critics' conception of procedure as a superficial, technical field unworthy of "real" reform or codification was an idea invented by the law reformers themselves in order to give their proposals a chance for political success. As the "mere machinery" of the law, procedure could become a domain where legislative reform could not be politically resisted merely because it was innovative. Critical accounts

[89] Gordon, "American Codification Movement," 434–39. See also Lawrence M. Friedman, "Law Reform in Historical Perspective," 13 *St. Louis University Law Journal* 351 (1969).

[90] Gordon identifies an Anglo-American "tradition of anti-legalism and law reform" running from at least the seventeenth century through the Jacksonian era. Yet Gordon's own account of this tradition describes not so much anti-*legalism* as what New Yorkers in the 1840s were calling anti-*lawyerism*. Gordon includes in this tradition demands for "publication of legal rules in a form accessible to the ordinary person's understanding, abolition of lawyers, curtailment of judicial discretion, . . . and reform of the processes for handling defaulting debtors." Gordon then argues that lawyers used "technical changes in procedures or forms" to stifle or subvert these "interests for real social change." It is difficult to imagine, however, how a common law lawyer or even a lay critic in the 1840s would distinguish between these "real" reforms and matters of "procedure and form" (indeed, "form" and "process" are two of the items on Gordon's list of radical reforms). The list of reforms Gordon itemizes might be summarized together as the lawyer's craft, and anti-lawyers sought to admit anyone to the craft, just as—in Enoch Strong's analogy at the state convention— anyone in the Early Republic could become a minister of religion. Strong summed up in one person the factions that Gordon's political vision tends to keep apart: anti-lawyering farmers and pro-creditor lawmakers, incidentally the essence of the Whig coalition at this time. Gordon, "American Codification Movement," 437–38.

[91] Amalia Kessler, "Deciding Against Conciliation: The Nineteenth-Century Rejection of a European Transplant and the Rise of a Distinctively American Ideal of Adversarial Adjudication," 10 *Theoretical Inquiries in Law* 423 (2009), 481–82; *Bouvier's Law Dictionary* (Boston Book Co., 1897), 2:764.

are correct to note that procedure became a crucial tool for keeping lawyers in control of law reform, but here again the machinery metaphor did much of the work. Where Loomis and Graham, for their purposes, used it to emphasize the triviality of procedure, Field had deployed it to note its complexity and "what delicate adjustment it requires" in the hands of a skilled mechanic. As the machinery of the law, procedure was therefore complicated enough to require expert lawyerly mechanics but superfluous enough to be recrafted by a legislature abstracted out from a context of partisan political battles.[92]

This argument was not limited to lawyers, as most of the Whigs who had opposed Peters's nomination had been fellow farmers and mechanics convinced that law reform required legal expertise beyond the skill of legislators. But as the threatening anti-lawyers made clear, the legal mechanics were expected to keep faith by producing the reforms they were commissioned for: the abolition of chancery, the simplification of form and process, the fair collection of debts, and the restructuring of the lawyers' guild and its fee system. The "mere machinery" claim was acceded to by many nonlawyers who were unwilling to trust the fundamental restructuring of civil justice to neophytes working at a rush. But its success was limited in New York, where legislators ultimately refused to hand over their lawmaking authority to expert lawyers. With its political capital exhausted at home, the code, like many New Yorkers at the close of the 1840s, would have to seek its fortunes in the West.

[92] [David Dudley Field], *A Letter to Gulian C. Verplanck, on the Reform of the Judicial System of this State* (1840), 3–4; "Report of the Commissioners," 4.

4

An Empire in Itself

The Migration of Field's Code

I

At the opening of the first Nevada legislature in 1861, Territorial Governor James W. Nye, a former New York lawyer, instructed the assembly that they would have to forsake the Mormon statutes of Utah Territory, out of which Nevada was carved. Those laws were ill-adapted to "the mining interests" of the new territory, but "happily for us, a neighboring State whose interests are similar to ours, has established a code of laws" that could attract "capital from abroad."[1] That neighbor was California, and Nye urged that California's procedure code be adopted as far as it could "be made applicable." Territorial Senator William Morris Stewart, the famed mining lawyer who would become a leading US Senator of Reconstruction, followed the instructions perhaps too well. As Figure 4.1 shows, the senator literally cut and pasted the latest *Wood's Digest* of the California Practice Act into a session bill, crossing out "state" and "California" and substituting "territory" and "Nevada" where necessary. Amidst all the work of organizing the territory, the bill did not gain passage until late in the hurried session when it was sent to Nye for his signature.

Nye wrote back in disgust. The bill—715 sections—had reached him along with other legislation late the night before the legislature was to adjourn. Even in the few hours he had to read it, Nye counted "so many errors in the enrolling of it, numbering probably more than three hundred." Some errors were severe. Nevada's Organic Act specified the jurisdiction of the district courts and justices of the peace, but the code overwrote these by copying California's arrangements. Error-riddled and unconstitutional as the bill was, Nye persisted in the conviction that a civil practice code—something that had not existed when Nye began his legal career—was a "universal necessity and public need."[2] Nye signed the code into law.

At least Nevada had made an effort at adaptation. When Nebraska Territory was organized in 1855, its legislature declared the code of Iowa to be in force, leaving its officers to figure out for themselves when "state of Iowa" meant "territory of Nebraska."[3] "The scissors and paste-pot we had heretofore confidently believed were implements peculiar to the newspaper sanctum," wrote a Colorado journalist, mocking codification efforts in his state.[4] Oregon legislators, however, featured their paste-pot in an

---

[1] Message of the Governor, in *Journal of the Council for the Territory of Nevada* (1862), 21.
[2] *Ibid.*, 261.
[3] 1855 Neb. Laws 41.
[4] *Rocky Mountain News* (Denver, Colo.), Jan. 20, 1877.

Law's Machinery. Kellen R. Funk, Oxford University Press. © Kellen R. Funk 2025. DOI: 10.1093/9780197543962.003.0005

CRIMINAL PRACTICE.   271

Sec. 9. A criminal action shall be prosecuted in the name of the people of the *21.3*
state of California, as a party, against the party charged with the offense.

Sec. 10. The party prosecuted in a criminal action is designated in this act as the defendant.

ART. 1386, Sec. 11. In a criminal action the defendant is entitled: 1. To a speedy and public trial. 2. To be allowed counsel as in civil actions, or he may appear and defend in person or with counsel; and 3. To produce witnesses on his behalf, and to be confronted with the witnesses against him in the presence of

Sec 11. p. 271 Strike out "by question & answer" & indorse "in writing by the witness."

timony of a witness on the part of the people, who is unable to give security for his appearance, has been taken conditionally in the like manner in the presence of the defendant, who has, either in person or by counsel, cross-examined or had an opportunity to cross-examine the witness, the deposition of such witness may be read upon its being satisfactorily shown to the court that he is dead or insane, or cannot, with due diligence, be found within the state.

ART. 1387, Sec. 12. No person shall be subject to a second prosecution for a public offense, for which he has once been prosecuted and duly convicted or acquitted.

ART. 1388, Sec. 13. No person shall be compelled, in a criminal action, to be a witness against himself, nor shall a person charged with a public offense be subjected, before conviction, to any more restraint than is necessary for his ...
to answer the charge.

Sec. 14. p. 271. Insert after "public offense" - "tried by indictment"

... a demurrer to the indictment in the case,
... in section two hundred and sixty-six [299]

II.—PREVENTION OF PUBLIC OFFENSES.

ART. 1390, Sec. 15. Lawful resistance to the commission of a public offense may be made: 1. By the party about to be injured. 2. By other parties.

Sec. 16. Resistance sufficient to prevent the offense may be made by the party about to be injured: 1. To prevent an offense against his person, or his family, or some member thereof. 2. To prevent an illegal attempt, by force, to take or injure property in his lawful possession.

Sec. 17. Any other person, in aid or defense of the person about to be injured, may make resistance sufficient to prevent the offense.

ART. 1391, Sec. 18. Public offenses may be prevented by the intervention of he officers of justice: 1. By requiring surety to keep the peace. 2. By forming a police in cities and towns, and by requiring their attendance in exposed places. . By suppressing riots.

Sec. 19. Whenever the officers of justice are authorized to act in the prevention of public offenses, other persons, who by their command act in their aid, are justified in so doing.

ART. 1392, Sec. 20. A complaint may be laid before any of the magistrates mentioned in section one hundred and four, [103] that a person has threatened to commit an offense against the person or property of another.

Sec. 21. When the complaint is laid before the magistrate, he shall examine, on oath, the complainant and any witnesses he may produce, and shall take their depositions in writing, and cause them to be subscribed by the parties making them.

Sec. 22. If it appears, from the depositions, that there is just reason to fear the commission of the offense threatened by the person so complained of, the magis-

Figure 4.1 Detail of a session bill for Nevada's procedure code (covering both civil and criminal process) shows that pages from *Wood's Digest of California Law* (1857) were borrowed and edited to produce the law of the new territory. Lawmakers had to use two copies of the book to paste the front and back of each sheet into the bill.

Council Bill 21, First Territorial Legislative Session (1861). Nevada State Library, Archives and Public Records.

advertisement noting that their procedural code was "taken, word for word, from the New York Code."[5]

In a way, the cut-and-paste code matched well with the cut-and-paste governments adopting it. The Field Code proved especially popular with the nascent territorial governments of the American Far West and the Reconstruction governments of the Deep South.[6] Nevada's assembly met in borrowed chambers and printed its business on borrowed presses.[7] Why not borrow the laws and even the typesetting from a nearby neighbor? Moreover, the exigencies facing the Union meant that Nevada's legislators in 1861—like the Carolinas' in 1868—were in a rush to form a recognizably republican government, one with the trappings of civil justice and procedure that conformed to the model of surrounding states. For aspiring governments in a hurry, a code offered a ready-made civil justice system in a box—or, as one leading historian has put it, "off the rack."[8]

This assumed convenience of a code, however, obscures the significant real costs of borrowing legislation in the mid-nineteenth-century United States. Jurists may blithely speak of an innovative statute being "soon copied in other jurisdictions," but that phrase papers over a world of labor, patronage, and politics. In every jurisdiction, the code had to be sent out by elite lawyers back in New York, physically imported and reproduced on frontiers where quality publishing could be quite costly, and then enacted by a legislature riven by the partisan battles of the day that ranged from secession to suffrage to silver. And while the American codification debates have long been understood as a struggle over the separation of judges from legislators, the Field Code's contested migration shows that American-style codification provoked far more unease over the problem of lawmaking by unelected commissioners. Pressed by political demands within the short time horizons of legislative sessions, codifiers faced the dilemma of squaring lawmaking commissions and borrowed legislation with the ideals of popular sovereignty and democratic representation.

At one time, most US jurisdictions—including almost all of the eventual Field Code states—had solved this dilemma by brief, often single-paragraph laws "receiving" the

---

[5] 1854 Or. Laws iii.

[6] Depending on how one counts territories that later divided, around thirty jurisdictions adopted some version of the code. See Robert Wyness Millar, *Civil Procedure of the Trial Court in Historical Perspective* (New York University Press, 1952), 54–55. The usual litany is Missouri (1849), California (1850), Iowa (1851), Kentucky (1851), Minnesota (1851), Indiana (1852), Ohio (1853), Oregon (1854), Washington (1854), Nebraska (1855), Wisconsin (1856), Kansas (1859), Nevada (1861), Dakota Territory (1862), Arizona (1864), Idaho (1864), Montana (1865), Arkansas (1868), North Carolina (1868), Wyoming (1869), Florida (1870), South Carolina (1870), Utah (1870), Colorado (1877), Oklahoma (1890), New Mexico (1897), and Alaska (1900). Tennessee, in 1858, adopted a Code that, while much of it was original, borrowed nearly three hundred sections from other states, combining Field Code provisions from Iowa and Nebraska with the Civil Code of Alabama. In 1850, Mississippi incorporated about fifty sections of the code's provisions on pleading into its broader civil code. In 1855, Congress reviewed but did not enact a Code for the District of Columbia that borrowed heavily from the Field Code. Two states that prepared a code without ultimately adopting them were Utah in 1859 (the state would borrow Nevada's Field Code in 1870) and Texas in 1855. See Utah Territory Legislative Assembly Papers, 1851–1872, MS 2919, Box 3, Folder 17, LDS Church History Library; The Code of Civil Procedure of the State of Texas, Rare Books Collection, Tarlton Law Library, University of Texas at Austin.

[7] See Effie Mona Mack, *Nevada: A History of the State from the Earliest Times Through the Civil War* (Clark, 1936), 229–30.

[8] Lawrence M. Friedman, *A History of American Law* (Simon & Schuster, 2d ed., 1985), 394.

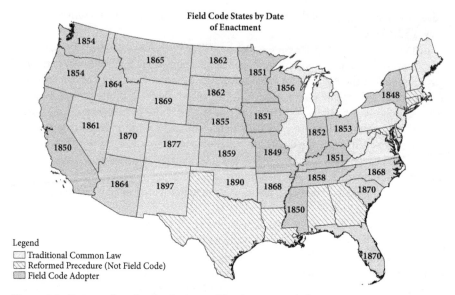

Figure 4.2 States and territories designated by the year each first adopted a version of Field's code.

Adapted from Charles McGuffey Hepburn, *The Historical Development of Code Pleading in America and England* (W. H. Anderson, 1897).

common law into force over a new territory.[9] Enacted directly by a legislature, such receptions avoided the problem of delegating lawmaking and left significant room for judges to adapt common law principles to future cases as they arose. Thus, borrowing law had always been a fundamental part of Anglo-American migration. But while receiving an amorphous and adaptable common law might accord with Jeffersonian visions of an expanding "empire of liberty," the migration of "foreign" codes created by a distant jurist for a distant people appeared to many critics to bring the empire without the liberty.[10]

Nevertheless, the Field Code won its way across the nation, as Figure 4.2 illustrates. Governor Nye's preferences for the laws of California over those of Mormon Utah give one clue to how codifiers overcame the charge of imperialism: they embraced it. The imagined expectations of distant capitalists fueled the codifiers' arguments that New York's remedial code was necessary to link newly formed governments to networks of wealth and credit flowing from the metropole. In time, even Mormon Utah adopted Nevada's new code, understanding that it originally derived from "the State

[9] See Ford W. Hall, "The Common Law: An Account of Its Reception in the United States," 4 *Vanderbilt Law Review* 791 (1951); Morris L. Cohen, "The Common Law in the American Legal System: The Challenge of Conceptual Research," 81 *Law Library Journal* 13 (1989). For a stark example of multiple such receptions (of Iowa law) in the Oregon Territory, see Sidney Teiser, "The Second Chief Justice of Oregon Territory: Thomas Nelson," 48 *Oregon Historical Quarterly* 214 (1947), 217.

[10] On the Jeffersonian idea of America as an empire of liberty, see Drew McCoy, *The Elusive Republic: Political Economy in Jeffersonian America* (University of North Carolina Press, 1980), 185–208; Robert W. Tucker and David C. Hendrickson, *Empire of Liberty: The Statecraft of Thomas Jefferson* (Oxford University Press, 1990).

of New York—a State which is an empire in itself and whose commercial transactions are far greater than those of any other State in the Union." Utah could be "rewarded by equal advantages" by copying its code.[11] On these imagined demands and rewards of capital from the Empire State, codifiers made an idiosyncratic New York law the uniform practice of a nation.

II

By November 1851, the *Sacramento Daily Union* could report that life was settling down in the golden hills of northern California. The booming gold rush population and national compromises with slavery had rushed California from a distant Mexican province to American statehood in less than two years. The editor took heart that civilization had taken root, as evidenced by professional specialization. Early migrants of all vocations washed their own clothes, crafted their own tools, and engaged in the mining frenzy, at least on the side. But now ministers were back to ministering, journalists were printing, and "the accomplished lawyer, now delver and digger in the mines, now trading, now cooking, is again assuming his legitimate place at the bar, re-perusing the huge works of the old guides to the principles and practice of law."[12] The editor's mistake was that, in 1851, those huge works of practice were not at all old.

By late 1851, California had already enacted the Field Code twice. Both adaptations came from the sort of multivocational lawyers the *Daily Union* described, men who came at the height of the gold rush to practice law while mining for gold, speculating for land, and running for office. Both codifiers were young New York lawyers, trained in Wall Street law firms, but, having departed New York in 1848, neither had much experience with practice under the code. Both were elected to the state senate and appointed to the judiciary committee, from whence they guided their versions of the code through the legislature without resorting to a commission as New York had. The first to arrive in 1849 was Elisha O. Crosby; the second, in late 1850, was Stephen J. Field, younger brother of David Dudley.[13]

Proud to think of himself as a Jeffersonian agrarian, Crosby would gain notoriety as a staunch defender of Mexican land claims. In his later career, he argued over a hundred cases for Mexican-descended land claimants at the congressionally established Land Commission and on appeal in the US federal courts. Crosby often criticized the slow and expensive legal proceedings required to confirm land titles, proceedings that frequently enabled well-funded Anglo land speculators to win claims despite the merits of a case. In the first session of the state legislature, however, Crosby counted it his finest achievement to defend traditional common law practice against

---

[11] *Journal of the Assembly of the Territory of Utah* (1870), 15.

[12] *Sacramento Daily Union*, Nov. 20, 1851. On the mixed labor regime in San Francisco, especially its gendered dimensions with an absence of white women, see Susan Lee Johnson, *Roaring Camp: The Social World of the California Gold Rush* (Norton, 2000).

[13] See Elisha Oscar Crosby, *Reminiscences of California and Guatemala from 1849 to 1864*, ed. Charles Albro Barker (Huntington Library, 1945); Stephen J. Field, *Personal Reminiscences of Early Days in California* (Washington, D.C., 1893).

the request of California's Hispanic bar—and the directive of the state's governor—to adopt European-style civilian procedure codes as the law of the state.[14]

In his first address to the legislature, Governor Peter Burnett urged the adoption of Louisiana's code of practice, which remained substantially as Edward Livingston had drafted it twenty years earlier. Treading carefully, the governor argued that civil law was "a system of the most refined, enlarged, and enlightened principles of equity and justice" so long as it "assumes to regulate" only the commercial "intercourse of men with each other" and "aside from its mere political maxims." Burnett reasoned that English law should otherwise provide the basis for criminal and constitutional law, reinforcing a distinction between commercial and constitutional law that would become common in future debates. Burnett added that "so great a portion of the cases that will arise in our courts"—implicitly, from Mexican grants—"must be decided by the principles of the civil law" that the state's bar might as well accommodate itself to civilian practice, as Louisiana's bar had. As if to reinforce the point, a memorial soon arrived signed by eighteen lawyers from San Francisco, the majority of Spanish or Mexican descent, urging retention of civilian law as the most practical option for the new state.[15]

In a lengthy report that would be celebrated by the state bar for decades to come, Crosby explained why the state could not import Louisiana's code. Countering the argument from expediency, Crosby offered practical reasoning of his own: "More than twenty-nine thirtieths of the emigration to this country is from Common Law States; and an equal proportion of the business of our people is now and will continue to be, carried on by Common Law men." Moreover, most emigrating lawyers read only English; "substitute the Civil for the Common Law, and it will be with great delay and expense, in limited supplies, and in strange tongues, that books can be procured which will be found absolutely necessary for the lawyer and the judge in the intelligent administration of the system." (Never mind that the daily papers advertised Louisiana's English procedure code and commentaries in the local bookshops.)[16]

The heart of Crosby's argument was civilizational. The works of Mansfield and Marshall, Kent and Story forged a "chain of memory which, stretching across the Sierra Nevada, binds [the lawyer] to the land and institutions of his fathers." The common law sprang from "the reformed religion and enlightened philosophy and literature of England." Civil law was "based upon the crude laws of a rough, fierce people, whose passion was war" but who had nevertheless descended into "luxurious and effeminate refinement." Some might argue the common law favored "the landed interest," but Crosby pointed out that it was in England and America where the landless laborer, merchant, and artisan contracted for the highest wages. Thus it was in the common law world where one found "the activity, the throng, the tumult of business life" and "the strength in freshness of manhood." Civilian countries

---

[14] Crosby, *Reminiscences of California*, 67–71, 58.

[15] *Journal of the Senate of the State of California* (1850), 33–35. Oscar Tully Shuck, "Adoption of the Common Law," in *History of the Bench and Bar of California* (Commercial Printing House, 1901), 47–53.

[16] Report of Mr. Crosby on Civil and Common Law, *Senate Journal* (California, 1850), 459–80, 477; Shuck, *History of the Bench and Bar*, 48–49. For the advertised codes and treatises on Louisiana law, see, for instance, *Daily Alta California* (San Francisco, Cal.), Oct. 1, 1850.

exhibited only "feebleness of intellect, timidity of spirit, and the crouching subservience of slaves."[17]

As stark as Crosby's contrast was, it was not unique. In debates over procedure codes, the comparison of civil law and common law frequently turned on the premise that, as an 1855 Maryland commission put it, "as far as their administrative principles and forms of procedure are concerned," the two systems were "the opposites of each other." Actual policy differences were rarely elaborated, perhaps supporting Governor Burnett's premise that practitioners knew few details about one another's system. Instead, themes of manliness and civilizational destiny abounded. The same Maryland commission argued that adopting civilian law "would rend the spiritual chain which connects us with our forefathers, and would reduce us from a mighty original race . . . to one developing its energies in the obsolete forms of a past civilization, produced by a people inferior to ourselves, and standing behind us in the providential order of history."[18]

According to common law defenders, the history of a civilization's legal institutions affected its present liberty and prosperity. To the Maryland commissioners, the common law supported the rule of law through its institutional organization (a limited executive and an independent judiciary) and by its regard for history (the binding force of precedent among the latter branch). The civil law supported only the rule of will through legislative supremacy and unfettered judicial discretion. But, argued the Maryland commissioners, "the notion that human institutions can be created anew . . . without regard to old organizations, is a doctrine of sheer despotism. The notion is founded upon an entirely false philosophy of history."[19]

Underlying these civilizational claims, especially in the political context of the 1850s, was a lurking fear that legal institutions might reduce even white men to effeminacy and servility. In ranking historical determinants, the Maryland report prioritized legal systems even over race, arguing that a people's civilization "is not determined more by peculiarity of race, than it is by the character of the institutions under which a people are developed." In that case, all Americans of whatever origin were "the Anglo-Saxon race on a grander theatre," a nation that spread Anglo-American common law over more places and peoples than even England had.[20] In this regard, Crosby's report to the California legislature was somewhat unusual in discussing actual policy differences between common law and civilian law. Each example illustrated the difference between manly independence and the subordination deemed appropriate to women, children, and slaves. Civil law did not emancipate minor boys until the age of twenty-five (and it committed the opposite sin by failing to regard a wife's legal identity subsumed by her husband's). Further, the "Common Law allows parties to make their own bargains, and when they are made, holds them to a strict compliance; whilst

---

[17] Report of Mr. Crosby, 465, 469, 471.
[18] *The First Report of the Commissioners to Revise the Rules of Practice and Pleadings* (Maryland, 1855), 7, 76. See also, e.g., William G. Bishop & William H. Attree, eds., *Report of the Debates and Proceedings of the Convention for the Revision of the Constitution of the State of New York* (Evening Atlas, 1846), 572; *Journal of the House of Representatives of the State of Minnesota* (1858), 517, 562; *Rocky Mountain News* (Denver, Colo.), Jan. 24, 1877. On the broader culture of manhood and (especially racial) dominance, see Gail Bederman, *Manliness and Civilization: A Cultural History of Gender and Race in the United States, 1880–1917* (Chicago University Press, 1996).
[19] *First Report* (Maryland 1855), 62–69, 75.
[20] *Ibid.*, 70, 72.

the Civil Law looks upon man as incapable of judging for himself, [and] assumes the guardianship over him." The civil law was overrun with implied warranties; the common law expected contractors to man up and live by the maxim "caveat emptor."[21]

The abhorrence of civil law was not, in many cases, a thin disguise for upholding status quo property rights. Common law property reformers like Crosby were not so worried about redistributing property as they were concerned that they could *become* property, reduced to servile dependency on a guardian state. Codification, rather than a narrow debate over institutional protection of property, squarely raised the broader problem of what Daniel Ernst calls "Tocqueville's nightmare." Alexis de Tocqueville, the French visitor to Jacksonian America, warned that American liberalism might degenerate into a dependency on an administrative "central power" to the point that Americans would lose "little by little the faculty of thinking, feeling, and acting by themselves, and thus . . . gradually falling below the level of humanity." In Tocqueville's stark dichotomy, a legal system could establish either emancipation or empire; there was "no other alternative than democratic liberty, or the tyranny of the Caesars."[22] This was the specter raised by codification. If all law became merely the positivist decree of a legislature, a civilization's history could be effaced in an instant, its development arrested, its people managed by centralized statutes rather than emancipated to flourish according to local customs.

And yet the same Crosby who denounced civilian codes as the harbinger of imperial subservience readily introduced California to New York's untested and nontraditional code. After the legislature accepted his anti-civilian report and drew up an act receiving the common law, Crosby submitted an adapted version of New York's 1849 amended Field Code without comment or report. It passed by a voice vote, presumably on the understanding that this code, unlike Louisiana's, was not antithetical to the common law. Apparently, the threat of imperial subjugation could sometimes be avoided if the code under discussion was a "mere" procedure code. When Crosby wrote back to New York to announce the code's success, he spoke only of the code regulating "practice" and "proceedings," never the law itself.[23]

Elsewhere, codifiers hailed the civilian affinity of Field's code as its leading virtue on the same grounds of civilizational pedigree. A committee of Minnesota legislators in 1858 celebrated the code for being "closely analogous in its pleadings and practice to the celebrated civil code of Justinian, the leading principles of which prevail in all the enlightened commercial countries of Europe, except England." Like California's Governor Burnett, the committee was careful to distinguish Europe's dangerously autocratic political and criminal law from the commercial attainments of its civilization, for which "no wiser or better code ever existed." The civilian-like procedures of chancery courts, admiralty courts, and the courts of Louisiana and Texas proved that civilian commercial remedies could be distinguished from the arbitrary positivism of civilian systems. Hedging its arguments, the Minnesota committee also reaffirmed the

---

[21] Report of Mr. Crosby, 467–68.

[22] Daniel Ernst, *Tocqueville's Nightmare: The Administrative State Emerges in America, 1900–1940* (Oxford University Press, 2014); Alexis de Tocqueville, *Democracy in America*, trans. Harvey C. Mansfield & Delba Winthrop (Chicago University Press, 2000), 301, 665.

[23] 1850 Cal. Laws 219, 428; *Troy Daily Whig*, Oct. 20, 1849.

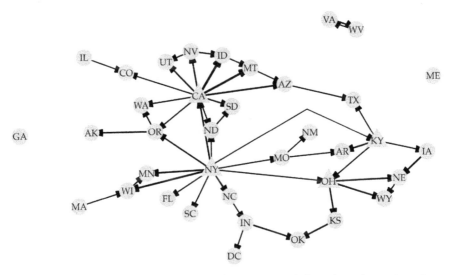

Figure 4.3 States and territories designated by the year each first adopted a version of Field's code.

The influence of one code on another is depicted by an arrow running to a "borrower" state based on the number and extent of textual borrowings from up to two source states. California, Ohio, and Kentucky were significant hubs of regional text families, though all three derived the majority of their texts from New York originally.

See Kellen Funk & Lincoln A. Mullen, "The Spine of American Law," 123 *American Historical Review* (2018), 132–64, for a guide to the creation of this graph and other family trees of the Field Code.

idea that a merely procedural code was neither civilian nor common law since it did not alter real law at all: "By showing our preference for . . . the New York Code, we in no manner show disrespect to the 'Common Law.' The code does not derogate one 'jot or tittle' from the common law."[24]

The code could thus pass as an uncontroversial revision of common law practice or as a total repudiation of that practice in favor of civilian procedure. Until the end of the century, the code would so pass in many jurisdictions, formerly common law, civilian, or the supposed legal wildernesses of the American Far West. Digital text analysis can help us understand how extensively American jurisdictions borrowed the Field Code. Most US procedure codes averaged nearly 750 sections spanning 200 pages. While one historian at the end of the nineteenth century valiantly attempted to compare all US codes by hand, computational analysis can more quickly and precisely offer an overview of the patterns of borrowing (see network graph in Figure 4.3).[25]

---

[24] *House Journal* (Minnesota, 1858), 559, 563. See also R.W. Wells, *Law of the State of Missouri Regulating Pleadings and Practice* (1849), 23; and at the end of the century, *Minutes of the New Mexico Bar Association* (1894), 34. For other civilian-favoring comparisons of civilization, see Bishop & Attree, *Report of the Debates and Proceedings*, 662; *Denver Daily Tribune*, Jan.10, 1877.

[25] For a nineteenth-century comparison of the codes, see Charles McGuffey Hepburn, *The Historical Development of Code Pleading in America and England* (W. H. Anderson & Company, 1897).

New York, as one would expect, sat in the center of the code universe, but not all satellites revolved around it. Rather, there were several regional text families, a couple stemming from midwestern states, and one stemming from California into other states of the Far West.[26]

It may be unsurprising that legislators would borrow from a nearer neighbor, but it is worthwhile to note cases that break from this pattern. Midwestern states drew directly from New York in the early 1850s, when there were few other codes from which to borrow, but that was not the case with the Reconstruction South. There was no southern code family—only direct borrowings from New York. Likewise, although western states drew their texts from California, the similarity between California and New York rendered the states of the Far West and the Coastal South one big text family, as some commentators noticed. One newspaper expected the Idaho legislature would "report substantially the Nevada code, which is the California code, which is the New York code."[27] The Lower Midwest and Upper South adopted some New York reforms while dispensing with others, and their reliance on the New York text was relatively slighter. But all along the American periphery, the law of each state conformed closely to the law of New York.

III

"Why the West?" Lawrence Friedman has asked about the nearly universal migration of the Field Code to the US frontier. Summarizing the literature, Friedman answers, "In none of the Western states did the bar have a strong vested interest in the continuance of old rules, especially rules of pleading. Codes were a handy way to acquire new law, a way of buying clothes off the rack, so to speak."[28] The accounts on which Friedman relies make much of the fact that eleven jurisdictions adopted the code in their first year of organization (whether as a state or territory), while six more adopted it at some point in their territorial days.[29] These numbers obscure the fact that a majority of Field Code adopters had a long history (at least a decade or more) of common law practice before codification, and many of the early codifiers—such as California's Elisha Crosby and Stephen Field—had no experience with code practice before introducing the legislation.[30] Considering nineteenth-century technologies for transmitting texts and nineteenth-century opposition to commissioner lawmaking confirms

---

[26] For a detailed account of the digital methods employed, including the construction of a corpus of American procedural legislation, see Kellen Funk & Lincoln A. Mullen, "The Spine of American Law: Digital Text Analysis and U.S. Legal Practice," 123 *American Historical Review* 132 (2018).

[27] *Boise News*, Feb. 13, 1864.

[28] Friedman, *History of American Law*, 394, 406.

[29] In the first year of territorial organization: Washington (1854), Nebraska (1855), Nevada (1861), Dakota Territory (1862), Arizona (1864), Idaho (1864), Montana (1865), Wyoming (1869), Oklahoma (1890); in the first year of statehood: California (1850), Colorado (1877); and during their territorial days: Missouri (1849), Minnesota (1851), Oregon (1854), Kansas (1859), Utah (1870), New Mexico (1897).

[30] Field Code states with more than a decade of common law experience include Arkansas, Colorado, Florida, Indiana, Iowa, Kentucky, Missouri, New Mexico, New York, North Carolina, Ohio, Oklahoma, South Carolina, Utah, and Wisconsin, as well as partial adopters of the Field reforms in Maryland, Mississippi, and Tennessee.

that codification was anything but an off-the-rack convenience in the West (or the South or Midwest).

Consider first the drain of codification on state treasuries. Most states that employed commissioners compensated them well. An antebellum commissioner in Iowa was paid $3,000 for revising and printing a code, the second-highest state salary next to the governor and significantly more than any public attorney. In the postbellum period, both of the Carolinas spent more than $10,000 a year on commissioner compensation.[31] These could be significant sums, especially for territories that had not yet established stable revenue streams. As one Colorado newspaper complained, procedural code commissions ranked "in the same category with $6,200 per year governors and $3,500 secretaries of state, which in the course of time we may be able to afford, but which at present we can readily exist without."[32]

Commissioner salaries were slight compared to the cost of printing the code. Legislatures commonly required 500 to 1,000 copies of proposed legislation, copies that would be amended in the course of the session and then destroyed.[33] Legislators often convened evening or extra sessions to consider (or at least give the appearance of considering) the bulky bills, and critical journalists also counted these expenses against a code.[34] Statutes that merely received the common law took up barely a page and then obligated private practitioners to see that their libraries were well stocked with books of precedent. As public legislation, however, codes required a secretary of state to provide sufficient copies to practitioners for reference—and those copies had to endure daily use. The Iowa legislature accordingly commanded that its code be "printed on good book paper . . . in one volume of royal octavo size, full bound in sheep."[35] Codes that ran to several hundred pages were thus a major expense and could raise sharp disputes over political patronage. The Iowa commission had to outsource the task to Connecticut printers to fulfill its mandate (not the farthest example of outsourcing—Arizona had its code printed in New York). The commissioners were then accused of self-dealing with the printing contract, a scandal that occupied the legislature and political press through the next two sessions.[36]

Critics of codification never discounted when they balked at the cost of the code, but in most cases, there was not much to discount. If a print run of a code lasted several decades, the annual expense per value might have been more reasonable. The problem was that few codes lasted so long. Not counting New York's many revisions, seventeen Field Code jurisdictions—a majority of them—recommissioned

---

[31] 1859 Report of the Auditor of the State, in *Legislative Documents of the General Assembly of Iowa* (1860), 11. *Reports and Resolutions of the General Assembly of South Carolina* (1870), 60.

[32] *Rocky Mountain News*, Jan. 27, 1877. Auditor's Statement of the Public Revenue, in 1870 N.C. Pub. Laws 405, 408, 418, 448.

[33] See, e.g., Clifford Powell, "History of the Iowa Codes of Law," 9–11 *Iowa Journal of History and Politics* 9:493, 10:3, 10:311, 11:166 (1913), 10:321; *Journal of the Assembly of the State of Wisconsin* (1856), 1186.

[34] *Rocky Mountain News*, Dec. 27, 1876.

[35] 1860 Iowa Laws 119–25. Wisconsin quickly exhausted its supply of six thousand copies of the Code and had to appropriate more funds to the Secretary of State for printing and distribution. *Appendix to the Senate Journal for the State of Wisconsin* (1858), 93.

[36] See Powell, "History of the Iowa Codes," pts. II & III. The California legislature that printed Crosby's Code designated printing costs the second-largest budget item for the state (behind only legislative salaries). Report of the State Comptroller, in *Assembly Journal* (California, 1850), 1174.

or readopted a substantial revision of the code less than a decade after its initial enactment, incurring the same costs over again.[37] On this point, Iowa was again noteworthy. The state hired a commission to write its code from 1848 to 1851 and another commission to rewrite it for another three years at the end of the 1850s.[38]

The further west one traveled, the higher off-the-rack prices soared. Mark Twain could joke about the absurdities of carrying the US Statutes at Large overland to Nevada, but his experience was familiar to the codifiers, who had to import physical copies of the bulky law to consult, copy, and distribute.[39] Nor did codification save practitioners from importing the many volumes of precedential law reports that a reception of the common law would have entailed. Instead, practitioners were encouraged to consult the New York reports to understand what the code meant. As more states adopted the code, the volumes of reports and treatises interpreting it increased, and many of these volumes became necessary companions of code practice.[40] These costs of codification remain invisible to those looking only at the reception of the code in the courts.

Yet perhaps the greatest cost of codification, one just as invisible in the case reports, was not to the public or professional fisc but to American ideals of popular sovereignty. Historians have typically viewed the codification debate as one about the institutional competencies of courts versus legislatures.[41] As David Rabban has illustrated, this was a primary concern for the "historical school" of American jurisprudence that largely resisted late-nineteenth-century efforts toward codification. Although many of the adherents of that school were politically progressive, they feared that legislators were more liable to capture by corporate interests than they were receptive to democratic appeals from the poor and working classes. On the other hand, independent judges could better adapt the law on the books to evolving social customs of the law in practice.[42] But outside of this intellectual debate, carried on almost exclusively within the Northeast and centered at Harvard Law School, critics of codification recognized that even the most perspicacious provisions of the code required judicial interpretation and that judges were unlikely to lose influence or power under an American

[37] Those states were Arizona, California, Dakota Territory, Iowa, Kansas, Kentucky, Minnesota, Missouri, Nebraska, Nevada, North Carolina, Ohio, Oklahoma, Oregon, South Carolina, Wisconsin, and Wyoming. For a comprehensive list of all US procedure codes in the nineteenth century, see Appendix C to Kellen Richard Funk, The Lawyer's Code: The Transformation of American Legal Practice, 1828–1938 (Ph.D. dissertation, Princeton University, 2018), 478–85.

[38] See Powell, "History of the Iowa Codes," pts. II & III.

[39] Mark Twain, Roughing It (American Publishing Co., 1872), 22, 30.

[40] Indeed, treatise literature sought to advertise its national scope through subtitles. See John L. Tillinghast & Thomas G. Shearman, Practice, Pleadings, and Forms in Civil Actions in Courts of Record in the State of New York ... Adapted Also to the Practice in California, Missouri, Indiana, Wisconsin, Kentucky, Ohio, Alabama, Minnesota, and Oregon (Lewis Brothers, 1865); William Angus Sutherland, A Treatise on Code Pleading and Practice: Also Containing 1900 Forms Adapted to Practice in California, Alaska, Arizona, Idaho, Montana, Nevada, New Mexico, North Dakota, Oklahoma, South Dakota, Utah, Washington, and Other Code States (Bancroft-Whitney, 1910).

[41] See James Willard Hurst, The Growth of American Law: The Law Makers (Little, Brown, 1950), 90–91; Robert W. Gordon, "The American Codification Movement," 36 Vanderbilt Law Review 431, 445–46 (1983); Morton J. Horwitz, The Transformation of American Law: The Crisis of Legal Orthodoxy, 1870–1960 (Oxford University Press, 1992), 118–21.

[42] David M. Rabban, Law's History: American Legal Thought and the Transatlantic Turn to History (Cambridge University Press, 2013), 27–31, 356–61.

code regime.[43] Many critics instead argued that codification undermined the law-making authority of the very legislators who passed the codes. The length and technical sophistication of the Field Code meant that few legislators could actually give it any meaningful review, and thus it was the commissioners who adapted and recommended it that were truly the lawmakers. Even the more abstract thinkers in the historical school recognized as much and charged the codifiers with hypocrisy when they hailed codification as democratic legislation against aristocratic judge-made common law. "The complaint," wrote the stalwart opponent of codification James Coolidge Carter, "really amounts to this, that *judges* make the law instead of *commissioners*."[44]

Criticism based on popular sovereignty greeted the code upon its earliest migrations. In 1851, Iowa, like a few other states, adopted the Field Code while consolidating its other legislation into a comprehensive state code.[45] While other states usually granted their commissions exceptional authority to revise the rules of pleading and practice, Iowa directed its commission to "prepare a complete and perfect code of laws, as nearly as may be," one of the few times a statutory commission was granted broad authority to revise the prior law of a state.[46] In place of the usual substantive limitations on revision and codification, the legislature placed strict procedural requirements on the commission. The commissioners were to meet in regular session and elect a president who would rule on points of order and break tie votes between the other two commissioners. A journal of all proceedings and votes had to be kept, and no commissioner could be absent without leave. The legislature prescribed a special oath for the commissioners, which bound them to discharge their duties "with an eye single to the good of the people of the State of Iowa."[47] The commissioners were not popularly elected, but in all these other regards the legislature had done its best to constitute the commission as a mini-legislature that promulgated laws for the public good through transparent, public processes.

Nevertheless, newspapers complained about the delegation. *The Miner's Express* remarked that the commission operated against "the general idea of Democracy." Despite its three-year term, the commission cut corners and appropriated significant pieces of legislation—including the procedure code—from other states, but "to be governed by a foreign law, especially when that law is not preknown to the people whose conduct is to be regulated thereby . . . is something repugnant to the idea of Democratic Republican government."[48] When the legislature debated the printing contract for the code, the paper read more into the decision than mere financial patronage. Printing the code seemed to commit the legislature to actually examine it as

[43] See, e.g., John Pickering, "A Lecture on the Alleged Uncertainty of the Law," 12 *American Jurist* 285 (1834), 293–98; Joseph Hopkinson, *Considerations on the Abolition of the Common Law in the United States* (1809); James Coolidge Carter, *The Proposed Codification of Our Common Law: A Paper Prepared at the Request of the Committee of the Bar Association of the City of New York, Opposed to the Measure* (1884), 85–86.

[44] Carter, *The Proposed Codification of Our Common Law*, 42.

[45] Including Arizona, Arkansas, Tennessee, New Mexico, North and South Carolina, Mississippi, and Montana. On Iowa, see Powell, "History of the Iowa Codes," pt. II.

[46] Cf. Report, *Appendix to the Journals of the Senate and Assembly of the State of Tennessee* (1857), 191; 1897 N.M. Comp. Laws 9; 1866 Ill. Comp. Laws at v; 1849 Wis. Rev. Stat., "Advertisement."

[47] 1848 Iowa Laws 42–44.

[48] *The Miner's Express* (Dubuque, Iowa), Feb. 26, 1851.

any other bill, "whether they should, in this matter, be the Legislators in fact, or a mere approbatory assembly [of an] irresponsible Commission."[49]

Against these complaints that Iowa's real legislating was being done "by this trio of Lawyers," pro-codification papers made the commission's unrepresentativeness and lack of accountability its main virtue. The three lawyers "were presumed to be . . . familiar with the bearing of all our laws and practice under them" as well as "the wants and interests of our entire population," explained one. "Otherwise, they never could have been appointed."[50] Another argued that the sound judgment and erudition of the commissioners stood in stark contrast to the legislators who would review the commission's work. The paper satirically reported a legislative session amending the code:

> The gentleman from "Buncombe" approves of the general sense of the section, but some of the details are a little different from what "they used to was" in the State of Kentucky . . . *whar* he was born, and he therefore moves to strike out the word "quantity" and insert the words "powerful sight"—the gentleman on his left seconds the motion, and suggests that the words "or smart chance" be inserted after the words "powerful sight."[51]

The representativeness of the legislature, when it came to Buncombe County, was the problem standing in the way of scientific legal progress. Therefore, another editor explained, "The devil is to get the legislature to let [the code] alone . . . without making ten thousand amendments." After all, "what was the utility of appointing Messrs. Woodward, Mason, and Hempstead to compile a code of laws if our Legislators possess legal talent so much superior?"[52]

One answer might be that compared to the legislature's brief sessions, a commission at least could enjoy the luxury of time to compile its code, yet the length and innovation of the Field Code presented a novel problem for American lawmaking. Even the shortest version of the code was significantly longer than any other state statute before the progressive legislation of the twentieth century. Practice codes were far longer than the relatively simple criminal codes of the early republic or the regulatory laws on corporations or railroads passed after the Civil War. Opening with a declaration of novelty, abolishing the hallmarks of prior practice, and instituting "hereafter" a new form of action with significant revisions to civil remedies, the Field Code over and again announced itself as an original and lengthy new law.[53]

Even multiyear commissions thus proved to be too short-lived to read the code with a critical eye and a revisionist's pen. Whether sitting on commissions or legislative committees, American codifiers constantly complained about a lack of time to give their subject full consideration and to adequately systematize procedural law. In Kentucky, "the Commissioners have not been able to perform all the duties assigned to them." In Ohio, "they have realized [their task] requires more time and research, than they

---

[49] *The Miner's Express*, Dec. 25, 1850.
[50] *The Miner's Express*, Feb. 19, 1851; *Burlington Tri-Weekly Telegraph*, Dec. 19, 1850.
[51] *Muscatine Journal* (Muscatine, Iowa), Jan. 11, 1851.
[52] *Burlington Tri-Weekly Telegraph* (Burlington, Iowa), Dec. 19, 1850.
[53] 1848 N.Y. Laws 510.

have been able to bestow." In Kansas, "the time within which the commissioners were required to perform their labors was too short," and in Wisconsin, "the limited time for completion of the work was very short." "Recognizing and regretting [the code's] deficiencies," the North Carolina commissioners "beg leave only to call attention to the very brief time" they had to craft it.[54] Of course, states that declined to appoint a commission had even shorter time horizons during a single legislative session. "It is folly to undertake to pass a code in a sixty day session," wrote the *Montana Post*, "and the best way would be for the Assembly to select one from a State or Territory which would come near meeting our wants, and slide it through with the fewest changes possible."[55]

Given these time constraints, adopting the Field Code tended to be an all-or-nothing proposition. Once in a while, that could work against the code, as it did in Texas, the only western state to reject the Field Code. When "the clerk then proceeded to read the code of civil procedure" in the Texas Assembly, "there was a general *stampede*, and the House adjourned, there not being a quorum to transact business." The code was not taken up again before the session expired.[56] Paired with a close reading of political commentaries on the Field Code, the macroscopic patterns of its borrowing intensify the question: Why the West? If codification of legal practice was not a natural convenience, if it provoked widespread complaints about the subversion of popular sovereignty, and if it invited the Tocquevillian nightmare of imperial servility to foreign law, why then did so many jurisdictions copy wholesale a text addressed to the idiosyncrasies of New York procedure and civil remedies? Why not rather follow Texas in its lonely rejection of the code?

As in other areas of postbellum study, one may learn a lot about the American West by turning to the American South. Scholars of Reconstruction have broadened the scope of their study to include both the American South and the American West as two sites in one "Greater Reconstruction." These studies have illustrated the ways in which military conquest, rapid industrialization, and the resettlement and education of ethnic minorities developed similarly in each region, guided by economic elites in New York and political administrators in Washington.[57] Twelve of the states and

---

[54] *Report of the Commissioners Appointed to Prepare a Code of Practice for the Commonwealth of Kentucky* (1850), vi; *Report of the Commissioners on Practice and Pleadings* (Ohio, 1853), iv; *Journal of the Senate of the State of Kansas* (1868), 71; *Revised Statutes of Wisconsin* (1858), iii; *The Code of Civil Procedure of the State of North Carolina* (1868), iii; *Revised Statutes of Arizona* (1887), 3.

[55] *Montana Post*, Jan. 21, 1865. Compared to Europe, the limited time horizons of American legislation could be quite short indeed. European commissions on civil procedure might sit for longer than a decade, even if they only produced what one scholar calls a "(bad) translation of the French Code." A. W. Jongbloed, "The Netherlands," in C. H. van Rhee, *European Traditions in Civil Procedure* (Intersentia, 2005), 69. The Dutch code of civil procedure took nearly fifteen years to prepare, while the French code went into effect five years after the commission was first issued. Later French commissions would sit for the entirety of the 1870s and from 1886 to 1892. The first German confederation code of procedure took four years to prepare and another seven years of drafting before it was transformed into Germany's *Zivilprozessordnung*. See *ibid.* at 5, 30, 42, 111–13.

[56] *Texas State Times* (Austin, Tex.), Dec. 15, 1855. See also William V. Dorsaneo III, "The History of Texas Civil Procedure, 65 *Baylor Law Review* 713 (2013), 717–18.

[57] Elliott West, "Reconstructing Race," 34 *Western Historical Quarterly* 6 (2003). See also Heather Cox Richardson, *West from Appomattox: The Reconstruction of America After the Civil War* (Yale University Press, 2007); Richard White, *The Republic for Which It Stands: The United States During Reconstruction and the Gilded Age, 1865–1896* (Oxford University Press, 2017); Sven Beckert, *Monied Metropolis: New York City and the Consolidation of the American Bourgeoisie, 1850–1896* (Harvard University Press, 2003);

territories that copied the Field Code mostly closely did so during the Civil War and Reconstruction era—four states in the former Confederacy and eight jurisdictions in the Far West.[58] Complaints about imperialism and servility to foreign law unsurprisingly intensified as the New York code appeared in the Reconstruction South. The codifiers' answer to the charge there would resound across the nation: capital demanded it.

IV

As Reconstruction in North Carolina faltered in the 1870s, and Democrats expected a chance to rewrite the constitution on more favorable terms, many counseled compromise on racial equality but stood fast against the new code of civil procedure. "The conditions upon which the State was restored to the Union, however unjust those conditions were, should not be disturbed," one partisan paper announced, but "the 'Civil Code of procedure' offends and oppresses all."[59] The state's speaker of the assembly argued that "this child of the carpet baggers" was among the worst impositions of Radical Reconstruction. As the partisan press prepared their wish lists for a new convention, repealing the procedure code and abolishing the code commission topped the lists each time. "One of the greatest curses inflicted upon North Carolina is the new system of laws that Judge Tourgée brought down here from New York," one such list concluded.[60]

"Judge Tourgée" was Albion W. Tourgée, a New York lawyer and one of the nation's leading racial egalitarians.[61] Tourgée sat on a commission alongside Victor C. Barringer, a leading Democrat and close personal friend of the ex-Confederate President Jefferson Davis (who had hid in Barringer's house on his unsuccessful flight to Georgia). Filling the third chair was William Blount Rodman, a lawyer with a substantial practice in the eastern part of the state. Although Rodman served in the Confederate Army, he early on discerned the turn of the war and became a devoted Republican, a "scalawag" in the local parlance.[62] Seating an elite Democrat, a Radical

---

Mark Wahlgren Summers, *The Ordeal of the Reunion: A New History of Reconstruction* (University of North Carolina Press, 2014). The major application of the Greater Reconstruction idea to legal history has been Sarah Barringer Gordon, *The Mormon Question: Polygamy and Constitutional Conflict in Nineteenth-Century America* (University of North Carolina Press, 2003).

[58] Those jurisdictions were Nevada (1861), Dakota Territory—which retained the Code when split into North and South (1862), Idaho (1864), Arizona (1864), Montana (1865), Arkansas (1868), North Carolina (1868), Wyoming (1869), Florida (1870), South Carolina (1870), Utah (1870), and Colorado (1877).
[59] *Weekly Standard* (Raleigh), Oct. 5, 1870.
[60] *Wilmington Journal*, Sept. 30, 1870; *Tarboro Southerner*, Feb. 16, 1870; *Wilmington Journal*, Feb. 25, 1870; *Tarboro Southerner*, Nov. 24, 1870; *Wilmington Journal*, Aug. 1, 1873.
[61] Otto H. Olsen, *Carpetbagger's Crusade: The Life of Albion Winegar Tourgée* (Johns Hopkins, 1965), 131–41; Mark Elliott, *Color-blind Justice: Albion Tourgée and the Quest for Racial Equality* (Oxford University Press, 2006).
[62] On the tropes of the carpetbagger and scalawag, see Eric Foner, *Reconstruction: America's Unfinished Revolution* (Harper & Row, 1988), 294–326. See the biographies of Barringer and Rodman kept with their personal papers. Barringer Family Papers, University of Virginia Library Special Collections; William Blount Rodman Papers, East Carolina University Library.

Figure 4.4 Victor C. Barringer, William Blount Rodman, Albion W. Tourgée, with a manuscript code in the foreground—the only known photograph of a nineteenth-century US code commission.
Albion W. Tourgée Papers, Box 1, Image 37, Chatauqua County Historical Society.

Republican carpetbagger, and a southern scalawag, North Carolina's commission was a virtual microcosm of (at least, white) Reconstruction politics (see Figure 4.4). And as with Reconstruction more broadly in 1868, the Radical had the most influence early on.

As a delegate to North Carolina's constitutional convention, Tourgée had pressed to entrench procedural reform in the constitution's text. Indeed, the state's first borrowing of the Field Code was in the constitution itself, which copied the opening provision that "the distinction between actions at law and suits in equity, and the forms of all such actions and suits shall be abolished, and there shall be in this State but one form of action."[63] Republicans thus ensured that even if they did not fare well at the forthcoming elections, the legislature would be constitutionally bound to adopt the Field Code, or something very like it. Republicans did fare well in the election, however, as reflected in the composition of the commission. Democrats could complain about the "stranger boy" Tourgée and the traitor to his people Rodman, but they could not muster the votes to defeat their appointment.[64]

---

[63] *Constitution of the State of North Carolina, Together with the Ordinances and Resolutions of the Constitutional Convention* (1868), 18–19, 79.
[64] *Wilmington Journal*, Apr. 3, 1868.

As soon as the commission was formed, Tourgée sought to link it to the network of other code states. He wrote to his colleagues that they must "organize immediately and communicate with the officials of the various states which are working under Code Procedure, and get copies of their codes." Included among Tourgée's correspondents was David Dudley Field, who had his carpetbagging nephew carry along "several volumes of my codes" to Tourgée.[65] As with other commissions, the workload was divided, but Tourgée assigned the main work of civil procedure to himself.[66] Tourgée's code closely accorded with Field's 1850 draft and was drawn up quickly. The printed code of 575 sections appeared less than two months after Tourgée's first letter organizing the commission.[67]

Secure with a constitutional mandate and sympathetic legislature, Tourgée's First Report boldly reminded the legislature of its constitutional duty to pass the code. Unlike most codifiers, Tourgée's report put no reliance on the argument that procedure was an exceptionally benign field open to reform and codification. Rather, it argued, procedure was the ground on which the constitutional reconstruction of race relations would be carried out:

> The changes which the last eight years have wrought in the fundamental relations of society, blotting out entirely one of the great classes of personal relations—that of master and slave—opening the ears of justice to those who were before dumb in her presence, and giving parity of right, authority and remedy, to the highest and lowliest; breaking down the barriers of the jury-box, and permitting the landless citizen and the man of African descent to come within its bounds, opening the forum, the bar and the bench, to the honorable competition of the colored man—all these mighty changes in the relations of the great component elements of society, demand equivalent changes in the laws and render the work both of the Legislator and the codifier, one of extreme difficulty and delicacy.

Access to courts, to remedies, to juries, and to the profession—this was the scope Field had given civil procedure, and in Tourgée's handling, civil procedure would be the tool to upend the law of master and slave. Accordingly, Tourgée "did not hesitate to take the Code of New York as the basis of that to be prepared for this State."[68] In the following months, as disgruntled Democrats insisted they could accept political racial equality but could not abide the code of procedure, they understood they were taking back with their left hand what they seemed to be offering with their right. As one complained, "Tourgée induced the late so-called Convention to do

[65] A. W. Tourgée to Wm. B. Rodman, June 8, 1868, Rodman Papers; D. Dudley Field to Hon. A. W. Tourgée, July 20, 1868, Field to Tourgée, July 30, 1868 (confirming receipt of codes sent with Field's nephew Fisk Brewer "some weeks ago"), Albion Tourgée Papers, Chautauqua County Historical Society.

[66] Rodman was responsible for sections on "special proceedings" and Barringer the code of criminal procedure. In correspondence between themselves, Rodman and Barringer called the civil procedure statute the "A.W. Tourgee code of procedure." V. C. Barringer to William Rodman, Oct. 16, 1868; Barringer to Rodman, Aug. 21, 1868; Barringer to Rodman, Mar. 26, 1869; Barringer to Rodman, Oct. 11, 1869; Barringer to Rodman, Nov. 24, 1869, Rodman Papers.

[67] *The Code of Civil Procedure of North Carolina* (1868).

[68] *First Report of the Code Commissioners*, x–xi; *Second Report of the Code Commissioners*, in *North Carolina Code of Civil Procedure* (1868) viii–ix, xvi.

away with ... pleading, and law and equity.... The Supreme Court is now a political, and not a judicial tribunal."[69] Political, because procedure had become the tool of Reconstruction policy.

Tourgée and his fellow commissioners took some steps to mitigate the sense of imposition. In their report they called for the bench and bar of the state to make the code their own and forward to the commission "such amendments as may occur to them, in practice under it, as necessary or valuable." Even then, however, they made their authority clear. Significant alterations of the law were to run through them, not through ordinary legislation. They concluded their report by instructing the legislature to pass their code "as it is," offering for a model "the Code of New York [which] was adopted in 1848 as it come from the hands of the Commissioners."[70]

Although Republicans had the votes to pass the code without amendment, the native bench and bar were less willing to accommodate Tourgée's code. "I don't quite know whether the Code will go from beneath the dark waters or not," Rodman wrote to Tourgée in the summer of 1869. "[Chief Justice] Pearson is against it and I fear the rest all are." Two state senators complained that "our present Judicial system is a servile copy of New York, a State less like ours than almost any other in the Union." Unlike the Californian defenders of the common law, North Carolinians readily conceded that civilian laws and practice codes were best suited for commercial empires, but North Carolina Democrats preferred rustic simplicity to being one more codified jurisdiction in New York's network. "New York is full of large towns and cities, and her people are extensively engaged in commercial and maritime pursuits. North Carolina is an agricultural State, with a rural people," the senate report continued. "The New York system was devised upon a model deemed suitable to a dense, commercial community." But such a system was, as many Democratic newspapers complained, "unadapted to the wants of our people."[71]

Such criticisms endured to the end of the century. One 1891 commentary in the inaugural issue of the *Yale Law Journal* argued, "The legal practice of the State was reconstructed by the adoption of the New York Code of Civil Procedure, with all its penalties and high-pressure machinery adapted to the conditions of an alert, eager, pushing commercial community."[72] Like pre-code New York, North Carolina summoned debtors to answer a complaint only when a court was in session, and in many parts of the state, a court sat only for one month out of the year, holding over trials to the next term if too much business had accumulated. By copying Field's provisions for default judgment, issued within twenty days by clerks in and out of term time, the code dramatically accelerated creditor remedies from around two years to three weeks.[73]

---

[69] *Wilmington Journal*, Apr. 3, 1868. Procedure could operate as a tool of Reconstruction policy at the level of the federal courts as well. See Edward A. Purcell, *Litigation and Inequality: Federal Diversity Jurisdiction in Industrial America, 1870–1958* (Oxford University Press, 1992).

[70] *Second Report* (North Carolina, 1868), iv, xvi. The latter remark was not strictly true, since the New York legislature had at least taken two weeks to make some two dozen minor amendments.

[71] *Wilmington Journal*, Feb. 25, 1870; *Tarboro Southerner*, Aug. 25, 1870. *Wilmington Journal*, Sept. 26, 1873; *Tarboro Southerner*, Feb. 16, 1870; *Weekly Standard*, Sept. 7, 1870.

[72] Harry H. Ingersoll, "Some Anomalies of Practice," 1 *Yale Law Journal* 89 (1891), 91–92.

[73] See Olsen, *Carpetbagger's Crusade*, 134–37; McAdoo v. Benbow, 63 N.C. 462 (1869).

From the code's accelerated remedies arose the frequent comparisons between "commercial" states like New York and "agricultural" states like North Carolina. Although proceduralists tend to think of a bias toward settlement as a twentieth-century phenomenon, common law lawyers frequently hailed the pressure for out-of-court settlements as a virtue of pre-codified procedure. While trover and assumpsit were creditor remedies, jurists wrote that common law process overall created a debtor's remedy through the languid pace of enforcement. The length of proceedings encouraged negotiations and settlement among the parties, and settlement almost always favored debtors, who ended up paying less than their strictly legal liabilities, especially by avoiding the court costs and lawyers' fees that fell on a losing litigant.[74] When protracted proceedings extended beyond a year, they allowed a season or more of harvests to influence these negotiations. Despite their dramatic rhetoric, North Carolinians were not exaggerating that their remedial system had undergone a fundamental change of orientation toward creditors and a more liquid mercantile economy.

Tourgée and other codifiers did not wish to deprive debtors entirely of their customary powers of negotiation and settlement, but they sought to locate these powers in substantive law rather than process. The substantive legislation became known as "homestead exemptions," which arose around the time states were abolishing imprisonment for debt. These laws set a minimum allowance of property—usually one's home and adjoining land, as well as subsistence farm animals or an artisan's tools—which creditors could not recover to satisfy a debt. Field was ambivalent about New York's exemptions. His code repeated New York's previous exemption of certain farm implements and mechanics' tools. Whether the exemption should extend to a whole homestead, Field—not usually deferential about reforms he favored—declared it "a high question of public policy, which it is for the legislature alone to entertain." New York did extend its homestead exemptions in 1850.[75]

Paired with homestead exemptions, the New York code seemed to strike the popular balance for a Radical Republican like Tourgée, who sympathized with the plight of freedmen. The code would accelerate the determination of creditors' rights and remedies, but homestead laws would forbid enforcement against poor smallholders and sharecroppers. Freedmen could be protected while credit could again flow in the state, largely on collections from large landowners who overextended themselves—that is, the white plantation class. It was no coincidence, then, that Democratic

[74] On the twentieth-century shift to settlement, see John H. Langbein, "The Disappearance of Civil Trial in the United States," 122 *Yale Law Journal* 522 (2012). On the common law preference for settlement (or "compromise" as it was usually termed), see Wells, *Law of the State of Missouri*, 94. Compromises were frequent and sophisticated enough that a whole body of law had developed for setting compromises aside when they appeared to be last-minute collusions to avoid lawyers' fees. See David Graham, *A Treatise on the Practice of the Supreme Court of the State of New York* (Banks & Gould, 3d ed., 1847), 285–96. See also Bruce H. Mann, *Republic of Debtors: Bankruptcy in the Age of American Independence* (Harvard University Press, 2002), 16–25.

[75] Such exemptions apparently originated in the South. See James W. Ely, "Homestead Exemption and Southern Legal Culture," in Sally Hadden & Patricia Minter eds., *Signposts: New Directions in Southern Legal History* (University of Georgia Press, 2013), 289–314; Paul Goodman, "The Emergence of Homestead Exemption in the United States: Accommodation and Resistance to the Market Revolution, 1840–1880," 80 *Journal of American History* 470 (1993); William B. Aycock, "Homestead Exemption in North Carolina," 29 *North Carolina Law Review* 145 (1950). *Final Report* (New York, 1850), 354. For the New York exemption, see 1850 N.Y. Laws 499–500.

lawmakers and journalists offered to trade Black political equality for the repeal of the code. The two were vitally linked. Code remedies threatened to break up the source of planters' political power before they could stabilize their lines of credit and maintain control over the most productive land.[76]

In reaction to the swift denunciation of code remedies, the same legislature that passed the code enacted a simple compromise later in the session: summonses to defendants would be "returnable to the regular term" of a court. Clerks, thereafter, could not issue swift default judgments out of term.[77] When a debtor tried to claim the statute's protection before Tourgée, who had become a superior court judge, Tourgée struck the statute down for violating the state's constitution. Not coincidentally, it was Tourgée who had worked at the convention to safeguard the powers of clerks to issue such judgments.[78] On further appeal, Chief Justice Pearson reversed Tourgée, writing that Tourgée "did not fully comprehend" the legislature's intent "to repeal so much of the Code as confers jurisdiction on the Clerk 'to give judgments,' and to restore the old mode of procedure, by which all judgments are rendered in term time." Pearson concluded that the legislature had put judicial powers back where they belonged. "The Clerk is no longer a subordinate Judge, but is divested of all judicial functions in civil actions, and is simply a Clerk."[79]

Of course Tourgée fully comprehended the effects of the new law, which is why he had struck it down. Believing that the state's war-torn economy could recover only if credit began flowing again, Tourgée remained opposed to "any 'Stay-law,' 'Suspension Law,' 'Jurisdiction Law,' or any other legislative humbug" that slowed creditor remedies. Writing to Rodman, Tourgée confided, "I have not got over cursing about" Pearson's decision more than a month after it was handed down. Rodman, now serving as Pearson's associate justice on the supreme bench, issued a dissent that focused on the equitable principle that "statutes which oust delay, and are for expedition of justice, shall be benignly construed." In such a constitutionally doubtful case, Rodman counseled sticking to the original code of procedure and its accelerated remedies.[80]

Although Tourgée hoped to see Pearson reversed by a future court, the commissioners did not have to wait so long. The legislation divesting clerks of authority carried its own expiration clause. Despite Pearson's separation of clerks and judges as a constitutional principle, the original code went back into effect on the first day of 1871, reviving complaints against the code and calls for a new constitutional convention.[81] Subsequent reports to the legislature from the code commission dropped

[76] See Olsen, *Carpetbagger's Crusade*, 134–45.

[77] 1868–1869 N.C. Laws 179–82.

[78] At the convention, Tourgée had tried to preclude this precise type of legislation, providing that only "issues of fact" could be "transferred to the Superior Courts" from a clerk's office. That is, only contested cases could be removed from the clerk's province, not uncontestable claims of debt.

[79] Norwood v. Thorpe, 64 N.C. 682 (1870), 683–84. *Norwood* was a follow-up case to *McAdoo v. Benbow*, 63 N.C. 461 (1869), the first reversal of Tourgée to which Rodman dissented. See also Backalan v. Littlefield, 64 N.C. 233 (1870). N.C. Const. of 1868, art. 4, § 17.

[80] Tourgée to G. W. Welker, Feb. 26, 1869, Tourgée Papers; Tourgée to Rodman, August 5, 1869, Rodman Papers; *Norwood*, 63 N.C. at 471 (Rodman, dissenting).

[81] Tourgée to Rodman, Aug. 5, 1869, Rodman Papers; 1868–1869 North Carolina Laws 182; *Tarboro Southerner*, Nov. 24, 1870.

the bold tone of the First Report. "For the changes made by the constitution the Commissioners are no wise responsible," they pleaded in an 1870 report. "We took them as accomplished facts; and our duty was as skillfully and as prudently as we could to bring the law of the State into harmony with them."[82] The defense was somewhat disingenuous, as the two Republican commissioners, Tourgée and Rodman, had sat on the convention committee that wrote the mandate for codification and practice reform into the constitution's text. The commissioners' Second Report no longer argued that procedure would be the vessel through which freedman's rights would be secured. Rather, it followed the original New York strategy of distinguishing procedure as "the machinery" of the law independent of the law's "principles," and it argued for the commissioners' authority on the basis that "none but those whose profession makes them necessarily familiar" with practice were fit to reform it.[83]

Receiving innumerable letters complaining that under the code, "no one will be benefited, except perhaps some Northern Capitalists," Rodman undertook an anonymous defense of the new code in *The North Carolina Standard*. He encouraged the bar to accommodate themselves to change, for "the New York system . . . bids fair to become national." Putatively offering an overview of the code, Rodman's articles were almost entirely about credit. "How can we create credit? By punctuality," he wrote. "And how create punctuality? by law, and by law alone. Let the law enforce punctuality; let the people of North Carolina learn that the great law of business is, that 'time is of the essence of the contract,' and incur no debt that they do not expect to meet at maturity." Under the old system, he argued, "the pleadings were most absurdly required to be made up in term time only," but under the more certain and speedy remedies of the code, "we may expect that the secret hoards of the frugal among ourselves will be offered to loan, and even that the vaults of the banks of New-York . . . will be open to our industry."[84] Although they had to compromise on stay laws and trim their rhetoric on the power of procedural reform, Tourgée and Rodman ultimately defended the adoption of the code on the promise that New York remedies would draw out and secure New York capital.

V

Like their southern counterparts, relatively long-time residents of the American West claimed that agitation for the code had been stirred up by "the carpet-bag crew who came here a few months since" hoping their careers would rise along with the elevation of territories to statehood.[85] Just as North Carolinians had complained the code was ill-adapted to local conditions, western attorneys warned that commissioners

---

[82] *Report of the Code Commissioners*, in *Executive and Legislative Documents of the Assembly of North Carolina*, No. 28 (1870), 2.

[83] *Second Report* (North Carolina, 1868), xvi.

[84] William A. Jenkins to Rodman, Jan. 14, 1868, Rodman Papers. Rodman's explication of the code appeared in three sequentially numbered articles in the *Standard* on August 14, 15, and 16, 1868, under the title "The Code of Civil Procedure." Rodman disclosed his authorship in private correspondence with Barringer. See Barringer to Rodman, Aug. 21, 1868, Rodman Papers.

[85] *Rocky Mountain News*, Jan. 21, 1877.

might be appointed who "had little or no knowledge of our statutes and practice" and would plunge local practice into "inextricable confusion."[86] Thus, westerners, no less than southerners, could view the code as a foreign imposition.

Codification in the West developed with the significant difference that most jurisdictions sought to bolster local political autonomy by avoiding lawmaking commissions. California, Colorado, the Dakotas, Idaho, Montana, Nebraska, New Mexico, Nevada, Oklahoma, and Wyoming adopted procedure codes through judiciary committees without appointing extra-legislative commissions. Often, the choice was explicitly rooted in concerns over popular sovereignty. When a Wyoming judiciary committee reported against a resolution to appoint a code commission, its chairman remonstrated that "the people have selected the different members of this body from their number and have commissioned us to act for them." If a procedure code served the public good (and the legislature decided later that session that it did), "the duty" to craft it "is upon us and not upon others."[87]

The same logic militated against a procedure commission in Colorado, a state that especially casts doubt on the notion that codification was an off-the-rack convenience for the West. For seventeen years after its organization as a territory, lawyers in Colorado adhered to the old common law forms of practice—indeed, they did so through a legislative borrowing, importing the practice acts of the staunchly anti-code state of Illinois. Although Colorado adopted the Field Code in its first year of statehood, its territorial history contradicts the notion that western states lacked an entrenched bar interested in maintaining traditional practices or that the Field Code was the only law available for importation.

Both ideas were expressly argued at the time. One lawyer wrote anonymously to the Denver papers that "I should regret very much to see the '*accumulated wisdom of the ages*' thrown aside for that new fangled abortion of legal quacks, denominated a 'code.'" If the state had to look elsewhere to update its practice laws, it could with more ease and less expense adopt the briefer and more moderate laws of Massachusetts or even England. Although the rules of common law practice there were scattered across volumes of case reports, New York's code was not a real alternative: "What constitutes a complaint in the New York code is contained in a definition, comprised in sixteen words. There are in the New York code reports *two thousand* decisions on these sixteen words. . . . So much for your code simplicity." Perhaps with an eye to the South, the lawyer concluded that the code had "fastened itself upon states which, were they now free to choose, would gladly go back to the so much deprecated common law practice."[88]

Other code opponents argued that they did not oppose codification in principle, but they were opposed to this particular code and the manner in which it was rushing through the legislature without due consideration. At a January 1877 meeting in Denver attended by most of the Colorado bar and legislative assembly, common law lawyers rallied behind J. Q. Charles, who concluded that "the strongest argument against the adoption of the code" during the present legislative session "is the want of

---

[86] *Rocky Mountain News*, Feb. 16, 1877.
[87] Report of Chairman William S. Rockwell, *Journal of the Council of the Territory of Wyoming* (1870), 39.
[88] *Pueblo Daily Chieftain*, Jan. 13, 1877.

time to do it well."[89] Western legislatures often sat for only sixty days every two years. At that pace, deliberative legislation over so vast a topic as civil remedies was impracticable. Sometimes constitutionally bound to put bills through three readings before passage, legislatures scheduled evening sessions for the reading. But in the satirized words of a "Granger" who sat in on one such session, "fifty fellers" were just "settin' around, some of them smoking, with their heels cocked up on their desks, some of 'em readin' newspapers, some of 'em talkin' and laughin'," but "not one of 'em legislated a bit."[90]

Code proponents conceded that "it hardly seems to the common mind that an entirely new system of practice can be properly framed and rightly adjusted in the limited time allowed by a single session of the Legislature." But, they argued, the expertise and experience of other states could avoid the dangers of novel legislation—as long as the text of other states was followed closely. "The code proposed to be adopted," noted a Colorado lawyer, "is the California code," and therefore "the time and thought spent upon the code of California by lawyers of that State accrue to the benefit of people of Colorado."[91] In place of arguments about local concerns and state popular sovereignty, code proponents substituted something of a national popular sovereignty, one rooted in a mobile bar of lawyers whose rules of practice could travel with them and generate similar experiences in different locales.

The argument that all due consideration for the code had essentially been outsourced to California did its required work in Denver. One of the most vocal legislative opponents of the code, Allison DeFrance, abandoned his criticisms after the code became identified with California law. Whereas earlier in the session, he had cited lack of time as a reason to defeat the code, he now reasoned that "he did not consider that he, or any other member of the General Assembly, with the time he had to examine it, was competent to criticize it. He understood the bill was almost an exact copy of the code of California, which had been framed by some of the ablest men in the land, and he could not criticize their work."[92] Now that the architect of California's code, Stephen J. Field, represented the West on the US Supreme Court, it would hardly do to continue calling his code the law of "sciolists, agitators, and revolutionists."[93]

The ultimate effect of forgoing commissions was that western states that refused to engage in commissioner lawmaking on the grounds of popular sovereignty copied the text of New York lawyers even more closely than did the postbellum southern commissions. The Denver press complained that Colorado's legislators "have clipped a section from one code and pasted it with a section from another, and so industriously have they labored that they have been enabled to present the work of their hands to the assembly in the limited space of fifteen or twenty days a complete code of procedure, which . . . has been 'assimilated,' as we are informed, 'to the character and requirements of our people,' whatever that may mean."[94]

---

[89] *Denver Daily Tribune*, Jan. 10, 1877.
[90] *Pueblo Daily Chieftain*, Feb. 15, 1877. Less humorous accounts stated the same position. See *Rocky Mountain News*, Feb. 9, 1877; *Journal of the Council of the Territory of Washington* (1854), 151.
[91] *Denver Daily Tribune*, Jan. 31, 1877.
[92] *Denver Daily Tribune*, Feb. 17, 1877.
[93] *Rocky Mountain News*, Jan. 24, 1877. See also *Pueblo Daily Chieftain*, Feb. 25, 1877.
[94] *Rocky Mountain News*, Jan. 20, 1877.

Considering the universal complaints that time was too short and legislators too inexpert to give the code due consideration, one might expect the code to have failed more often or at least to have faced more competition from other workable statutes. The Louisiana code that California's governor wished to adopt remained a live option, as did the variety of southern codes that abandoned the common law forms of action.[95] If settlers believed law had to be imported into the West, Colorado immigrants proved that the common law of Illinois was just as amenable to statutory importation as a New York code.

What codifiers saw when they looked at New York, more so than Louisiana, Alabama, or Illinois, was the Empire State of commercial capital. And the putative fears, demands, and desires of a personified Capital continually wielded promises—and threats—in the debates over procedural codification. The western codifiers parried charges that a code would be a "new-fangled" contrivance by pointing to the fact that it had been "adopted twenty-nine years ago by the Empire state of the Union" as well as "the wealthy and populous states of Ohio, Indiana, Wisconsin and Missouri." They contended that the code of the nation's uniquely commercial empire would bring wealth in its wake.[96]

Whether the actual demands of capital were anything like the perceptions of anxious merchants and miners along the periphery is hard to say. When a Colorado legislator scoffed at the idea that capitalists could possibly care about the difference between old common law and modern code remedies, his adversaries rebuked him. "Mr. Hamill replied that he knew of one California company of capitalists who were deterred from investing in mining property here wholly on account of the practice of the courts in mining cases. If we had had this code years ago, Colorado would now have a larger amount of California capital in her mines." Beyond occasional hearsay like this, codifiers never produced direct evidence that financiers expected to find New York's code operating in the mines. More often, codifiers argued from the logic of capital to infer what the capitalists desired. On this account, procedure was at least as important as the substantive rules of property and contract, because procedure secured the remedies that actually protected investments. "Men of capital and enterprise will not make investments and devote their time and energies to those works of internal improvement so necessary for the speedy development of our natural resources, and for the settlement and building up the country," Nebraska's governor reasoned, "unless ample protection is afforded them, by legal enactment, for the capital invested and labor employed." Therefore he urged swift passage of the Field Code. On the same understanding, another western lawyer succinctly summarized the difference between the code and the common law as "whether a merchant had better try to collect a $500 note or burn it up."[97]

The creditors' remedies in the code gave the codifiers their leading argument against criticisms rooted in the ideology of popular sovereignty. "There is no doubt

[95] Although Tennessee adapted nearly 225 sections of its code from Field codes in 1848, the state also incorporated nearly 50 sections of the 1852 Code of Alabama, which did not particularly rely on Field.

[96] *Pueblo Daily Chieftain*, Feb. 25, 1877.

[97] *Denver Daily Tribune*, Feb. 17, 1877. Governor's Message, in *Journal of the House of Assembly of the Territory of Nebraska* (1857), 12. *Denver Daily Tribune*, Jan. 10, 1877.

but the people are in favor of anything that promises to hurry up that proverbially slow and blind old female called Justice, and they will go for the old code," one Colorado newspaper announced. New York's "code practice is the best in excellence," stated another, "and when I say *best* I do not mean best for lawyers only, but best for the people—the commonwealth." If the People favored economic progress, certainty of remedy, and efficiency in proceedings, they favored the New York code, whether they understood or cared about the technical rules of pleading and joinder. Thus, in their arguments, codifiers imagined themselves champions of popular sovereignty, for they accomplished what the People desired. Since legislative commissions and committees sought the proper end of the People's good, codifiers downplayed the legislative short-cuts they used, arguing that "as long as the mass of the people represented by the non-legal portion of the legislature are in favor of a code, it matters little how much dust of ages the anti-code lawyers and their [newspaper] organs kick up."[98]

A central irony in the migration of the New York code, premised on the demands of New York capital, was that the migrating code was not the law of New York. The version of Field's code that was copied the most was the 1850 draft—the one never enacted in New York. In 1876, just as Colorado debated the code, New York replaced what remained of Field's original draft with a new code framed by a commission under the leadership of Montgomery Throop. A count by a "friend" of Field's found that only three sentences of the Field Code had carried over word for word into the Throop Code. However, hardly a line of the Throop Code appears in any of the post-1870s procedure codes or revisions of other states.[99]

Thus, by the end of Reconstruction, New York's domestic empire of capital and creditors' remedies bore a remarkable resemblance to the international empire administered by the British. While reforming the practice of law, both jurisdictions largely rejected codification within their borders but encouraged it among their economic dependents. The English Parliament commissioned a complete codification of law for India and colonies in Singapore, while further codifications produced by Field in New York covering civil and penal law were adopted in California and other western jurisdictions but defeated in Field's home state.[100] In both places, leading arguments against codification were again civilizational: advanced societies could not codify their law, for to do so would be to freeze the progress of legal science. What appeared to some to be a hopeless mass of confusion was to common law defenders the sign of true legal sophistication. Science was, after all, sophisticated.[101] The Throop Code came in for censure in its first year and in following

---

[98] *Denver Daily Times*, Jan. 12, 1877. *Denver Daily Tribune*, Jan. 31, 1877. *Pueblo Daily Chieftain*, Jan. 25, 1877.

[99] Only Montana's revised procedure code in 1895 borrowed any material from the Throop Code—about two dozen sections on liens in a code of 3,484 sections.

[100] See Gunther A. Weiss, "The Enchantment of Codification in the Common-Law World," 25 *Yale Journal of International Law* 435 (2000). For a thorough study of the ideology of codification in India, see Robert A. Yelle, *The Language of Disenchantment: Protestant Literalism and Colonial Discourse in British India* (Oxford University Press, 2012).

[101] See, for instance, James C. Carter's classic defense of the common law against codification, *The Ideal and the Actual in the Law, Address to the American Bar Association*, August 21, 1890, at 28 ("ascertaining and declaring existing customs . . . is the work of experts who can qualify themselves only by the devotion of their lives.").

decades precisely for trying to capture all the sophistication of the New York legal system within an unwieldy 3,300 rules.[102] Codification, however, could help developing societies along law's frontier take a progressive leap forward. As India's chief codifier, Thomas Macaulay, explained, codification "cannot be well performed in an age of barbarism," but also "cannot without great difficulty be performed in an age of freedom." As India balanced between the two, however, "it is the work which especially belongs to a government like that of India—to an enlightened and paternal despotism."[103]

In the United States, Macaulay's tool of enlightened despotism spread with the anxiety that capital from the nation's economic center would remain scarce without a code of remedies that, if not in fact the law of New York, was at least endorsed by New York lawyers and their monied clients. In the two most populous and commercially advanced western states, Texas and Illinois, New York capital failed to move state legislators to adopt the code at the expense of popular sovereignty (although there were concerted efforts in both jurisdictions).[104] Lacking the self-sufficiency of those two jurisdictions, the other states of Greater Reconstruction adopted a foreign code, at times through extra-legislative means, but lawyers, legislators, and their supporters claimed the authorization of popular sovereignty in doing so. Even in North Carolina, whose Democratic newspapers daily called for the repeal of the code as an imperial imposition from New York, Republican editors proclaimed that "the movement" toward procedural codification "comes from the people, from the instinctive logic by which an unprejudiced mind grasps the advantages of the system."[105]

The history of codification on the American periphery challenges cherished notions about American federalism. On the one hand, those suspicious of centralized power and critical of national governance since the New Deal have relied on narratives that tout the equality of sovereign states to set their own policies, foster local diversity, and "experiment" with legislative solutions to local issues.[106] However, the history of legal practice and civil remedies is one in which the localism fostered by common law practice rapidly gave way to uniform regulations transmitted by a network of New York lawyers without the slightest interference of a centralized federal government. While recent histories have sought to demonstrate that nineteenth-century Americans could be quite comfortable with administrative law, accepting it as a normal part of the constitutional order, the migration of the Field Code shows how lawmaking by commission generated significant political controversy and raised

---

[102] See, for instance, "Notes," 29 *Albany Law Journal* 141, 142 (1884); Millar, *Civil Procedure of the Trial Court*, 55–56.

[103] 19 *Hansard Parliamentary Debates* 531.

[104] Texas commissioned the preparation of a code of civil procedure in 1855, and the legislature scheduled an extra session to consider it but ultimately never passed the law. 21 *Texas Reports* (Hartley) xi (1882); *Texas State Times*, Dec. 15, 1855. Reformers in the 1869 convention in Illinois attempted to pass a provision similar to the one in New York's 1846 constitution, which would have required the legislature to appoint a commission to revise practice and pleadings along the lines of the Field Code. See *Debates and Proceedings of the Constitutional Convention of the State of Illinois* (1870), 1496–98.

[105] *Weekly Standard*, May 26, 1869.

[106] See, for instance, the summary of the states-as-laboratories literature in Brian Galle & Joseph Leahy, "Laboratories of Democracy? Policy Innovation in Decentralized Governments," 58 *Emory Law Journal* 1333 (2009).

grave questions about popular sovereignty that over time were merely dodged rather than answered.[107]

The notion that lawyers were trading in a false populism to serve their own interests frequently followed the Field Code during its cross-country migration. The claim of public good, one Colorado lawyer wrote, "comes from a half-dozen or less of lawyers, who demand in the name of the people, that which these lawyers want for themselves. In other words, these lawyers want a 'code' and forthwith they shout 'vox populi.'" In the view of this common law lawyer, the People "do not pretend to understand the principles of practice and pleading at law, any more than they pretend to understand the principles of any other particular science."[108] Although he may have been just as professionally interested in maintaining his accustomed practice, the lawyer's criticism at least had the merit of accurate observation. In both the West and the South, codifiers transmuted democratic theory into support for a remedial code that elected legislators had neither the time nor inclination to read. Popular support for commercial development was taken to indicate popular support for New York's civil remedies, especially the cheapened and accelerated collection of debts.

While the quickening pace of economic time created pressures to adopt New York's creditor remedies, and while the brief spasms of legislative time spurred the wholesale adoption of Field's code, the cadences of professional legal time eventually helped to entrench what had entered so many US jurisdictions in a rush. In the same North Carolina papers that hoped to overturn the code, a news item appeared on December 16, 1870, showing just how entrenched the code had become: the bar exam was coming up. The first day would cover real property; the second day, the code of civil procedure.[109]

---

[107] On the new administrative histories, see Ernst, *Tocqueville's Nightmare*; Jerry L. Mashaw, *Creating the Administrative Constitution: The Lost One Hundred Years of American Administrative Law* (Yale University Press, 2012); Gautham Rao, *National Duties: Custom Houses and the Making of the American State* (Chicago University Press, 2016).

[108] *Rocky Mountain News*, Feb. 2, 1877.

[109] *Wilmington Journal*, Dec. 16, 1870.

5

The Code American

The Institutes of Code Practice

I

In 1888, David Dudley Field became the eleventh president of the American Bar Association. Founded in Saratoga Springs ten years earlier, the Association's charter promoted "the administration of justice and a uniformity of legislation throughout the country." But the Association's members—who hailed from solid code states like Missouri, common law states like Michigan, and Anglophile reform states like Massachusetts—disagreed over what "legislation" meant and whether national uniformity in legislation was even desirable.[1] Field hoped to use his presidency to press for national codification, but recent experience instructed that he would have to launch his efforts from a familiar point of departure: achieving codification by starting with procedure.

Two years earlier, Field had pursued a very different approach, co-drafting a resolution with municipal law theorist John F. Dillon "that the law itself should, so far as possible, be reduced to a statute."[2] Field and Dillon clarified that their proposal was a modest first step, asking "the real question[,] whether the American people should be governed by legislation or by litigation." Field pitched the resolution in nationalist terms, calling unwritten law "un-American" and concluding that "the law of the legislature, as distinguished from the law of the courts, is the necessary sequence of the American doctrine." The Association should take a stand on this general principle, Field advised, regardless of members' views on particular codification efforts.[3]

Common law lawyers quickly saw through the ploy. Henry Budd, from the anti-code state of Pennsylvania, offered what was by now a standard objection to codification. Even if a binding American code could somehow be formulated and enacted, "the code won't execute itself, [and] must be interpreted." Without a "body of jurisconsults to meet together to discuss problematical questions and decide them," there would "still be law-making by litigation as before." Budd was especially disparaging of Field's belief that codification fit naturally with American political development. According to Budd, the legal foundation of American politics was not legislative

---

[1] John A. Matzko, *Best Men of the Bar: The Early Years of the American Bar Association* (Talbot, 2019); Henry Martyn Field, *Life of David Dudley Field* (Charles Scribner's Sons, 1898), 307; Simeon E. Baldwin, "The Founding of the American Bar Association," 3 *American Bar Association Journal* 658 (1917), 695.

[2] *Report of the Ninth Annual Meeting of the American Bar Association* (1886), 11. Two other signatories to the report were George G. Wright of Iowa and Seymour D. Thompson of Missouri. *Ibid.*, 358. Wright dissented from the report because he thought it too disparaging of civil jury trials. *Ibid.*, 359. On Dillon's jurisprudence, see Hendrik Hartog, *Public Property and Private Power: The Corporation of the City of New York in American Law, 1730–1870* (Cornell University Press, 1989), 220–27.

[3] *Report of the Ninth Annual Meeting of the American Bar Association*, 328–29.

Law's Machinery. Kellen R. Funk, Oxford University Press. © Kellen R. Funk 2025. DOI: 10.1093/9780197543962.003.0006

supremacy but the federated system of independent states. But a national code was the antithesis of American-style federalism. Recasting arguments made all along the American frontier, Budd argued that codes were inherently a tool of imperial administration because only an imperialistic regime could enact a single piece of legislation across an entire continent. Things might be different if a code could "be put before the legislatures of the thirty-eight states." However, no legislation could run that gauntlet without fracturing into many inconsistent drafts. In sum, the dilemma of American codification was that no single code could achieve national consensus, and to proceed anyway was to impose legislation on unconsenting sovereigns.[4]

The prominent New York case reporter Austin Abbott offered a practical compromise, amending Field's resolution to state that "the law, so far as in its substantive principles it is settled, should be reduced to the form of a statute." The amended resolution clarified that any resulting code would not change substantive policy but only gather settled precedents in one place, somewhat like a treatise with legislative force behind it. Abbott defended the proposal as a practical question of "whether it will facilitate the labors of the profession and of the bench." Abbott knew from experience that case reports had vastly increased from the time that Jacksonian-era lawyers complained about the crushing bulk of precedential law. "Reports are multiplying so that their authority is breaking down by the mere mass of them," Abbott contended.[5] If nothing else, codification could be a labor-saving device, and that was American enough.[6]

As president in 1888, Field decided to start over, hoping to avoid the debates over the nature of legislation in general by advocating for codification only in the narrow field of procedure. Field reported a recent conversation with Senator Francis Cockrell of Missouri to work out a plan for a federal code of procedure. Field believed that the Association's support could overcome resistance in the Senate, and he urged a resolution that the Association go on record advocating a federal procedure code. Field described the resolution as more than simply adjusting practice in the federal courts. "If a Federal code of procedure is once made," he reasoned, "the codes of procedure in the various states (for I believe there will be one in every state eventually) will naturally assimilate themselves to the code of Federal procedure." In his closing remarks, Field revealed that he was both heartened but ultimately disappointed by the haphazard migration of his code. "Do gentlemen know what has already happened?" Field asked. "Do they know that the code of procedure of New York which was framed and passed in 1848, which abolished the distinction between law and equity, has gone the circuit of the world?" Yet the state that had adopted his partial draft in 1848 had rejected his final draft in 1850 and recently overwritten much of his work, and every other jurisdiction had a similar history of resistance and accommodation. Federal codification held out the promise of standardization. Resistance to the procedure code in Field's home state and along the eastern seaboard could be transcended at the federal level.[7]

---

[4] *Ibid.*, 20.

[5] *Ibid.*, 45–47.

[6] On the rise of efficiency and the "scientific management" of labor in the postbellum era, see especially John C. Wood & Michael C. Wood, eds., *F.W. Taylor: Critical Evaluations in Business and Management* (Routledge, 2002); Catherine Fisk, *Working Knowledge: Employee Innovation and the Rise of Corporate Intellectual Property, 1800–1930* (University of North Carolina Press, 2009).

[7] *Report of the Eleventh Annual Meeting of the American Bar Association* (1888), 69.

In retelling the story of his code's migration, Field betrayed just how much substantive import and ambition could be smuggled into a code of procedure. Referring in part to the adaptation of his code in western and southern states and in part to reformed English procedure for which he took credit, Field proclaimed that his "code has been followed in twenty-six states and territories of this Union, and it is followed in almost every colony where there is an English speaking people. It is in Australia, it is in Singapore, it is in Hong Kong, it is in China." The litany of Field's procedural colonies bore a remarkable resemblance to an address Field had given thirty years earlier at Albany Law School. Field stressed to the students then that codification was the key to measuring New York's stature against all other sovereigns. "Shall this imperial State be outstripped in the noble race by either of her sisters, or by that queenly island, mother of nations, which having been our parent, is now our rival?" No, he answered. In the race for empire, the Empire State would be the first to "win the well-deserved prize; that we shall have a book of our own laws, a CODE AMERICAN, not insular but continental, . . . and that work will go with our ships, our travelers, and our armies; it will march with the language, it will move with every emigration, and make itself a home in the farther portion of our own continent, in the vast Australian lands, and in the islands of the southern and western seas." Like the Code Napoleon, the Code American would be a monument of civilization. Unlike the French code, it would be "as simple as so vast a work can be made, free in its spirit, catholic in its principles!"[8]

Field's proposal to the American Bar Association in 1888 essentially proclaimed his Albany prophecy fulfilled. The Code American turned out to be a procedure code, his procedure code. It had crossed the continent and even, in Field's telling, the Western seas. It had traveled with emigrants to the West and with armies to the South. The seemingly narrow ambit of procedure was a chimera, for the procedure code had disrupted and revolutionized legal practice in more ways than a civil code could have. But the dominance that state sovereignty and American federalism afforded to the code also left its authority fragmented, its revolution incomplete. Some states avoided codification, and some, like Field's home state, took half measures that distorted his intentions. "Now," he pleaded with the Bar Association, "let us make a code of procedure for the Union, and that will lead to what we all desire, I think; to an assimilation of the practice in all the states. I hope the resolution will be adopted without a dissenting voice." It was.[9]

Fifty more years would elapse before Field and the ABA's call for a "code of procedure for the Union" would be realized in the 1938 Federal Rules of Civil Procedure. The project of federal codification would outlive Field and his Jacksonian colleagues and be carried out by a new generation of codifiers and proceduralists trained in Field's system. For that to happen, the Field Code had to win its way in the law schools and the educational regimens of young lawyers trained to view procedure as machinery and codification as modern technology. The code asked lawyers to think of procedure as nothing—the mere machinery of the law—and as everything—the summation of legal practice. In time, students caught on and became the professors in turn, though

---

[8] *Ibid.*; David Dudley Field, *Legal Reform: An Address to the Graduating Class of the Law School of the University of Albany* (1855), 32.
[9] *Report of the Eleventh Annual Meeting of the American Bar Association* (1888), 70, 79.

the task took far longer than Field had envisioned. But just as it had migrated from state to state, the Field Code eventually marched through the institutions of treatise literature, law school education, and finally, federal legislation.

II

The most important early popularizer of Field's code was not Field himself but a law clerk he encountered at a chance meeting in 1860. In one of his many failed attempts at elected office, Field found himself fighting with Albany Whigs for a chance to join the Republican nominating committee that fateful year. A young lawyer found the politicking distasteful and rose in a public session to give a fiery denouncement of the Albany machine. Field lost anyway, but the law clerk's oratory intrigued him. The next week, Field tracked down the clerk at the library of the New York Law Institute. So it was that Field became acquainted with Thomas G. Shearman, with whom he would found one of New York's most notable—and wealthiest—law firms. But when asking Shearman what he was working on at the time, Field must have been surprised to learn that the novice attorney was preparing a thousand-page commentary on Field's own code.[10]

Shearman had taken the job offer from the law librarian, "a very old lawyer, who had retired from practice" yet who was intent on publishing the definitive treatise on New York practice anyway. But of the reformed practice "he knew about as little as I did," Shearman fondly recalled. Shearman consulted the librarian several times "without the slightest benefit," and so "concluded to make the book as well as I could in my own way." Not until the work was nearly completed did Shearman gain a law license without which he could not have practiced any of the things he was writing about. "I often laugh to recall myself, a mere beginner at the study of law, without the least experience or instruction in its practice, gravely writing a book to teach lawyers and even judges how that practice should be conducted," he wrote in his memoirs.[11]

As Shearman's tale indicated, just about anyone could write a treatise. And many lawyers or would-be lawyers in the nineteenth century did, with one database of US treatises counting over ten thousand volumes during the period. Some treatises, like James Kent's *Commentaries on American Law*, produced dozens of editions and attempted to synthesize all legal knowledge to a high level of generality. Others could be more specialized, detailing practices in particular states or even particular courts. Indeed, legal treatises took such diverse approaches that modern scholarship has struggled to precisely define the genre. Many treatises introduced their subject to neophytes entering the profession, while others sought to persuade the master jurists on arcane points of legal development. Treatises took varying stances concerning objectivity, audience, and goals. Joseph Story, a prolific treatise author in the 1820s, thought

---

[10] Shearman Memoirs, 1: 99–101; Papers of Thomas G. Shearman, Shearman & Sterling Law Library. On the history of Field & Shearman, see Charles Parlin & Walter Earle, *Shearman & Sterling, 1873–1973* (Shearman & Sterling, 1973), ch. 1.

[11] Shearman Memoirs, 1:94–95. The book appeared as John L. Tillinghast & Thomas Gaskell Shearman, *Practice, Pleadings, and Forms in Civil Actions in Courts of Record in the State of New York* (Lewis & Blood, 1861).

treatises could be steppingstones to codification, while Herbert Wechsler, a prolific codifier in the 1950s, believed that codes were steppingstones to great treatises.[12]

Almost no one thought that treatises could *substitute* for codes. The authority of the twenty-five-year-old Shearman was a poor exchange for actual legislation, and the unregulated treatise market meant that purportedly synthetic "authorities" multiplied almost as rapidly as case law itself. Shearman figured that his first attempt at a treatise "ha[d] many great faults" and was valuable principally for the stipend it paid and the legal education it provided him personally.[13] While more than self-interest lay behind the publication of most treatises, it was never easy to tell just how accurate and helpful a treatise would be until it was used in practice.

Many of the early treatises after the Field Code give the sense that their authors turned a profit by presenting quick comparisons between existing New York practice and code legislation. One "treatise" did little more than reprint the code itself.[14] Others tried to follow the structure that Field's co-commissioner David Graham had used in his magisterial treatise on common law practice before the code. These treatises followed the progress of a suit at common law, quoting the code's text and commenting on predicted or observed changes to traditional practices.[15] Basically no one in the early days of the code attempted to explicate the code's possible effects on equitable practice. Since many equity proceedings were specially provided for in New York's Revised Statutes of 1829 and had not been overwritten by the code drafts New York had adopted, practitioners seem to have found the old treatises serviceable enough in the domain of equity.[16]

Alongside treatises, a new case reporter appeared in July 1848, when the code first took effect in New York. The so-called Code Reporter was complimentary toward Field, with indirect evidence that a close associate might have played an editorial role.[17] The first issue printed early judicial opinions interpreting the code, alongside

---

[12] Historiographical interest in legal treatises was revived by Angela Fernandez & Markus D. Dubber, *Law Books in Action: Essays on the Anglo-American Legal Treatise* (Bloomsbury Publishers, 2012). For responsive essays, see Richard A. Danner, "Foreword: Oh, the Treatise!," 111 *Michigan Law Review* 821 (2013); Steven Wilf, "The Legal Treatise," in Simon Stern, Maksymillian del Mar, & Bernadette Meyler, eds., *The Oxford Handbook of Law and the Humanities* (Oxford University Press, 2020). For the classic trilogy of treatise historiography, see G. Edward White, *The Marshall Court and Cultural Change, 1815–1835* (1988), 81–104; A. W. B. Simpson, "The Rise and Fall of the Legal Treatise: Legal Principles and the Forms of Legal Literature," 48 *University of Chicago Law Review* 632 (1981); Morton J. Horwitz, "Treatise Literature," pt. 3, 69 *Law Library Journal* 460 (1976). On Story, see chapter 1. On Wechsler, see Barry Wright, "Renovate or Rebuild? Treatises, Digests and Criminal Law Codification," in *Law Books in Action*, 181–201.

[13] Shearman Memoirs 1:95.

[14] John Townshend, *The New Practice in Civil Actions in the Courts of Judicature in the State of New York* (J. S. Voorhies, 1848).

[15] See, for instance, Henry Whittaker, *Practice and Pleading Under the Codes, Original and Amended* (E.O. Jenkins, 1852); George van Santvoord, *A Treatise on the Principles of Pleading in Civil Actions under the New York Code of Procedure* (Little & Co., 1852). Both are discussed at length in chapter 6.

[16] See chapter 3 on the code's repetition of the Revised Statutes of 1829 on equity practice, and chapter 9 for code practice in equity after the 1860s.

[17] A later volume of the Code Reporter gave the address of the publisher as 80 Nassau Street, an office building where numerous law partnerships operated, including among them Charles O'Connor's firm. At the time, O'Connor still supported codification and appeared alongside Field as counsel in various cases interpreting the code's meaning, including cases reported in the volumes. See, for instance, Bennett v. Hughes, 1 Code Rep. 4 (N.Y. Sup. Ct. 1848); Re Philip Walker, 1 Code Rep. 9 (N.Y. Sup. Ct. 1848); Cruger v. Douglas, 2 Code Rep. 123 (N.Y. Sup. Ct. 1850).

essays and practitioner guides such as one called "How to Read a Statute." More issues followed until 1851, when decisions interpreting the code had "become so numerous, and were often so conflicting, and so much difficulty was sometimes experienced" that the editor instead offered a digest of opinions that were being published by in other reporters. Soon there were too many cases for the digest even to index.[18]

By 1860, the early scramble to become the definitive commentary on the code had passed, and the Civil War wiped out demand for law books, causing Shearman to lament that his inaugural treatise appeared in 1861 when sales were scarcest. But as the war wound down, he was ready to try again. By then he had become a licensed attorney and Field's office manager, assisting Field with new codification projects. Although Shearman published a "second edition" of his treatise in 1865, the preface acknowledged that it was actually a fresh start. Rather than a digest of cases and holdings, the new work was a prose narrative about the code's aims and its reception in the courts. Unlike the first volume, "decisions, supposed to be erroneous, are criticized," and "there is throughout a free expression of the author's opinions."[19]

Written in Field's office, Shearman's treatise offered an insider's view of the code, and Shearman declared himself a true believer. He reported that the "conviction has grown on me more and more" that the codifiers had achieved something special. Put all other accolades aside, he continued, "It has been my chief ambition to . . . persuade the bench and bar to co-operate in building up that single and uniform system which the Code has so long offered to them in vain." The next twelve hundred pages avoided the term "equity" and rarely referred to pre-code practice. The code's preferred term, "special proceedings," appeared hundreds of times instead, and Shearman's materials followed the code's organization rather than tracking the progress of a common law case.[20] Thus, two decades after its appearance, the two-hundred-page Field Code had received a twelve-hundred-page gloss that adopted its outlook on practice and either ignored or criticized readings that failed to appreciate the code's aims.

As a work on "practice, pleadings, and forms," Shearman's treatise did not quite achieve the scope of what John H. Langbein describes as "institutionalist literature"—the attempt to comprehend all of private law within its scope and system, often in nationalist terms. Yet it would be a mistake to regard the multivolume work on practice as simply a narrow treatise on pleading. Practice, if it did not quite contain the whole of private law, was still a very large domain, and Shearman's didactic approach aimed to comprehend the whole of practice and convert practitioners to the reformed system. It even, in its way, bid to describe the code system of New York as a national system, reassuring readers by its subtitle that the work was "adapted also to the practice in

---

[18] "How to Read a Statute," 1 Code Rep. 23 (pt. I); 1 Code Rep. 34 (pt. II). On the announcement of the digest, see 2 Code Rep. 3.

[19] Shearman Memoirs 1:107, 118–21. John L. Tillinghast & Thomas G. Shearman, *Practice, Pleadings, and Forms in Civil Actions in Courts of Record in the State of New York* (Lewis Brothers, 2d rev. ed., 1865), 1:iii. While his name remained on the title page, Tillinghast had retired by the time Shearman began work on the second volume.

[20] Tillinghast & Shearman, *Practice, Pleadings, and Forms,* 1:v. For more on the substance of the treatise, see chapter 6.

California, Missouri, Indiana, Wisconsin, Kentucky, Ohio, Alabama, Minnesota, and Oregon." A code on its way to becoming American.[21]

III

The code's command over legal education took far longer than its uptake by the treatise writers. In 1838, when David Graham Jr. was appointed to the law faculty at New York University, the newly formed legal program had three departments with three professors. Reflecting Blackstone's division of the law, Benjamin F. Butler taught "the Law of Real Property," William Kent taught "the Law of Persons and Personal Property," and Graham, the future co-commissioner with David Dudley Field, taught "the Law of Pleading and Practice." This division was typical of American law schools early in the century, and over time, the "substantive" law categories expanded to include contracts, sales, partnerships, and equity. Virtually every law school also maintained a course on practice and pleadings—usually with the shortened title "Pleading"—as part of its core curriculum.[22]

"Pleading" hardly conveyed all of what went into courses on practice. Classes not only included joinder and jurisdiction, they also covered trial procedure and execution; the trajectory of litigation starting with summons or arrest and bail; and the elements necessary for claims involving contracts, property, and trusts. Only in the twentieth century would many of the latter elements be reclassified as "substantive" law. As a synonym of "practice" that eventually seemed almost redundant, "pleading" courses touched on nearly the entirety of law—only the law of property had at this point emerged with something like its own self-contained curriculum.[23]

Even into the twentieth century, Henry John Stephen's treatise on English pleading, written twenty years before the Field Code, was the standard textbook for pleading courses at most American schools. Although the treatise was revised for an American audience and sometimes annotated to keep pace with current developments, it continued to make "single-issue" pleading under the common law the foundation of legal practice.[24]

---

[21] John H. Langbein, "Chancellor Kent and the History of Legal Literature," 93 *Columbia Law Review* 547 (1993), 586–87. A decade after Shearman completed his work, another admiring treatise appeared from the California jurist John Norton Pomeroy. The work was often known by its shorthand title *Code Remedies*, and it might likewise be described in institutionalist terms. Pomeroy's work became a major vehicle for instruction on the Field Code, especially in western states. John Norton Pomeroy, *Remedies and Remedial Rights by the Civil Action, According to the Reformed American Procedure* (Little, Brown, 1876); Douglas Laycock, ed., *Modern American Remedies: Cases and Materials* (Wolters Kluwer, 4th ed., 2010), 1–2.

[22] See *Inaugural Addresses Delivered by the Professors of Law in the University of the City of New York at the Opening of the Law School of That Institution*, ed. E. B. Clayton (1838); Mary B. McManamon, "The History of the Civil Procedure Course: A Study in Evolving Pedagogy," 30 *Arizona State Law Journal* 397 (1998).

[23] For details of curricular coverage, see note 28 below.

[24] See McManamon, "The History of the Civil Procedure Course," 407, 413; Bruce A. Kimball & Pedro Reyes, "The 'First Modern Civil Procedure Course' as Taught by C.C. Langdell, 1870–78," 47 *American Journal of Legal History* 257 (2005), 259, 267, 272–73. On Stephen's treatise and single-issue pleading, see chapter 2.

At some schools, professors worked the code in, but rarely to the exclusion of Stephen's treatise. Still, the opening line to a lecture course on pleading at Columbia Law School shows just how far the codifiers' influence reached by the turn of the century. "The term civil procedure . . . includes all the machinery of law, and might be called the mechanics of law," Professor Jens Westengard announced. Yet Westengard freely admitted that it was difficult, perhaps even impossible, to teach "civil procedure" as the codifiers had envisioned it. The increasingly common term for procedure was "adjective law," rules that were external and collateral to substantive law. The term echoed the metaphor of procedure as merely the machinery of law, a field where policy experimentation could occur without affecting substantive law. But it was especially difficult to teach procedure as an independent field or to begin educating practitioners with the code itself. Professors like the Harvard-trained Westengard believed they could teach the code only comparatively, with lengthy instruction in and frequent reference to the practices the code was seeking to alter. "There is a difference between wrongs and rights," Westengard concluded his opening lecture, "and in order to present our case clearly we must go through the old process more or less."[25]

The old process, "more or less," dominated education about pleading and practice for many decades after the code had secured its place in the treatise literature of the 1870s. The earliest known course on code pleading was taught in 1871 by the president of Columbia's law department, Theodore Dwight. Following the code's chapter divisions, Dwight presented cases to interpret its obscure provisions and elucidate its major reforms, especially the acceleration of debt collection before clerks of court. Throughout the lectures, however, Dwight warned students that the code remained seriously incomplete as a system. "Proceedings in the Courts of Justice are termed remedies. The Code gives no definition of a remedy," began Dwight's opening lecture. Echoing Westengard, Dwight reminded students that "the former law must in some extent be resorted to in order to determine" the application of the code's rules.[26]

Henry Redfield, Columbia's code professor after 1900, complained that the "adjective" view of procedure was badly distorting legal education, but his solution was the same as his predecessors': to teach the code only after covering its historical antecedents in depth. Surveying the catalogs of forty-five law schools, Redfield reported with dismay that "on an average, less than one-tenth of the entire number of hours . . . is awarded to adjective law," a steep descent from midcentury when Pleading and Practice dominated the law school curriculum. Quite apart from the practical value of training lawyers in procedure, Redfield emphasized that "it will not be safe to put the substantive law on one side and the adjective law on the other." Legal science itself was incomplete "until the student knows how to make his knowledge of the substantive law practically effective for his clients," and in that sense procedure was both the

[25] R. W. Gifford student notebook on pleading, 1898–99, Jens Iverson Westengard, instructor, Alia Tutor Law Library Special Collections, Columbia Law School. Westengard's pedagogy is described more fully in "Jens Iverson Westengard," 32 *Harvard Law Review* 93 (1918).

[26] Geo. Miller student notebook on Lectures on Actions under the Code of Procedure in the State of New York, 1871–72, Theodore W. Dwight, instructor, Alia Tutor Library Special Collections, Columbia Law School.

root and the summit of legal science. Redfield asked what importance a substantive right of recovery could possibly have if procedural rules blocked enforcement. The only solution in Redfield's mind was for procedural education to cover everything "practice" did, not in one course of lectures but in several. Start with "a few introductory lectures" stressing the interrelation "of the adjective to the substantive law." Then survey the courts and remedial powers, then parties and pleadings, then details about investigation and presentation of evidence. "But whatever method is chosen, no proper course in pleading under the reformed system is possible unless it is based upon prior courses in pleading under the systems which it has succeeded," Redfield concluded, because often the theoretical principles of procedure were disclosed only by the systems rejected or modified in the codes.[27]

Attempts to replicate Redfield's now-lost data suggest that legal education was not quite as distorted as the procedural professor exclaimed. Perhaps the instructional hours were not as many as Redfield would have liked, but most law schools required students to enroll in procedure courses every term, and many curricula mirrored Columbia's by featuring a full year of common law pleading, a year of code pleading, and usually an optional year of equity pleading. Civil procedure may have hardened into a mainstay of the law school curriculum, but as the catalog sequence implies, professors found it impossible to confine civil procedure to Field's code or even to begin there.[28]

Indeed, the touchstone for modern legal education at the time did its best to ignore code practice entirely. The first synthetic course titled "Civil Procedure" came under the auspices of the famous reformer of American legal education, Christopher Columbus Langdell. As Harvard Law School's dean in 1870, Langdell's Pleading course was one of the first to employ Socratic legal education under the "case method." Until the fall of 1874, Langdell and his protégé James Barr Ames assigned individual cases while Ames compiled and edited a casebook, "Civil Procedure at Common Law." From 1874 to 1878, Langdell offered an elective on "Civil Procedure under the New York Code," but Langdell never formalized his case notes into a textbook and never resumed the brief experiment on teaching the code after 1878, even as he continued to teach and refine his Civil Procedure at Common Law class for decades thereafter.[29]

---

[27] Henry S. Redfield, "A Defect in Legal Education," 25 *Annual Report of the ABA* 545 (1902), 550–52, 549 (quoting an address by Iowa's Chancellor Emlin McClain), 554–55.

[28] This account is based on a survey of the extant catalogs from the law schools or law departments of Albany Law School, the University of California Hastings College of Law and Berkeley (Boalt Hall) School of Law, the University of Chicago Law School, Columbia Law School, Cornell Law School, Georgetown University Law Center, Harvard Law School, the University of Iowa College of Law, Indiana (Maurer) School of Law, New York University School of Law, Northwestern (Pritzker) School of Law, Notre Dame Law School, the University of South Carolina School of Law, the University of Texas Law School, Tulane Law School, Vanderbilt Law School, the University of Virginia School of Law, and Yale Law School. For a detailed guide to the extant archives and analysis of the catalog's text, see Legal Curriculum Project, Making Law Modern, https://legalmodernism.org/.

[29] Kimball & Reyes, "The 'First Modern Civil Procedure Course,'" 266–68; Daniel R. Coquillette & Bruce A. Kimball, *On the Battlefield of Merit: Harvard Law School, the First Century* (Harvard University Press, 2015), 346–47, 376–77 n.12. Langdell's notes for his code procedure course—mostly a list of cases covered—can be found in Miscellaneous (1871–1883) Handwritten Syllabi, Box 12, Folder 16, C. C. Langdell Research Notes and Correspondence, 1852–1902, Harvard Law Library.

Langdell's pedagogical method was to choose a jurisdiction and period that was deliberately foreign and outmoded, thus exhibiting to students a "fixed and definite system." Every year, his opening lecture announced that he would "confine myself wholly" to English practice of the King's Bench in the year "1830 as the standard" for analysis. Painstaking work by Bruce Kimball, Daniel Coquillette, and Pedro Reyes shows that Langdell often strayed from his baseline to comment on current developments, but that was the point. "In studying for practice," he maintained, "one's great object should be to acquire a knowledge of a system as such; every separate question should be considered with reference" to that benchmark. Thus, Langdell taught legal practice from King's Bench in the 1830s to law students in 1880s Boston because the system was just foreign enough in space in time. Langdell described the practices as "uniform," meaning they were comprehended within a single jurisdiction, and "fixed," meaning they were frozen by history, standing still long enough for the student to observe them. Left implicit was the conviction that common law procedure exhibited a timeless coherence that could not be effaced by superficial reforms as lawyers in either Boston or New York Americanized or else abolished the forms of action.[30]

Code procedure thus fell into severe neglect at Harvard, especially compared to other law schools. No matter their proximity to New York or its codes, basically all American law schools by the end of the century offered courses on code procedure taught by full members of the academic faculty, but not Harvard. Before the fall term in 1892, Langdell wrote in annoyance to Harvard's president to inform him that under student pressure, Langdell was returning code procedure to the curriculum, but the course would be offered only for an hour on Saturdays. The leading candidate for the position was a New York law office manager who was writing a treatise on New York practice, but Langdell worried that while the man "would presumably know the routine of practice by heart," he would "know very little of its theory or principles." Langdell preferred finding "a graduate of our school" rather than taking "the great risk in bringing a total stranger from New York." Even decades after Langdell's deanship ended, code procedure occupied the same disfavored status at Harvard. It was offered usually every other year as an after-hours elective and never taught by a member of the faculty. Even as Langdellians appropriated the code's title "civil procedure," Harvard primarily trained and tested students in the common law forms of action that the code formally abolished[31] (see Figure 5.1).

As Langdell's method of teaching law primarily through appellate case decisions spread to other programs, professors gradually applied it to code instruction as well.

---

[30] Quoted in Kimball & Reyes, "The 'First Modern Civil Procedure Course,'" 271, 278–79. On the history of procedural reform in Massachusetts, see William E. Nelson, *Americanization of the Common Law: The Impact of Legal Change on Massachusetts Society, 1760–1830* (University of Georgia Press, 1994 [1975]). Perhaps Langdell, like others, had begun to notice that New York's code remained seriously incomplete. See especially chapter 6.

[31] Christopher Columbus Langdell to Charles Eliot, August 22, 1892, Records of the President of Harvard University, Charles W. Eliot. UAI 5.150 Box 22, Folder: 1892, L-M. Harvard University Archives. See also "The Law School," 6 *Harvard Law Review* 150 (1892) (announcing the new course). The candidate was only referred to as "Miller" in the letter but was almost certainly George A. Miller, a long-time associate of James C. Carter's firm in New York City and author of *An Introduction to Practice with Special Reference to the New York Code of Civil Procedure* (Leslie J. Tompkins, 1903).

LAW SCHOOL OF HARVARD UNIVERSITY. 1891–92.

CIVIL PROCEDURE.

[Give reasons in all cases.]

I. Declaration, bad in form. Plea, bad in substance. Replication, bad in form. Special demurrer. Judgment for whom?

2. ASSUMPSIT for non-payment of the price of a horse. Plea that the sale was induced by fraud on the part of the plaintiff, in that he failed to disclose the unsound condition of the horse, of which he was well aware. Demurrer. On the argument of the demurrer the counsel for the defendant contended that even if mere silence as to a known defect was not of itself a defence, yet the demurrer admitted the allegation of fraud in the plea, and, therefore, the defendant must have judgment. Is this reasoning sound?

3. TRESPASS by A against X for assault and battery. Plea, not guilty. At the time X offered evidence that he was endeavoring to separate his dog from an attacking dog and in so doing raised his cane and unintentionally and without knowing it struck A who was standing behind him, which was the alleged trespass. The evidence was excluded. X moves for a new trial. Should it be allowed?

4. CASE by A against X for publicly uttering the words, " A is an incorrigible scold," whereby M was induced to break his engagement to be married to A. Plea that M at the time was already married to another woman. Special demurrer. Judg-ment for A or X?

5. CASE by A against X for suffering the sparks to escape from a locomotive set in motion by X on his railway, whereby A's house was burnt down. Plea that X had been authorized by the State to use locomotives on the said railway. Replication that the destruction of the house was due to the carelessness with which X managed the locomotive. Demurrer. Judgment for A or X?

6. CASE by A against X for a malicious prosecution. Plea that the prosecution was still pending at the time of action brought. Special demurrer. Judgment for A or X?

7. ASSUMPSIT. In consideration that A promised to abandon a pending action against M, X promised to pay A the amount of his claim. Averment, that A abandoned the action. Breach, non-payment by X. Plea, *non-assumpsit*. X offered evidence that the action against M was groundless, and known

Figure 5.1 Draft civil procedure examination at Harvard Law School, 1892.

Harvard Law School Scrapbooks, 1870–1913, Historical & Special Collections, Harvard Law School Library.

The first casebook on code pleading was published by the prolific digester Austin Abbott, who taught code procedure at New York Law School in 1893.[32] Courses and casebooks on the code were ubiquitous by the first decade of the twentieth century, many with a regional focus on code practice in Ohio, Missouri, or New York, including special editions for law students at Columbia.[33] In 1913, Professor Edson Sunderland authored one of the more prominent code pleading casebooks for his four-part procedure curriculum in the emphatically uncodified state of Michigan, covering a wide range of common law pleading, code pleading, trial practice, and appellate practice.[34] But while casebooks on the code abounded, most treated their subject as one subpart of a broader procedure curriculum, as in Sunderland's series.

The first attempt to treat code procedure as a field unto itself was Charles E. Clark's 1928 *Handbook of the Law of Code Pleading*, written just before Clark assumed the deanship of Yale Law School (see Figure 5.2). The *Handbook* opened with an expression of regret that "except for local and semi-local practice and form books," likely a reference to Shearman's treatise, "one must go back to the early days of the codes to find any attempts to set forth the subject as a unified whole." Clark aimed to provide that unity "notwithstanding the chance intervention of state lines." By focusing on "the code system of pleading which followed the New York Code reform of 1848," Clark essentially described code practice as a stateless system, the practice of nowhere in particular. Like Langdell's 1830s version of King's Bench, code practice in Clark's manual was a construction of his own making so that students could grasp a sense of the system *as* a system and appreciate what Clark frequently praised as the "modern" innovations of the reformed system.[35]

"Modern" seemed to be Clark's highest term of approbation. Much of his procedural scholarship declared one or another device the leading edge of legal modernity. "No procedure can be considered really modern which does not strive for the union of law and equity actually obtaining in the more advanced code States," he pronounced in one article. In another, he defended his preference for pleading in the alternative as "the most modern view." As these illustrations suggest, Clark defined legal modernity not through high theory but through reference to practical procedural devices. Clark similarly described to the ABA an "underlying philosophy" that "basic provisions" of his forthcoming draft code would share with "all pleading reform of modern times." Instead of discussing metaphysical principles of law or normativity, Clark offered as his "basic philosophy" a description of concrete procedural devices only a lawyer

---

[32] Austin Abbott, *Select Cases on Code Pleading with Notes* (2d rev. ed., 1895).

[33] Charles M. Hepburn, *A Selection of Cases and Statutes on the Principles of Code Pleading* (W.H. Anderson and Co., 1901); Edward W. Hinton, *A Selection of Cases on the Law of Pleading Under Modern Codes* (Callaghan & Co., 1906); Henry S. Redfield, *Selected Cases on Code Pleading and Practice in New York* (Banks Law Publishing, 1903).

[34] Edson R. Sunderland, *Cases on Procedure Annotated: Code Pleading* (Callaghan, 1913). The other leading casebooks on code pleading before Sunderland's works appeared were Edwin Bryant, *The Law of Pleading Under the Codes of Civil Procedure* (Little, Brown, 1894); Philemon Bliss, *A Treatise Upon the Law of Pleading Under the Codes of Civil Procedure* (F.H. Thomas and Co., 1879).

[35] Charles E. Clark, *Handbook of the Law of Code Pleading* (West, 1928), iii. To put it in Kuhnian terms, Clark's *Handbook* was the first major pedagogical work to treat the code as normal science, the paradigm by which all other data were rationalized the agenda for future research set. See Thomas S. Kuhn, *The Structure of Scientific Revolutions* (Chicago University Press, 3d ed., 1996 [1962]).

Figure 5.2 A portrait of Charles Edward Clark by the Kaiden-Kazanjian studio, taken around 1938, when Clark had just overseen the drafting of the Federal Rules of Civil Procedure.

Historical & Special Collections, Harvard Law School Library.

could love: "the generality of allegation and the free joinder of claims and parties."[36] For Clark, modernity inhered in procedure itself.

At one point in his commentary on procedure codes, Clark replaced the word "modernity" with "the universal trend of Anglo-Saxon procedural reform," but the "Anglo-Saxon" in Clark's usage had lost the civilizational determinism it bore for earlier codifiers. "Anglo-Saxon" was a historically accurate descriptor, Clark believed, because he was talking about procedures in England and America since the seventeenth century, but history showed only a series of accidents, not destiny. Clark contrasted procedure's history to "some inherent or fundamental necessity," and elsewhere, he explained that legal history's "most important function is still perhaps to demonstrate

---

[36] Charles E. Clark, "Procedural Reform and the Supreme Court," 8 *American Mercury* 445 (1926), 447; Charles E. Clark, "The Code Cause of Action," 33 *Yale Law Journal* 817 (1924), 826; Charles E. Clark, "The New Federal Rules of Civil Procedure: The Last Phase—Underlying Philosophy Embodied in Some of the Basic Provisions of the New Procedure," 23 *ABA Journal* 976 (1937), 976.

the falsity of so much of what passes in its name." While Harvard soaked its students in historical pleading materials to help them understand the superficiality of the codes and their attempted reforms, Clark's classes at Yale reverted to the same histories so that students could appreciate the errors of the past and the brilliance of modern reform. Where earlier codifiers had surmised that a code's common law or civilian origins could mark a disastrous departure down the path of servility, Clark maintained that modernity had no provenance. It inhered in the pragmatic experience of what worked and did not work in litigation over time. And for Clark, "the first modern system of practice," was "the New York Code of 1848, the work of David Dudley Field and his associates, and the model of the code reform of pleading which has been adopted in a majority of American states."[37]

Despite his penchant for modernity, Clark opted to use the older term "pleading" instead of "procedure" in his *Handbook*. His text omitted material on jurisdiction, trial, and enforcement, yet it exhibited the resilient capaciousness of "pleading" by covering summonses; remedies; "particular actions" such as those for debt, negligence, fraud, and title; and all manner of joinder actions, including class actions. The most significant omission from the book was a systematic treatment of common law practice, which, unlike his casebook-writing predecessors, Clark did not think necessary to understand code pleading as a system. The history of the common law was set out in two pages, and rarely did the text reference practice "before the codes." Langdell had reached back fifty years into the semi-foreign jurisdiction of King's Bench to find a representative model of procedure, a way to map and articulate practices that everywhere resisted articulation. Fifty years later, Clark found his map in Field's code. As Clark began his efforts at procedural codification in the next decade, he claimed his own code, prepared for the federal courts, "represent[ed] a present-day interpretation and execution of what are at bottom the Field principles."[38] Clark's code was not Field's all over again, of course, but when the federal code Field had called for finally arrived, it was what Field had dreamed: a draft that treated code procedure with the reverence and gravity that only the common law had previously garnered.

IV

After Field died in 1894, the drive for national uniformity continued in the ABA, but it was carried on by a new generation of administrator lawyers who did not share Field's

---

[37] Clark, "The New Federal Rules of Civil Procedure," 977; Charles E. Clark, "The Challenge of a New Federal Civil Procedure," 20 *Cornell Law Quarterly* 443, 444 (1935); Charles E. Clark, "The Handmaid of Justice," 23 *Washington University Law Quarterly* 297, 305 (1938).

[38] Clark, *Handbook of the Law of Code Pleading*, iii–viii; Charles E. Clark, "Code Pleading and Practice Today," in Allison Reppy, ed., *David Dudley Field: Centenary Essays* (New York University Press, 1949), 64. Stephen Subrin's leading account argues that Clark "misled [students] about the relationship of the Field and the Federal Rules" because "calling on the past" was a way of "reducing opposition" in the political present. Stephen N. Subrin, "David Dudley Field and the Field Code: A Historical Analysis of an Earlier Procedural Vision," 6 *Law & History Review* 311 (1988), 312–13. His study is not wrong to note that "Field's nineteenth-century world and his codes are vastly different from the twentieth-century world and the Federal Rules of Charles Clark and the legal realists," but "vastly" is an overstatement, as Part II of this volume illustrates.

Jacksonian ideas about an artisan bar struggling with overwork and inadequate fees. New technologies like the West system of digests and Frank Shepard's citational index helped practitioners to navigate the blizzard of new precedents. At the same time, Field and Shearman's example showed lawyers how unregulated fees could produce spectacular wealth from corporate clients. As late as 1888, Field insisted that codification's chief virtue would be comprehending an entire legal subject in one volume.[39] By contrast, legal luminaries at the turn of the century, including Harvard Law's dean Roscoe Pound and Secretary of State Elihu Root, saw codification's virtue as the systemization of law at a higher level of abstraction instead of a comprehensive synthesis of legal details.

For an ABA law reform committee in 1909, Pound drew up a guiding principle for turn-of-the-century codification: "Whenever in the future practice acts or codes of procedure are drawn up or revised, the statutes should deal only with the general features of procedure, ... leaving details to be fixed by rules of court." In 1912, when the US Supreme Court promulgated a chaotically organized set of detailed Equity Rules, Root issued a similar call: "The method [of code procedure] is wrong; the theory is wrong; and ... the true remedy is to sweep from our statute books the whole mass of detailed provisions and substitute a simple Practice Act containing only the necessary, fundamental rules of procedure."[40]

Root's invocation of a "Practice Act" conjured examples from close to home and across the Atlantic. Connecticut had adopted a reformed Practice Act in 1879 that drew not on the Field codes but rather on the English Judicature Acts of the 1870s. Likewise, Pound's proposals sounded strikingly similar to the philosophy expressed in the great German civil code, the *Bürgerliches Gesetzbuch* (BGB), promulgated on the first day of the new century. In German legal theory, the point of a code was not to gather together all of the law currently in force—the early Anglo-American ideal shared by Field, William Sampson, and Jeremy Bentham—but to systematize the theory of law, to provide a framework and an outline, the details of which would only gradually be worked out locally. General principles were the stuff of codification. Details—including detailed exceptions to the general principles—were better left to be enumerated elsewhere, if at all. In England's Judicature Acts, the new generation of codifiers saw an early illustration of this approach. Shorter than any American code, the English acts had in a dozen pages outlined a procedural system and then consciously turned that system over to case law and ministerial regulation for further refinement.[41]

---

[39] On the West digesting system, see Robert C. Berring, "Full-Text Databases and Legal Research: Backing into the Future," 1 *High Tech Law Journal* 27 (1986), 29–33; on Shepard, see Patti Ogden, "Mastering the Lawless Science of Our Law: A Story of Legal Citation Indexes," 85 *Law Library Journal* 1 (1993). David Dudley Field, *Legal Reform: An Address to the Graduating Class of the Law School of the University of Albany* (1855); Field, "The Study and Practice of the Law," 14 *Democratic Review* 345 (1844), 345–47; *Report of the Eleventh Annual Meeting of the American Bar Association* (1888), 69.

[40] *Report of the Thirty-Fourth Annual Meeting of the American Bar Association* (1909), 595. For a biography of Pound that connects his common law reformism to the large-scale organization of litigation, see John Fabian Witt, *Patriots and Cosmopolitans: Hidden Histories of American Law* (Harvard University Press, 2007), 211–78. Elihu Root, "Reform of Procedure," 34 *New York State Bar Association Report* 87 (1911), 89.

[41] *The Practice Act of the State of Connecticut* (1879); The Supreme Court of Judicature Act, 36 & 37 Vict. c. 66 (1873); The Supreme Court of Judicature Act, 38 & 39 Vict. c. 77 (1875). See Roscoe Pound, "Some

The new codifiers also had a salient negative example: New York's revised code. In 1876, a code commission chaired by Montgomery H. Throop, a well-bred lawyer from Utica, promulgated a code of civil procedure that, unlike Field's code, aimed to codify practice without altering it. Over six painstaking years of full-time effort, Throop assiduously avoided changing anything he understood to be the governing law of practice while trying to incorporate every interpretation, ruling, and application New York's courts had given the Field Code into enumerated sections. The result was a code of almost four thousand articles bereft of guiding principles and carrying over only a few sentences from Field's originals. Since it made no meaningful changes to the law, the code sailed through enactment. Yet from the day it was published, the Throop Code was met with derision from all quarters—traditionalists, code partisans, and especially ordinary lawyers just trying to navigate the unwieldy new statute.[42] Like a map drawn at the same scale as its subject, the Throop Code showed the new theorists of codification that a truly comprehensive code of practice would, ironically, be most impractical.

For the new codifiers, Throop's failures were just an exaggerated version of what had gone wrong with the original Field codes. Comprehensiveness of legislation rather than systemization was, in this account, bound to fail. The New York jurist Learned Hand wrote in private correspondence that "I live in a State where the practice is as barbarous as could well be designed. . . . The truth is that judicial procedure is like history and that nation is happiest which has the least." Throop's attempt to tediously describe every possible exception to otherwise clear rules "is at present thoroughly discredited I think in all responsible circles," Hand concluded. By now, codifiers' disillusionment with the legislative process was reaching a zenith. Hand stated that "after repeated efforts," it was clear "nothing can be done in the legislature." Another lawyer complained that "the laymen have legislated for us until they have clothed every step in procedure, both civil and criminal, with a maze of technicality." As one Seventh Circuit judge noted, the proper legislation advocated by Pound and Root could take years of lobbying and still be derailed by horse-trading politics, if it could even secure "legislative attention" in the first place.[43]

Principles of Procedural Reform," 4 *Illinois Law Review* 388 (1910), 447; "The English Judicature Act and the American Codes," 64 *Central Law Journal* 105 (1907), 105. On the theory of the German code, see Roger Berkowitz, *The Gift of Science: Leibniz and the Modern Legal Tradition* (Harvard University Press, 2010), 137–58. On the ferment of intellectual exchange across the Atlantic at this time, see generally Daniel T. Rodgers, *Atlantic Crossings: Social Politics in a Progressive Age* (Belknap, 1998).

[42] For the definitive edition, see William Wait, *The Code of Civil Procedure of the State of New York, Enacted 1876, and Amended 1877* (William Gould and Son, 1877). For Throop's report with his commentary, see Montgomery H. Throop, *The New Revision of the Statutes of the State of New York: The Code of Remedial Justice* (Weed, Parsons and Co., 1876). [Walter D. Edmonds], *Memorial of the Honorable Montgomery H. Throop* (1892), 9–11. On the early criticisms, see Note, 29 *Albany Law Journal* 142 (1884); Current Topics, 1 *Kansas Law Journal* 393 (1884); David Dudley Field, *The Latest Edition of the New York Code of Civil Procedure* (1878).

[43] Learned Hand, U.S. Court of Appeals for the Second Circuit, to Thomas Walsh, May 25, 1926; C. L. Young, President of the North Dakota Bar Association, to Thomas Walsh, May 21, 1926; Samuel Alschuler, U.S. Court of Appeals for the Seventh Circuit, to Thomas Walsh, June 12, 1926. Thomas J. Walsh Papers, Library of Congress Manuscript Division. See also *New York State Bar Association Report* 16 (1893), 51; J. Newton Fiero, "David Dudley Field and His Work," 51 *Albany Law Journal* 39, 43 (1895).

Edson Sunderland, a Michigan law professor who had studied in Berlin and would eventually help draft the Federal Rules, showed how interest in codification could perfectly combine with disparagement of legislators in this era. The need to get the legislature out of the way of codification was the great lesson of legal history in Sunderland's account. "If David Dudley Field had been a more thorough student of the history of the common law," Sunderland wrote, "he would not have been so readily fascinated by the novel principle of legislative control of judicial procedure." Working through legislation "seemed to offer unlimited possibilities," but, thought Sunderland, ordinary legislators could barely comprehend "the delicate adjustment of machinery necessary to an efficient administration of justice."[44]

The Field commissioners had used images of machinery to shift control of procedural reform toward the legislature. By contrast, twentieth-century architects of a federal code used that imagery to wrest control *away* from idiosyncratic legislators. Sunderland explained that, even if lawyer-legislators drafted bills, "the political atmosphere of a legislative assembly is not friendly to the close and painstaking study of an intricate mechanism which is necessary for successful regulation." Legislation generally exhibited "crude draftsmanship," but when it came to forging modern procedures, such crude drafting threatened "to disorganize the entire machinery of justice."[45]

Field, too, appreciated the "delicacy" of the procedural machine and insisted experts like himself would best rebuild the machine. But in Field's day, calling procedure "machinery" signaled its relative unimportance *so that* the legislature could get involved in its reform. As the "mere machinery" of the law, procedure was both desacralized and denaturalized, left open to political experimentation on the legislative floor. Now "machinery" elevated procedure beyond the competence of any legislature, and the new codifiers cared little if the results were undemocratic. "The New York legislature believed that the courts could be entirely regulated by the clumsy and alien hand of the popular assembly," Sunderland sneered, "and yet suffer no loss either in technical skill or in capacity to respond to the public demand for service."[46] Though the significance of "machinery" had shifted subtly, two generations agreed that seasoned practitioners should control the regulation of legal practice. The difference between Field and Sunderland was that Field thought he had to work with a legislature to accomplish codification. The new codifiers wondered if there might not be a way around the legislature entirely, at least when it came to the machinery of the law.

The new codifiers thus drew inspiration from Continental and English practice acts, recoiled from the tedious detail of the Throop Code, and preferred to work apart from the normal legislative process when they could. Altogether, modern codification theory coalesced around these themes. When yet another code commission was

---

[44] Edson Sunderland, "The Regulation of Legal Procedure," 35 *West Virginia Law Quarterly* 301 (1929), 308. The machinery metaphor was used this way again by Thomas W. Shelton in reporting a draft federal code prepared by the ABA. See Hearings on ABA Bills Before the House Committee on the Judiciary, 63d Congress, 2d Session (1914), 22–23.

[45] Sunderland, "The Regulation of Legal Procedure," 305.

[46] *Ibid.*, 310. See also Alschuler to Walsh, June 12, 1926; John Owen Roberts, "Trial Procedure—Past, Present and Future," 15 *ABA Journal* 667 (1929), 668.

formed in New York in 1915, its report summarized three principles drawn from the lessons of second-generation codification. First, "substantive" law belonged outside the machinery of procedure and could be left to the legislature to prescribe. This category included much that had crept into the original Field codes, including the jurisdiction of the courts as well as politically contentious rules such as executions of judgments against debtors. The New York report explained that the Field Code had covered too many substantive topics in its quest for comprehension. In a modern rearrangement of the law, "so many provisions formerly in the code [should be] inserted in substantive statutes." In the commissioners' view, only depoliticized procedural machinery would remain for proper codification.[47]

Second, procedure had to be regulated by a relatively small set of general principles or rules. Commentators frequently referred to this ideal as a "practice act," but paradoxically wished to drain the term of legislative import. How an "act" was to gain authority without legislative initiative was not spelled out in the report, but the commissioners were clear that legislators were ill-suited to be the primary draftsmen. Instead, the commissioners urged courts to take the lead in drafting procedural rules, including by delegating the task to a panel of experts, perhaps with nothing more than an up-or-down vote of legislative approval for the practice act as it emerged. Such a structure would, the commissioners argued, reach a happy medium "between the two extremes of regulating procedure substantially by rules of court and that of regulating procedure substantially by statute." The trick was to capture the authority of the legislature without compromising expertise in the drafting.[48]

Third, the codification of general principles would leave the details of practice to case law or local court rules. Such decentralization would allow small issues to be quickly and easily addressed by courtroom administration rather than by the drawnout politicking involved in repealing or replacing statutory law and would avoid the disorganization that legislatures inevitably produced. The new conviction that a proper code eschewed comprehension in favor of guiding principles was widely acclaimed. While New York's commission was getting organized, the ABA created a committee to report on uniform judicial procedure. William Hornblower, a longstanding critic of Field, served on both the New York board and the ABA committee. In both venues he encouraged his colleagues to avoid Field's "statutory idea," whereby the legislature regulated even the "details of practice by statute," but he also discouraged following the "English idea," which did the opposite by leaving courts totally in control of practice without legislative guidance. The "intermediate procedural system which might be called the advanced American system" would have a statute deal with "important matters of procedure, jurisdictional and otherwise, leaving the details of practice to court rules."[49]

---

[47] *Report of the Board of Statutory Consolidation on the Simplification of the Civil Practice in the Courts of New York* (J.B. Lyon, 1915), 1:176–77.

[48] Ibid., 173–75; *Report of the Board of Statutory Consolidation of the State of New York on a Plan for the Simplification of the Civil Practice in the Courts of this State* (J.B. Lyon Co., 1912), 9.

[49] *Report of the Board of Statutory Consolidation* (1915), 165–67. For Hornblower's critique of Field, see William B. Hornblower, *Is Codification of the Law Expedient? An Address Delivered before the American Social Science Association* (1888). *Report of the Board of Statutory Consolidation* (1912), 23–24, 29–30.

In 1917, the ABA supported efforts by Senator George Sutherland (a future Supreme Court Justice) to legislate this "American system" for the federal courts, preserving Congress's power over "fundamental" matters in theory but not always in effect. The proposed bill gave the Supreme Court authority to prescribe "the forms for and the kind and character of the entire pleading, practice, and procedure to be used in all actions, motions and proceedings at law," but left to Congress "jurisdictional and fundamental matters." The ABA's Committee on Uniformity clarified that Congress would maintain control over "the legal machine through which justice is to be administered, as distinguished from the actual operation thereof," which would now be the Court's to regulate.[50] Thus, concluded the ABA, the legislature would continue to hardwire the mere machinery of the law as it had, in theory, since the early days of the Field Code. Although turn-of-the-century codifiers rejected Field's aims for codification, the potent image of procedure as machinery continued to wield its double-edged meaning for legislative authority. Procedure as the mere machinery of the law invited legislative oversight, yet it simultaneously pointed up the inadequacies of amateur legislators to rework its tools. Academics like Edson Sunderland hoped to free law's machinery from legislative interference altogether, but for reformers who worked in Congress on federal codification, law's machinery continued to stand as an invitation to legislative involvement and experimentation.

V

While the ABA spoke of federal codification as an inevitability in 1915, opponents pushed back for two long decades. Neither the Sutherland bill nor a substantially revised act by William Howard Taft (which threw the fusion of law and equity into the mix) came close to passage, although the ABA promoted them with annual statements of support during the 1920s. Instead, the enabling legislation for an "American system" of procedure was continually stymied by a remarkable populist senator from the West, the heart of Field Code country.[51]

Thomas J. Walsh came from a true Field Code state. Not only had Montana operated under Field's procedure code for nearly half a century when Walsh became a US senator in 1913, it also followed California by enacting Field's civil, criminal, and political codes in 1895.[52] Walsh sympathized with Field's aspiration to promulgate the "Code American," noting in a speech about procedure that "Field entertained the hope that his code, or something modeled upon it, would come into universal use." Walsh could not himself "understand why it has not. Having been

<hr/>

[50] S. 4551, 64th Congress, 1st Session (1916); "Report of the Committee on Uniform Judicial Procedure," 6 *ABA Journal* 509 (1920), 517. For a marvelously detailed legislative history of the Rules Enabling Act and its many false starts in Congress, including the influence of New York reform proposals, see Stephen B. Burbank, "The Rules Enabling Act of 1934," 130 *University of Pennsylvania Law Review* 1015 (1982). On the distinction between form and fundamental jurisdiction, see *ibid.*, 1066 n.228.

[51] See Burbank, "The Rules Enabling Act of 1934," 1069–1098; S. 2061, 68th Congress, 1st Session (1924); see also 65 *Congressional Record* 1074 (1924).

[52] See Andrew P. Morriss et al., "Debating the Field Civil Code 105 Years Late," 61 *Montana Law Review* 371 (2000).

bred under it, I am convinced it approaches as near simplicity and perfection as any mere human work may."[53] Despite endorsing Field's proposals for other states, however, Walsh adamantly opposed any plan to have Congress legislate a national uniform code.

Walsh arrived in the Senate just in time to thwart the best hope the ABA had had in years for their federal code project. Before his term, the ABA had forwarded a draft code of 381 sections to Congress. After the House bill died in a Senate committee, code proponents shifted tactics. Instead of drafting the code themselves, the ABA's Committee on Uniform Judicial Procedure advised on *how* a code should be put together. Their next proposal offered simpler legislation that would allow the Supreme Court or an advisory commission to draw up a code of procedure. Walsh held up the proposal, now known as an "enabling act," both when it was introduced in 1917 and until the end of his twenty-year career in the Senate. Walsh told a disgruntled lobbyist, "I have never conducted anything like a filibuster against the [procedural reform] bill before the committee or sought at any time to delay its consideration," protesting that, although he came to hearings prepared to argue against the proposal, each time he "found there was no quorum present." Some speculated Walsh was not so innocent, and may have had a hand in keeping a quorum from forming.[54]

Either way, Walsh made significant efforts to rally opposition. He sent surveys to every US attorney's office and every federal judge, including the Justices of the Supreme Court. Of those who wrote back, twenty-seven federal judges opposed codification, along with six US attorneys, as compared to nineteen judges and one US attorney favoring it.[55] Walsh received lengthy but shallow letters supporting codification from Supreme Court Justices Sutherland and McReynolds, while Justice Brandeis wrote back cryptically, "I am unreservedly against the measure. Ten years ago—before my experience on the Court—I thought otherwise," with no other explanation. Justice Holmes, mingling his characteristic deference to legislatures with his cynicism that any progress would thereby result, opined only that "I see the objection much more clearly than I can see the possible, I hesitate to say probable, advantages," without stating what the objection was.[56] The more detailed correspondence rehearsed the arguments against codification that had resounded through the debates of the past century: codification required more skill than American legislators possessed, while delegating the work of drafting to unelected commissioners contravened democratic principles; procedure remained an undefined category, so a procedure code invited mischievous expansions; even the simplest code would

[53] Thomas Walsh, *Reform of Federal Procedure: Address Delivered at the Meeting of the Tri-State Bar Association at Texarkana* (April 23, 1926), 8.

[54] See H.R. 15,578, 63d Congress, 2d Session (1914); 51 *Congressional Record* 10,615 (1914); S. 2061, 68th Congress, 1st Session (1924); see also 65 *Congressional Record* 1074 (1924)—what Burbank refers to as the "Sutherland Bill." Burbank, "The Rules Enabling Act of 1934," 1075–76. Thomas Walsh to Charles B. Letton, May 27, 1926, Thomas J. Walsh Papers.

[55] Answers Received from United States Judges and District Attorneys to Letters Sent Asking Their Opinion on the Procedural Bill S. 477, undated memorandum, Thomas J. Walsh Papers.

[56] George Sutherland to Thomas Walsh, May 29, 1926; Oliver Wendell Holmes Jr. to Thomas Walsh, May 22, 1926; Louis D. Brandeis to Thomas Walsh, May 14, 1926; James Clark McReynolds to Thomas Walsh, June 9, 1926; Harlan F. Stone to Thomas Walsh, May 17, 1926; Willis Van Devanter to Thomas Walsh, June 22, 1926, Thomas J. Walsh Papers.

contain ambiguities and accrete hundreds of interpretations little better than the system the code was replacing.[57]

Walsh had some sympathy with the democracy argument—his own state had not relied on an extralegislative commission either time it adopted Field's codes—but Walsh's objections to a federal code turned almost entirely on protecting the monopoly of a local bar over its local, practical knowledge. Walsh wrote to the prominent New York attorney Robert H. Jackson that a federal code would "foist upon the public a system that would require ninety-nine out of every hundred lawyers to learn two procedures of practice," the local system and the federal. Walsh's concern for localism crystallized in his popular slogan: "I am for the one hundred [lawyers] who stay at home as against the one who goes abroad."[58]

Elsewhere, Walsh handwaved at the idea that procedure "should remain . . . for local experiment in prompt effectiveness," but states as laboratories of procedure were clearly a secondary concern to Walsh's protectionism on behalf of the local bar. Walsh repeatedly emphasized that lawyers who stayed home should only need to know state court procedure. When critics charged that Walsh thought his constituents too "lazy or unintelligent that they cannot learn the new [federal] rules without great effort," his defenders retorted that it was the other way around: it was the elite national attorneys who rarely bothered to learn local procedure, and having the recourse to a nationally uniform federal code would mean they would never need to.[59]

The defense was elaborated by one of Walsh's admirers, a West Virginian lawyer named Connor Hall. In a lengthy editorial that the ABA continually refused to publish, Hall voiced his frustration that proponents of federal codification "speak of uniformity as if it were some excellence in itself, something transcendental and absolute; or at least as an undoubted blessing, as health, happiness, and virtue." But Hall thought that procedural uniformity would only "augment the importance of large aggregations," thereby tending "toward centralization and the further destruction of local character and influence." Such corporate centralization had become obvious in legal practice. Distinctive state court procedures forced the large corporate law firms to hire local counsel to litigate or advise in remote locales like Montana and West Virginia, but a system of federal courts with uniform practices would allow elite corporate lawyers to feel at home everywhere. It would allow "a firm in a great city" on its own to "conduct the main parts of the litigation and reduce the local lawyers substantially to filing clerks," Hall predicted.[60]

---

[57] See William L. Walls to Thomas Walsh, October 26, 1927; Chester I. Long, President of the American Bar Association, to Thomas Walsh, June 5, 1926; George C. Scott, U.S. District Court for the Northern District of Iowa, to Thomas Walsh, June 5, 1926, Thomas J. Walsh Papers.

[58] Thomas Walsh to Robert H. Jackson, April 19, 1927, Thomas J. Walsh Papers; Walsh, *Reform of Federal Procedure*, 2. For an overview arguing for the "modernity" of a populism that both criticized centralization and corporatism but also emulated them for an effective politics, see Charles Postel, *The Populist Vision* (Oxford University Press, 2007).

[59] Thomas Walsh to S.R. Childs, June 25, 1926; Charles B. Letton to Thomas Walsh, May 22, 1926, Thomas J. Walsh Papers.

[60] Connor Hall, "Uniform Law Procedure in Federal Courts," unpublished editorial sent to the *ABA Journal*, dated October 15, 1926, Thomas J. Walsh Papers. See also George W. McClintic, U.S. District Court for the Southern District of West Virginia, to Thomas Walsh, May 20, 1926, Thomas J. Walsh Papers;

Critiques of federal uniformity thus briefly revived Jackson-era arguments about artisan legal practice and fears of a degraded bar. Only this time, the threat was not that low-class pettifoggers would crowd the docket with frivolous filings but rather that legal amateurs would insert themselves at the top, stifling real practitioners from atop New York's business firms. "Uniformity increases the influence and importance of the great city firm, having at its head, perhaps, some business man masquerading as a lawyer," Hall thought.[61] Rather than perpetual journeymen unable to earn a competency, lawyers' nightmares had modernized into a vision of lawyers as cogs in a machine run by professionals who were no longer masters of legal science but of the scientific management of business.

Just as uniformity distinctively favored national corporate interests, so did the flexible category of "procedure." Senator Walsh was especially sensitive that a federal code might delve into numerous substantive policy disputes. Would limitations on the time or maximum recovery of remedies be a procedure regulated by the codifiers or a substantive policy set by Congress, Walsh's interlocutors wondered? Would "procedure" dictate if imprisonment were an allowable remedy in civil cases—on a party's mere affidavit, or with something more required? What about jurors—were women eligible to serve? Most importantly, would the national code that answered these questions speak with the voice of a progressive Congress or a conservative Court?[62]

In answering Walsh's survey, some proponents of federal codification accepted their populist rivals' factual assumptions. The US attorney for Wyoming wrote that "as a rule those appearing in important matters in the federal court make federal court practice more or less of a specialty," and he did not want to see the elite federal bar "handicap[ped]" by federal courts following local procedure. Similarly, a district judge in Alabama, Henry Clayton, advised local lawyers to learn whatever new federal code came along or get out of the business. Local lawyers could "master the simple rules promulgated by the Supreme Court" rather than insist that the rest of the national bar condescend to their common law traditions.[63]

What federal codifiers disputed was the political salience of mere procedure. "We know that the substantive law is the very essence of government, and that ... the adjective law is in theory, and ought always to be in fact, the efficient aid of the substantive law," Clayton stated. Without answering the difficult questions of where substantive rights ended and procedural remedies began, Clayton piled up analogies about the distinction. Procedure was the rules of the game, not the rules of law itself. Substance was the master of the law; procedure was "no more than its hand-maiden." Whatever the precise line between procedure and substance, the point of procedure was to

Stephen N. Subrin, "Federal Rules, Local Rules, and State Rules: Uniformity, Divergence, and Emerging Procedural Patterns," 137 *University of Pennsylvania Law Review* 1999 (1989).

[61] Hall, "Uniform Law Procedure in Federal Courts."
[62] Walsh, *Reform of Federal Procedure*, 7–8; Judge Walter C. Lindley, U.S. District Court for the Eastern District of Illinois, to Thomas Walsh, May 26, 1926; McClintic to Walsh, May 20, 1926, Thomas J. Walsh Papers.
[63] Albert D. Walton, U.S. Attorney for the District of Wyoming, to Thomas Walsh, May 22, 1926, Thomas J. Walsh Papers. Henry D. Clayton, *Uniform Federal Procedure: Address Before the State Bar Association of Missouri* (1916), 2, 19.

ensure the "game is square" at "the lowest practicable cost." Traditions of localism and amateur legislating had to give way to the efficiencies gained by the techno-expert apostles of scientific administration who would transcend the local and the accidental with their rigorously principled national code.[64]

VI

Procedure as the "Handmaid of Justice" became the enduring image of the field for Charles Clark, the disciple of Field who finally managed to wrangle a federal codification into the 1938 Federal Rules of Civil Procedure. For Clark, legal systems failed when they made procedure the "mistress" of the law—by which Clark meant a female master, not a lover. Procedure was to be subject to the rules of justice and not the other way around. Clark argued that he was not offering a new vision for procedure but was describing what was inherent to American legal practice. "Lawyers and judges in the old days might appear to worship form and obey formal rules," he observed. "Yet they had a penchant for getting things done, and so they used the rules, with the aid now and then of some convenient fiction or subterfuge, to accomplish results without unnecessary trouble." In "modern" times, lawyers and judges had lost their capacity to use fictions and technicalities to arrive at just results, so the positive law of codes had to get them there more efficiently.[65]

The way forward, for Clark, was not to codify the rules of procedure exactly as Field had done but to essentially deregulate procedure by turning codes into flexible maxims designed *not* to be taken too literally. "Regular procedure is necessary to secure equal treatment for all," he seemed to concede, but then he followed, "It is necessary, too, for the quite as important factor of the *appearance* of equal treatment for all." A code of principles rather than rules kept up a semblance of order and maintained the pretense that like cases were decided alike and all received equal justice, but "the Court ought not to be so far bound and tied by rules, which are after all only intended as general rules of procedure, as to be compelled to do what will cause injustice in the particular case." Unlike the rules of justice, the rules of procedure were meant, like a servant, to bend and, if needed for the good of the household, to break.[66]

Because a procedure code could consist of flexible rules, Clark thought it could actually achieve what had so long eluded the codifiers: simplicity. Here Clark retold the story of Walsh's opposition not in terms of populist distrust of elite centralizers but as a matter of "a complicated metropolitan practice" being "forced upon the lawyers of various remote states in place of the simple practice they knew." But when procedure properly served as a handmaid, a procedure code could achieve the simplicity Walsh sought. There would be no need to write out every exception for every rule as one arose in the case law. Let the articulated principle stand, and let judges honor it in the breach as needed.[67] By advocating a code of general, malleable principle, Clark

---

[64] Clayton, *Uniform Federal Procedure*, 3, 16.
[65] Charles E. Clark, "The Handmaid of Justice," 23 *Washington University Law Quarterly* 297 (1938), 297, 309.
[66] *Ibid*, 297, 299, 308.
[67] *Ibid.*, 308, 319–20.

significantly departed from Field's ideal for codification, but in his description of procedural law subordinated to a substantive law of right and in his preference for expert codifiers over elected legislators, Clark and Field could hardly have been in closer agreement.

Thomas Walsh died in March 1933, and the Senate approved a Rules Enabling Act with an uncontroversial one-page report less than a year later. The Act—almost exactly the same words that had been proposed for a decade—authorized the Supreme Court to issue rules of procedure in common law and equitable cases or to combine the two jurisdictions if the Court wished. The Act further allowed the Court to take recommendations from an advisory committee, and it quickly became apparent that the committee would be the real architects of the procedural code, much as state commissioners had been a century before. The committee's key figure would be its reporter, and Clark lobbied for the job about as strenuously as Field sought his commission in 1847.[68]

The legislative history of the Federal Rules strikingly resembled that of the state code commissions from the Civil War era, but that history had been largely forgotten by 1938. Although the Rules Enabling Act allowed Congress to disapprove particular rules, the commissioners emphasized their expert authority over the legislature's. Clark argued that "attempts at reform by legislative acts run all the risks of indifference and political manipulation which inhere in popular bodies, coupled with the peculiar difficulties that the general populace is not interested in technical details of pleading." Procedure was once again viewed as a domain that the legislature could delegate to experts because of its superficiality, and should delegate to experts because of its technicality. Yet the boundaries between procedural and substantive law remained as unclear as ever. As late as 1937, the advisory committee had only a working definition of procedure which read as much into the codification mandate as the committee figured it could get away with. As one member candidly wrote to another: "The general policy I have acted on is that where a difficult question arose as to whether a matter was substance or procedure and I thought the proposed provision was a good one, I have voted to put it in, on the theory that if the Court adopted it, the Court would be likely to hold, if the question ever arises in litigation, that the matter is a procedural one."[69]

The time for drafting the Federal Rules was quite limited, as it had been for the earlier state codes. The advisory committee that was appointed in June 1935 produced a draft code in 1936 after sporadic meetings of the part-time commissioners. Though he was the principal draftsman, Clark retained his deanship and teaching responsibilities while serving as reporter. When the final draft reached Congress in 1938, Senator William King opposed it because Congress and interested parties did not have sufficient time to examine the code, much as New York senators had complained in 1850. Former Attorney General William D. Mitchell, one of the advisors, replied that the

---

[68] Rules Enabling Act, 48 Stat. 1064 (June 19, 1934), codified at 28 U.S.C. § 2072. See Burbank, "Rules Enabling Act of 1934," 1097–98; Peter Charles Hoffer et al., *The Federal Courts: An Essential History* (Oxford University Press, 2016), 300–01.

[69] Letter from William D. Mitchell to the Hon. George Wharton Pepper (December 19, 1937), quoted in Burbank, "Rules Enabling Act," 1134 n.530.

committee's work "was not a star chamber process." He insisted that the committee had created the code after three-and-a-half years of labor, and "thousands of copies were printed" so that "every class of lawyers" and "every bar association" could review them.[70] Ultimately, Congress adjourned without taking action on the Rules—but here, the story unfolded differently than it had in New York, because the Rules Enabling Act required Congress's affirmative vote to *defeat* the rules. Because Congress adjourned, ostensibly lacking time to consider the code, the Federal Rules took effect at the end of the congressional session.[71]

Still, 1938 was not 1848. The science of the codifiers had traded Field's ideal of comprehensiveness for systemization which resulted in a shorter, more ambiguous code than Field-era drafts. Protestant valorization of the written word gave way to Legal Realism's veneration for the "situation sense" of judges, who experienced words alone as feeble constraints.[72] With these changes in the philosophy of codification came a subtle but fundamental transformation of the professional audience that was expected to receive the code. Field was a consummate trial lawyer, who wrote his code for lawyers. His ideal of comprehensiveness aimed to help practitioners by condensing all relevant rules in one handy volume. That exhaustive collection of detailed rules (exceptions to exceptions included) would ensure that litigators never missed a step.[73]

Clark's professional sympathies were the opposite. Clark rarely wrote about lawyers or the perspective of practitioners, and when he did, he reduced the lawyer's craft to a mere "game where you try to catch the other fellow in an admission caused by his saying too much while you say as little as you can."[74] Clark typically imagined his audience as judges. Clark was not yet a judge when he drafted the federal rules, but his twenty-year tenure on the Second Circuit—whence he relished telling trial courts how to improve their procedures—gives some indication of his early temperament. Clark elevated the Field Code to the federal level as a matter of substance: law and equity were fused in the same terms and with the same compromises as the Field Code, the forms of action were abolished, party testimony was enhanced by discovery procedures developed under code practice, creditor plaintiffs received a host of advantages, and some of the more foundational rules copied the very text of 1848.[75] But as a matter of tenor, it was no longer a lawyer's code. Clark proposed that his codified

[70] Rules of Civil Procedure for the U.S. District Courts, Hearing Transcript, Subcommittee of the Committee on the Judiciary, U.S. Senate, April 18, 1938, 2–8. King continued to press for a deeper examination of the rules, calling expert witnesses such as the Georgetown professor Charles Keigwin to testify on the doubtful constitutionality of the proposed Rules. Rules of Civil Procedure for the U.S. District Courts, Hearing Transcript, 20–24.

[71] Hoffer et al., *The Federal Courts*, 298–310.

[72] The classic statement of Realist "situation-sense" is Karl N. Llewellyn, *The Common Law Tradition: Deciding Appeals* (1960), 60–61, 122–23. See also Shyamkrishna Balganesh, "The Constraint of Legal Doctrine," 163 *University of Pennsylvania Law Review* 1843 (2015); Shyamkrishna Balganesh & Gideon Parchomovsky, "Structure and Value in the Common Law," 163 *University of Pennsylvania Law Review* 1241 (2015).

[73] On Field's outlook, see especially the Law Reform tracts he published, discussed in the Part II introduction.

[74] Clark, "The Handmaid of Justice," 314.

[75] See especially chapters 6, 8, and 9. Rules that closely copied the Field code include Rule 8 (minus the codes' undefined "facts"), and Rule 54, the rule empowering judges to award any relief consistent with the evidence, including relief not sought in the pleadings.

rules "indicate the purpose sought to be achieved. They may give the *guiding principle* to the court, but this must be worked out by the court itself, and a large measure of discretion is necessary."[76] The new theory of codification went hand in hand with this outlook. A code of general principles was a code designed for judges. The structures of litigation might be imported from a nineteenth-century world of litigators, but it could not help but be transformed in the coming age of managerial judges.[77] Whether or not procedure under the Federal Rules would become the handmaid of justice, Clark's code would have it become the handmaid of the judiciary.

Like Field's code, the Federal Rules of Civil Procedure enjoyed remarkable influence beyond their original jurisdiction. Many states adopted the Federal Rules either by emulation or directly by copying.[78] Unlike Field's code, Clark's system of federal practice quickly became the polestar of civil procedure education in law schools. Richard H. Field (no relation) and Benjamin Kaplan's 1953 *Materials for a Basic Course in Civil Procedure* focused exclusively on practice under the Federal Rules in the federal courts. As one commentator noted, "reviewers praised this move because it gave the students a sense of direction. The advantages of using the federal system were also recognized: it was simple, and it was influencing the procedure of the states."[79] In reality, federal practice could vary significantly from judge to judge and circuit to circuit thanks to local rules and conflicting precedents. What Field and Kaplan offered was what Langdell had offered in the King's Bench procedure of 1830, and what Clark had offered in his *Handbook*: not so much procedure as practiced but as an artificial system representing what procedure could be. A survey conducted in 1999 found that current procedure textbooks are "updated but fundamentally unchanged version[s] of the 1953 Field & Kaplan course."[80]

VII

With the Federal Rules came new ideas about codification and a renewed focus on the role of the judge in litigation, but as the second half of this volume illustrates, the Rules themselves continued in force many of the practices innovated by the Field Code, practices that gave lawyers new or intensified powers over the framing, conduct, and results of litigation. Though Clark rarely thought of the lawyers as he drafted a federal version of the Field Code, his code of general principles could not entirely efface the prominence of the professional bar in the ur-text of the American procedure codes. Slowly but unmistakably winning over treatise writers, law professors, and the architects of federal codification, the Field Code's structures for practice receded into

[76] Clark, "History, Systems and Functions of Pleading," 551. See also Edson R. Sunderland, *Judicial Administration* (Callaghan & Co., 2d ed. 1948).

[77] See Judith Resnik, "Managerial Judges," 96 *Harvard Law Review* 374 (1982); Steven S. Gensler, "Judicial Case Management: Caught in the Crossfire," 60 *Duke Law Journal* 669 (2010).

[78] See John B. Oakley, "A Fresh Look at the Federal Rules in State Courts," 3 *Nevada Law Journal* 354 (2003).

[79] McManamon, "The History of the Civil Procedure Course," 436.

[80] Paul D. Carrington, "Teaching Civil Procedure: A Retrospective View," 49 *Journal of Legal Education* 311, 329 (1999).

bedrock principles of "modern practice," even as modernity rejected the code's outlook on what a code should be.

The magisterial comparativist R. C. Van Caenegem once argued that a jurisdiction's distinctive legal history and legal culture were largely controlled by the institution that became preeminent during nineteenth-century codification controversies. In France, that institution was the legislature; in Germany, the professoriate. In England, codification was controlled—and thus successfully resisted—by the judiciary.[81] Van Caenegem largely ignored the United States as having no codification controversy to speak of, and many European accounts of codification have followed his lead. The political and intellectual history given here shows the incompleteness of this account. In America, it was the professional bar that gained power and preeminence through the fortunes of codification. The United States did indeed witness a long-running controversy over codification, but one that is easy to miss if one adopts the codifiers' assumption that procedure was an unimportant and therefore uncontroversial supplement to the real law. In fact, the controversial Code American was a "mere" procedure code, but a lawyer's code for all that. For it was in procedure that the lawyers found their power.

---

[81] R. C. Van Caenegem, *Judges, Legislators and Professors: Chapters in European Legal History* (Cambridge University Press, 1987).

II

THE GARDEN

Upon returning from a celebratory trip to England in 1852, David Dudley Field established a Law-Reform Association in New York City. Inspired by Lord Henry Brougham, whose Law Amendment Society had received significant press coverage for its reform proposals and model legislation, Field's Association republished some of Lord Brougham's commentary on Field's reforms.[1] But as far as the newspaper archives show, the American association never held a meeting, and no one ever claimed to be a member. The association seems to have existed only to publish a half dozen "Law Reform Tracts" in the 1850s that were otherwise anonymous. At least, technically anonymous. Even if his brother had not revealed Field's authorship, the acerbic tone and intimate knowledge of New York's practice commission made the attribution obvious enough.[2]

Field's first tract was his most trenchant. He wrote that "hostile judges" were "confounding, misconstruing, and denouncing" the code, "pervert[ing] an opinion upon its construction into a lecture upon its policy," reviving the kind of judicial legislation codes were meant to overthrow. The pamphlet attacked two judges by name and advised that voters should not return them to the bench. Then, on second thought, with elections so far in the future, the tract urged legislative impeachment as a "remedy justly to be applied to a willful perversion of the law, or neglect to study and apply it."[3]

Field heaped most of his criticism on John Worth Edmonds, a trial judge in New York City. In an 1850 decision, Edmonds had declared that "the principles of pleading are left untouched" by the code reforms. "And as, before the Code, no party was obliged to use the forms then existing, it would seem to follow that the abolition of the forms, in reality, amounted to nothing." Field marveled that "this could have been said by any rational and reflecting man." Field considered the abolition of the medieval forms of pleading one of the central reforms of the code and counted Judge Edmonds's decision a personal insult he was eager to return. Judges like Edmonds, he remarked, "are usually advanced beyond the middle period of life; trained from their majority in habits of

---

[1] On the Law Amendment Society, see Michael Lobban, "Preparing for Fusion: Reforming the Nineteenth-century Court of Chancery," pt. II, 22 *Law & History Review* 565 (2004). The tracts containing Lord Brougham's republished material were *Law Reforms Tracts No. 2: Evidence on the Operation of the Code* (1852) and *Law Reform Tracts No. 4: Competency of Parties as Witnesses for Themselves* (1855).

[2] Henry Martyn Field, *The Life of David Dudley Field* (Charles Scribner's Sons, 1898), 69. In addition to the two tracts in the note above, the Association published *Law Reform Tracts No. 1: The Administration of the Code* (1852); *Law Reform Tracts No. 3: Codification of the Common Law* (1852); and *Law Reform Tracts No. 5: A Short Manual on Pleading Under the Code* (1856).

[3] *Administration of the Code*, 6, 8, 9.

subservience to precedent; reposing on other men's studies; thinking the thoughts of their predecessors; looking only at the past, with their backs to the future."[4]

As the code traveled to state after state, the conservatism of "old judges" and "elderly lawyers" became a byword of the codifiers. "In every state and country so far as we know [the code] has been violently opposed by some of the older members of the bar, and has received the cordial support of the younger members," wrote a proponent of codification in Michigan (one of the few midwestern states to reject the code).[5] More modern commentators have shared the view that old conservative judges and lawyers stunted the code's progress in reforming the law. "Much of what is now accepted as a matter of course in legal procedure," wrote Roscoe Pound, Dean of the Harvard Law School, "could have been attained at least eighty years [earlier] if Field's Code of Civil Procedure had been developed and applied in its spirit."[6] According to this view, the codifiers were naïve to believe reform could be carried through a legislature alone, and the story of the Field Code is the story of how conservative judges used their powers to alter the statutes they received, turning texts toward the exact opposite result of what was intended.[7]

The following chapters challenge the premise of this reception history. They argue that the code must be taken seriously as a code before it can be understood as an artifact of decisional case law. The motive for this approach is simple: It turns out that some of the judges who most "misinterpreted" the code were not gray-haired conservative adversaries of reform but some of its warmest supporters. Judge Edmonds, for instance, avidly supported the code and became the first sitting judge to publicly advocate its adoption in 1848. His remarks at the time show that he largely understood Field's goals, especially to reform pleadings, which Edmonds thought "promise[d] such great benefits, that I cannot persuade myself that we can soon return to the evils from which we are now so suddenly relieved." Like Field, Edmonds worried that an elderly bar "who have fitted themselves by a long period of preparation for practice, should resist every change." He therefore urged on the profession "a ready and cheerful obedience" to the new legislation.[8]

And in the next term, Field called for Edmonds's impeachment. Did the judge have a sudden change of heart? If not, how could two good-faith readings of the code arrive at opposite conclusions about its central reform? Field's displeasure shows that we can be too quick to seek a reception history in the courts, to assume the coherence of statutory intention, and to treat a code as a product of judicial construction before

---

[4] Dollner v. Gibson, 3 Code Rep. 153 (1850); but see Judge Edmonds's hand-corrected copy at 2 Edm. Sel. Cas. 253; *Administration of the Code*, 5, 18. On the precedential force of *Dollner*, compare Henry Whittaker, *Practice and Pleading Under the Codes of New York* (Edward O. Jenkins, 1852), 159–60; and *New York Herald*, March 7, 1852.

[5] Samuel Maxwell, "Alfred Russell's Objections to a Code of Civil Procedure," 2 *Michigan Law Journal* 367 (1893), 374.

[6] Roscoe Pound, "David Dudley Field: An Appraisal," in Alison Reppy, ed., *David Dudley Field Centenary Essays: Celebrating One Hundred Years of Legal Reform* (New York University Press, 1949), 14.

[7] See Alison Reppy, "The Field Codification Concept," and Charles E. Clark, "Code Pleading and Practice Today," in Alison Reppy, ed., *David Dudley Field Centenary Essays*, 7, 55; Lawrence M. Friedman, *A History of American Law* (Simon & Schuster, 2d. ed., 1985), 393–94; Charles M. Cook, *The American Codification Movement: A Study in Antebellum Legal Reform* (Greenwood Press, 1983), 210; Robert Wyness Millar, *Civil Procedure of the Trial Court in Historical Perspective* (New York University Press, 1952), 53–54.

[8] John W. Edmonds, *An Address on the Constitution and the Code of Procedure* (1848), 3–4, 6.

appreciating it as an object of legislation. Across the eight hundred pages of the Final Report of the code, the commissioners attempted a variety of reforms whose systematic coherence was questionable at best. In order to understand what appeared to be judicial opposition to the code, one must have a better sense of how the code itself could speak at cross purposes, draw on disparate cultural assumptions, and—despite its stated aim at comprehensiveness—leave huge gaps in the law of practice.

Critics of the code often understood, even if they could only imperfectly express, that practice had its own life and logic and that a code could not simultaneously abolish practical logics and rely on them to fill in the code's gaps. Against the machinery metaphor of the procedure code-writers, their critics posed images of nature. Judges like Edmonds instructed the legislature that it could not accomplish what it had intended, not because of any constitutional bar in the modern sense of that term but because the legislation ran up against natural barriers no skill in drafting could surmount. "I do not deny that it was the intention of the legislature to blend the modes of proceeding at law and in equity," wrote one judge, "but I insist that it would be unjust to the legislature itself to impute to it the design of abrogating differences which are inherent in the nature of things." Against the insinuation that judges were constructively repealing the code, another judge replied, "It repeals itself. It has been meddling with a subject not understood; and has come into collision with a 'higher law,'—the law of nature—which it cannot overcome. For the distinctions which mark law and equity are laid broad and deep in the nature of things."[9]

For the most part, these jurists were not trying to associate themselves in any deep way with the natural law tradition that had grown out of seventeenth-century liberal thought or to work out a systematic theory of law. On the contrary, they were making the point that the garden of legal practice was too complex, wild, and unpredictable for any one-volume systemization to succeed. Their aims in invoking nature sought to remind the codifiers that they did not draft on a blank slate. Legal practices had their reasons that Reason could not always articulate within the structured regulations of a code. Attempting to obliterate what was "natural" in practice was only to invite the garden to break back into the machine in unpredictable ways and in unexpected places.[10]

Each chapter that follows takes one piece of the machinery the codifiers thought foundational to their reformed system of practice and considers the ways the code both altered and was altered by the logics of practice it encountered. Chapter 6 begins with what Field considered the code's central reform, the requirement to plead plain facts while ignoring the common law forms of action. Chapters 7 and 8 consider the code's changes to witness testimony and the closely related reforms to pretrial investigation. Chapter 9 takes up the philosophically complex puzzle of merging law and equity practice, and Chapter 10 concludes with an overview of the code's reforms to attorney fee structures and legal ethics.

---

[9] Wooden v. Waffle, 6 Howard 145 (N.Y. Supreme Court 1851) (Selden, J.), 151; Le Roy v. Marshall, 8 Howard 373, 376 (N.Y. Supreme Court 1853) (Barculo, J.).

[10] In these ways, code critics anticipated more modern critiques. See Hendrik Hartog, "Snakes in Ireland: A Conversation with Willard Hurst," 12 *Law and History Review* 370 (1994), 375; Robert W. Gordon, "Critical Legal Histories," 36 *Stanford Law Review* 57 (1984), 111; Oliver O'Donovan, *The Ways of Judgment* (Eerdmans, 2005), 190.

6

No Magic in Forms

Fact Pleading and the Forms of Action

I

Whether judges in the late 1840s thought the code reforms advisable or not, they generally kept their views to themselves. A notable exception was Judge Seward Barculo, a trial judge who despised the code and openly mocked the codifiers in his courtroom and in published opinions. When counsel in one case argued that Barculo's interpretation effectively overruled the code, the judge retorted, "If this were true, I should deem it not an unpardonable offense."[1]

During a protracted litigation before Judge Barculo, one plaintiff hired Field himself to argue the construction of the code on appeal to the general term where Barculo, joined by a panel of two other judges, would review Barculo's decision from the court below. Barculo drew Field into a heated exchange after declaring that "to anyone acquainted with the law as it stood prior to the Code, it is quite obvious that this section is mainly an embodiment of the rules of pleading as they existed, with some omissions and numerous imperfections." A lawyer who attended the hearing reported that Field, "after contending for his view of the case, exclaimed 'I know that was the *intent* of the legislature.'

'I beg your pardon,' said the judge, 'the legislature meant exactly what they have said and nothing else.'

'Well,' replied the counsel, 'I know the codifiers meant so.'

'Ah!' responded the judge, 'very likely! They seem to have *meant* one thing and *said* another very often, if your argument is good.'"

Barculo ruled against Field, concluding that "it seems to me quite clear that the terms of the section and . . . the settled principles of good pleading, are irreconcilable with the views of the learned expounding author."[2]

Shortly after this decision, Field produced his scathing law reform tract expressing ill-disguised contempt for Barculo. "Embodiment of the rules of pleading!" he wrote. "What principles does he refer to? Is he ignorant, that there are other rules of pleading than those of the common law?" To Field, it was obvious the code had prescribed

---

[1] Le Roy v. Marshall, 8 How. 373 (N.Y. Sup. Ct. 1853), 374, 376. See also [David Dudley Field], *Law Reform Tracts No. 1: The Administration of the Code* (1852).

[2] Alger v. Scoville, 6 How. 131 (N.Y. Sup. Ct. Gen. Term 1852), 139–140. The description of the oral argument was provided in a eulogy of Barculo, who died in 1854. John Thompson, "Judge Barculo," in 20 *Barbour* 661 (appendix to New York reports) (1883 [1st. ed. 1855]), 668–69.

Law's Machinery. Kellen R. Funk, Oxford University Press. © Kellen R. Funk 2025. DOI: 10.1093/9780197543962.003.0007

what used to be deemed equitable procedures for the case at hand, yet Barculo had judged it by common law formulas.[3]

Despite Barculo's unusually outspoken hostility to the code, his clash with Field demonstrates several common features in the early judicial reception of the code. It shows, for instance, how quickly the problematic role of code commissioners was effaced as the code came before judges for interpretation. Like Barculo, most judges shrugged off arguments about commissioner intent and attributed authorship of the code to a legislature that had passed it unexamined and largely unread. That move from commissioner intent to legislative intent was an easy one to make because judges often discerned intent from the text itself or from their background understanding of common law practice, rarely or never referring to the political debates that had prompted constitutional conventions, reform commissions, or the various drafts of a code.[4]

What Field considered the code's most obvious and important reform as a matter of legislative intent produced one of the code's most obscure texts: a requirement to plead "facts constituting a cause of action." Because the code required what we now call "fact pleading" without defining any of its operative terms, jurists were left to puzzle out how common law and chancery had distinguished material claims from frivolous arguments and whether those methods were compatible with each other in a fused system. Supporters of codification both then and now claimed that common law judges deliberately misinterpreted the code and refused to bend from tradition in their old age. "They who had mastered" the old system "in youth, had forgotten the distaste with which they then regarded it, and had come to consider it as something necessary and unalterable," the Field Commission lectured the legislature. Left unmentioned by the commissioners was that their opponents were not the graybeards of the bar but their own contemporaries and often their former supporters (see Figure 6.1). Judge Barculo was four years Field's junior and had supported early calls for codification.[5] The problem was that even friends of the code struggled to figure out what it meant.

Ultimately, the code's aim to sunder substance and procedure was partially realized, but not in the way the codifiers, least of all Field, had intended. Through the slow development of case law and treatise literature, practitioners gradually came to think of the old common law pleading requirements as independent "elements" of a rights claim. In time, the practitioner's sense inverted itself: instead of looking to pleadings to learn the law, apprentice lawyers could look to "the law" to figure out what to plead. But instead of this revolution bursting in with the passage of the code, it developed slowly, case by case, as jurists initially confused by the code's lack of guidance thought back through the logic of the writ system and wrenched its principles into something like a substantive law of right.

[3] *Administration of the Code*, 24–25.
[4] See, for instance, Linden v. Hepburn, 3 Sand. 668 (N.Y. Super. Ct. 1851); Giles v. Lyon, 4 N.Y. 600 (1851); Williams v. Hayes, 5 How. 471 (N.Y. Sup. Ct. 1851); Millikin v. Cary, 5 How. 272 (Sup. Ct. 1850); Knowles v. Gee, 8 Barb. 300 (Sup. Ct. 1850), as well as cases discussed below.
[5] *Third Report* (New York, 1849), 4. See also *Report of the Code Commissioners to the Eighth General Assembly of the State of Iowa* (1859), 294. On Barculo's initial support for codification, see Thompson, "Judge Barculo," 659–61.

Figure 6.1 Two engravings and a photographic portrait of three of the most influential New York Supreme Court judges who interpreted the Field Code in its first decade: John Worth Edmonds, Samuel Lee Selden, and Seward Barculo. Although Field believed his code was abused by elderly judges who refused to conform to the new system, Edmonds and Selden were only five years older than Field, and Barculo was several years younger.

John Livingston, *Livingston's Law Register for 1852* (1852), front piece.

Ray B. Smith, ed., *History of the State of New York Political and Governmental* (Syracuse Press, 1922), 2:432.

Edmund Platt, *The Eagle's History of Poughkeepsie from the Earliest Settlements 1683 to 1905* (Platt & Platt, 1905), 132.

II

The foundational principle of the Field Code was that legal practice needed to become more truthful. Historians have widely noted the rise of a Victorian culture of sincerity and earnestness across the nineteenth century in England and America, although the roots of this broad cultural trend remain obscure. English scholars have drawn attention to a rising theology of evangelical authenticity early in the century, while historians of Whig republican theory have traced an emphasis on the virtues of honesty and candor as critical to the health of the state.[6] Evangelical piety and republican virtue theory were, of course, widespread in the early United States as well, further cultivated by ideals of political and religious "plain speech."[7] No less true for the American experience was the recent observation of an English legal historian that Victorian earnestness in the quest for truth "was negotiated and manufactured in the courtroom as much as it was in the catechism."[8]

In the Early Republic, courtrooms were consistently hailed as "temples of justice," but codifiers pushed the imagery further. Courts might not teach divine religion directly, reasoned the Iowa codifier Charles Ben Darwin, but "a court-house, is in a sort, a school" where "good morals" were preached. And, Darwin continued, "the lawyer is the priest who more than the judge announces those lessons," since lawyers mediated the lessons of the law both to their clients and to the juries before whom they spoke.[9] This reliance on priestly imagery was especially striking because codifiers generally railed against the "mystery" and "priestcraft" of traditional common law practice. Casting themselves as priests could only play into the hands of the anti-lawyers, who charged that lawyers used the mysticism of technical doctrine to keep their profession closed to ordinary citizens. Nevertheless, directly engaging the anti-lawyers, Darwin emphasized the comparison between priestcraft and lawyering: "Take these ministers of public vengeance from your court-houses, and . . . you have broken the chief altar, and silenced and ejected the priest, and your temple of justice, has become a mercenary shamble where profit and loss is selfishly bartered."[10]

---

[6] On piety, see Walter E. Houghton, *The Victorian Frame of Mind* (Yale University Press, 1957), 218–21, 425–26; Martin J. Weiner, *Men of Blood: Violence, Manliness and Criminal Justice in Victorian England* (Cambridge University Press, 2004), 13–14; V. Markham Lester, *Victorian Insolvency: Bankruptcy, Imprisonment for Debt, and Company Winding-Up in Nineteenth-Century England* (Clarendon Press, 1995). On Whig republicanism, see J. G. A. Pocock, *The Machiavellian Moment: Florentine Political Thought and the Atlantic Republican Tradition* (Princeton University Press, 1975); Daniel T. Rodgers, "Republicanism: The Career of a Concept," 79 *Journal of American History* 11 (1992).

[7] Gordon S. Wood, *The Creation of the American Republic, 1776–1787* (University of North Carolina Press, 1969); Daniel Walker Howe, *The American Whigs: An Anthology* (Wiley, 1973). On the union of evangelical piety with republican theory, see especially Mark Noll, *America's God: From Jonathan Edwards to Abraham Lincoln* (Oxford University Press, 2002). On "plain speaking" in the Jacksonian era, see Kenneth Cmiel, *Democratic Eloquence: The Fight Over Popular Speech in Nineteenth-century America* (University of California Press, 1990), ch. 2.

[8] Wendie Ellen Schneider, *Engines of Truth: Producing Veracity in the Victorian Courtroom* (Yale University Press, 2015), 5–6.

[9] *Report of the Code Commissioners* (Iowa, 1859), 322–24. On courts as temples of justice, see Michael Kammen, "The Iconography of Judgement and American Culture," in Maeva Marcus, ed., *Origins of the Federal Judiciary* (Oxford University Press, 1992), 248–80.

[10] *Report of the Code Commissioners* (Iowa, 1859), 234. On the criticisms of the common law as "priestcraft," see Kunal M. Parker, *Common Law, History, and Democracy in America, 1790–1900: Legal Thought Before Modernism* (Cambridge University Press, 2011), 121–22.

Darwin's statements echoed Field's 1850 Final Report of the code. "The courts are, or should be, schools of morals," Field wrote. "Of all the institutions in society, they should be most sacred to truth."[11] A church-going Unitarian and brother to a prominent Presbyterian minister, Field was not casually forgetting about churches when he designated courtrooms the most sacred spaces for truth in American society. Field believed "the separation of church and state" to be one of the "greatest accomplishments" of American history, one that had succeeded in making religion a purely private affair. But, as the historian of religion Mark Noll has written, a fully privatized religion made the few remaining institutions of public morality all the more important to a republic that relied on public virtue to counter tyrannical corruption. Even especially to devout Protestants like Field and his law partner Thomas G. Shearman, truth-speaking became a sacred obligation in *court*, one upon which the health of the polity depended. Monarchical England, with its established church, might tolerate falsehoods and the nonsense of traditional legal practice, but codifiers argued that a republic required a legal priesthood to maintain the sanctity of its courts.[12]

Truth-telling became an obsessive focus of practice codification reports. "The tendency of our age, is to look for the truth wherever it may be found," Field announced as a guiding principle for the code. "The commissioners feel that they would be sinning against the light of truth" if they did not adopt the Field reforms, wrote the Maryland codifiers. "The object of every rule of evidence ought to be to attain the truth," wrote Judge Wells of Missouri. "The benefit of all may be lost, or turned to evil, unless there is provided a tribunal . . . with the means of arriving at the truth," wrote the Kentuckians.[13]

All of these reports agreed with Field that no single rule could turn the prior practice of the courts from fiction and falsehood toward truth and common sense. Rather, they argued that three key reforms would work together as a system to bring the truth into court: pleading facts, verified by oath, with parties competent to stand the scrutiny of cross-examination at trial. In time, "fact pleading" became the label that represented the entire system of code remedies and procedure, what many jurists referred to simply as "the American system."[14]

---

[11] *Final Report* (New York, 1850), 274.

[12] David Dudley Field, "American Progress in Jurisprudence," 44 *American Register and Law Review* 541 (1896), 545–46. Noll, *America's God*, 203–16. See also Perry Miller's posthumously published account of the "tension between law and Christianity in America." Perry Miller, *The Life of the Mind in America: From the Revolution to the Civil War* (Mariner, 1965), 186–206. For further examples from the codifiers, see especially [Jesse Higgins], *Sampson Against the Philistines, or The Reformation of Lawsuits* (1805); Thomas Smith Grimké, *An Oration on the Practicability and Expediency of Reducing the Whole Body of the Law to the Simplicity and Order of a Code* (1827).

[13] *First Report* (New York, 1848), 246; *The Final Report of the Commissioners to Revise the Rules of Practice and Pleadings* (Maryland, 1855), 150; R.W. Wells, *Law of the State of Missouri Regulating Pleadings and Practice* (1849), 73; *Report of the Commissioners Appointed to Prepare a Code of Practice for the Commonwealth of Kentucky* (1850), iii. See also *Report of the Commissioners on Practice and Pleadings* (Ohio, 1853), 20.

[14] See, for instance, John Norton Pomeroy, *Remedies and Remedial Rights by the Civil Action According to the Reformed American Procedure* (Little, Brown, 1876); E.F. Johnson, "The American (or Code) System of Pleading," 2 *Michigan Law Journal* 376 (1893); Charles E. Clark, *Handbook of the Law of Code Pleading* (West, 1928).

In the First Report of the code to the New York legislature in 1848, Field argued that "truth, which ought to be the first essential in the proceedings of courts of justice" was "not only disregarded generally, and upon system" in traditional practice, "but that the disregard of truth is forced upon the parties by the present system of pleading." In Field's view, the requirement to plead fictions was a requirement to lie. In every use of the common counts or general issue, a litigant pleaded "a denial of what he would not deny in conversation."[15] Nevertheless, a solution seemed inherent in the system. Field believed that although parties often delayed until trial to do it, at some point, they presented the "facts" upon which the "law" was to operate.

The distinction between law and fact was at least three centuries old by the time Field codified it in New York. In a wide-ranging rhetorical analysis, Barbara Shapiro argues that the very concept of facticity arose in sixteenth-century English legal practice and only later migrated to journalism, philosophy, and the natural sciences. In its early legal usage, she observes, "fact" did not denote "an established truth but an alleged act whose occurrence was in contention." A man might be "taken in the Fact" of committing arson while others spoke of "false facts."[16] Facts were thus inherently disputed. They might be true or false, provable or not. Law, on the other hand, was fixed and knowable, even when very difficult to discern. Major jurists of the sixteenth century, such as Lord Coke, accordingly transformed the distinction between law and fact into an institutional distinction. After a long period of training, judges declared the law and guided litigants in legal disputes; lay jurors weighed the proofs and decided which facts were so. The Field Code offered no definition of law or facts, although it often relied on the distinction. Instead, the code followed Lord Coke by resting the distinction not on metaphysics but on institutional competence: juries declared the facts, judges the law. Even for juryless courts like chancery and admiralty, the jury offered a paradigm by which to draw the distinction. Factual propositions could be related in "ordinary language" to laymen, who could evaluate their truthfulness based on the presentation of evidence. The legal effect of the facts, on the other hand, required technical training and might not be obvious to nonlawyers.[17]

Many commentators have focused on traditional prohibitions of juries deciding questions of law, showing how often these rules were contested or, at best, honored in the breach.[18] But even in the province of facts the boundaries could be murky. "Two parties signed a contract" was technically a legal conclusion, where "parties" and "contract" (and even "signed") were terms of art. But the occurrence was so common and well understood that "ordinary language" might treat the statement as

---

[15] *First Report* (New York, 1848), 145, 153.

[16] Barbara J. Shapiro, *A Culture of Fact: England, 1550–1720* (Cornell University Press, 2000), 11, 44–45

[17] See William Forsyth, *History of the Trial by Jury* (Lawbook Exchange, 1994), 216–48; Ellen E. Sward, "The Seventh Amendment and the Alchemy of Fact and Law," 33 *Seton Hall Law Review* 573 (2003); Stephen A. Weiner, "The Civil Jury Trial and the Law-Fact Distinction," 54 *California Law Review* 1867 (1966). *Final Report* (New York, 1850), 2:317–21.

[18] See John Phillip Reid, *Controlling the Law: Legal Politics in Early National New Hampshire* (Northern Illinois University Press, 2004); Morton J. Horwitz, *The Transformation of American Law, 1780–1860* (Oxford University Press, 1977), 28–29, 141–43; Brenner M. Fissell, "Jury Nullification and the Rule of Law," 19 *Legal Theory* 217 (2013); Renée Lettow Lerner, "The Rise of Directed Verdict: Jury Power in Civil Cases Before the Federal Rules of 1938," 81 *George Washington Law Review* 448 (2013).

a factual proposition of what happened at a particular time and place. As one codifier explained, "'[Party] A promised,' looks quite like a fact-statement, until the objector starts to question whether the promise was legal or not, and then the proposition is seen to be a legal one, capable of being divided into its elemental facts of consideration—capacity of promissor—illegal constraint, etc."[19] But then, even these "elemental facts"—consideration, capacity, and duress—relied on a further set of legal conclusions.

Nevertheless, Field considered the difference between fact and law clear enough as a matter of practice. Whenever counsel summed up their case to a jury, the concluding points of those arguments were the facts. Whenever judges instructed juries to return special verdicts stating particular findings (rather than general verdicts), those too were facts. What was important to Field was that these factual statements should appear at the beginning of a controversy rather than on the day of trial. "Since the facts give the right to relief, it must be proper that they should be stated as they exist," Field wrote. "It is impossible, that there can be a good reason, why they should be stated untruly, or in any other language" from the outset.[20]

Accordingly, Field began his code of practice with pleading as the cornerstone reform. "All the forms of pleading heretofore existing, are abolished" the code declared in its first title on civil actions. The code mandated that "there shall be in this state, hereafter, but one form of action" called a "civil action." In this single form of action, the complaint was to state "the facts constituting the cause of action, in ordinary and concise language, without repetition, and in such a manner as to enable a person of common understanding to know what is intended."[21]

Field's phrasing met immediate derision from some quarters of the bar, who thought "ordinary language" and "common understanding" conceded too much to vulgar democracy and the impulse to make every man his own lawyer.[22] The code was not a serious attempt to democratize the bar, but Field did argue that courtroom procedure in a democratic republic ought to be legible to citizens. "Heretofore the records of the courts, have been sealed books to the mass of the people. Though concerned in them as suitors, and participating in them as jurors, they were repulsed by strange forms, and technical language," the Final Report declared. Fact pleading would restore to public proceedings "at least the same regard to truth, that prevails between members of society, in their daily communications with one another."[23] In pleadings, the language of the law had to adopt the ordinary language of commerce, of electioneering, of preaching. Like the Puritans of his Massachusetts homeland, Field preferred public speech to be "plain." The code produced a "plain and rational system of procedure" that required pleading "a plain statement" simple enough that "a plain man" could understand it. "There is no magic in forms," the First Report concluded.

---

[19] *Report of the Code Commissioners* (Iowa, 1859), 204.

[20] [David Dudley Field], *Law Reform Tracts No. 5: A Short Manual on Pleading under the Code* (1856), 12–13; *First Report* (New York, 1848), 141.

[21] 1848 New York Laws 510, 521; *Final Report* (New York, 1850), 225–26, 263–64.

[22] See for instance, *Diary of George Templeton Strong*, ed. Allan Nevins (Macmillan, 1952 [Sept. 28, 1848]), 1:301; Orestes Brownson, "Cooper's Ways of the Hour," *Brownson's Quarterly Review* 5:3 (July 1851), 285.

[23] *Final Report* (New York, 1850), v; *First Report* (New York, 1848), 153.

The forms of action were merely "old jingles of words, invented somewhere about the times of the Edwards."[24] In Field's view, their perseverance was not only an unreasoning superstition but a commitment to falsehood in a republic that could not suffer corruption in its courts.

III

Although the jury was crucial to marking the distinction between law and fact, Field gave comparatively little attention to the jury as an instrument of truth-seeking. Across all their reports, the New York commissioners emphasized that proper pleading was the only key to truth-seeking in the civil courts. "If the party be not confined in his pleading to what he believes, no adequate reform in pleading can ever be affected," the Final Report concluded.[25] Other American codifiers echoed the New York emphasis on factuality, and, like Field, all generally treated the right to a jury trial as incidental to truth-seeking reforms. Because most state constitutions preserved the right to a jury trial (at least in cases where it "has been heretofore used," as New York's did), codifiers were generally content to repeat these preservation clauses with little comment. Only those commissions that reported adversely on the Field Code, such as Maryland's, poeticized jury participation as "the great end of government."[26]

The codifiers' indifference to the jury is at odds with historical commentary on the Field Code. Some accounts present the code as a jury-empowering attempt to thwart judicial tyranny, a product of Jacksonian democracy that expanded lay participation in civil justice.[27] A literal reading of the law provides some support for these views. Since the codifiers hoped to provide "a uniform course of proceeding, in all cases," and since by constitutional mandate they had to make jury trial available in some cases, the codes accordingly allowed factual disputes in any case to be resolved by a jury. Commentary on the rules occasionally noted that equity's juryless proceedings arose when jurors "could neither read nor write" and might have been led astray by gullibility or ignorance. But, wrote Missouri's codifier, in modern America, "their daily business and intercourse with all classes enables them to know more of men, their passions, interests, feelings, and prejudices, and the influence these may exercise over them, than the judges do."[28]

Most code reports had a different focus, however. Pleading reform might help a juror better understand his duty, Field granted, but he and the other codifiers hoped

---

[24] David Dudley Field, "The Study and Practice of the Law," 14 *Democratic Review* 345 (1844); David Dudley Field, *What Shall be Done With the Practice of the Courts? Shall It Be Wholly Reformed?* (1847), 21–22; *First Report* (New York, 1848), 141; David Dudley Field, *Legal Reform: An Address to the Graduating Class at the University of Albany* (1855), 20; Field, "Study and Practice of the Law," 349.

[25] *Final Report* (New York, 1850), 274. See also *Second Report* (New York, 1849), 12.

[26] N.Y. Const. of 1846, art. 1, § 2. See *First Report* (New York, 1848), 51. *The First Report of the Commissioners to Revise the Rules of Practice and Pleadings* (Maryland, 1855), 17.

[27] See Sephen N. Subrin, "David Dudley Field and the Field Code: A Historical Analysis of an Earlier Procedural Vision," 6 *Law and History Review* 311, 318–19; 333–34 (1988). On the legal system's increasing reliance of the jury over time, see George Fisher, "The Jury's Rise as Lie Detector," 107 *Yale Law Journal* 575 (1997).

[28] *First Report* (New York, 1848), 76–77. Wells, *Law of the State* (Missouri, 1849), 45–46, 70–71.

to excuse jurymen from that duty altogether. Along with an expanded right to a jury trial came an expanded right to waive a jury. Renée Lettow Lerner has shown that the Field Code's encouragement of waiver represented a watershed moment in the gradual vanishing of the American civil jury. "One of the most burdensome duties of the citizen, is the performance of jury service," Field wrote. "If that burthen can be lessened . . . we shall regard it as a great benefit." If jurors were now better educated, more industrious, and generally wiser in the ways of the world, all the more reason for the legal system to stay out of their way and let them contribute to the bustling economy.[29] Nothing in the jury system inherently promoted the search for truth, Field thought. The commissioners preferred "the rapid examination which takes place on common law trials before juries," but figured "a judge is as competent to estimate the weight of testimony as a juror, and can do it as rapidly." It was the oath-bound cross-examination by skilled counsel that "leads to the truth," rather than the presence of lay jurors.[30]

In contrast to the jury, Field's code accorded much more power and responsibility to the judiciary than commentators have appreciated. Given the importance of candid pleading to his system, the code could hardly have done otherwise. Field may have chided judges for being stuck in the past, but his ideal vision for pleading was actually inspired by an even deeper past. In the thirteenth and fourteenth centuries, English "sarjeants-at-law" conducted their pleadings orally before the judges, exchanging views on theories of liability and raising factual considerations until a dispositive issue arose for trial. "When the presence of the judge was withdrawn," Field observed, pleading "lost an essential part of its original character."[31]

Oral pleading, as Field understood it, had involved an element of give and take among lawyers and judges. Judges could advise on the spot about the legal effects of any particular plea, and lawyers could disclose the actual facts of their cases piece by piece until they reached a disputed point to be resolved by a jury. "The substitute for that now is the trial," Field observed. The evasions of common counts and general issues in modern written pleadings allowed counsel to plead multiple causes and defenses and then present their best evidence at trial. Using procedures that mimicked medieval pleading, lawyers at the commencement of the trial orally negotiated disputed points and offered their proofs before the judge determined which points and which proofs would go to the jury. Field admitted that a system that relied exclusively on oral pleading would be impractical in a large commercial state where parties litigated complex multiparty and multi-issue transactions, but he nevertheless hoped to turn written pleading back toward the judicially managed give and take of medieval practice. Factual pleadings rather than formulaic fictions would inform parties about the nature of the dispute and the proofs they would need to gather well before trial— as long as judges did their part to keep pleaders honest.[32]

---

[29] Renée Lettow Lerner, "The Failure of Originalism in Preserving Constitutional Rights to Civil Jury Trial," 22 *William & Mary Bill of Rights Journal* 811 (2014), 835–36; *First Report* (New York, 1848), 189.

[30] *First Report* (New York, 1848), 178. See also N.Y. Const. of 1846, art. 6, § 10, and for background, Amalia Kessler, "Our Inquisitorial Tradition: Equity Procedure, Due Process, and the Search for an Alternative to the Adversarial," 90 *Cornell Law Review* 1181 (2005).

[31] *A Short Manual on Pleading*, 28–29.

[32] *First Report* (New York, 1848), 144; *A Short Manual on Pleading*, 28–29.

Accordingly, the code empowered judges to force amendments to the pleadings "when the allegations of a pleading are so indefinite or uncertain, that the precise nature of the charge or defence is not apparent." Or the court could even amend the pleadings directly "by adding or striking out the name of any party, or by correcting a mistake ... in any other respect, or by inserting other allegations material to the case." If upon trial there arose a variance between the pleadings and the proofs, the court could order "immediate amendment" of the pleadings to conform to the evidence presented—this in addition to the direction that the court must grant "any relief consistent with the case made by the complaint." Taken literally, all these provisions of the code granted judges full power to redraft pleadings, even to the extent of granting unrequested remedies against previously unnamed parties based on allegations or arguments never raised by counsel.[33] The original draft of the code had restrained judges from "substantially" changing "the cause of action." Field dropped this language in the 1849 amendments, explaining, "There is so little danger of the courts going too far, in allowing amendments, that the qualification can be omitted without danger. It is the intention of the commissioners to allow and encourage amendments of every kind, whenever justice will be promoted by them."[34]

Both treatises and the early cases that construed the code demonstrate that jurists largely understood Field's aim to move the looser, more informal negotiations of oral pleading from trial to a preparatory pretrial phase. Judge Edmonds announced that before the code, "it has been very seldom ... that I have taken occasion to examine the [written] pleadings." He instead relied on legal counsel to inform him orally of the dispute at trial. Edmonds declared his optimistic hope that the code could bring the same level of candor to written pleadings before trial. Judge Augustus Hand expressed similar appreciation that the code was attempting to produce candor at an earlier, less hurried stage of proceedings. "When the law and the fact are decided by the judges, ... the judge selects the points in the pleadings to which the proofs are to be applied," he wrote. "But when this is done in the haste of a jury trial it is more difficult, and casts upon the court great power and responsibility, and this selection often takes the counsel by surprise."[35]

Although he admired the attempt at upfront candor, Judge Hand worried that Field's effort to produce facts without any regard to rules of form and to accord liberal powers of amendment to judges would have troubling consequences. Without "certain settled principles by which good pleading is tested," he reasoned, "doubt, uncertainty and perplexity, to say nothing of constant novelty and diversity, will tend to render the administration of justice at least tardy, precarious and irregular, if not capricious."[36] Indeed,

---

[33] 1848 N.Y. Laws 525–26 §§ 145–52; 1849 N.Y. Laws 648 §§ 159–60; *Second Report* (New York, 1849), 29; *Final Report* (New York, 1850), 281.

[34] 1848 N.Y. Laws 526 § 149; *Second Report* (New York, 1849), 29–30.

[35] Edmonds, *An Address on the Constitution and the Code of Procedure*, 14. Judicial commentary on the code is, as this chapter notes, vast. For a good representative cross-section, see Boyce v. Brown, 7 Barb. 80 (N.Y. Sup. Ct. 1849) (Augustus Hand, J.) (trespass action in the rural upstate); Dollner v. Gibson, 3 Code Rep. 153 (N.Y. Sup. Ct. 1850) (John W. Edmonds, J.) (commercial dispute that would have used the "money counts" before the code); Wooden v. Waffle, 6 How. 145 (N.Y. Sup. Ct. 1851) (Samuel L. Selden, J.) (complex case seeking an equitable injunction); Alger, 6 How. at 131 (Field's disputed points with Judge Barculo in a fraud action that would have employed a "creditor's bill" before the code).

[36] *Boyce*, 7 Barb. at 87.

although Field was one of the more prominent critics of "judge-made law," his code had the curious quality of legitimizing and extending the very activities of the oracular judge that had troubled reformers like Jeremy Bentham and William Sampson. Upon the code's enactment, judges gained new powers to declare the law by passing judgment on the sufficiency of pleadings apart from traditional restraints on the forms of action. And, as the cases showed, when "conservative" judges refused to apply the code "in its spirit," they frequently acted to maintain the rule of law in the sudden absence of the rule of writs.

IV

For treatise writers seeking to explain the code, the most striking feature of the legislation was that nowhere in an eight-hundred-page code of pleading could one find precise instructions on how to plead. "It *abolishes* but it does not *reconstruct*; it tears down an old system, but it does not build up a new and complete one it its place," complained a prominent early expositor of code practice in New York, George van Santvoord. Another author, Henry Whittaker, wrote that under the code, "each step in pleading has its own peculiar rules as to sufficiency or insufficiency," but the code contained few of these "peculiar rules." It required sufficient facts "constituting the cause of action," but defined none of those words and offered no guidance on what even a basic contract claim ought to look like. By speaking of causes of action without defining any of them, the code appeared to incorporate the common law by reference, or so early readers figured.[37]

Field thought such readings were an attempt to overthrow his code and preserve common law practice exactly as it was, so he tried to supply the missing definitions in his law reform tracts. "What are the 'facts' to be stated in a pleading, is really a question of no difficulty, if the code be read, and fairly administered," Field wrote in one tract criticizing early judicial interpretations of the code. "The 'facts constituting the cause of action,' or 'constituting a defense,' are the facts, to which the law is to be applied." Field's tautological definition was hardly an improvement. Neither did the Final Report of the code define "fact" (and indeed, it engaged in its own tautology by declaring that "judicial remedies are such as are administered by the courts"), nor were other codifiers able to offer more precision. "Indeed, facts are facts," the Iowa code affirmed.[38]

As jurists continued to struggle with the requirements of fact pleading, Field's Law-Reform Association published another tract in 1856 titled "A Short Manual of Pleading Under the Code." Its second rule (after "pleadings must be true") declared that "*facts only must be stated.* This means the *physical facts*, cognizable to the senses, or capable of being shown to a jury without the aid of legal inferences; the *facts* as

---

[37] George van Santvoord, *A Treatise on the Principles of Pleading in Civil Actions under the New York Code of Procedure* (Little & Co., 2d ed., 1855), 12, 14, 62; Henry Whittaker, *Practice and Pleading under the Code* (E.O. Jenkins, 2d ed., 1854), 1:325.

[38] *Administration of the Code,* 18. *Final Report* (New York, 1850), 10 § 5; *Report of the Code Commissioners* (Iowa, 1859), 204.

contradistinguished from *the law*, from *argument*, from *hypothesis*, and from *the evidence* of the facts." The rule that pleadings should not state the law or arguments, however, "does not imply that the rules of logic, the rules which lie inherent in the nature of things, exist for pleading no longer. They must exist in every system." How, then, did one avoid pleading the frivolous details of evidence on the one hand without conclusory statements of law on the other? "What is and what is not essential, an uninstructed person might not readily discover," the guide admitted, "but a lawyer ought not to be in doubt."[39] Thus even the codifier of pleadings and practice ultimately relied on unwritten practice in order to explain his codification of pleading.

Field did make a further attempt to articulate what it was lawyers did in practice. "The following question will determine, in every case, whether an allegation be material: Can it be made the subject of a material issue; in other words, if it be denied, will the failure to prove it decide the cause in whole or in part?" If so, it was neither evidence nor law but an "ultimate fact" that belonged in a pleading. Field, however, considered the material elements of a claim to be the essence of substantive law and thus beyond the scope of a procedure code. When Field undertook the codification of civil law in the 1860s, he proceeded on this principle, defining property and contract rights as enumerated lists of material elements, the violation of which could be easily pleaded by going down the list. In the meantime, Field figured substance and procedure worked together in the same way—the substantive elements being merely scattered across case reports rather than collected in a code.[40] Elements were to be defined by substantive law and not by procedural form.

Thus Field paradoxically declared that "the facts vary, with the cases as they occur, and no fixed form can be given, which will correspond with their ever-changing phases" while he simultaneously produced a "book of forms" to guide pleaders.[41] While Field asserted that pleadings under the code had no stable form and that an attempt to force any two cases with their infinite variety of facts into one form could reintroduce artifice and technicality into the system, he nevertheless recognized "natural" classifications in the law that distinguished, for instance, claims arising on contracts from those based on physical injury, recovery from a trespasser on real property versus recovery of assets from one's trustee. The form book indicated that these various types of claims would indeed have standard elements pleaded across all claims of the same type, but Field imagined that the elements arose from a substantive body of law rather than being dictated by a fixed menu of pleading forms.[42]

It was on this point that practitioners struggled to follow Field, for most lawyers had learned the law not as discrete bodies of substantive doctrine (say, contract and tort) but as so many genres of pleading. One knew which contracts required express consideration not because of a substantive law of contracts but because one knew which cases required consideration to be pleaded and which permitted it to be implicit. Practitioners were thus astonished when a code of pleading offered none of this

[39] *A Short Manual on Pleading*, 10, 13–14.

[40] Ibid., 15. See *The Civil Code of the State of New York Reported Complete by the Commissioners of the Code* (1865).

[41] *Administration of the Code*, 18. *Book of Forms Adapted to the Code of Procedure* (1860).

[42] See *First Report* (New York, 1848), 261–71; *A Short Manual on Pleading*, 18–28; *Book of Forms Adapted to the Code of Procedure*.

information, and treatise writers worked to supply the deficiency. Both Whittaker and van Santvoord devoted hundreds of pages of their treatises on pleading to provide a primer on the law of contracts, tort, real and personal property, and van Santvoord produced an additional treatise on pleading "in former equitable cases" that offered an introductory guide to mortgages, guardianship, and other matters of equitable jurisdiction.[43] "It is not true then," van Santvoord explained, "that the main *rules* of pleading, founded as they are in sound logic and solid reason, are utterly abolished, though the *forms* may be." Just as treatises on "pleading and practice" before the code had run over a thousand pages covering major bodies of Anglo-American law, so early treatises on code practice continued to include broad surveys of legal rules in their treatments on pleading. "Pleading, as we have seen, is a matter of substance and not of form, under the Code," van Santvoord concluded, but the old forms were the only guides to the new substance.[44]

After writing his pleading manual and book of forms, Field took a further step toward clarifying his reforms by subsidizing a new treatise written by his clerk and soon-to-be-partner Thomas G. Shearman. Shearman thoroughly adopted the outlook of his mentor, writing in his preface "that the failure of the profession in general to appreciate and accept the radical change effected by section 69 of the Code is, more than any and all things else, the source of the confusion and uncertainty which have infected our practice for the last sixteen years." At the time, Section 69 was the one that "abolished" the forms of action and instituted only one "civil action."[45]

Instead of "forms of action," Shearman preferred to speak of "kinds of relief." He introduced the term when defining a "cause of action," connecting the latter to the traditional idea that common law remedies rectified a defendant's wrongful act: "A cause of action, although for the sake of brevity we shall call it a *claim*, is nevertheless not accurately described by that word. For upon a single cause of action the plaintiff may be entitled to several distinct kinds of relief. The *cause* of action is the defendant's wrongful act, and not the remedy which the plaintiff seeks." Having pointed out the false equivalency of claims for relief and causes of action, Shearman nevertheless used the terms synonymously through the remainder of his treatise. He classified claims for relief into those seeking recovery of a debt, those seeking damages for personal injury, and those affecting specific property. And like the other treatises, Shearman advised that in each claim, "every fact which, at common law or in equity, was necessary to sustain the pleader's case, must be alleged in his pleading." Thus, Shearman too included a long primer on the law of contracts, illustrating material elements case by case, although his presentation had a Fieldian cast to it. Decisions

---

[43] Whittaker, *Practice and Pleading Under the Code*, 1:164–87 (surveying essential requisites in a variety of cases), 259–72 (surveying grounds for demurrer for insufficiency in a vary of case types); van Santvoord, *A Treatise on the Principles of Pleading*, 216–69 (contracts), 271–93 (tort, real and personal property—under the general heading of trespass), 293–08 (real property in equity); George van Santvoord, *A Treatise on the Practice in the Supreme Court of the State of New York in Equity Actions Adapted to the Code of Procedure* (1860).

[44] van Santvoord, *A Treatise on the Principles of Pleading*, 12, 14, 17.

[45] John L. Tillinghast & Thomas G. Shearman, *The Practice, Pleadings and Forms in Civil Actions in the Courts of Record in the State of New York* (Lewis Brothers, 2d rev. ed., 1865), 1:v. See John Townshend, *The Code of Procedure of the State of New York as Amended to 1868* (1868), 85 § 69. On the evolution of Shearman's treatise, see chapter 5.

at common law and in equity were treated as providing a set of "rules" for contracts, and these rules informed the requirements for what facts ought to be pleaded in particular cases.[46]

Despite the contentious tone taken by Field and several New York jurists, both sides basically agreed that substance and form might be distinguishable without being separable. In Shearman's rendering, substantive law defined the material elements of a right to recover a remedy, and the material elements dictated the form of pleading and procedure. Traditional practitioners, however, reversed this logic. When jurists like Edmonds wrote that "the principles of pleading are left untouched," they were not seeking to repeal the code. Rather, they were replying to Field that substantive rules were, in fact, found in the old rules of pleading. Van Santvoord summarized his understanding of the code with the maxim: "The forms of action are abolished, but their substance and the principles which govern them are preserved." And Judge Barculo agreed that "there is *substance* in the distinction between actions." Either way, it was in the old rules of pleading where lawyers could inform themselves about the substantive content of the law.[47]

Several decades after the rise of code practice, the English legal historian Henry Maine wrote his famous observation in *On Early Law and Custom* that "so great is the ascendancy of the Law of Actions in the infancy of Courts of Justice, that substantive law has at first the look of being gradually secreted in the interstices of procedure; and the early lawyer can only see the law through the envelope of its technical forms."[48] Maine did not fully appreciate that the reversal of his aphorism had occurred in his own lifetime. His "early lawyer" described American practitioners in the 1860s quite well. Applying the code in practice, jurists believed the old forms of action best apprised lawyers of what elements of a claim they would have to prove at trial—the envelope of technical form continued to carry the substantive law within.

After a couple of decades of self-consciously extracting substantive rules from old formulary pleadings, traditionalist lawyers gradually turned Field's theoretical prescriptions into an actual description of the law in practice. The very language of writs and rights shifted over time, as Figure 6.2 illustrates. Treatises on "practice" in general became scarce, while treatments of "procedure" grew slimmer as they focused less on the general rules of civil obligations. As G. Edward White has noted, with the abolition of the formulary system, tort became a distinct legal domain by the end of the century, a substantive body of law with its own doctrines and rules. As in torts, so also in contracts and a growing number of subfields: "substantive law" now defined the elements of rights claims, and pleaders had to learn their content from these substantive rules.[49]

[46] Tillinghast & Shearman, *The Practice, Pleadings and Forms in Civil Actions*, 57, 17, 82–88 (equitable claims), 89–101 (contract claims), 102–10 (tort claims).

[47] Dollner v. Gibson, 3 Code Rep. 153 (N.Y. Sup. Ct. 1850), 154; van Santvoord, *A Treatise on the Principles of Pleading*, 56; Le Roy v. Marshall, 8 How. 373, 376 (N.Y. Sup. Ct. 1853).

[48] Sir Henry Summer Maine, *On Early Law and Custom* (London, 1890), 389. On Maine's historicism, see David M. Rabban, *Law's History: American Legal Thought and the Transatlantic Turn to History* (Cambridge 2013), 115–49.

[49] G. Edward White, *Law in American History, Volume 2: From Reconstruction Through the 1920s* (Oxford University Press, 2016), 230–80.

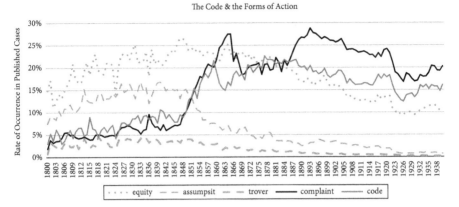

The Code & the Forms of Action

Figure 6.2 References to specific common law forms of action like assumpsit and trover as well as the distinct domain of equity declined in reported cases after the advent of the code in 1848, while reference to the code and its preferred locution of "complaints" became standard vocabulary.

Data drawn from Harvard Law School's Caselaw Access Project. See https://old.case.law/trends/.

The separation of substance from procedure did not happen immediately and, as jurists tried to tell Field, could not happen immediately. "The science of pleading is broken up. Its foundations are now to be relaid," wrote Judge Selden. "Let each one whose duty it may become to aid in the erection of the new edifice, lay his block."[50] Without any guidance from the code, the substantive elements of each common law claim had to be built up piece by piece, judge by judge, and case by case. Each would have to inquire how a claim would have been pleaded under the old forms, which parts of those forms created material substantive elements, and which were mere "technical" or fictitious requirements. Some inquiries would be more difficult than others. In trover (money damages for wrongful taking of personal property), the allegation that one casually lost the goods was clearly a fiction that need no longer be pleaded. But what about an allegation that the plaintiff had demanded the return of the goods and been refused? Most trover cases never went to issue over the sufficiency of the plaintiff's pretrial demands, but a few had. Was a demand then a disposable fiction or a material element the plaintiff had to plead to justify a recovery? Van Santvoord advised that in some cases, the demand was material (e.g., bailment and the physical taking of goods), while in others, it would be a needless fiction (e.g., the wrongful sale or destruction of property).[51]

In its ultimate practical effect, the Field Code did not abolish the forms of action—it multiplied them exponentially. Whereas before the code a pleading using the form of trover could introduce nearly a dozen claims relating to the wrongful conversion of personal property, now each theory had its own form, defined by its material

---

[50] Wooden v. Waffle, 6 How. 145, 148 (N.Y. Sup. Ct. 1851).
[51] van Santvoord, *A Treatise on the Principles of Pleading*, 276–77.

elements, all of which had to be pleaded in proper order and with sufficient supporting facts. Shearman's treatise provided over three hundred form pleadings, which was
"much reduced from what was contemplated," leaving out many forms for formerly
equitable actions.[52] Paradoxically, the procedure code may have contained much
more material than civilians considered to be "procedure," but it contained far less
material than Anglo-American jurists had considered to be the law of "pleading and
practice," which the commission purported to codify.

   Judges were left to fill in the gaps, defining the material elements of each remedial
claim and thereby creating the very oracles that codification was supposed to destroy.
By making causes of action substantive and leaving them undefined in the procedure
code, Field created the conditions for judges to declare the substantive law directly
rather than deciding mere rules of proof or pleading as early modern practitioners
had described their practices. At times, judges expressed their worries that the code
"casts upon the court great power and responsibility," but instead of drawing attention
to the need to declare substantive law, judges more often proclaimed faithful adherence "to certain settled principles by which good pleading is tested."[53]

V

The transformation of the old formulary system into sets of substantive material
elements for each claim raised a further complication in light of the code's fusion of
law and equity because the very notion of materiality appeared to differ in each tradition. "The allegations in a pleading at law, consist of a *chain* of facts, all tending
to establish some definite legal right," Judge Selden explained. "An equity pleading,
on the contrary, frequently, if not generally, consists of an accumulation of facts and
circumstances, without logical dependency, but the accumulated weight of which is
claimed to be sufficient to raise or defeat an equity." Following the same metaphor,
Judge Barculo pithily explained that "the one is a chain which is worthless if a single
link fail; the other a rope composed of numerous strands, some of which may give
way, and yet enough remain to secure some relief."[54] In effect, each system had used a
different standard of materiality. At common law, "material" meant *dispositive* of the
case; in equity, "material" meant *considerable*.

   The dilemma judges faced was that any decision to define a claim's material elements was likely to run afoul of some provision of the code. Common law pleadings
were plain and concise, but often conclusory. Equitable pleadings were factually detailed and devoid of fiction, but they were rarely "simple" and concise as the code
seemed to require. An early consensus developed among New York judges that it was

---

[52] On the multiplicity of claims that could come under a single form of common law action, see Wells,
Law of the State (Missouri, 1849) 44; *First Report* (Maryland, 1855), 44–45; Tillinghast & Shearman, *The
Practice, Pleadings and Forms in Civil Actions*, 1:iv. Cf. William P. LaPiana, "Just the Facts: The Field Code
and the Case Method," 36 *New York Law School Law Review*, 287, 313 (1991).

[53] Boyce v. Brown, 7 Barb. 80, 86 (N.Y. Sup. Ct. 1849).

[54] *Wooden*, 6 How. at 152; Le Roy v. Marshall, 8 How. 373, 375 (N.Y. Sup. Ct. 1853). See also van
Santvoord, *A Treatise on the Principles of Pleading*, 75.

better to err on the side of decisive, conclusory statements that mimicked common law pleading.[55]

One of these cases—a debt collection—was the one that opened a rift between Field and Judge Edmonds. Plaintiffs Dollner and Potter had sold nearly $600 worth of stearin (a fat used in candle making) to Adam Maitland, an agent of defendant Gibson, but Gibson never paid the bill. How should Dollner have complained? Was it a material "fact" that the partners sold stearin "to the defendant"? That seemed to involve several conclusions of law, particularly the rules of how agents bound their principals. Were the facts, then, that the partners sold to Maitland, and "Maitland acted with the knowledge and assent of said defendant, and as his agent"? That might stray too far into immateriality, for those statements would not have been decisive of the case at common law (express agency might be disproven, but Gibson's liability would still stand). Dollner and Potter's counsel opted for the latter strategy to include more facts.[56]

In hearing the defendant's motion to strike out the complaint, Edmonds, who had sympathetically explained the code to law students two years earlier, now showed some peevishness in having to apply the code in daily practice. He opined that "among the many questions of doubt and difficulty which have arisen under the Code—and those have been very numerous which flow from the imperfect and inartificial use of the language in which it is expressed—there has been none which has given rise to as much diversity of opinion as that in regard to pleading." Even in the paradigm case of a simple creditor's remedy, the line between evidence, fact, and law was difficult to draw. In Edmonds's experience, pleaders "are misled by their familiarity with the old mode of pleading in equity . . . . That whole thing, however, is changed."[57] Edmonds understood the requirement for "simple," straightforward pleadings to refine the old common law forms by stripping away their fictions and leaving "the dry allegation of the fact, without detailing a variety of minute circumstances, which constitute the evidence of it." In this case, the material element was the sale and delivery of goods, so the "dry allegation of the fact" should have stated merely that, not the immaterial actions of intermediate agents.[58]

Edmonds's rule was easy to administer in former common law actions, which may have been why so many other judges adopted it at first. Nearly the same pleadings as before could be used and reused as long as overt fictions were discarded. As Figure 6.3 shows, the publishers of law blanks lost no time running off new common law-style pleadings for use under the new code. The standard was difficult to apply in equity-style claims, however. In one early case Judge Selden presided over a complicated real property controversy in which the plaintiff sought an injunction. The plaintiff's

[55] See, for instance, Dollner, 3 Code Rep. at 153; Millikin v. Cary, 5 How. 272 (N.Y. Sup. Ct. 1850); Boyce, 7 Barb. at 80; Shaw v. Jayne, 4 How. 119 (N.Y. Sup. Ct. 1849).

[56] Dollner v. Gibson, 3 Code Rep. 153; 2 Edm. Sel. Cas. 253 (N.Y. Sup. Ct. 1850).

[57] Equitable pleading, according to Edmonds, "was not merely a mode of setting out a claim, but was a means of obtaining evidence of particular facts to substantiate that claim, and it necessarily dealt in probative facts as well as in the legal effects of them." 3 Code Rep. at 153–55; 2 Edm. Sel. Cas. at 253–55. Numerous cases commented that although the code seemed to recommend equitable pleadings, the pleadings should omit the evidentiary examinations that had been common in chancery. See, for instance, Wooden v. Waffle, 6 How. 145, 155 (N.Y. Sup. Ct. 1851); van Santvoord, A Treatise on the Principles of Pleading, 79.

[58] 3 Code Rep. at 153–55; 2 Edm. Sel. Cas. at 253–55.

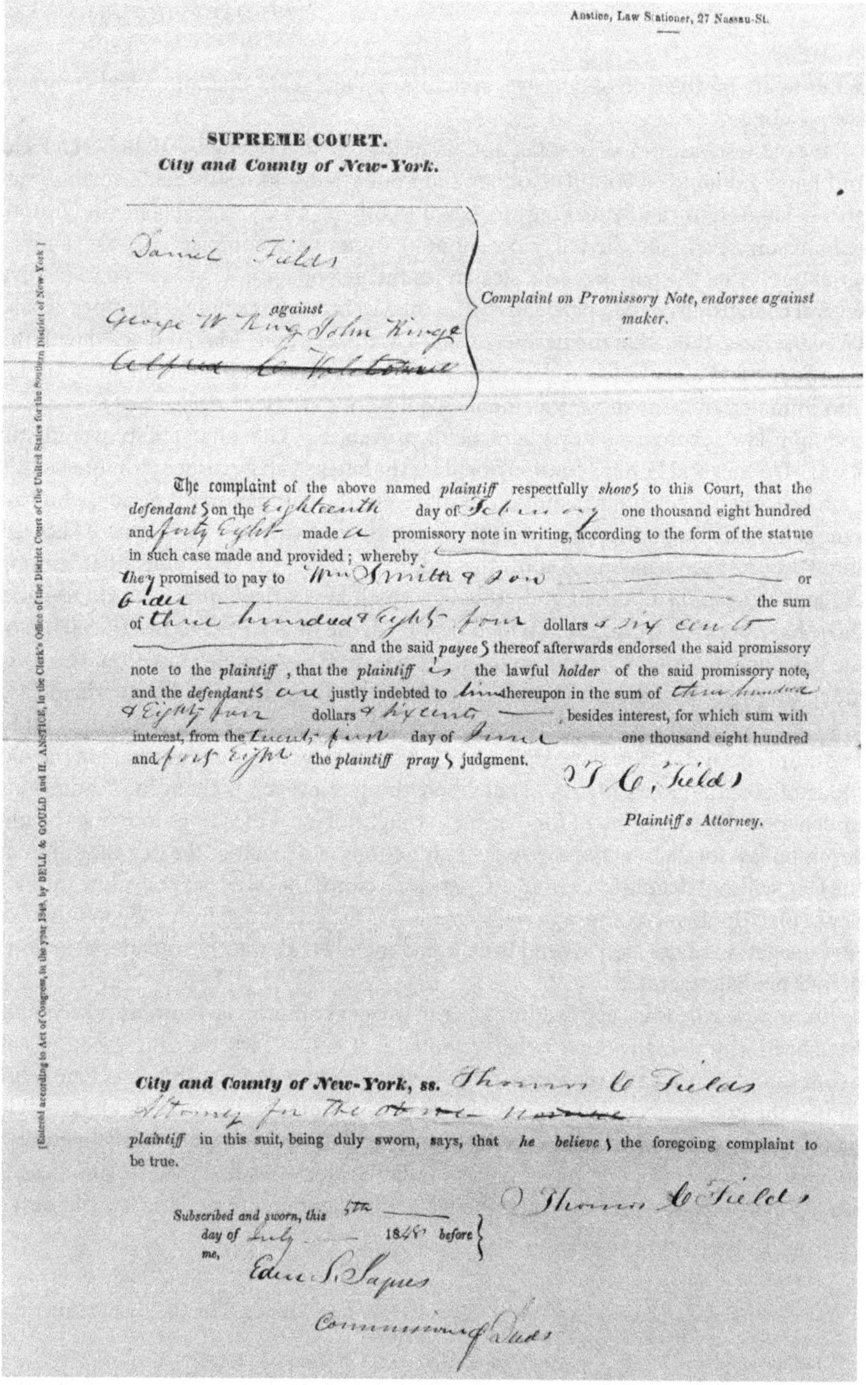

Anstice, Law Stationer, 27 Nassau-St.

SUPREME COURT.
City and County of New-York.

Daniel Fields

against

George W. King, John King &
Alfred C. Valentine

Complaint on Promissory Note, endorsee against maker.

The complaint of the above named *plaintiff* respectfully *shows* to this Court, that the *defendant*s on the *Eighteenth* day of *February* one thousand eight hundred and *forty Eight* made *a* promissory note in writing, according to the form of the statute in such case made and provided; whereby *they* promised to pay to *Wm Smith & Son* or *order* the sum of *three hundred & Eighty four* dollars *& six cents* and the said *payee*s thereof afterwards endorsed the said promissory note to the *plaintiff*, that the *plaintiff* *is* the lawful *holder* of the said promissory note, and the *defendant*s *are* justly indebted to *him* thereupon in the sum of *three hundred & Eighty four* dollars *& six cents*, besides interest, for which sum with interest, from the *twenty first* day of *June* one thousand eight hundred and *forty Eight* the *plaintiff* pray s judgment.

T. C. Fields

Plaintiff's Attorney.

City and County of New-York, ss. *Thomas C. Fields*
Attorney for the above named
plaintiff in this suit, being duly sworn, says, that *he* *believe*s the foregoing complaint to be true.

Thomas C. Fields

Subscribed and sworn, this *5th* day of *July* 184*8* before me, *Edwin S. Sames*

Commissioner of deeds

Figure 6.3 A law blank filed just after the code went into effect. The pleading is around eight hundred words shorter than the money counts (compare Figure 1.2), and it states the actual amount of the debt, $384.06. The lawyer's signature at the bottom swears to the truth of the allegations.

Pleadings of the Supreme Court of Judicature Collection, PL-1848-F-26, Fields v. King et al., New York City Municipal Archives, Office of the New York County Clerk.

complaint consisted of 41 pages, the defendant's answer 458 pages. Even after Selden struck most of the answer for stating immaterial evidence and argumentation, he thought it clear "that the term 'material issue' cannot be applied to an equity pleading in the common law sense, as an issue decisive of the whole case."[59]

Further explaining his approach to interpreting the code, Selden argued that despite the code's attempt to abolish the distinction between law and equity, each tradition proceeded on fundamentally different ideas about disputed issues. Selden urged that the centrality of the jury to common law proceedings had created this difference. Through "the use of simple and settled forms of issues," Judge Hand agreed, "juries can generally respond yea or nay."[60] Because common law actions had developed through the binary judgment of the jury's yea or nay, material issues at common law could always be decisive. The plaintiffs either sold and delivered the goods to the defendants or they did not. That "fact" was not to be a question of degree, shifting with particular circumstances, but of stark occurrence or non-occurrence. As rule-bound and precedential as equity may have become by the 1840s, its dispositive issues still raised questions of relative weight for a judge to assess. Was an injunction deserved, all things considered? For a limited time or permanently, given the circumstances?

Thus after initial consensus on adopting the common law standard of materiality, judges gradually reversed the early decisions, at least as they might apply to equitable claims and defenses. Summarizing the new line of cases, van Santvoord reasoned that, despite the supposed fusion of law and equity, "the statement of facts in a pleading is to be made in accordance with the particular kind of relief demanded." For common law remedies, say upon simple contracts, pleaders were to allege decisive facts with an eye to their "legal effects," but for equity-style remedies, pleaders were best advised to state "a variety of facts and circumstances," any of which "might become in the failure of proof of other allegations, a material fact to entitle the party to particular relief sought."[61]

Field and Shearman disagreed with this newly developing consensus because it kept alive the distinction between law and equity that the code in its famous Section 69 had expressly abolished. Moreover, pleading "legal effects" or "legal conclusions" in common law claims threatened to return pleadings to the "artificial system" that had obscured truthful facts beneath fictions pleaded to satisfy the elements of common law pleading. Field insisted that "a legal inference, or conclusion from the facts, should not be stated; that is not the province of the pleadings under our system." But Field and Shearman continued to struggle to define "facts" in a way that distinguished them from the legal conclusions which were the exclusive "province of the court."[62] Shearman's attempt in his treatise held forth:

Facts, within the meaning of the Code, are in general actual occurrences—physical facts, capable of demonstration by evidence without any reference to municipal law,

[59] *Wooden*, 6 How. at 152.

[60] *Ibid.*, 150; *Boyce*, 7 Barb. at 86.

[61] van Santvoord, *A Treatise on the Principles of Pleading*, 75, 244. See *Millikin*, 5 How. at 272; *Minor v. Terry*, 6 How. 208 (N.Y. Sup. Ct. 1851); *Williams v. Hayes*, 5 How. 471 (N.Y. Sup. Ct. 1851); *Fry v. Bennett*, 5 Sand. 54 (N.Y. Super. Ct. 1851); *Buddington v. Davis*, 6 How. 401 (N.Y. Sup. Ct. 1851); *Field and Stone v. Morse*, 7 How. 12 (N.Y. Sup. Ct. 1852).

[62] *A Short Manual on Pleading*, 10, 13–14.

and from which the court can draw the legal conclusions necessary to sustain the pleader's case. . . . Thus, if A. borrows money of B., the borrowing is a fact, and the non-payment is a fact, but the consequent inferences that B. *owes* A. the money, and that A. is *entitled* to have it, are conclusions of law, and not actual facts.

As courts frequently pointed out, such subtlety could be difficult to apply in practice. How, for instance, could one factually state a claim to land without invoking "ownership" or "possession" or, at the very least, the "delivery" of a deed? Yet all of these terms were also legal constructions. Could they not, then, in Shearman's phrasing, be "actual facts"?[63]

Shearman admitted that "the rule excluding conclusions of law is not . . . to be enforced too rigidly. Mixed allegations of law and fact are frequently allowed, sometimes to avoid prolixity, and in other cases because such allegations are quite as much in harmony with the ordinary usages of speech."[64] But in that case, responded Judge Selden, the code failed to state an administrable rule, and "to determine precisely *how great* an infusion of law will be allowed to enter into the composition of a *pleadable* fact, precedent and analogy are our only guides."[65]

Whittaker's treatise advised lawyers "to state not one word, not on syllable more" than necessary, as "every unnecessary allegation" gave "an advantage to the adversary." Nevertheless, out of caution, most lawyers pursued the opposite strategy, and Shearman recorded by 1870 a consensus "that the rules of pleading applied in chancery to the *stating* part of a bill, are the best rules left from the old practice as a guide in the new." The eminent trial lawyer Charles O'Conor agreed with Shearman's assessment. Like Edmonds, O'Conor had eagerly advocated for the code when it appeared in 1848. Like Edmonds, O'Conor had also become disaffected by the code in practice and supported his law partner James Coolidge Carter's crusade against Field's civil code. In O'Conor's experience of code pleading, "the common practice is to tell your story to the court, precisely as your client tells it to you, and just as any old woman, in trouble for the first time, would narrate her grievances" to her neighbor.[66]

Making due allowance for O'Conor's exaggerations, the code's preference for equity practice was striking, especially considering the power it accorded judges to frame cases and, thus, the law that would decide them. As another practitioner wrote in criticism of the code, "the net result" of the new system "has been to throw upon the courts the burden of analyzing the contents of the complaint and of determining in each instance what is the substance of the cause of action set forth or sought to be set forth, and whether equitable or legal, tortious or contractual rights are involved." Pre-code treatises had warned that this was the precise danger of civilian pleading: it allowed judges to frame the questions to which they were to provide the legal answers. Equity could make limited use of that power as long as it followed behind and analogized

---

[63] Tillinghast & Shearman, *The Practice, Pleadings and Forms in Civil Actions*, 1:9–10. See Dows v. Hotchkiss, 10 N.Y. Leg. Observer 281, 283–84 (N.Y. Sup. Ct. 1852).

[64] Tillinghast & Shearman, *The Practice, Pleadings and Forms in Civil Actions*, 1:12.

[65] Dows, 10 N.Y. Leg. Observer at 284.

[66] Whittaker, *Practice and Pleading under the Code*, 1:326; Tillinghast & Shearman, *The Practice, Pleadings and Forms in Civil Actions*, 1:3. See "Some Recollections of Charles O'Conor," 29 *Century* 725 (1885); "Mr. O'Conor and the New York Code," 1 *Albany Law Journal* 302, 303 (1870).

itself to the processes of the common law.[67] Those processes abolished, every case under the code became an equity case, and every judge an unguided chancellor.

VI

Even judges who supported the code tended to decline the powers it afforded them, at least when they could. When Judge Edmonds agreed to strike the needlessly detailed facts of agency in the *Dollner* case, it left the complaint without any allegation of the defendant's liability. Edmonds accordingly ruled that the claim must fail. Under the specific provisions of the code on amendments as well as the general instruction that pleadings "must be liberally construed, with a view to substantial justice between the parties," Edmonds could have ordered the pleading amended to state that Dollner sold directly to Gibson, and Gibson was thus liable. Edmonds was well aware that "the subject of amendments is put forth quite prominently in the Code, as being as liberal as could be devised," but like most judges, both in New York and elsewhere, he refused to employ the powers the code had conferred on him to edit party pleadings.[68]

Another prominent code-friendly judge who refused such powers was Field's brother, Stephen Johnson Field, chief justice of the California supreme court from 1859 to 1863 and the legislator who had introduced the Final Report of the New York Code into California law in 1850. Like Edmonds, Stephen regularly expressed frustration with counsel who failed to heed the rule "that facts, and not the evidence of facts, should be alleged." He may have had an even harder time dealing with western lawyers who used the pleadings as a chance to spin colorfully detailed stories of frontier life that, as Stephen supposed, "subserve no useful purpose, and are only calculated, when read to the jury, to excite prejudice against the defendants." In one such case, Stephen reproduced nearly all of David Dudley's pleading manual as the official decision. Nevertheless, like Edmonds, Stephen Field did not order an amendment on the court's own motion; he granted motions to edit the pleadings only if raised by opposing counsel.[69]

What, then, explains the apparent conservatism of judges under the code? Some, like Barculo, may have been reflexively hostile to its attempted reforms, but many, like Edmonds and Stephen Field, were professed allies of the reformed system. Even Barculo's biographer declared him to be an earnest advocate of the code's reforms until he had to administer them in practice.[70] In some cases, judges professed the need to restrain themselves in light of the powers the code had placed upon them. In a case that recognized both the expansion of equitable pleading under the code and the need for judges to declare anew the substantive elements of each remedy claimed,

---

[67] Hornblower, "Fifty Years of Reformed Procedure," 290. On the pre-code treatises, see chapter 2. See also B. Tucker, *Principles of Pleading* (Little, Brown, 1846), 1–4; S. Croswell & R. Sutton, eds., *Debates and Proceedings in the New-York State Convention* (Albany Argus, 1846), 444.

[68] 3 Code Rep. at 155–56; 2 Edm. Sel. Cas. at 256–57; 1848 N.Y. Laws 524; Edmonds, *An Address on the Constitution and the Code of Procedure*, 36. See also *First Report* (1848), 158 (commissioners "provide a means of amendment of the most liberal character, as liberal, indeed, as we could devise").

[69] Coryell v. Cain, 16 Cal. 567 (1860); Green v. Palmer, 16 Cal. 571 (1860).

[70] Thompson, "Judge Barculo," 659–61.

Judge Selden declared that if any judge could do it "with unshaken nerve, I am not the man."[71] Whether or not all judges shared Selden's sentiment, two other practical barriers prevented judges from acting like the oracular chancellors the code proclaimed them to be.

The first problem was that, as Judge Barculo had written, the code seemingly "repeal[ed] itself" in the way it both demanded "liberality" in the joinder and amendment of claims yet also prohibited arguments in the alternative. Since Field's "rule number one" was that "pleadings must be true," both the code and the official commentary on it made clear that arguments in the alternative could not be permitted in the reformed system. "Obviously," Shearman wrote, code pleading's central "purpose would be entirely defeated, if the plaintiff should be allowed to put his demand in an alternative or hypothetical form." One of the earliest cases brought under the code provided an apt illustration. The defendant answered that he did not cross the plaintiff's land and trample a garden, but "if" he did, he had an easement that the garden obstructed. The court struck the answer as insufficient. It could not have been true that the defendant both did and did not cross the plaintiff's land.[72]

Field's prohibition on arguments in the alternative was at the root of his altercation with Judge Barculo. The code's provision for the joinder of claims in the same action between the same parties enumerated seven classes of actions and stated that "the plaintiff may unite several causes of action in the same complaint," provided that "the causes of action so united must all belong to one only of these classes." The classes included contracts express or implied, injuries by force, injuries without force, injuries to character, claims to recover real property, claims to recover personal property, and claims against a trustee. Field wrote elsewhere that "our own opinion is decided, that the plaintiff should be left free to unite, in the same action, all his controversies with the same parties, if he be so inclined," citing former practices in equity and admiralty. The intent of the joinder restriction seems to have been to ensure that plaintiffs did not resort to the old "common counts" of common law pleading, whereby the same claim could be argued under different theories of recovery and joined in one action. But with the code's abolition of the forms of action, it was not entirely clear what claims fit into which categories. Did the failure to deliver goods give rise to a claim upon implied contract? Or a claim to recover property? Or maybe a bailment claim against a trustee? "Had the old phraseology with which the profession was familiar been retained, fewer mistakes would have been made in this respect," van Santvoord opined. Almost all trusteeships were created by contract, so could trustee claims be joined with contract claims under the first class, or did they have to be separately litigated since they had their own class? That was the issue of the case Field argued before Barculo, and Barculo ruled that trust claims could not be joined to contract claims under the plain meaning of the code's enumerated classes.[73]

---

[71] Wooden v. Waffle, 6 How. 145, 148 (N.Y. Sup. Ct. 1851).

[72] A Short Manual on Pleading, 10; Tillinghast & Shearman, The Practice, Pleadings and Forms in Civil Actions, 1:114; Boyce v. Brown, 7 Barb. 80 (N.Y. Sup. Ct. 1849).

[73] 1848 N.Y. Laws 525 § 143. Administration of the Code, 21–24; van Santvoord, A Treatise on the Principles of Pleading, 346. Alger, 6 How. at 131.

On joinder and amendment, the code thus instructed judges to simultaneous liberality and constraint. Actions could be freely united and amended at the option of the parties, but they could not be united or amended if doing so would become a means of arguing in the alternative, joining different hypothetical claims to improve one's chances at trial. Of course, the difficulty was that judges could not know in advance how parties and their counsel were strategically using their pleadings. That created the second problem for judicial activism under the code. Although the code required (and Field's tracts urged) judges to be active in policing the pleadings to force candor from the parties, recreating the give and take of oral negotiation, the legislation provided insufficient details about how this process should work through written pleadings and motions. The entire regulation on this point, in the Amended Code of 1849 read:

> § 160. If irrelevant or redundant matter be inserted in a pleading, it may be stricken out, on motion of any person aggrieved thereby. And when the allegations of a pleading are so indefinite or uncertain that the precise nature of the charge or defense is not apparent, the court may require the pleading to be made definite and certain, by amendment.

Nowhere else did the code define or regulate "motions" or clarify how motions differed from demurrers which sought the entire dismissal of an action for failure to plead a valid cause of action or defense.[74] Treatise literature recognized these issues would have to be resolved by case law.[75]

In practice, litigants preferred to file demurrers—winning a claim outright was better than merely forcing an amendment on one's adversary. But whether parties moved for amendments or demurrers, judicial decisions on these motions became matters of record that could then be challenged on appeal.[76] By attempting to formalize in written pleadings the informal oral negotiations that had taken place at trial, the Field Code essentially abolished those negotiation practices altogether. The oral back and forth between judges and counsel had often escaped the record books, and thus, no precedents could accumulate to bind these practices to particular rules. By forcing those negotiations into the record, the Field Code made judges more reluctant to exercise their newfound powers. In court, the idea of editing written pleadings

---

[74] 1849 N.Y. Laws 648. A demurrer permitted a party to argue that even if everything his adversary said was true as a matter of fact, it failed as a matter of law because there was no remedy a court could offer on that set of facts. David Graham, *A Treatise on the Practice of the Supreme Court of the State of New York* (Gould & Banks, 2d ed., 1836), 754. The original code permitted demurrer on the grounds that (1) a plaintiff did not have capacity to sue, (2) the action was redundant with another action already pending between the parties, (3) there was a defect of joinder, either of parties or issues, and (4) the complaint did not "state facts sufficient to constitute a cause of action." 1848 N.Y. Laws 521–522, § 122. As in the rest of the code, that last phrase went undefined.

[75] van Santvoord, *A Treatise on the Principles of Pleading*, 348–54; Whittaker, *Practice and Pleading under the Code*, 1:352–55; Tillinghast & Shearman, *The Practice, Pleadings and Forms in Civil Actions*, passim, 1:131–201.

[76] See, e.g., 1849 N.Y. Laws 680 § 329 (permitting an appeal after judgment to review any intermediate order, involving the merits, and necessarily affecting the judgment"). On the application of this provision to a demurrer, which in some cases operated as a final judgment and in other as an intermediate order, as well as motions to edit the pleadings, see Whittaker, *Practice and Pleading under the Code*, 2:200–05.

to create liabilities and requests for relief where they had not existed before seemed unthinkable.

Or, more probably, the idea seemed too lawyerly. One western lawyer exclaimed that the judicial power of amendment was "a monstrosity in judicial procedure." It was for counsel to plead and amend pleadings, and if one side made a mistake, counsel on the other side could take tactical advantage of it by moving to strike.[77] And counsel wished only to strike defective pleadings, not cure them to help their adversary's case. Rather than risk the appearance of impartiality by supplying winning arguments and formulas to defective pleaders, judges ignored the code. They deferred to the lawyers, granting—only when requested—motions to remedy defective pleadings by striking them.

VII

The Field Code would have to wait another generation to find its most sympathetic reader on the bench. Like Field himself, that reader was not overeager to name his direct influences. Nevertheless, Charles E. Clark, a young dean of the Yale Law School and then judge of the Second Circuit Court of Appeals, grasped Field's aims better than many present-day commentators have, and accounts that portray Clark as "revolutionizing" practice unjustifiably discount his claim that the Federal Rules essentially elevated the Field Code to the federal level. Almost the entirety of Clark's academic work focused on the history of code pleading and remedies. Clark especially tried to rescue what he understood as the codifiers' aims in pleading a "cause of action" and in defending their views on the fusion of law and equity.[78]

Indeed, the ground on which Clark and Field most agreed was in their theory of pleading, though modern commentary has often overlooked this connection. From their inception, the 1938 Federal Rules were understood to implement a regime of "notice pleading"—pleading that suffices as long as it merely puts the opposing party on notice that a lawsuit concerning some particular event has been filed—as against the Field Code's "fact pleading" with its technical distinctions between evidence, ultimate facts, and conclusions of law. The triumph of Clarkian notice pleading over Fieldian fact pleading was a cornerstone of Supreme Court doctrine for half a century, and the Field Code's latest citations in Supreme Court opinions came in 2007 and 2009 dissents that criticized the majorities for mistakenly resurrecting fact pleading in the Federal Rules—a charge echoed by numerous other jurists.[79]

---

[77] "A Code Lawyer on the Code," *Rocky Mountain News* (Denver, Colo.), Jan. 24, 1877.

[78] See, e.g., Charles E. Clark, "The Code Cause of Action," 33 *Yale Law Journal* 817 (1924); Charles E. Clark, "Union of Law and Equity," 25 *Columbia Law Review* 1 (1925); Charles E. Clark, "The New Federal Rules of Civil Procedure: The Last Phase—Underlying Philosophy Embodied in Some of the Basic Provisions of the New Procedure," 23 *ABA Journal* 976 (1937). Compare Federal Rule of Civil Procedure 1, 8 (1938), with 1849 N.Y. Laws 630–631 § 59, § 142.

[79] See Ashcroft v. Iqbal, 556 U.S. 662, 678 (2009) ("Rule 8 marks a notable and generous departure from the hypertechnical, code-pleading regime of a prior era."); Bell Atlantic Corp. v. Twombly, 550 U.S. 544, 574–75 (2007) (Stevens, J., dissenting); Kevin M. Clermont, "The Myths about Twombly-Iqbal," 45 *Wake Forest Law Review* 1337 (2010), 1340–59 (surveying the literature of the fact-pleading critique).

The perceived opposition between Clark and Field is understandable, since Clark presented his work as a dramatic break from fact pleading as it had developed in New York. But Clark was highly critical of New York's implementation of the code, not the theory of the code itself. One of his favorite quotations came from Chief Justice John B. Winslow of Wisconsin, who wrote of the "cold, not to say inhuman, treatment which the infant code received from the New York judges."[80] Clark was careful in his writings, especially before the enactment of the Rules, to insist he was not elevating New York procedure to the federal system, leading him occasionally to conflate New York practice with the early New York commissioners in his criticism. As often as he could, Clark claimed Livingston's Louisiana code or the English judicature and practice acts as progenitors of his work—or, more often, he combined both of them with the Field Code into a "modern" procedure of no clear provenance. Other times, Clark sought to divorce criticism of New York from criticism of the New York code system. "New York is often pointed to as an example of the lack of success of the code system," he observed. But, in his view, New York "is not actually" a code state at all, given the "conflicting statutory enactments and diverse rulings of the court" that had made a mess of the code over time. Instead, "the success of such widely divergent states as California, Minnesota, and Connecticut indicates the real effectiveness of [code] procedure."[81]

Clark criticized Field and the other codifiers for their inelastic view of "facts," but Clark's theory of fact pleading was not so much a departure from Field's ideas as a refinement of them. He wrote that "the codifiers and the courts failed to appreciate that the difference between statements of fact and statements of law is almost entirely one of degree only." As early critics of Field recognized, *A is married to B* might in one case be an uncontroversial background "fact," but in another case (such as a prosecution for bigamy) it would be the ultimate legal judgment to be supported with other factual evidence. But where common law lawyers concluded that pleading had to be guided by formulary systems gradually worked out by the peculiar reasoning of the common law, Clark saw the solution as simply less insistence on the factuality of the facts or, as he put it, to "expect less of pleading."[82]

The problem with code pleading, Clark believed, was not fact pleading itself but fact pleading done poorly—pleading *just* facts. "We think of 'facts' as things definite and concrete, as representations of past events now a part of history and thus fixed and unchangeable," he explained, before countering: "Actually the stating of facts involves a mental process of *selecting* from among observed phenomena those which are important *in view of our particular purpose*, and *interpreting them in the light of that purpose*." Clark agreed with the codifiers that merely stating legal conclusions did not make for appropriate pleading. In that sense, Clark had no use for actual notice

[80] McArthur v. Moffet, 143 Wis. 564, 567, 128 N.W. 445 (1910). Quoted, for instance, in Charles E. Clark, "Addresses on the Proposed Rules of Civil Procedure," 22 *ABA Journal* 787 (1936), 787; Clark, "Union of Law and Equity," 2–3.

[81] Charles E. Clark, "History, Systems, and Functions of Pleading," 11 *Virginia Law Review* 517 (1925), 531–37; Charles E. Clark & James Wm. Moore, "A New Federal Procedure—I. The Background," 44 *Yale Law Journal* 387 (1935), 393–94.

[82] Clark, "History, Systems, and Functions of Pleading," 534, 542; Charles E. Clark, "The Complaint in Code Pleading," 35 *Yale Law Journal* 259 (1926), 264–265.

pleading if that meant simply notifying the other party that a suit was forthcoming on some legal ground and not another. Elsewhere, Clark explained that "we are helped, rather than hindered, by thinking of our problem as simply giving a bit of past history," which Clark also called "a segment of private history between the litigants."[83]

In essence, skillful pleading in Clark's ideal system perfectly combined public law with private history. The public law of substantive rights gave pleadings their narrative organization and guided lawyers as to which facts from a private encounter between parties needed to be included. *A negligently breached his duty of care and damaged B* stated only the public elements—the plot points—and was insufficient even if it gave B clear notice of the grounds of a lawsuit. *Jack, while driving blindfolded on June 15, struck Lucy on the knee, which required $10,000 of surgery to repair* tracked those same elements with case-specific facts. So far, Clark's advice followed point for point Field's guidance in his manual on pleading and the book of forms Shearman had offered.[84]

A private history of Jack's antics and Lucy's knee could be told in a thousand variations of more or less detail. Would the statement given above be a sufficient pleading? Clark's answer was indefinite. To Clark, there was "no absolute definite definition, no mathematical test to be applied as a rule of thumb." There was "no royal road to pleading for either bench or bar." Like Field, Clark believed reformed procedure had to be essentially formless. But what then would constrain the pleaders, keeping them from being too taciturn and withholding crucial details or being too prolix and wasting the court's time? Like Field, Clark trusted the judiciary to keep the pleaders in bounds. "How specific the plaintiff's recital must be, and how much of the story we shall expect to hear from the defendant rather than the plaintiff" would be a task for judges to "work[] out in each case pragmatically with an idea of securing convenient and efficient dispatch of trial business."[85]

Clark lamented that it was "somewhat depressing, to observe the gradual development of an involved and technical practice from the piling up of precedents on an originally simple code." To him, "the moral seems clear. The ministers of justice must be eternally on the job of keeping their tools keen and bright. It is not a misfortune for a code of procedure to require revision; it is its nature." Clark never seemed to realize that the cure he prescribed was the very cause of his problems, for it had been the same solution Field offered eighty years earlier. Seeking to decide like cases alike, jurists published thousands of opinions explaining what a "plain" statement of facts should look like in particular kinds of cases. In this they were even guided by Field and Shearman's book of forms, despite the codifiers' claims to have invented a formless procedure. Clark's advisory committee too offered a book of forms. And so in the twentieth century, as in the nineteenth, a formless procedure of fact pleading only resulted in multiplying the forms of action, from the common law's twelve or so "technical" devices of fiction and flexibility to the hundreds and thousands of causes

---

[83] Clark, "The Complaint in Code Pleading," 264–265; Clark, "The Code Cause of Action," 832; Clark, "Union of Law and Equity," 5; cf. *A Short Manual on Pleading Under the Code*, 12–13.

[84] Clark did have a major disagreement with Field about pleading in the alternative, which Clark thought a positive good given how often plaintiffs might not know the exact circumstances of their injuries. For more on the problem of asymmetric information between the parties, see chapter 8. On Clark's view of hypothetical pleading, see Clark, "The Code Cause of Action," 826.

[85] *Ibid.*, 830–32, 837.

of action under modern American litigation, each now with its own generic—and no less "technical" —form for stating one's private history before the public tribunals.[86]

VIII

To be sure, the Field Code and the Federal Rules that followed it dramatically changed significant aspects of the practice of pleading. Overt fictions like the finding and losing of trover quickly receded, and the length of pleading significantly diminished even though straightforward common law claims became more factually detailed.[87] Even when van Santvoord and Whittaker produced their second editions in the mid-1850s, lawyers were routinely organizing their allegations into enumerated propositions designed to track the settled "elements" of various classes of claims. Early confusion about whether statements of ownership or delivery were actual facts or legal conclusions became settled with positive answers from the courts.[88]

But as they had done before the code, practitioners needed to consult the case law and the treatises to find these prescriptions. The code declared there to be but one form of action even as the commissioners' official form book provided several hundred forms for different "classes" of actions. In his most sympathetic reading of the code, Judge Edmonds figured substantive law would have to fix procedural form. "So long as other parts of the Law, not connected with the pleadings or practice of the Courts, recognize substantial distinctions, ... there will and must be substantial differences in the causes of action in respect to those subjects," Edmonds declared in his laudatory address on the code. But while the "Code has swept away from our jurisprudence the old forms of action," he remarked, "it has not blotted from our minds or our books the old learning on that subject." As Edmonds recognized, sheer truthfulness could not be an administrable principle. For a dispute to resolve, some "material issue upon some important part of the subject matter" had to be culled from the messy facts of everyday life. Cases could hardly proceed if they had to "set out all the circumstances" as they actually happened.[89] If the codifiers were ever to achieve their goal of a scientifically systematized and coherent substantive law, some artifice would be required to make the messy truths of any given case conform to the expected elements of legal rights.

That had been the use of the forms of action. But now that law's machinery called for facts while abolishing form, jurists surmised that forms of legal pleading would

[86] Clark, "History, Systems and Functions of Pleading," 545; *Book of Forms Adapted to the Code of Procedure* (1860); Federal Rule of Civil Procedure 84 & cmt. For a short and humorous "parable" to similar effect, see Samuel L. Bray, "The Parable of the Forms," 93 *St. John's Law Review* 623 (2019).

[87] About a quarter of plaintiff filings from 1849 New York consisted of a single page, a circumstance rarely attained before the code. See, e.g., Pleadings of the Supreme Court of Judicature Collection, PL-1849-B-1–B-50, New York City Municipal Archives.

[88] See Henry Whittaker, *Practice and Pleading Under the Code, Original and Amended, With Appendix of Forms* (E.O. Jenkins, 2d ed., 1854); George van Santvoord, *A Treatise on the Principles of Pleading in Civil Actions under the New York Code of Procedure* (Little & Co., 2d ed., 1855).

[89] Edmonds, *An Address on the Constitution and the Code of Procedure*, 22–24; Dollner, 3 Code Rep. at 155; 2 Edm. Sel. Cas. at 255–56. See also William Hornblower, "Fifty Years of Reformed Procedure," 6 *American Lawyer* 288 (1898), 290 ("Forms of actions are abolished, but kinds and classes of action remain.").

have to be inferred from the nature of law and legal right itself. That enterprise took far longer than the codifiers expected because the quest for "real" law continually led back to the pleadings lawyers had used before the code. No matter how much they supported the code and its aims, judges, lawyers, and jurists found their practices could not immediately dispel the magic of forms.

7

The Swearer's Prayer

Oathtaking and Witness Testimony

I

On a Sunday in the autumn of 1859, David Dudley Field's soon-to-be law partner Thomas G. Shearman sat awed by America's most famous preacher. "I never was so *quickly* affected by any sermon I ever heard—it seemed to reach my heart at once," Shearman scribbled in his journal, adding with winking humor that his public display of emotion made his wife "quite cross" with him. Although Shearman was still relatively new to the congregation, his journal marked Sunday, October 9, as the day he found a spiritual home under the preaching of Brooklyn's Henry Ward Beecher.[1]

Beecher, the son of a revivalist Presbyterian and brother to the author of *Uncle Tom's Cabin*, was renowned for his imaginative metaphors and soothing pulpit oratory. Comparing Beecher to Charles Finney, the firebrand revivalist of an earlier era, Beecher's successor at the Plymouth Church in Brooklyn remarked that "Dr. Finney drove men to repentance; Mr. Beecher drew them." Indeed, the sermon that Shearman said "melted me right down from the very beginning," was titled "The Gentleness of God."[2]

While most of the sermon might strike more modern ears as so many comfortable bromides, Beecher's conclusion about eternal destiny ended with surprising ambivalence:

Sometimes, in dark caves, men have gone to the edge of unspeaking precipices, and, wondering what was the depth, have cast down fragments of rock, and listened for the report of their fall, that they might judge how deep that blackness was; and listening—still listening—no sound returns; no sullen plash, no clinking stroke as of rock against rock—nothing but silence, utter silence! And so I stand upon the precipice of life. I sound the depths of the other world with curious inquiries. But from it comes no echo and no answer to my questions. No analogies can grapple and bring up from the depths of the darkness of the lost world the probable truths.

Beecher left the connection of this passage to the theme of God's gentleness implicit for his audience. The connection was clear to Shearman, though. When he wrote his memoirs in the 1880s, Shearman devoted the first hundred pages telling not how he

---

[1] Diary of Thomas G. Shearman, October 9, 1859, Papers of Thomas G. Shearman, Shearman & Sterling Law Library.
[2] Henry Ward Beecher, "The Gentleness of God," Sermon Preached at Plymouth Church, Brooklyn, New York, October 9, 1859, in Gaius Atkins, ed., *Master Sermons of the Nineteenth Century* (Willett, Clark & Co., 1940), 84–102; Lyman Abbott, *Henry Ward Beecher: A Sketch of His Career* (1887), 94–95; Shearman Diary, October 9, 1859.

Law's Machinery. Kellen R. Funk, Oxford University Press. © Kellen R. Funk 2025. DOI: 10.1093/9780197543962.003.0008

Figure 7.1 Printed reproduction of a film portrait of Thomas G. Shearman around 1860, when David Dudley Field hired him to perform clerical work. Shearman and Field later became law partners, the predecessor to today's Shearman & Sterling LLP.
Papers of Thomas G. Shearman, Shearman & Sterling Law Library.

became one of New York's wealthiest lawyers or an implacable courtroom litigator but rather how his years-long struggle to remain a devout Christian while rejecting doctrines of perdition finally ended in repose at Beecher's pulpit (see Figure 7.1). In Beecher, Shearman found a kindred spirit, a respectable New Yorker of reputable orthodoxy who nevertheless relaxed Protestant teaching on damnation that had been so crucial to an earlier generation of American revivalists.[3]

In the same era that mainstream American evangelicals might publicly doubt that a gentle God could damn souls to hell, Field's practice code sought to sunder any remaining connection between the legal system and Christian ideas of perdition by transforming the civil law's most explicit link to theology: the testimonial oath. While devout jurists and moral theologians in the eighteenth and nineteenth centuries insisted that the obligation of an oath depended on the swearer's belief in supernatural and usually eternal consequences for oath-breaking, Field, Shearman,

---

[3] Beecher, "The Gentleness of God," 98; see Memoirs of Thomas G. Shearman, vol. 1, esp. 40–92, Shearman Papers. At this time, a confidant observed, "Mr. Beecher believed in retribution . . . more definitely than he did subsequently." Abbott, *Henry Ward Beecher*, 94.

and their fellow codifiers sought to relocate the obligations of truth-telling entirely within a temporal legal system. Under the code, perjury prosecutions and especially the skillful cross-examination of counsel were thought to sufficiently deter and detect falsehood without further reliance on theology.

But history did not unfold as neatly as the codifiers expected. "Premodern" and "modern" evidence regimes did not succeed one another but rather swirled together as lawyers rethought their methods of truth-seeking in a civil justice system. Instead of replacing oaths, the codes exponentially multiplied them, dramatically increasing the legal system's reliance on swearing. And although the theological ground under-lying the oath shifted over time, many American lawyers remained committed to the notion that some threat of divine displeasure was required to make the oath do its work. Instead of spurring a secular rationalization of evidence law,[4] the codifiers' up-take of racial science eventually convinced them of the limits of forensic investigation. Concerned that racialized minorities could not be forced by temporal penalties into testifying truthfully, code lawyers ultimately refused to consign threats of perdition to a premodern legal past.

II

The legal oath had a history that was even more ancient than that of the common law forms of action. Across the High Middle Ages, controversies could be resolved upon which party agreed to swear for the legitimacy of his claim. Ecclesiastical authorities at the time made clear that false swearing was a mortal sin, liable to everlasting punish-ment in the afterlife.[5] Perhaps for that reason, civil authorities in the sixteenth and seven-teenth centuries became extremely guarded in their allowance of oath-taking. Unwilling to become accessories to a witness's damnation, magistrates might permit criminal defendants, children, or "infidels" to speak in court, but they spoke unsworn, disallowed to stake the ultimate wager of their souls on the truthfulness of their testimony. Civil parties, those especially tempted to swear falsely for mere monetary gain, were mostly banned from testifying. The only partial exception—discovery procedure at chancery—developed at the time the chancellery was an ecclesiastical office, and the chancellor could administer an oath in his dual capacity as priestly confessor and secular jurist.[6]

---

[4] Cf. George Fisher, "The Jury's Rise as Lie Detector," 107 *Yale Law Journal* 575 (1997); Kenneth S. Abraham & G. Edward White, "The Transformation of the Civil Trial and the Emergence of American Tort Law," 59 *Arizona Law Review* 431 (2017). Barbara Shapiro has vigorously disputed Fisher's account that the legal system did not permit conflicts of testimony before the rise of party qualification, especially in civil cases. Barbara J. Shapiro, "Oaths, Credibility and the Legal Process in Early Modern England," I & II, 6–7 *Law & Humanities* 145 (2012–2013).

[5] John S. Bekerman, "Procedural and Institutional Change in Medieval Manorial Courts 1250–1550," 10 *Law and History Review* 197 (1992), 203–04; R. H. Helmholz, *The Ius Commune in England* (Oxford University Press, 2001), 101–02.

[6] See William Wake, *A Practical Discourse Concerning Swearing* (Richard Sare, 1696), 25–35; Jean Domat, *The Civil Law in Its Natural Order*, trans. William Strahan (London, 1772), 462–66; Michael R. T. McNair, *The Law of Proof in Early Modern Equity* (Duncker & Humblot, 1999), 204–19; John H. Langbein et al., *History of the Common Law: The Development of Anglo-American Legal Institutions* (Aspen, 2009), 247–48. See also, R.H. Helmholz, *The Spirit of the Classical Canon Law* (University of Georgia Press, 2010), ch. 6.

Like early treatments of pleading, early modern treatises on evidence were entirely focused on guiding practitioners through the technical details of practice. Guides on legal evidence elaborated the cases in which oaths were required or excused, but they usually did not undertake to explain what an oath was, what it was for, and how it was supposed to work.[7] A limited exception was one of the earliest works on evidence, the mid-eighteenth-century treatise by Geoffrey Gilbert, who wrote that excluding certain witnesses from swearing an oath was a matter of "Piety." Gilbert tentatively explained that "the Reason seems to be" that such witnesses "are not admitted to hurt their Consciences by Swearing."[8]

Commentators like Gilbert seemed reluctant to admit that jurists relied on religious devotion to make fundamental practices of the legal system workable. Barbara Shapiro has shown how frequently assize sermons before court sessions focused on the oath, explaining its theological significance and the necessity of religion to create, as one cleric stated, "the most firm and sacred bond that can be laid upon all that are concerned in the administration of public Justice." But these ubiquitous sentiments in assize sermons do not appear to have been preserved in the judicial instructions or opinions handed down at the assizes.[9] For all the advances of eighteenth-century jurisprudence, the law was not yet autonomous, as jurists were loath to admit.

A similar division of labor continued into the nineteenth century: Treatises on evidence gave the rules on oath-taking without explaining the act's significance, while moral theologians worked to make up the deficiency. William Paley's *Principles of Moral and Political Philosophy* explained that "whatever be the form of an oath, the *signification* is the same. It is the calling upon God to witness, *i.e.*, to take notice of what we say, and it is invoking his vengeance, or renouncing his favor if what we say be false."[10] Paley thought that English overuse of the oath might drain it of its solemnity. He encouraged lawmakers to assess "penalties proportioned to the public mischief of the offence" of false testimony. But as long as the legal system continued to rely on the oath, Paley insisted that oaths "carry with them no *proper* force or obligation, unless we believe that God will punish false swearing with more severity than a simple lie."[11]

Half a century later, moral theologians widely cited and elaborated on Paley's definition of the oath. While the everyday conversation of the marketplace appeared to some codifiers as offering ideal, unvarnished truth, the mid-nineteenth-century moral theorist William Whewell reasoned that everyday commercial talk was precisely the

---

[7] See, e.g., William Nelson, *The Law of Evidence* (R. Gosling, 1717); John Morgan, *Essays Upon the Law of Evidence* (E. Lynch, 1789); S. M. Phillips, *Treatise on the Law of Evidence* (Gould, Banks & Gould, 1816); John F. Archbold, *A Summary of the Law Relative to Pleading and Evidence* (R. Pheney, 1824).

[8] Geoffrey Gilbert, *The Law of Evidence* (Henry Lintot, 1756), 159.

[9] Barbara J. Shapiro, "Oaths, Credibility and the Legal Process in Early Modern England: Part One," 6 *Law and Humanities* 145 (2012), 151–52 (quoting John Tillotson, *The Lawfulness and Obligation of Oaths* (1681)).

[10] William Paley, *The Principles of Moral and Political Philosophy* (London, 1785), 162. The leading practical treatise on evidence law in the United States was Simon Greenleaf, *A Treatise on the Law of Evidence* (1842); see also Abraham & White, "The Transformation of the Civil Trial," 450 ("Greenleaf devoted 104 pages of his treatise to discussion of the rule, its permutations, and its exceptions" without addressing its purpose or policy).

[11] Paley, *The Principles of Moral and Political Philosophy*, 164–65.

problem oaths were meant to correct. If juridical actors spoke "with the carelessness and perversion of truth and right, which men often allow themselves in common conversation; the administration of justice would be impossible," Whewell wrote in his work, *The Elements of Morality: Including Polity*. Legal testimony required more solemnity and care than ordinary conversation, and oaths offered a "natural way of acknowledging and marking this moral solemnity" by "declaring that we will act, as in the presence of God." Professional jurists might be embarrassed to acknowledge the law's heavy reliance on religious piety, but Whewell declared that oath-taking was the fundamental basis of legality itself, "for a State, not claiming a moral reality for its acts, by means of religious solemnities [i.e., oaths], could not stand against a great body of citizens bound together by religion." Without due regard for the oath, the state itself and its legal apparatus vanished, leaving to any religious oath-taking body the right of revolution.[12]

Popular explications of the legal oath followed similar lines. During the first half of the nineteenth century, one of the most widely disseminated tracts—of any kind— was titled "The Swearer's Prayer, or, His Oath Explained" (see Figure 7.2). Its lengthy translation of "so help me God" ran in part: "O God! thou hast power to punish me in hell forever: therefore let . . . every lie that I have told . . . rise up in judgment against me, and eternally condemn me!" "Swearer," the tract announced, "*this is thy prayer!!!*"[13] And for some laymen, the threat of hell was the foremost, or even the exclusive, safeguard of an honest oath. As late as 1852, a poor Irishman could testify that "I know what perjury is, and that the punishment of perjury is damnation; I never heard that a man could be transported for perjury; I never heard that a man would be punished by the law of the land for perjury."[14]

Accordingly, treatises pitched to justices of the peace or magistrates, those who straddled the line between laymen and professionals, were often more explicit about the need for piety to make oaths legally useful. Thomas Peake's early *Compendium of the Law of Evidence* explained that children under the age of fourteen could be sworn only if they appeared to have "the sense of religion." New Yorker Oliver Barbour's "practical treatise," *The Magistrate's Criminal Law*, likewise counseled that "a man wholly without religion . . . shall not be received to give evidence in any case whatever."[15]

Whether or not the legal treatises made it explicit, the sacral logic of the oath remained largely undisturbed into the early days of the American Republic. When John Locke famously excluded atheists from his plans for religious toleration, he did so on the basis that atheists denied an afterlife and, therefore, offered worthless oaths.

---

[12] William Whewell, *The Elements of Morality: Including Polity* (1845), 2:87–88.

[13] [William Rust,] "The Swearer's Prayer, or His Oath Explained," Virginia Religious Tract Society (1813), 1–2; reprinted by the Newark Cent Society, 1814; the Religious Tract Societies in the Western Country, 1818; Lincoln & Edmands, 1820; the New-York Religious Tract Society, 1820; the Religious Tract Society (England), 1839; the Presbyterian Church in the Confederate States of America, 1861. The American Tract Society reported distributing 42,000 copies of the tract in Andover alone. *The Publications of the New England Tract Society* (1820), 5:236.

[14] Testimony of Jordan, *Report of the Trials at the Petty Sessions of Achill* (1852), 20.

[15] Thomas Peake, *A Compendium of the Law of Evidence* (Thomas & Thomas, 2d ed., 1804), 123; Oliver L. Barbour, *The Magistrate's Criminal Law* (W. & A. Gould, 1841), 380.

CONSTITUTION

OF THE

AMERICAN TRACT SOCIETY,

WITH

ADDRESSES TO CHRISTIANS

RECOMMENDING THE

DISTRIBUTION OF RELIGIOUS TRACTS,

AND

Anecdotes

ILLUSTRATING THEIR BENEFICIAL EFFECTS.

—I handed him the *Swearer's Prayer*, and went on my journey.—

See p. 24.

PRINTED FOR

THE AMERICAN TRACT SOCIETY,

BY FLAGG AND GOULD.

Figure 7.2 "The Swearer's Prayer" was such a popular tract that there were tracts about the tract, lauding its widespread distribution and transformative reception. Here an illustration of the tract's distribution prefaces an annual report of the American Tract Society.

Front piece, *The Publications of the American Tract Society*, vol. 1 (Flagg & Gould, 1824), New York Public Library.

Likewise, when George Washington urged in his Farewell Address that "religion and morality are indispensable supports" to "political prosperity," his argument relied solely on civil oath-taking. "Let it simply be asked: Where is the security for property, for reputation, for life, if the sense of religious obligation desert the oaths which are the instruments of investigation in the courts of justice?" Accordingly, state after state received the common law rule barring non-Christians from oath-taking.[16]

III

If Field expected statements of fact to disenchant pleadings, the second major reform in his system appeared at first to reenchant them. "Every pleading," read section 133 in the original code, "must be subscribed by the party" and "verified by the party, his agent or attorney, to the effect that he believes it to be true." That is, as the note explained, the code proposed to "test" pleadings by requiring "a verification by the oath of the party."[17] Oaths may have had a long history of crossing the sacred and secular divide in the common law tradition, but for that very reason, they had not usually been required of so mundane an activity as pleading. The application of the oath to pleadings raised several immediate difficulties for the commissioners, but not the one that would have been obvious even a generation earlier: the risk of perdition. Far from reintroducing any "magic" eliminated with the forms of action, Field's expansion of the oath shows how much American legal practice had become secularized by mid-century.

The conviction that the threat of hell secured the solemnity, and thus truthfulness, of an oath rapidly deteriorated in early nineteenth-century America. Recent scholarship suggests that the spread of Christian Universalism at the turn of the nineteenth century directly contributed to the demise of state restrictions on oath-takers. Though they never attracted significant numbers, Universalists counted among their members leading statesmen and moral reformers, who seemed to prove by their example that virtue and veracity could be founded on something other than the fear of everlasting perdition. By the 1830s, the exclusion of Universalists and other varieties of Christian heterodoxy raised significant concerns that the judicial system was subverting constitutional law by preferring certain religious sects and denying religious expression to others. Many states, including New York, amended their constitutions to forbid religious discrimination in oath-taking.[18]

---

[16] John Locke, *A Letter Concerning Toleration* (London, 1796), 56; Jeremy Waldron, *God, Locke, and Equality: Christian Foundations in Locke's Political Thought* (Cambridge University Press, 2002), 223; John C. Patrick, ed., *The Writings of George Washington: From the Original Manuscript Sources, 1745–1799* (Government Printing Office, 1931–1944), 35:229; Sarah Barringer Gordon, "Blasphemy and the Law of Religious Liberty in Nineteenth-Century America," 52 *American Quarterly* 686 (2000).

[17] 1848 N.Y. Laws 525; *First Report* (New York, 1848), 145.

[18] Jud Campbell, "Testimonial Exclusions and Religious Freedom in Early America," 37 *Law and History Review* 431 (2019); Kathryn Gin Lum, *Damned Nation: Hell in America from the Revolution to Reconstruction* (Oxford, 2014), 28–35. See N.Y. Const. of 1846, art. 1, § 3; Nev. Const. of 1864, art. I, § 3, *Fuller v. Fuller*, 17 Cal. 605 (1861). On the broader debates over Christian oaths and office-holding or witness testimony, see Steven K. Green, *The Second Disestablishment: Church and State in Nineteenth-Century America* (Oxford University Press, 2010), 142–49, 172–218.

The speed at which the theological foundation of the oath disappeared was dramatic. As late as 1820, a New York appellate court had banned a Universalist from taking a testimonial oath.[19] Yet the sacral logic of future divine retribution was completely absent from every commissioner report on civil procedure three decades later, both in New York and elsewhere. In his 1847 tract laying out an ideal procedure system, Field expressed incomprehension that "some persons are very tender of the consciences of parties, thinking that the temptation to perjury will prove too strong for human frailty,... if I understand the drift of their argument." Focus on an individual's conscience seemed misplaced to Field, for all that mattered was whether parties' oaths were more likely to disclose or to conceal the truth. Gone was the concern that a court might become complicit in condemning a soul to hell, or that divine retribution secured veracity. Concern for conscience thus struck Field as a "palpable absurdity, that because, in some cases, the motive of interest is stronger than the principle of honesty, therefore those truths which are only known to interested parties shall forever be hidden."[20] A few truthful statements in the public record were more valuable than numerous falsehoods or nagging guilt within private consciences.

Rather than resacralizing civil proceedings, Field meant oath requirements to be a further step in the disenchantment of procedure. In the Final Report, Field counseled the legislature to "abolish oaths altogether," as long as pleading and other solemn affirmations still carried temporal penalties for perjury. The rest of the commentary was devoted to other secular concerns. In order to protect state constitutional rights against self-incrimination, the commissioners decreed that no admissions in civil pleadings could be used as proof in a criminal trial.[21]

The secularity of the oath and of Field's code featured in a curious joke that appeared in the western newspapers in the 1870s. A woman rushed her husband into a clerk's office and demanded her husband take an oath "that he will not strike me again." The clerk protested that he was not empowered to administer oaths, but " 'it don't make any difference,' said the woman. 'He's got to take an oath on the big book, before you, that he won't lick me again.' " His protests ignored, the clerk "took down from one of the shelves a copy of the code of Civil Procedure and laid it before the man, who placed his hand upon it and repeated ... 'I solemnly promise that I will never beat or abuse my wife again, and if I should so far forget myself as to do so, this promise which I now make may be used against me in aggravation of punishment in any criminal proceeding.' " The couple thanked the clerk and left satisfied, the woman affirming, "John, you are a good man after all, and I know you'll keep your promise."[22]

---

[19] Jackson ex dem. Tuttle v. Gridley, 18 Johns. (N.Y.) 98 (1820). Within three years, the future Chancellor of New York confined the reach of Jackson by ruling that a witness could testify as long as he "believes that he will be punished by his God even in this world, if he swears falsely." People v. Matteson, 2 Cow. 433, 433 (N.Y. Ct. Oyer & Terminer 1824).

[20] David Dudley Field, What Shall Be Done with the Practice of the Courts? Shall It Be Wholly Reformed? (1847), 11.

[21] 1848 N.Y. Laws 525; Final Report (New York, 1850), 2:275, 787. On the complicated conflation of party disqualification rules with privileges against self-incrimination, see John Fabian Witt, "Making the Fifth: The Constitutionalization of American Self-Incrimination Doctrine, 1791–1903," 77 Texas Law Review 825 (1999).

[22] Denver Daily Tribune, Jan. 24, 1877.

In the anecdote, the penalty for oath-breaking was described in purely temporal terms—an aggravated criminal punishment. By replacing the Bible with Field's Code of Civil Procedure, the tale drew its humor from the understanding that there could be no magic, no objective spiritual consequence to such an oath. But like its more solemnly administered counterpart, the mock oath could perform its function as long as those using it believed in it.

IV

The third prong of reformed procedure was closely related to the first two. If parties were now obligated (1) to state the facts of their dispute, (2) under oath in their pleadings, it was but a short step to (3) permit parties themselves to be called to the stand to testify under oath at trial. And if parties were competent witnesses, there could be no reason to exclude any other witness who might have an interest (usually defined as a financial stake) in the litigation. The short step toward party competency, however, turned into a decade-long struggle in New York, where legislators reluctantly incorporated party testimony into the code only in 1857.[23]

The code's original enactment in 1848 permitted interested (nonparty) witnesses to testify but allowed only a limited form of party testimony. As with the oath requirement, Field insisted that "the only just enquiry is this; whether the chances of obtaining the truth, are greater from the admission or the exclusion of the witness." In Field's experience, the likeliness of truthful testimony was clear. "In the great majority of instances the witnesses are honest, however much interested, and in most cases of dishonesty the falsehood of the testimony is detected, and deceives none," the First Report concluded.[24] Nevertheless, the commissioners did not extend their logic on interested witnesses to party testimony. Instead, they allowed party testimony only as a substitute for the old equitable bill for discovery (which the code then abolished). A party could be called to the stand only by an adverse party, and testimony on one's own behalf was discouraged. To replace discovery's function as a means of securing pretrial admissions, the examination could be conducted before trial, but then the party could not be called to the stand again at trial.[25]

The continuing distinction between parties and interested witnesses showed the sizable gulf between written pleadings and oral statements before a court. When Lord Brougham's Law Amendment Society surveyed New York lawyers on their opinions about the code reforms, extending testimonial competency to parties received the most hostile answer, even among those who otherwise supported the new code. "If had at all," explained Myron Wilder, a lawyer from rural Canandaigua, party examination should be conducted only "before the day of trial." For "after the excitement of the trial has commenced" and lawyers had "animadverted upon the parties and 'badgered the witnesses,' it is in effect setting a trap for the soul when you call the party on

[23] See 1857 N.Y. Laws 1:744.

[24] First Report (New York, 1848), 246.

[25] 1848 N.Y. Laws 559.

the stand to testify."[26] A written pleading solemnly prepared in a lawyer's office—and with his careful counsel—guarded against perjury in ways the spontaneous and emotionally charged proceedings in a live trial would not.

But once again the commissioners spent no time arguing about traps for the soul. In the Final Report, they declared that "in this completed code, we are for abolishing the remaining portion of the rule of exclusion, and for declaring parties competent as well as others" to testify. The completed code adopted an almost comically expansive rule that rendered any person having "organs of sense" a competent witness, regardless of interest or party status. The code exempted only children and the insane, and it privileged spouses, attorneys, clergy, and physicians from testifying. A party who chose to testify automatically waived all privileges. Even then, the commissioners worried they were too liberal with privileges and invited the legislature to scale back. Parties could still be deposed before trial to secure admissions, but the Final Report went further, and allowed parties to be called again at trial to sift their testimony.[27]

The "excitement" of an oral trial might have dissuaded some lawyers from permitting party testimony, but the codifiers argued that it was precisely the live, oral proceedings that extracted the truth from parties. Generally opposed to technical, Latinate phrases, they made an exception in their frequent praise for *viva voce* testimony—testimony made with "the living voice" and open to challenge by the living voices of opposing counsel. "A written deposition taken in private, is not the best means of eliciting the truth," Field explained, because it was only in public trials before counsel and possibly before juries that witnesses "are subjected to the most searching and often offensive examination."[28]

"Offensive examination" was central to Field's ideal system. Through cross-examination, the skilled lawyer could overwhelm an obfuscating witness, frightening him with the consequences of perjury while probing his story from every direction. On this point, Field could draw on sources outside New York, as Connecticut and even England had begun experimenting with party testimony. The Final Report quoted a report by Lord Brougham, who reasoned that "the *party* knows that his testimony will be sifted with more than ordinary care, and this knowledge must have a tendency to restrain any inclination to falsehood."[29]

"Sifting the conscience" was an old phrase that originated in ecclesiastical writings but was now frequently applied by Field and Lord Brougham to truth-seeking in the secular civil courts. And the ministerial analogy did not end there. Renée Lettow Lerner and Sarah Barringer Gordon have traced how early nineteenth-century

---

[26] *Evidence on the Operation of the Code*, 11–13.

[27] *Final Report* (New York, 1850), 714 § 1708, 726–27, 767–72 §§ 1821, 1830–32. Stephen Subrin's account of the Field Code overlooks this intended expansion of party testimony and pretrial examination and accordingly undervalues the influence of equity on the Field Code. See Stephen N. Subrin, "David Dudley Field and the Field Code: A Historical Analysis of an Earlier Procedural Vision," 6 *Law & History Review* 311 (1988), 332–33, 338.

[28] *First Report* (New York, 1848), 244. See also Wells, *Law of the State* (Missouri, 1849), 68–69.

[29] Conn. Rev. Stat. tit. 1, ch. 10. § 141 (1849); An Act for Improving the Law of Evidence. 6 & 7 Vict. ch. 85. § 1 (1843); An Act for the More Easy Recovery of Small Debts and Demands in England. 9 & 10 Vict. ch. 95, § 83 (1846). *Final Report* (New York, 1850), 715–25.

lawyers adapted the "emotional speechifying" of itinerant revivalists.[30] If closing arguments mimicked the altar call, as Lerner contends, then cross-examination, according to the codifiers, sought the conviction of sin. Putting their own gloss on Field's report, the Ohio commission, like contemporary preachers, detailed the terrors that awaited sinners on the witness stand. "The witness is aware of the suspicion which rests upon him," by "this imposing array" of judge, jury, and opposing counsel. "They are fully determined not to be deceived. . . . Their eyes are bent upon him with the keenest solicitude, they watch with eagerness the most trifling movement; the slightest hesitation in his answers does not escape their notice; they observe the expression of his countenance, his attitude and demeanor, and the very intonations of his voice."[31] Never mind perdition; cross-examination would be hell enough to deter dishonest litigants.

Deterrence was the crucial point. However much English and American reformers praised cross-examination as a means of detection, they did not expect they would have to use it that way often. As Lord Brougham had phrased it, "the dread of detection and of consequent punishment, even in the absence of every moral sentiment, will in the great majority of instances check the commission of perjury." The point was important, because Anglo-American evidence law continued to respect the sanctity of another kind of oath: the juror's. By their oath, jurors, too, were risking their souls by participating in litigation (note that when Myron Wilder complained about "a trap for the soul," he did not specify whose soul—the defendant's or the jury's—he had in mind). If two parties offered exactly conflicting testimony, at least one was committing perjury, and the jury would be called upon, in effect, to declare which soul was damned, a dangerous enterprise given Christ's commandment to "judge not, lest ye be judged."[32] But in their early reports, the codifiers did not believe that allowing party testimony would seriously increase conflicting testimony. "There is a natural tendency to declare the truth which is never wholly eradicated," the Ohio codifiers wrote. Based on this tendency, the fear of detection would deter perjury from even occurring in the first place.[33]

V

The code replaced the theological foundations of legal formulary systems, oath-taking, and examination with a secular rationale. Whatever the afterlife might hold

---

[30] See Samuel Warren, *A Popular and Practical Introduction to Law Studies Civil, Criminal, and Ecclesiastical* (1846), 234; Dennis R. Klinck, *Conscience, Equity and the Court of Chancery in Early Modern England* (Routledge, 2010); Renée Lettow Lerner, "The Transformation of the American Civil Trial: The Silent Judge," 42 *William & Mary Law Review* 195 (2000), 233–39; Gordon, "Blasphemy and Religious Liberty," 691.

[31] *Report of the Commissioners* (Ohio, 1853), 130.

[32] Campbell, "Testimonial Exclusions and Religious Freedom," 436; John Longley, *Observations on the Trial by Jury* (1815), 30; Eli Price, *Discourse on the Trial by Jury* (1863), 19. For the medieval origins of this idea, see James Q. Whitman, *The Origins of Reasonable Doubt: Theological Roots of the Criminal Trial* (Yale University Press, 2016), 186–92.

[33] *Report of the Commissioners* (Ohio, 1853), 140.

for oath-breakers, the codifiers contended that the ultimate threat of a perjury prosecution and the penultimate unpleasantness of a live cross-examination would deter falsehood and render civil proceedings altogether more truthful. Although their commentary often traded in abstractions and generalizations, codifiers in New York and around the states and territories specified the benefits of their system for one case in particular, that of a debt collection. When they tried to illustrate what they meant by fact pleading, when they argued for the necessity of an oath, and when they touted the efficiencies of extracting testimony from the parties themselves, they continually recurred to the example of an action on a promissory note or bill of sale as a paradigm case.[34]

In their schedule of forms, the New York commissioners showed how fact pleading should work in the case of an unpaid debt. The pleader should not state, on the one hand, all the trivial details of a transaction through one's agents, nor, on the other, legal conclusions that one party contracted with or owed money to another. Instead, the complaint should state that the plaintiff sold goods and the defendant agreed to pay but had not. The answer should state, if true, whether the defendant had in fact paid or whether the plaintiff's goods had been defective.[35]

The oath would then secure the key piece of information: the exact amount owed. Under the "common counts" of former practice, a demand for $100 might be stated four different ways, thus pleading $400 damages, although the actual trial would limit the recovery to the original $100. By forbidding repetition and abolishing the various forms of action to recover on an obligation, the commissioners expected to force plaintiffs to state in one line the exact amount owed, whatever the theory of recovery.[36]

Upon this system of verified pleading, the commissioners provided additional rules to speed up remedies in proceedings upon debt. Default judgment would issue if a complaint were not answered within twenty days, and the code abolished the customary thirty-day waiting period between judgment and enforcement. The Final Report offered even more summary proceedings that cut the twenty days to five. The clerk could enter default judgment at any time in the year, not just during court sessions as under former practice. A defendant's answer might delay judgment until the court term, but as defendants, too, had to verify their answers under oath, the commissioners hoped to foreclose sham defenses that only caused delay. They even expected most defendants would accept default judgment, which they cited as a prime feature of the code. Courts would be relieved of cases where the amount owed was not really in dispute, and if defendants had to accept a default, at least they did not have to incur the additional expenses of hiring a lawyer.[37]

---

[34] As Jed Rubenfeld has explained in a constitutional context, a paradigm makes the abstract intentions of lawmakers more definite by providing concrete applications, usually in the form of cases the lawmaker was seeking to provide for or prohibit going forward. Jed Rubenfeld, "The Paradigm-Case Method," 115 *Yale Law Journal* 1977 (2006).

[35] *First Report* (New York, 1848), 261–68.

[36] Ibid., 139–40; Wells, *Law of the State* (Missouri, 1849), 92–93, 99–102. See also *Report of the Code Commissioners to the Eighth General Assembly of the State of Iowa* (Iowa, 1859), 185; *Report of the Commissioners* (Ohio, 1853), 50–52, 65–66.

[37] *First Report* (New York, 1848), 182–83 § 202, 197; *Final Report* (New York, 1850), 570–74.

Indeed, the commissioners sounded almost antilawyerly in how strongly they stated their desire "to relieve defendants, as far as possible, from the necessity of employing a lawyer." Default judgment could never exceed the damages stated in the original complaint. If "the defendant is not disposed to controvert" the pleaded amount, explained the report, "he may, with perfect safety, permit judgment by default, as the law limits the recovery, in that case, to the amount specified." Ideally, the commissioners wrote, most trials could be avoided when "credit requires that the remedy should be speedy."[38]

The commissioners further explained that competent party testimony could remedy "one of the worst evils of our judiciary system": nondisclosure of assets by defaulting debtors. The ability to call an adverse party was "designed to furnish a cheaper and easier method of discovering the concealed property of a judgment debtor," Field explained. The debtor might be the only person fully informed about his ability to pay his debts, but the disqualification of party testimony prevented disclosure unless a plaintiff resorted to the expensive and time-consuming discovery proceedings of a creditor's bill in chancery. Many smaller debts were not worth litigating at chancery, and thus, explained codifiers in Ohio, "there are innumerable cases, where the dishonest man escapes the payment of his debt or the performance of his obligations, by the inability of the adverse party to adduce the requisite legal proof, which his own testimony would always supply."[39]

Perhaps no one better embodied the exchange of traditional theologies of the oath for oaths of purely commercial significance than the New York trial judge John Worth Edmonds, an early proponent of Field's code. After the death of his wife in 1850, Edmonds sought comfort in spiritualist séances, and by 1853, Edmonds had resigned his seat on the state supreme court bench to become one of America's more prominent spirit mediums and apologists for Spiritualism. In his memoirs, Edmonds recounted how spirit guides had revealed to him the true nature of the afterlife—not a binary of heaven and hell, but rather a graduated series of stages toward enlightenment. If anything like a hell existed, it was equivalent to earthly life in the here and now.[40]

Edmonds shared a distaste for hell with Shearman and a common juridical approach with Field. He explained to law students in 1848 that temporal penalties alone would allow the oath to restore "to pleadings their truth-telling character." Edmonds praised the democratic, plainspoken nature of code pleading and complimented code practice as "a valuable substitute for the creditor's bill." He concluded that testimonial qualification and oath-taking by parties marked "the shadowing forth of an important aid to creditors . . . against the efforts of a fraudulent debtor."[41] From the parts to the whole, Edmonds understood the code on its own terms: terms of marketplace conversation and merchant credit.

In the debates over procedural codification, debt collection provided a concrete application through which codifiers could think about the metaphysics of formulary

---

[38] *Final Report* (New York, 1850), 256, 571; *First Report* (New York, 1848), 238–39.

[39] *First Report* (New York, 1848), 201; *Report of the Commissioners* (Ohio, 1853), 135.

[40] Gin Lum, *Damned Nation*, 151–57; Hon. J. W. Edmonds, "Personal Experience," 1 *The Shekinah* 265 (1852), 270–71.

[41] John W. Edmonds, *An Address on the Constitution and the Code of Procedure* (1848), 15, 31, 38, 42–43.

systems and testimonial oaths. When codifiers attempted to illustrate the absurdities of traditional practice, they most often pointed to cases in trover and assumpsit— the actions used to recover unpaid obligations.[42] Code opponents instead turned to noncommercial forms, such as those for assault and battery, to argue that pleadings were sufficiently clear and concise already.[43] When the English bar interrogated Field about the New York reforms, they peppered him with hypothetical cases of real estate encumbered with multiple mortgages of unclear priority. Field waved off realty questions as uninteresting or uncomplicated under the code. Instead, he focused on how oath-bound pleadings and party testimony in cases of personalty settled "an immense mass of business, which occupies a great deal of time in your Court of Chancery."[44] Tiring of all the focus on commercial credit, one western legislator observed that he "never knew one of these professionals who undertook to write up the beauties of the New York code, . . . that he did not also break out somewhere with 'take for instance the case of an action on a promissory note,' as though the collection of notes was about all there could be any law needed for!"[45]

VI

On the face of it, Field's statute requiring all pleadings to be verified by oath seemed like it should have been easy to implement. In practice, the rules of oath-taking became one of the more complicated departments of code pleading. Remarkably quickly, lawyers in all the early code states abandoned their faith in cross-examination and prosecution as a deterrence to perjury, arguing instead that their skillful cross-examinations could, if not deter, at least detect the violation of the oath and thus secure the truth in court. Some argued that they were forced to this position when the code seemed to demand perjury from the parties.

From the earliest days of code practice, some lawyers doubted whether perjury could even be committed under code pleading. One New York attorney wrote to the *Code Reporter*, a magazine founded to share judicial decisions and professional discussion on the new code. The lawyer noted that the code required pleadings to be verified "but does not state, *in terms*, that it shall be *verified by oath*." The attorney wondered, then, "Can a party who verifies a complaint or answer on oath, knowing it to be wholly false, be convicted of perjury?" The editor bemusedly answered, "We cannot imagine how any doubt can arise on the subject," but in subsequent issues, the *Reporter* admitted the question was more difficult than it first appeared.[46]

---

[42] See, for instance, *Report of the Commissioners* (Ohio, 1853), 6; Wells, *Law of the State* (Missouri, 1849), 101–04.

[43] See, for instance, *Journal of the House of Representatives of the State of Minnesota* (1858), 514–15.

[44] *Evidence on the Operation of the Code*, 28–29, 33. After the survey of New York attorneys, the reform tract republished the minutes of an examination of Field, "taken before the Commissioners appointed to inquire into the Process, Practice, and System of Pleading, the Court of Chancery.—Monday, December 22nd, 1851." The questions were posed by Lord Romilly, England's Master of the Rolls.

[45] *Denver Daily Times*, Jan. 27, 1877.

[46] 1 Code Rep. 26–27 (1848–49).

The literal provisions of the code seemed to put defendants in an intolerable dilemma. Although a plaintiff generally bore the burden of proof, the defendant could not put the plaintiff to his proof without denying a material allegation under oath, at the risk of perjury. But if a defendant could not deny an allegation he suspected, believed, or even knew to be true, the plaintiff would be relieved of the burden of proof the law assigned to him. "Can a party be convicted of the crime of perjury," a Minnesota lawyer exclaimed, "under a law *requiring* him upon *oath* to deny '*all the material facts in the case*'?" If so, the code basically forced defendants into testifying against themselves. If they sought to hold plaintiffs to their proof, as traditions of due process demanded, they opened themselves to criminal prosecution for perjury on their pleadings. Thus, the *Code Reporter* ultimately concluded, "The Code does not render it necessary to verify pleading on oath, but if it does, then it is unconstitutional."[47]

The commissioners remained resolute in their Second Report, waiving verification only when admission would subject a party to prosecution for "an infamous crime" (other than perjury) and expressing "regret, that a more stringent rule in respect to the verification of pleadings is required, but they have reason to believe, that the spirit of the code in this respect has not been always regarded."[48] The legislature overruled the commissioners with two new provisions designed to ameliorate the oath requirement.

First, the oath was made optional unless the parties themselves insisted on it, which largely reinstituted the rules of discovery pleading at chancery. To force an admission under oath from the defendant, a plaintiff would have to swear to his own facts, often including an allegation that he could not come by the needed information any other way than the defendant's admission. Under such a rule, it was no longer clear when an oath was "voluntary" or "required by law," yet this distinction was crucial for the traditional laws of perjury. Under long-standing rules of equity derived from biblical injunctions against needless swearing, a voluntary oath was an "unlawful" oath and could not support a charge of perjury. The same year as the New York amendment, the *Code Reporter* favorably cited an Ohio chancery decision restating the voluntary oaths rule. New York courts applied the rule to code practice a few court terms later.[49]

Second, the legislature took Field's commentary on the code and made it a point of law. "It is not required of a party, that he state absolutely, that the matters pleaded are true, inasmuch as his knowledge may not extend to the whole case," the Second Report had explained, "but it is intended to put him upon his veracity, and to require him to state nothing, that he does not believe to be true." The legislative amendment accordingly specified that with the oath, a party swore not that the facts were true but that they were believed to be true at the time of pleading, a more difficult burden

[47] Report of Aaron Goodrich, *House Journal* (Minnesota, 1860), 220; 1 Code Rep. 2 (1848–49). See also Henry Whittaker, *Practice and Pleading Under the Codes* (E.O. Jenkins, 1852), 169 (advising plaintiffs always to verify their complaints so to effectively shift the burden of proof to defendants).
[48] *Second Report* (New York, 1849), 28.
[49] On the antiquity of the rule, see Helmholz, *The Spirit of Classical Canon Law*, 156. Silver v. State 17 Ohio 365 (Ohio Ch. 1847); 2 Code Rep. 29; People v. Travis, 4 Parker's Criminal Reports 213 (Buffalo Super. Ct. 1854).

for a prosecutor to prove perjury.[50] Henceforth, parties were required to distinguish in their pleadings between their "knowledge"—that is, direct experience of the facts alleged—and facts known only by "information and belief."[51]

The quasi-voluntary nature of the civil oath and a heightened knowledge requirement rendered perjury convictions on civil pleadings largely impractical. Over the next three decades, virtually no perjury prosecution on civil pleadings appears in the case reports or newspapers. The sole exception is one peculiar case in 1875 when the county court in Tompkins upheld a perjury conviction when a defendant lied in his pleading about paying off a promissory note and sought to escape punishment by arguing that the pleading did not directly claim the note was paid, only that "the defendant says" it was paid, that is, a true allegation of a false statement.[52] About one or two perjury prosecutions per year arose from false affidavits gathered during discovery, but not from the pleadings.[53]

When the English began admitting party testimony in civil cases, according to a recent study, perjury prosecutions (and convictions) nearly tripled in the early 1850s, gradually declining as lawyers came to trust cross-examination as the greatest "engine of truth" in civil trials.[54] In America, however, perjury trials based on civil pleadings were scarce, even as many lawyers recognized that parties lied with regularity. "Under the New York code the provisions concerning verification of pleadings are completely evaded and rendered of no avail," griped one emigrating New York lawyer in the 1870s, "and no man has ever been convicted of perjury under them to this day, although the spirit of the provisions are violated in almost every action brought."[55]

Notably, the English did not adopt Field's rules for pleading under oath. American judges thus faced additional pressure to overlook potentially perjured testimony, because such testimony was often offered just to be consistent with the pleadings. If it seemed unfair to relieve plaintiffs of the burden of proof through a defendant's verified pleadings, it seemed abusive to prosecute parties for sticking to their pleaded stories when put on the stand. Commentators reported a common belief "that the

---

[50] New York law had made it perjury for any person to "wilfully and corruptly swear, testify, or affirm falsely, to any material matter," making it ambiguous whether intentionally swearing to facts one did not know to be false constituted perjury. 2 Rev. Stat. 681 § 1.

[51] See John L. Tillinghast and Thomas G. Shearman, *The Practice, Pleadings and Forms in Civil Actions in the Courts of Record in the State of New York* (Lewis Brothers, 1870), 39.

[52] People v. Christopher, 4 (11) Hun 805 (Thompkins Cnty. Ct., N.Y. 1875).

[53] See, e.g., Frank F. Brightly, *A Digest of the Decisions of All the Courts of the State of New York from the Earliest Period to the Year 1892* (1893), 3:5924–27; People v. Burroughs, 1 Parker Crim. 211 (Sup. Ct. Gen. Term 1851); People v. McGinnis, 1 Parker Crim. 387 (Sup. Ct. Gen. Term 1853); People v. Sweetman, 3 Parker Crim. 358 (Sup. Ct. Gen. Term 1857); People v. McKinney, 3 Parker Crim. 510 (Sup. Ct. Gen. Term 1857); People v. Townsend, 5 How. Prac. 315 (Sup. Ct. N.Y. Cnty. 1850); People v. Albertson, 8 How. Prac. 363 (N.Y. Cnty. Ct. 1853); People v. Harriot, 3 Parker Crim. 112 (N.Y. Oyer & Term. 1856); Wood v. People, 59 N.Y. 117 (1874); Harris v. People, 64 N.Y. 148 (1876); Jones v. People, 79 N.Y. 45 (1879); Guston v. People, 4 Lans. 487 (Sup. Ct. Gen. Term 1st Dep't 1871); Burns v. People, 59 Barb. 531 (Sup. Ct. Gen. Term 3d Dep't 1871); Ortner v. People, 4 Hun 323 (Sup. Ct. Gen. Term 4th Dep't 1875); People v. Christopher, 4 Hun 805 (Sup. Ct. Gen. Term 3d Dep't 1875); Case v. People, 14 Hun 503 (Sup. Ct. Gen Term 1st Dep't 1878); Lambert v. People, 14 Hun 512 (Sup. Ct. Gen. Term 1st Dep't 1878); People v. Vail, 57 How. Prac. 81 (Sup. Ct. N.Y. Cnty. 1879); People v. Pearsall, 46 How. Prac. 121 (Sup. Ct. N.Y. Cnty. 1873).

[54] Wendie Ellen Schneider, *Engines of Truth: Producing Veracity in the Victorian Courtroom* (Yale University Press, 2015), ch. 1 & ch. 2.

[55] *Rocky Mountain News* (Denver, Colo.), Jan. 24, 1877.

verification of a pleading under the Code can not, under any circumstances, consti-tute perjury." If that were true of the pleadings, critics complained, then written and vocalized "perjury seems to be fast becoming legalized under the corrupting influ-ences of the 'Code.'"[56]

Even in states that adopted Field's more "stringent" rule, the threat of perjury pros-ecution failed to deter false pleading—or false testimony. In 1853, the Ohio commis-sioners adopted Field's rules noting their trust "in the rigor of the criminal laws of the State to deter the dishonest from perjury." But by the end of that same decade, Ohio's judges had abandoned the hope of deterrence and clung only to the promise of detec-tion. When interviewed by another code commission, judges on the Ohio Court of Common Pleas agreed that perjury had become rampant under the reformed system, but none found the epidemic particularly troubling. "If perjury is committed, it is very soon disclosed" Judge James L. Bates assured his correspondents. Another responded, "Much perjury exists in the swearing of parties. It is really alarming, but in many cases does conduce to truth." Another judge, B. F. Hoffman, wrote that it was "almost always . . . easy to see who has the truth on the point in dispute. The point must be naked and isolated indeed, the contradiction plump and evenly balanced in manner, matter, etc., not to tell where the real truth is."[57]

Rather than undertaking the English experiment of exemplary prosecutions, American lawyers essentially made their peace with perjury. Ignoring criminal sanc-tions, Ohio's Judge Hoffman reasoned that perjurers "will soon find their true so-cial and trading position at the lower end of the scale, and out of the good opinion of honest men." The handicap to bargaining was apparently all the just punishment perjury required. Some judges continued to insist into the 1860s that "where, in the course of legal proceedings, the oath of a party is required, the intention is to appeal to his conscience and to his religious sense." But in echoes of Field's code reports, Judge Hoffman waved off such concerns, concluding that he "would not be tender of [par-ties'] internal mental condition, at the expense of others' rights and dues."[58]

VII

"Admission is the rule here," Field explained in defense of the rules making parties competent witnesses at trial. "Exclusion is the rule of the common law. Let in all the light possible, we ask. Not so the common law; exclude the light, it says, lest perchance it deceive you; unmindful, as it appears to us, that poor light is better than none." The apparent rise of perjured testimony under the code may have meant that the light was much poorer than Field had expected. Still, at least the compromises of the code allowed truth-seeking that former practices had foreclosed. Even as it became evi-dent that party testimony had opened the floodgates to falsehood, some previously

[56] McCrory v. Skinner, 2 Ohio 268 (1860); *House Journal* (Minnesota, 1860), 220. See also *Report of the Code Commissioners* (Iowa, 1859), 288.

[57] *Report of the Commissioners* (Ohio, 1853), 140; *Report of the Code Commissioners* (Iowa, 1859), 234–36.

[58] *Report of the Code Commissioners* (Iowa, 1859), 234–35.

excluded truth was streaming in as well, and Field shared the same confidence as the Ohio judges that lawyers could easily elicit the truth. "Let us not fear, that judges and juries will be deluded into a belief of an improbable or untrue story, though the parties themselves be the persons who utter it," he urged.[59]

Field's policy was commended outside of New York. "I entirely concur with your opinion, that all rules for the exclusion of evidence are rules for the exclusion of light," the Missouri codifier R. W. Wells wrote to Field. In his report, Field reprinted the recommendations of William Storrs, Chief Justice of the Supreme Court in Connecticut, a state that had recently abolished party disqualifications. "For although, it is obvious that there will be much false swearing by parties in their own behalf under it," Storrs admitted, juries could "make the proper allowance for the interest and situation of the witness, especially as he is personally before the Court, and is subjected to the searching operation of a cross-examination." The Ohio Commission concurred: "The tests of truth are almost innumerable, and tried by them, falsehood is laid bare and recoils upon the head of him who utters it."[60]

But just when lawyers in state after state were learning to live with perjury, confident in their ability to detect the truth, many states introduced a new policy of testimonial exclusion in their codes. It began in one of the earliest adopters of the code, California. As enacted by the legislature, the state's Practice Act tracked the 1849 version of Field's code by permitting the examination of adverse parties and abolishing the disqualification of nonparty interested witnesses. The act then provided that "no black, or mulatto person, or Indian, shall be permitted to give evidence in any action to which a white person is a party, in any Court of this State." When his brother Stephen J. Field introduced David Dudley's completed draft in the next session, Stephen incorporated the racial exclusion, merely adjusting the blood quantum defining "negro" (upward) and "indian" (downward) from the levels set in 1850.[61] The state assembly briefly considered mitigating the absolute exclusion for the latter category. Perhaps "Christianized Indians whom two disinterested white persons, citizens of the State, shall, on oath, testify, in open court, that they are known to them, and that they consider their testimony under oath worthy of credit" could testify, "leaving the credibility of such Indians to the jury." With a tied vote, however, the assembly decided to leave the exclusion absolute.[62] Neither Stephen nor the other codifiers commented on their change to the New York code. Testimonial exclusions of racialized peoples were not new in American law, and the language of the California rule closely tracked the laws of midwestern states from which many Californians had emigrated.[63]

Commentary would be provided three years later by an infamous case in the state supreme court, *People v. Hall*, which extended the testimonial exclusion of Indians to Chinese witnesses. *Hall* has become widely noted for its strained attempts to include Chinese people in the statutory construction of "Indian," as well as for its reasoning that if "a race of people whom nature has marked as inferior" were admitted to testify,

---

[59] *Final Report* (New York, 1850), 715; *First Report* (New York), 246.

[60] *Final Report* (New York, 1850), 715–17; *Report of the Commissioners* (Ohio, 1853), 129.

[61] 1850 Cal. Laws 455 § 306; 1851 Cal. Laws 114 § 394. Stephen Field's code changed the blood quantum to consider a person an "indian" from one-half to one-fourth, and a "negro" from one-eighth to one-half.

[62] *Journal of the House of Assembly of the State of California* (1850), 990–91, 1000.

[63] See 1807 Ohio Laws 54; Jordan v. Smith, 14 Ohio 499 (1846); 1839 Iowa Laws 379.

they would next clamor for "all the equal rights of citizenship, and we might soon see them at the polls, in the jury box, upon the bench, and in our legislative halls."[64]

What accounts have failed to notice, though, is how thoroughly the case subverted legislators' professed faith in cross-examination as the great test for truth at trial. Most of the opinion in *Hall* sought semantic connections between Native American *Indians* and the West *Indies* to bring all Asian peoples under the terms of the statute. In the final pages, the opinion pivoted and argued that "even admitting the Indian of this Continent is not of the Mongolian type," the legislature clearly intended a policy that excluded all non-white testimony in court. "The evident intention of the Act was to throw around the citizen a protection for life and property, which could only be secured by removing him above the corrupting influences of degraded castes," the majority wrote. In elaborating this racial degradation, *Hall* focused on a supposed inability to respect the oath among the Chinese, "whose mendacity is proverbial" and who were "incapable of progress of intellectual development" to respect a testimonial oath. The most vital clue to legislative intent, the opinion concluded, was the comparison to "domestic Negroes and Indians, who not unfrequently have correct notions of their obligations to society." Surely, the legislature did not mean to protect white citizens by excluding the oft-true testimony of California's Black and Native populations only to allow foreign races to testify without inhibition.[65]

As a matter of legislative intent, *Hall* may have had the interpretation right. The point of the statute had not been to exclude certain races specifically but to generally exclude non-white testimony. The specific mention of "negro" and "indian" had been to set the legal levels of blood quantum that would assign race, and a later legislature affirmed *Hall* and clarified the law by adding "Mongolians" and "Chinese" to the Indian clause with its requisite one-half blood quantum.[66]

Yet *Hall's* concession that racial disqualifications excluded the frequently true testimony of racialized witnesses for the sake of policy highlighted a tension with one of the code's key reforms. As the codifiers often reported, if anyone's mendacity had become proverbial by the early 1850s, it was that of white parties and interested witnesses. Nevertheless, the codifiers had argued, within the totality of the trial, truth was easy to discover and self-interested lying easy to detect. Sensing the contradiction that white lawyers in front of white juries could easily sift truth from white witnesses but not from "inferior" races, Montana's governor Sidney Edgerton vetoed his territory's entire code of civil procedure over its proposed borrowing of California's racial exclusions. "Our Juries and Courts are composed exclusively of white men and I consider the Caucasian race competent to weigh evidence coming from any witness of

---

[64] People v. Hall, 4 Cal. 399 (1854). The case was a criminal prosecution for murder committed by a white man, but all three witnesses to the murder were Chinese. As the criminal and civil procedure codes contained identical language on the exclusion of testimony, *Hall* was understood to apply to civil cases as well. See Speer v. See Yup Co., 13 Cal. 73 (1859). William J. Novak, "The Legal Transformation of Citizenship in Nineteenth-Century America," in Meg Jacobs et al., eds., *The Democratic Experiment: New Directions in American Political History* (Princeton University Press, 2003), 85–119; John R. Wunder, "Chinese in Trouble: Criminal Law and Race on the Trans-Mississippi West Frontier," in Gordon Morris Bakken, ed., *Law in the West* (Garland Press, 2001), 75–92; D. Michael Bottoms, *An Aristocracy of Color: Race and Reconstruction in California and the West, 1850–1890* (Oklahoma University Press, 2013), ch. 1.

[65] 4 Cal. at 403.

[66] 1863 Cal. Laws 60.

any race wisely, justly and well," he wrote to the territorial assembly. The legislature overrode the veto without comment.[67]

In the standard history of American evidence law, George Fisher argues that witness disqualification rules were an "anachronistic survival" of an age that trusted "the truth-assuring powers of the oath." Noticing that in New England especially, party disqualification was abolished close to the same time racial exclusionary rules were, Fisher surmises that states "maintained the old bar against civil parties because their lawmakers saw no good way to reconcile testimony by parties with their racial exclusion laws." He further surmises that by prohibiting racial exclusions, the Fourteenth Amendment's Equal Protection Clause freed legislatures to dispense with anachronistic party disqualifications. Until then, legislators "chose to avoid an awkward clash between [racial exclusion rules] and rules permitting testimony by civil parties simply by resisting the latter as long as they retained the former." But forced to admit testimony on a racially equal basis, states had no reason to continue the prohibitions on party testimony.[68]

By overlooking the codes that governed most American jurisdictions through the nineteenth century, the conventional account gets the history backward in several key ways. It misunderstands, first, that oaths and party examination were not one-for-one substitutes. The Field Code, as noted, dramatically expanded its reliance on both at the same time.[69] Second, it treats party qualification as an all-or-nothing proposition, thereby assuming that states (and so far histories of evidence have focused mainly on states, not territories) disqualified party testimony completely until they allowed it, again completely. But the political history of the Field Code was more complicated. Its three drafts from 1848 to 1850 differed significantly on the scope of party qualification and the rigor with which it required sworn pleadings.[70] Those variant drafts made a difference as the code migrated west.

Start again with California. By so swiftly adopting Field's code in 1849, California enacted an intermediate draft of the code that did not completely abolish the disqualification of party testimony but that nearly did so. Parties were not fully competent to testify as other witnesses, but they nevertheless offered oath-verified pleadings and could examine one another adversely at or before trial. Further, if an adverse examination did not produce anticipated admissions, the examining party could then introduce his own affirmative testimony. The difference between California's first code and full party competency was thus only a relatively minor rule of sequence.[71]

California's testimonial rules—both the near-qualification of party testimony and the disqualification of racial minorities—then migrated to other jurisdictions, enjoying an influence almost as widespread as the original Field Code. Altogether, fifteen states and territories—a majority of pre-Reconstruction adopters—overwrote Field's preferred

---

[67] *Journal of the House of the Territory of Montana* (1865), 201–02, 207–10.

[68] Fisher, "The Jury's Rise as Lie Detector," 661–62, 673–74.

[69] See also Witt, "Making the Fifth," 885. That is not to say that Fisher's detailed history of party qualification in New England is off base, just that it accounts for a relatively narrow and uncodified region of the United States. See Fisher, "The Jury's Rise as Lie Detector," 683–90.

[70] Compare 1848 N.Y. Laws 523, 559–60; 1849 N.Y. Laws 648, 691–92; *Final Report* (New York, 1850), 272–73, 714–15, 784–86.

[71] 1850 Cal. Laws 455. See also 1851 Cal. Laws 117.

competency rules with racial exclusions, even while allowing party testimony into the trial.[72] Indeed, the only Field Code family that admitted party testimony without racial exclusions was in the postbellum South—a further sign, critics complained, that the code was the imposition of northern radicals. In southern states, the Field Code overwrote the infamous Black Codes, several of which had themselves qualified party testimony while at the same time barring "negro" testimony against white people.[73]

Outside the South, Field Code jurisdictions maintained these rules for years or even decades after Reconstruction. Nebraska was the extreme case. Its 1866 amended code excluded "Indians and Negroes who appear incapable of receiving just impressions of the facts respecting which they are examined, or of relating them intelligently and truly." That, too, was a textual borrowing—from Field's original exemption of children under ten years old from testifying. Because the provision "permit[ted] all persons of sufficient capacity to understand [the oath's] obligations to be witnesses," as the Nebraska Supreme Court reasoned in 1880, the exclusion arguably survived the Fourteenth Amendment's equal protection requirements. Apparently, lawyers could, in fact, live with the "awkward clash" of rules allowing party testimony for the sake of truth-seeking while excluding potentially truthful racialized testimony. Nebraska's arrangement remained in place until 1925.[74]

VIII

Over time, lawyers gave a variety of explanations for the racially exclusionary "policy"—a frequently invoked term that indicated that code provisions on witness testimony did not sound in a constitutional or natural law register but were simply matters of local politics. When the question arose whether a mulatto victim could testify against a white defendant in a criminal trial, Stephen Field—now as Chief Justice of the California Supreme Court—read the code to answer no, blithely noting that "instances may arise where, upon this construction, crime may go unpunished." But, he concluded (over a dissent), the "policy, wisdom, or consequences of legislation" were for the legislature to decide.[75]

The New York Field Commission itself showed how to reason about the policies underlying witness testimony. When the practice commission turned its attention to criminal procedure in 1849, it made clear that truth-seeking could *not* be the animating policy behind witness examination. If it were, "the French practice" of using cross-examination to "extract from the defendant evidence of his guilt" might be appropriate.

---

[72] In addition to California, the other code jurisdictions to exclude racialized testimony were Arizona, Idaho, Indiana, Iowa, Kansas, Kentucky, Missouri, Nebraska, Nevada, Montana, Oregon, Tennessee, Washington, and Wyoming.

[73] See 1866 N.C. Laws 102; 1866 S.C. Laws 263; Fla. Const. of 1865, art. XVI, § 2. Cf. 1866 Ala. Laws 98; 1867 Ga. Code 334.

[74] 1866 Neb. Rev. Stat. 449; Priest v. State, 6 N.W. 468, 469 (Neb. 1880). For a detailed breakdown of disparate dates of party admission and the end of racial exclusions, see Kellen Funk, "An Oath on the Big Book: Oaths and Examinations in American Codes of Procedure," in Pamela Klassen et al., eds., *Making Promises: Oaths, Treaties, and Covenants in Multi-jurisdictional and Multi-religious Societies* (University of Toronto Press, 2025).

[75] People v. Howard, 17 Cal. 64, 65 (1860).

Under the New York constitution, however, truth-seeking in criminal proceedings had to be secondary to protecting the civil rights of the accused. The proposed code of criminal procedure thus did not make criminal defendants competent to testify, even though the commission pressed to abolish civil party disqualifications the same year. Rather, the criminal code allowed a defendant to offer exculpatory statements without facing the rigors of cross-examination "proceeding on the assumption of his guilt" and driving him "to the alternative of equivocating as to facts, or of denying circumstances plainly true, or of what is occasionally his resort, declining to answer."[76]

Many of the jurisdictions that adopted Field's code apparently refused to maintain this distinction between civil and criminal practice. If a policy of protecting civil rights could trump the purposes of fact-finding on the criminal side, it might do so in civil practice as well. And in many western states, codifiers reasoned that the civil rights of white litigants—the protection of their property, their trades, and in some cases their liberty—outweighed the truth value of testimony from what the California supreme court had called the "degraded castes."[77]

Critics of the exclusions often used the same language of "policy" even as they disagreed about the animating principles behind the exclusionist policies. John Henry Wigmore's foundational treatise on evidence sanguinely explained that "the condition of public feeling in [California] against the economic encroachments of Chinese laborers explains and extenuates (while it may not excuse) this blunder in the policy of the testimonial law." The Radical Republican Albion Tourgée vehemently objected that underlying economic anxiety was "the idea that it would be a degradation of the white man to allow the colored man to take the witness-stand and traverse the oath of a Caucasian." For that reason, Tourgée thought his adoption of the Field Code over North Carolina's Black Code wrought "one of the hottest political struggles since the war." One of Tourgée's novels explained:

> To reverse this [exclusionary] rule, grown ancient and venerable by the practice of generations, to open the mouths which had so long been sealed, was only less infamous and dangerous than to accord credence to the words they might utter.... [I]t passed the power of language to portray the anger, disgust, and degradation which it produced in the Southern mind. To be summoned before the [court], confronted with a negro who denied his most solemn averments, ... was unquestionably, to the Southerner, the most degrading ordeal he could by any possibility be called upon to pass through.

Thus, policy talk thus had its manifold uses. For Stephen Field and Wigmore, it relieved responsibility over rules that could be safely criticized as local eccentricities. In Tourgée's hands, policy safeguarded responsibility to remake laws no matter how venerable their pedigree or deep their entrenchment.[78]

---

[76] *Fourth Report of the Commissioners on Pleading and Practice: Code of Criminal Procedure* (New York, 1849), xxv–xxix.

[77] People v. Hall, 4 Cal. at 403 (1854).

[78] John Henry Wigmore, *A Treatise on the System of Evidence in Trials at Common Law* (Little, Brown, and Co., 1904), 1:645–46; Albion W. Tourgée, *Bricks Without Straw*, ed. Carolyn L. Karcher (Duke University Press, 2009 [1880]), 159, 204.

Where policy talk ran thin was in legislative justifications of racially exclusionary rules. In this context, lawmakers revived a language of nature and natural law to place their rules beyond the realm of policy and safeguard them in the realm of necessity. Key to this revived language was, indeed, the old language of revival: of hell, the after-life, and spiritual consequences for violating sacred rites.[79] Cross-examination could make a witness sweat, shift his eyes, or stutter his speech, wrote one journalist, only be-cause the witness was under oath and dreaded the cosmic penalties for oath-breaking. In the case of California's Chinese, however, "it was difficult to shape an oath solemn enough to bind them." In their perception of Chinese spirituality, western lawyers concluded that merely temporal penalties did not, in fact, make witnesses nervous enough that their prevarication could be detected by cross-examination, even by skillful (white) lawyers. Notwithstanding ubiquitous constitutional and legislative provisions that "no person shall be rendered incompetent to be a witness on account of his opinions on matters of religious belief," codifiers transformed sacral capacities into racial ones, arguing that Chinese, Indian, or Negro testimony had to be excluded, not because it was frequently untrue, but because it had become impossible to discern truth from falsehood in the mouths of racialized speakers.[80]

Lawyers repeated these arguments numerous times before a California senate com-mittee convened in 1870 to consider "the Chinese Question." At the time, California's procedure code continued to bar the testimony of Natives and the Chinese (al-though Black exclusions had been abolished after the adoption of the Fourteenth Amendment).[81] San Francisco's white attorneys insisted the ban had to remain. Chinese "think no more of taking an oath than they do of eating rice," one lawyer tes-tified, a sentiment echoed numerous times in the proceedings. "They do not appear to realize the sanctity of an oath," another testified, "and it is very difficult to enforce the laws, where they are concerned, for that reason." Despite widespread evangelization efforts among California's Chinese, the lawyers professed to know "not more than half a dozen" Chinese Christians, and even then, they doubted the religious sincerity of "Chinamen who pretend to be Christians." In contrast to the boastful codifiers who believed in their skills to detect perjury, the San Francisco bar frankly admitted that the Chinese "will tell such well concocted stories that it is almost impossible to get at the truth as we can with white persons."[82]

Contending against the lawyers was the Reverend William Speer, a Presbyterian missionary who, as it happens, had been the interpreter for the Chinese witnesses in *People v. Hall*. In his *Answer to the Objections to Chinese Testimony*, Speer refuted the

[79] American linkages between racial exclusions and religious orthodoxy date back at least as far as a 1715 ordinance of Lord Baltimore's that forbid Negro or Indian testimony in any cause "wherein any Christian White Person is concerned." The following section permitted such testimony against other Negros and Indians, implicitly defining them outside the category of Christian. Thomas Bacon, *Laws of Maryland at Large* (1785), 140.

[80] Frank Tuthill, *The History of California* (H.H. Bancroft & Co., 1866), 373. See also "On Chinese Oaths and Swearing," 3 *Chinese Recorder and Missionary Journal* 103, 105 (1871); Memorandum of a Conversation Between William King, esq., of Savannah, and Carl Schurz, *Senate Executive Documents for the Thirty-Ninth Congress*, No. 29 (1866), 2:83–84.

[81] See 1868 Cal. Practice Act 485–86, § 394.

[82] The Chinese Question: Report of the Special Committee on Assembly Bill No. 13 (California, 1870), 48, 60, 75–76, 81–83, 93, 108, 112–18, 124, 143.

racist logic of *Hall* point by point. "If the Chinese are Indians, then *we* are Indians," he declared in derision of *Hall*'s attempt at demography. The common law of England recognized no racial incompetencies, and statutes in derogation of the common law should have been more strictly construed. In short order, Speer had no doubt, immigrating Chinese would learn of the American "civil crime of 'perjury'" and respect its temporal penalties.[83]

Turning from *Hall*, Speer had to contend with an argument of recent innovation: "We are told that the advance of science has established an *ethnological difficulty*; that the Chinese are of a diverse, and inferior, species of mankind; a colored 'caste,' ordained by the Creator to serve." Against this intermingling of theology and modern racial science Speer's lawyerly argument broke into a revivalist's polemic. Polygenesis was "no 'advance' of science," but a "figment" of "national pride" and "heathenish ignorance," a retrograde in civilization. "Call it 'new'? It is as old as the primeval ages of barbarism . . . . Call it 'science'? It exists in hideous shapes wherever superstition is moonless and starless, throughout the heathen world."[84]

In the next legislative session, California's code commission silently repealed the remaining racial exclusions for witness testimony, but across the nation, the "ethnological difficulty" against which Speer had argued remained deeply entrenched. In case after case, racial and religious competencies remained entangled as courts passed on the admission of testimony.[85] In these cases, what the legislature had decided as a matter of policy retreated into the background as courts decided as a matter of legal and natural necessity who could be believed.

In Nebraska, a Native witness named Holly Scott:

Q. By Mr. Marks, (prosecuting attorney:) State whether or not you understand, if you tell a lie in this case, that God, the Great Spirit, would be displeased with you. A. I will tell the truth; I don't want to tell any lies.

Q. By the court: You may ask the witness if the Indians have anything in their affairs which answers or is like the oaths that we use. A. He says that they had some kind of a way to have that, but still he was going to tell the truth; and he thought that he

---

[83] William Speer, *An Answer to the Common Objections to Chinese Testimony and an Earnest Appeal to the Legislature of California for their Protection by Our Law* (1857), 7–8. Speer repeated his arguments in a book-length work, *The Oldest and the Newest Empire: China and the United States* (S.S. Scranton & Co., 1870), 561–63, 628–30.

[84] Speer, An Answer to the Common Objections to Chinese Testimony, 8–9.

[85] See 1872 Cal. Code of Civ. Proc. 493–94, §§ 1879–80. On the entanglement of Christian theology and nineteenth-century race science, see especially Terrence Keel, *Divine Variations: How Christian Thought Became Racial Science* (Stanford University Press, 2018); Jennifer Snow, *Protestant Missionaries, Asian Immigrants, and Ideologies of Race in America, 1850–1924* (Routledge, 2006). On the emergence of race science generally, see Lee D. Baker, *From Savage to Negro: Anthropology and the Construction of Race, 1896–1954* (University of California Press, 1998); Philip Gleason, "Americans All: World War II and the Shaping of American Identity," 43 *Review of Politics* 483 (1981); Carl Degler, *In Search of Human Nature: The Decline and Revival of Darwinism in American Social Thought* (Oxford University Press, 1991), 187–211; Peggy Pascoe, "Miscegenation Law, Court Cases, and Ideologies of 'Race' in Twentieth-Century America," 83 *Journal of American History* 44 (1996); Matthew Frye Jacobson, *Whiteness of a Different Color: European Immigrants and the Alchemy of Race* (Harvard University Press, 1999); Henry Yu, *Thinking Orientals: Migration, Contact, and Exoticism in Modern America* (Oxford University Press, 2001).

was going to ask a question right away; so he was waiting for you to ask the questions of him.

Q. By the court: Do you know that it is wrong to swear to a lie? A. He don't know that. He says if you want him to testify he wants to know so; he wants to tell his evidence—that is all he is waiting for.

Q. By Mr. Marks: State whether or not you know that God, the Great Spirit, would be displeased if you should tell a lie. A. He says he don't know that. He says he is sworn to tell the truth, and thought that he was going to tell his questions. That is about all that he was waiting for, he says. He says if God was going to dislike him, or anything of that kind, he didn't know it.[86]

In New Mexico, a Chinese witness known as Jo Chinaman:

By Mr. Green:

Q. I will ask you if you believe in the Chinese Joss house where they worship, where they have their religious services? Do you ever go with Chinamen in this country where they worship? Do you understand what a God is? A. I don't know what it is. Yes, I believe the Chinese religion.

Q. Have you ever changed from Chinese to Christian religion since you came to this country? A. I am a Chinaman, and believe in the Chinese religion.

Q. Was you ever a witness in Court before? A. Yes.

Q. Do you know anything about the obligations of an oath under the Christian religion? A. I don't know it.[87]

In Tennessee, a freedman named Dick Johnson (related for the purpose of humoring a bar association):

Q. Squire, I wish to know whether this negro understands the solemnity of an oath. Let him swear to what he believes. . . . I want to know whether the witness believes in a state of future rewards and punishments, and I wish that question propounded to him. . . . Now, Dick, if you swear to a lie about this matter, what will be the result?

A. Judge, if they catch me, they would whip me.

Q. That is not the question. If you swear to a lie here, and they don't catch you in this world, and you go to the next world, what will be the result?

A. Judge, if they caught me there, they would whip me.

From this, a Tennessee lawyer concluded that racial exclusions were no matter of policy, but of "experience and common sense from the time when the memory of man runneth not to the contrary," unaltered and unalterable by legislation, the natural roots of the common law itself.[88]

---

[86] Priest v. State, 6 N.W. 468, 469 (Neb. 1880). See also Deborah Rosen, *American Indians and State Law: Sovereignty, Race, and Citizenship, 1790–1880* (University of Nebraska Press, 2007), 122–23 (surveying Native incompetency rules in other jurisdictions).

[87] Territory v. Yee Shun (N.M. 1882), Trial Transcript, 49–50, San Miguel County District Court Records, New Mexico State Archives. The transcript is largely reprinted and discussed in John R. Wunder, *Gold Mountain Turned to Dust: Essays on the Legal History of the Chinese in the Nineteenth-Century* (University of New Mexico Press, 2018), ch. 2.

[88] *Proceedings of the Tenth Annual Meeting of the Tennessee Bar Association* (1891), 18–19.

In these and other cases, courts reached a variety of conclusions, sometimes admitting testimony based on far less than assurance of Christian orthodoxy, sometimes not. But even in cases in which testimony was admitted, racial others had to submit to a theological examination rarely administered to their white counterparts. In cases in which proof lay in the testimony of the Chinese, Natives, Blacks, or mixed-race speakers, a discarded theology of sacral oaths thus became powerful once again.[89] Lawyers who had dismissed the threat of hell and divine retribution in adopting the new law of civil testimony later pleaded that degraded races lacked the requisite spirituality to make temporal perjury and keen cross-examination trustworthy instruments of seeking out the truth. Field might have been ready to abandon oath-taking and all pretense of spiritual punishment, but the reform ran headlong against the racial prejudices of the western bar, which insisted that cross-examination required some degree of Euro-American piety to work its magic.

The Field Commission thought it could use desacralized oaths to force truth into civil pleadings, even to the point it avoided the need for trial. It did not anticipate the tensions its rules would create with the traditional rule that plaintiffs bear the burden of proof, even when defendants could not mount strong defenses. Nor did the codifiers anticipate how dramatically admitted perjuries would increase under their expansion of the oath to pleadings. While many lawyers thought they could abide the perjury while detecting truth through their skillful cross-examination, the rise of scientific racism convinced many others that secular oaths and witness examinations were unable to secure true testimony among racialized witnesses. Just as the code multiplied legal forms in the attempt to abolish form altogether, the code's abrogation of sacral oaths greatly multiplied their use and power in the civil trial, and with the oaths came popular conceptions of theological meaning and obligation. Codifiers like Field and Shearman may have learned to live without hell under a benevolent God, but across the American West, their fellow codifiers and workaday lawyers dreaded to litigate without the fear of God.

---

[89] Perhaps the most striking codification of this phenomenon was Oregon's original procedure code, which in one section declared that no person "shall be disqualified from being a witness on account of the want of religious belief," and in the very next section required belief "in the existence of a Supreme Being, who will punish false swearing" in order to deem a witness competent to testify. 1854 Or. Laws 111.

8

The Want of Information
Discovery Before Trial

I

In early November 1872, Thomas G. Shearman solemnly visited his pastor, the Rev. Henry Ward Beecher. The prior month had seen both the zenith and the nadir of Beecher's storied career at the Plymouth Church in Brooklyn. A week of services, lectures, and parties had celebrated Beecher's Silver Anniversary—twenty-five years of service as pastor (see Figure 8.1). Shearman and his wife had rented rooms across the street to catch as much of the action as possible during the week and were among the 2,500 guests filling the auditorium to capacity night after night. Then, on October 28, a shocking editorial accused Beecher of adultery. Well known for upsetting the gender conventions of his day in preaching a "feminist" gospel, Beecher nevertheless adhered strongly to Victorian rules of chastity and monogamy. The adultery charge not only impugned his character and middle-class standing, it struck at the very root of his— and his congregation's—pietist theology.[1]

Over tea with the Beechers, Shearman relayed the advice of his law partner David Dudley Field, who urged Beecher "strongly to maintain absolute silence and to talk with no one upon the subject." Beecher replied that some other lawyer friends had offered the same advice that morning. The trouble was that Beecher had already spoken. For over two years, Beecher had been attempting to cover up something that had happened between him and Elizabeth Tilton, the wife (twenty years Beecher's junior) of Theodore Tilton, a charismatic orator and sometimes editorial rival of Beecher. To this day, it remains unclear what that something was. Theodore, the source of the editorial, believed that Beecher had confessed in 1870 to the act of adultery. Beecher would always maintain that his only sin was naively mistaking Elizabeth's love for the chaste adoration of her spiritual adviser. Modern investigative accounts locate the truth somewhere in the middle: Henry and Elizabeth seem to have fallen in love to the extent Beecher had something to be ashamed about, even— perhaps especially—if it had stopped short of physical consummation. In any event, the trio had conferred multiple times and enlisted multiple confidants and referees since the first disruption between Henry and Theodore, a dire episode, Shearman's

---

[1] Clifford E. Clark, *Henry Ward Beecher: Spokesman for a Middle-Class America* (University of Illinois Press, 1978). The editorial appeared in the October 28, 1872, issue of *Woodhull & Claflin's Weekly*. Shearman's activities are recorded in his printed Memoirs, vol. III, 390–94, Papers of Thomas G. Shearman, Shearman & Sterling Law Library.

Law's Machinery. Kellen R. Funk, Oxford University Press. © Kellen R. Funk 2025. DOI: 10.1093/9780197543962.003.0009

Figure 8.1 Portraits of Henry Ward Beecher and the interior of the Plymouth Church in Brooklyn on the occasion of Beecher's twenty-fifth anniversary as pastor.
"The Plymouth Church Silver Wedding," *Harper's Weekly*, October 19, 1872, 812.

law partners thought, of " 'working things out between ourselves' without consulting a lawyer."[2]

Shearman set about investigating the case immediately—but not in the law courts. Careful to keep his influence off the public record, Shearman drummed up a Committee of Inquiry at the Plymouth Church to sift Tilton's account, making sure to appoint "deacons with special reference to their fitness for the work of investigation."[3]

---

[2] Shearman Memoirs, III: 394; Walter K. Earle, *Mr. Shearman and Mr. Sterling and How They Grew* (Yale University Press, 1963), 97. See Richard Wightman Fox, *Trials of Intimacy: Love and Loss in the Beecher-Tilton Scandal* (University of Chicago Press, 1999). 97.

[3] Shearman Memoirs, III: 393.

Theodore and Elizabeth were both members of the church, but Theodore's turn to Unitarian theology gave the committee ample reason, in conjunction with his "slandering" of Beecher, to excommunicate him. After the committee work resolved in Beecher's favor in 1874, Tilton launched a civil suit seeking damages from Beecher for the affair. Beecher immediately retained Shearman to lead the defense.[4]

The Great Brooklyn Scandal, as the ensuing trial became known, is a set piece of Reconstruction history. Its verdict proved inconclusive on the fact of adultery but decisive on a broader cultural turn away from Beecher's liberal individualism and the "religion of gush," as one paper derided it, toward a more steely-eyed social gospel that would meld the public and private spheres as it addressed the ravages of urban industrialization.[5] Many works have chronicled the 112-day trial that brought to the stand 86 witnesses including Theodore and Henry but not Elizabeth. With only slight exaggeration, one account declared the trial the only thing that "drove Reconstruction off the front pages for two and a half years."[6]

Yet, so far, the story of the scandal has not been told from the lawyers' perspective. Turning to the litigators' experience reveals a feat more impressive than the trial itself: Somehow, in the few months between Shearman's retention on August 19, 1874, and the opening of the trial on January 11, 1875, Shearman and his law clerks had determined with reasonable confidence all the proofs that Tilton would bring to trial. To do so, they had to rely in no small part on Shearman's church investigations carried out in the private realm and with the soft coercion of church discipline and negative publicity. For the rest, Shearman had to navigate the complex ways his law partner Field had modernized the ancient chancery device of "discovery" in the New York Code.[7]

Originally an equitable action used to interrogate one's adversary (in writing), discovery is now used as a catchall term describing pretrial fact investigation, whether consisting of subpoenas for the production of documents, written affidavits and stipulations, or oral depositions of parties and witnesses. Michigan law professor Edson R. Sunderland, the architect of modern American discovery, wrote in 1932 that "discovery before trial" covered the variety of devices that addressed "the want of information" that kept litigants and their counsel from knowing "the real nature of the respective claims and the facts upon which they rest." Inspired by practice under the Field Code, Sunderland believed that "no procedural process offers greater opportunities for increasing the efficiency of the administration of justice" than empowering lawyers to become more effective discoverers of the facts before trial.[8]

---

[4] On the Committee of Inquiry proceedings, see Barry Werth, *Banquet at Delmonico's: Great Minds, the Gilded Age, and the Triumph of Evolution in America* (Random House, 2009), 80–82. For Shearman's retention, see the firm's journal entries in Earle, *Mr. Shearman and Mr. Sterling*, 102.

[5] See Fox, *Trials of Intimacy*, 36–39, 244–46; T. Jackson Lears, *No Place of Grace: Antimodernism and the Transformation of American Culture 1880–1820* (University of Chicago Press, 1983), 22–24; "The Lesson of the Scandal," *New York Herald*, Sept. 22, 1874.

[6] Walter McDougall, *Throes of Democracy* (HarperCollins, 2009), 551.

[7] For a discerning reading of the lawyers' strategies and constructions of the record, see Fox, *Trials of Intimacy*, 15, 19–20, 100, 105. Understandably, many have overlooked the lawyers' internal papers and strategy documents because they remain housed in the law firms like Shearman & Sterling LLP and not in professional archives.

[8] Edson R. Sunderland, foreword to George Ragland Jr., *Discovery Before Trial* (Callaghan & Co., 1932), iii. On Sunderland's role in producing and promoting Ragland's book, see Stephen N. Subrin, "Fishing

As the Beecher-Tilton affair illustrates, much more could be at stake in pretrial discovery than just the efficiency of the trial. A history of Shearman's firm estimated the costs of the Tilton investigation to be $118,000, a good deal more than the $100,000 Tilton was seeking in damages. Never mind the plaintiff's burden of proof, Shearman understood that for Beecher to be vindicated, the defense would have to go as far as possible to disprove Tilton's claims affirmatively, whatever they might be. Field's code offered several resources for this endeavor, but their use was not without complication. Of all the code's provisions, those allowing for the discovery of information before trial revealed the scars from what Shearman called the "hasty codification of 1848."[9] As other states quickly outpaced New York in how far they would implement Field's more deliberate experiments with discovery, the Beecher-Tilton trial exhibited the last gasps of an old order, one dedicated to the public control of private disclosures.

II

For many New York lawyers in the days before the code, discovery was more of a *who* than a *what*. The techniques of forcing or disclosing information were inseparable from chancery's personnel who oversaw their use: the master or, in more minor actions, the examiner. These public officers were the workhorses of the chancery system. Since chancery was famously a one-judge court—only the decree of the lone chancellor resolved disputes in the classical equity system—many more hands were needed to oversee the preliminary steps in chancery litigation and to prepare the record for the chancellor's review. Even after New York expanded chancery's staff to include ten vice chancellors (three full-time plus seven common law judges with expanded jurisdiction), the caseload in equity was far beyond what the bench alone could process. New York did not keep exact records on its court personnel, but by 1846 Field estimated that the state's chancery system employed around three hundred masters and examiners, giving equity a comparably sized staff as the common law system with its supreme court judges and their lower-level counterparts, the justices of the peace.[10]

"Masters" earned their name from their mastery of case records. Masters were chiefly responsible for gathering and compiling the proofs in a litigation, reducing everything to a series of written records and recommendations for the chancellor's review. That task often entailed examining witnesses and preparing synopses (not exact transcripts) of the testimony. As the name implied, examiners also conducted witness interviews. The difference between the offices was that masters had more discretion

---

Expeditions Allowed: The Historical Background of the 1938 Federal Discovery Rules," 39 *Boston College Law Review* 691 (1998), 702.

[9] Earle, *Mr. Shearman and Mr. Sterling*, 121 n.10. 1 Abbott 28.

[10] [David Dudley Field], "Civil Officers," *New York Evening Post*, July 13, 1846; Murray Hoffman, *The Office and Duties of Masters in Chancery and Practice in the Master's Office* (Gould and Banks, 1824). See also Michael R. T. Macnair, *The Law of Proof in Early Modern England* (Duncker & Humblot, 2013); Kellen Funk, "Equity Without Chancery: The Fusion of Law and Equity in the Field Code of Civil Procedure, New York 1846–76," 36 *Journal of Legal History* 152 (2015).

to expand the investigation beyond the lawyers' written interrogatories, summon additional witnesses, or subpoena additional documents to make up a sufficient record. The quasi-judicial nature of the office thus rewarded legal learning, as masters who understood the legal relevance of the materials could conduct their investigations more sharply and efficiently. Chancellor James Kent made this legal learning the basis of his defense of chancery when the New York legislature considered abolishing the master's office in 1821. "The masters in chancery are sworn officers, whose habits, and study, and knowledge, fit and prepare them for such duties," Kent submitted in a report. Because their "business is made a matter of distinct profession and science," Kent believed the public trust of the office cultivated "the skill and capacity" that should be rewarded with "exclusive employment" as state officers.[11]

Herman Melville offered a fairly different view of the master's office in his famous short story *Bartleby the Scrivener*. The somewhat unreliable narrator of Bartleby's story was a former master in chancery, who, despite an obvious effort to maintain a gregarious manner and easygoing style, could not restrain his temper over New York's treatment of chancery. Steadfastly maintaining the philosophy that "the easiest way of life is best," the master presented himself—and those of his office—as "one of those unambitious lawyers who never addresses a jury, . . . but in the cool tranquility of a snug retreat, do a snug business among rich men's bonds and mortgages and title-deeds." The master's position "was not a very arduous office, but very remunerative," and the narrator was indignant at the "wrongs and outrages" of New York's lawmakers in prematurely terminating the master's "life-lease of the profits" when the state's court of chancery was abolished in 1846.[12]

Melville implicitly rebuked Kent's emphasis on the public-minded character of the master by putting the workaday concerns of the private practitioner on full display. As the story indicated, a master's commission was usually not a full-time commitment to public service but rather contract work that could be layered on top of a lawyer's ongoing private practice. While Kent reported that "nothing is more complicated than the investigation and settlement of accounts between partners in a trade," Melville described the work of chancery as easy enough for a professional and typically overcompensated for the effort involved.[13] And, central to the story, most of those efforts devolved not on the master but on the other critical personnel of chancery, the master's law-copyists, otherwise known as the scriveners.

Although centrally important to a jurisdiction that valued the written word as highly as chancery did, scrivening was understood to be a mere trade, unconnected to the science of law. Copying was its own profession—even scriveners who worked with legal documents for decades usually never practiced law themselves, as exemplified by the sixty-year-old copyist nicknamed Turkey in the Bartleby tale. Lawyers avoided

---

[11] James Kent, Report on an Act to Alter the Mode of Taking Evidence in the Court of Chancery, in Nathaniel H. Carter & William L. Stone, *Reports of the Proceedings and Debates of the Convention of 1821* (E. and E. Hosford, 1821), 506. See also Amalia D. Kessler, *Inventing American Exceptionalism: The Origins of American Adversarial Legal Culture, 1800–1877* (Yale University Press, 2017), 74–75, 90–92.

[12] "Bartleby," in Herman Melville, *Piazza Tales* (1856), 31, 33. The story was first published in 1853 in *Putnam's Monthly* under the title "Bartleby, the Scrivener: A Tale of Wall-Street."

[13] Kent, Report on an Act to Alter the Mode of Taking Evidence, 506; Kessler, *Inventing American Exceptionalism*, 73.

doing their own copy work whenever they could. Indeed, the dread that lawyers were becoming mere scriveners was a constant theme of the lawyers' complaints about law as a swiftly degrading craft. The chief problems with the forms of action, with repetitious fictions, and with filing law blanks were all of a piece: legal practice had been reduced to mere copy work. A lawyer's "labor is thrown away," Field lamented, "and so many fine heads and strong hands are condemned to the servile, the belittling employment of writing out old jingles of words." Whereas the practice of law should have been "the noblest which the citizen can exercise in a free state," the pressure to copy over forms in sufficient numbers to collect fees pegged to the page count meant that only "a feverish restlessness, and an overtasked mind, are the present concomitants of a leading position in the profession."[14]

Field's sense of the "mere drudgery" of copying legal documents found vivid expression in Melville's *Bartleby*. Typically read as a young novelist's struggle with either writer's block or the stifling constraints of conventional literature, *Bartleby the Scrivener* chose the law office as its central site of professional ennui. Bartleby's desultory reaction to everyday tasks, standing still with the repeated refrain, "I would prefer not to," is odd (for its nonconformity) but understandable, given the tedious and unending nature of the work of chancery. Bartleby first refuses work, then refuses to leave, taking up residence in the master's office. The final straw for the master is Bartleby's denial of the master's authority in front of his lawyerly colleagues, a public display of what had been the master's private indulgence. When "the room was full of lawyers and witnesses and business was driving fast," Bartleby tranquilly refused a request "to run round to [a] legal gentleman's office and fetch some papers for him," the most basic task of the master's charge. From there, the tale spirals into a tragedy, ending with Bartleby's imprisonment and death.[15] Among the technical changes to discovery, Field's code set out to rescue lawyers from a similar intellectual confinement and atrophy. But unlike the law of pleading, Field was not out to build a system from the ground up.

III

Chancery's written procedure underwent dramatic transformation decades before the Field Code appeared. Equity's powers to compel the production of documents migrated to common law courts, while the oral adversarial culture of common law gradually crept into chancery proceedings.

Both common law and equity prohibited testimony from a party or witness interested in the outcome of the case. The answer to an equitable bill, however, was supplied by a party in writing and verified by oath, and the opposing party could

---

[14] David Dudley Field, "The Study and Practice of the Law,"14 *Democratic Review* 345 (1844), 345–49. See also R.W. Wells, *Law of the State of Missouri Regulating Pleadings and Practice* (Missouri, 1849), 112–14. Michael Zakim's labor history of merchant clerks in the nineteenth century would have accorded with the experience of law clerks as well. Michael Zakim, "The Clerk at Work," in Michael Zakim & Gary J. Kornblith, eds., *Capitalism Takes Command: The Social Transformation of Nineteenth-Century America* (Chicago University Press, 2012), 223–47.

[15] "Bartleby," 70–72, 88–89, 90–106.

then use the sworn statement in subsequent litigation both in equity and at common law.[16] When the interrogation of a party was the only remedy sought, the pleading was called a "bill of discovery." Discovery had a narrow purpose: to compel a defendant's admission to a material element of a case when other evidence was unobtainable. Equity courts intended discovery "to enable the applicant to prove his case: not to get information as to whether he had a case, much less to explore his adversary's case." It was the task of the pleadings to prove that a requested discovery was material and necessary and not "a mere fishing bill."[17] Bills for discovery appended long lists of "interrogatories" prepared by the lawyers. Masters and examiners dutifully read out and recorded the answers to the interrogatories, but the records were kept secret until all examinations were finished. Masters could then employ their freedom to range beyond the written interrogatories to request additional witnesses or documents if needed to complete the record.[18]

Masters could also compel a party to deliver to the court "books, deeds, letters, accounts, and other papers relating to the matters at issue" for the other party's inspection. Often the interrogatory process was used to figure out what documents were available to subpoena. Relevance depended on a party having an "interest" in the document, for instance, if the party was named in a deed or receipt of payment, or if a partner sought the accounting books for the partnership. For documents held by a nonparty witness, either party could request a subpoena *duces tecum* ordering a witness to produce the documents for examination by a master or the chancellor, but neither the documents nor any nonparty witness was made available for pretrial examination by parties.[19]

At the beginning of the nineteenth century, depositions by masters and examiners were conducted without the presence of lawyers, who could only submit their written interrogatories in advance and could not view the synopses of the testimony until the record had closed. As Amalia Kessler has shown, lawyers like Field gradually inserted themselves into the deposition process by the 1830s, reducing the master's role to refereeing the skirmishes between the lawyers' live, oral, and adversarial investigations.[20]

At the same time that lawyers sought to bring the oral, adversarial style of examination from common law to chancery, they complained about the lack of chancery procedures at common law. Reformers in the 1830s and 1840s especially complained about their lack of access to testimony evidence until the day of trial in open court. Field's co-commissioner Arphaxad Loomis thought the practice contributed to verbose pleadings, as lawyers were "multiplying words to meet every possible contingency in the memory or expression of witnesses" they could not get on record until

---

[16] See Joseph W. Moulton, *The Chancery Practice of the State of New York* (O. Halsted, 1829), 1:181.

[17] Christopher Columbus Langdell, *A Summary of Equity Pleading* (Charles W. Sever, 1877), 196; Moulton, *Chancery Practice*, 1:182–83. Joseph Story provided a classic definition of fishing bill as the effort of a plaintiff to "file a bill, and insist upon knowledge of facts wholly impertinent to his case, and thus compel disclosures in which he had no interest, to gratify his malice or his curiosity or his spirit of oppression." Joseph Story, *Commentaries on Equity Jurisprudence as Administered in England and America* (Hilliard, Gray & Co., 1836), 2:822.

[18] See Moulton, *Chancery Practice*, 1:292–94; Kessler, *Inventing American Exceptionalism*, 32–33.

[19] Oliver Barbour, *A Treatise on the Practice of the Court of Chancery* (Gould, Banks & Co., 1843), 1:229–32, 279–80; 2:431.

[20] Kessler, *Inventing American Exceptionalism*, 62–111.

the hearing. Moreover, the uncertainty of what witnesses would say and what precise issues might resolve the dispute meant that in complicated matters, parties had to demand that all possible witnesses appear on the day of trial, even if only one or two were ultimately needed—fees paid to attending witnesses all the while.[21]

The one exception to the rule against witness examinations before trial was the deposition *de bene esse*, also known as the conditional deposition. Parties could seek permission from the trial court to examine a witness outside of court conditioned on the witness's likely absence at trial due to a debilitating illness or impending relocation out of the jurisdiction of the state. The deposition was supposed to be taken and recorded by a neutral lawyer commissioned for the purpose, much like the examination procedure before chancery's masters. In actual practice, the examining party's counsel was often the one who conducted and recorded the deposition; objections from an adverse party were merely reserved for the judge to resolve at trial.[22]

The Revised Statutes of 1829 extended "the principles and practice of the court of chancery in compelling discovery" to the common law courts, while equitable examinations increasingly looked like oral and adversarial common law trials.[23] To the extent the code preserved these practices and continued the use of the subpoena *duces tecum* (while discarding the Latin) and the conditional deposition, the code was "non-revolutionary," as Professor Kessler put it.[24]

Yet discovery practices could not remain unaffected by one of the code's most revolutionary changes, the admission of testimony from parties and interested witnesses. A signal reform in the quest for truth-seeking, party qualification was expected to solve Loomis's problem of subpoenaing hosts of witnesses to meet every possible contingency. Testimony straight from the parties was expected to bring the most complete and accurate information upfront and obviate the need for additional witnesses or hypothetical alternatives—after all, it was usually the parties themselves who knew best what had happened between them.[25] But such a dramatic change in trial practice necessarily raised questions about how pretrial investigations would be affected. Codifiers were virtually unanimous in their agreement that live examination at trial was preferable to recorded examinations outside of court. "A written deposition taken in private, is not the best means of eliciting the truth," Field wrote in his 1848 report. The report accompanying Missouri's code the next year agreed that "private examination in an office is not so likely to obtain the truth" and explained why: "the witness will be less apt to prevaricate, when thus examined in open court and in the presence

---

[21] Arphaxad Loomis, *Historic Sketch of the New York System of Law Reform in Practice and Pleadings* (1879), 5; Report in Part of the Committee on the Judiciary in Relation to the Administration of Justice, in *Documents of the Assembly of the State of New York*, 65th sess., no. 81 (1842), 5:6.

[22] *Revised Statutes*, 2:392, § 5, 398–99, §§ 35–41; Moulton, *Chancery Practice*, 1:94. A party could take a deposition in a judge's chambers or at any other location agreeable to both parties. See Henry Whittaker, *Practice and Pleading Under the Codes* (1852), 632. Although Whittaker concentrated on practice under the code, he demonstrated that the particulars of conditional depositions differed little from prior practice.

[23] See *Revised Statutes of the State of New York* (1829), 2:199–200, §§ 21–27; *Rules of Practice of the Supreme Court of the State of New York at Law and Equity* 12, Rules 27–28 (1847).

[24] See 1848 N.Y. Laws 560, § 355. 1846 N.Y. Const., art. VI, § 10. Kessler, *Inventing American Exceptionalism*, 112ff.

[25] See A Letter from D. D. Field, Esq. of New York, on Law Reform, to Representative John O'Sullivan, in *Documents of the Assembly of the State of New York*, 65th Sess., No. 81 (1842), 5:1; Loomis, *Historic Sketch*, 5–6.

of the party against whom he is testifying."[26] The code thus aimed to limit pretrial investigations to facilitate the live, oral investigation of unmuzzled parties at the trial itself.

The code's primary change to pretrial discovery can be understood in this light. "No action to obtain discovery under oath in aid of [either party] shall be allowed," the 1848 draft declared. Commentators have sometimes overread the regulation to mean that the code "extremely limited discovery," but the commissioners' emphasis was on the opening words: no *action*—that is, no separately filed case whose only remedy was the disclosure of information—would be permitted under the code. Instead, all of the code's provisions for the discovery of information would be available in *every* action. No longer would practitioners need to file one action in equity to aid another case proceeding at common law.[27]

But how far would those investigative powers extend? Here, the multiple drafts of the code complicated matters. Although Field would have preferred to admit party testimony without restriction while entirely abolishing pretrial procedures for written testimony, his initial draft compromised on both issues. Parties could be put on the stand only by their adversaries for limited purposes. "In lieu" of calling the party to the stand, the examining party could conduct its examination in a pretrial deposition, similar to the former practice in chancery. Any such deposition would be taken by partisan lawyers instead of a court-appointed examiner, with objections reserved for the trial.[28] The commissioners' report argued that a single examination in open court was sufficient to do justice between the parties. With that as the goal, depositions were unnecessary but allowed as a transitional phase in the code's reform. The commentary explained, "If the examination be once had, we would not permit it to be repeated, else it might become the means of annoyance."[29] To the commissioners, anything more than one examination of a witness was excessive.

In the Final Draft of the code—the one never enacted in New York but taken up by many other jurisdictions—Field succeeded in making parties and all other interested witnesses fully competent to testify at trial. Without explanation, however, the code's provision for pretrial examination was continued, and the limitation that such an examination would be "in lieu" of calling the party or witness at trial was dropped.[30] The edits may well have been indeliberate. Nothing in Field's writings indicates a change of heart in preferring all examination to happen once at a live trial. Field generally held discovery in low regard because of his belief that pleading could adequately inform adversaries of each other's case and supply necessary admissions of fact. As long as the judge saw to it that the pleadings were properly conducted, the pleadings would "bring before the court, and to the knowledge of one's adversary, the precise

---

[26] *First Report* (New York, 1848), 244; R. W. Wells, *Law of the State of Missouri Regulating Pleadings and Practice* (1849), 68–69.

[27] 1848 N.Y. Laws 559, § 343; cf. Stephen N. Subrin, "David Dudley Field and the Field Code: A Historical Analysis of an Earlier Procedural Vision," 6 *Law & History Review* 311, 332 (1988).

[28] 1848 N.Y. Laws 559, § 343–56; Whittaker, *Practice and Pleading Under the Codes*, 631–32.

[29] 1848 N.Y. Laws 560, § 354 (materiality requirement) & 559, § 345 (pretrial examination in lieu of examination at trial); *First Report* (New York, 1848), 244–45, notes to § 350; David Dudley Field, *What Shall Be Done with the Practice of the Courts? Shall It Be Wholly Reformed?* (1847), 11.

[30] *Final Report* (New York, 1850), 2:767–68 § 1821.

questions in dispute, and . . . insure truthful allegations by the sanction of an oath." For Field—a lawyer more at home in the oral common law trial than in the scrivener's office at chancery—the live trial remained the primary site of fact investigation, not a stage on which to recite what lawyers had learned elsewhere.[31] While Field thought fact pleading would clear up major sources of surprise, he was comfortable with the occasional unexpected development at trial. The limits, frustrations, and stratagems induced by such a system quickly became apparent in New York practice and made especially stark by the Beecher-Tilton trial.

IV

Tilton and Beecher felt a severe "want of information" before their trial but in different ways. Tilton had to prove a physical act of adultery, even though there were no eyewitnesses to what occurred between Henry and Elizabeth except the couple themselves. The only purported confession, written by Elizabeth, had been destroyed years earlier at Theodore's own hand in an act of Christian forgiveness (or self-preservation). Recent amendments to the New York Code forbid Theodore from calling his wife to testify, and putting New York's most famous orator on the stand in her place was hardly a consolation. The case had to proceed circumstantially, relying on vague apologies and expressions of grief that Henry and Elizabeth had made in various writings over the years.[32]

On the other side, Beecher was desperate to know the extent of Tilton's inculpatory evidence. The complaint alleged adultery "on or about the tenth day of October, 1868, and on divers other days and times . . . before the commencement of this action."[33] That created a six-year span for which Beecher might have to produce alibis or rebut surprise witnesses. For sake of his public image, Henry made as sweeping a general denial of any improper relations with Elizabeth as he could, and although the code would have let Beecher's lawyers sign the answer in his case, Beecher insisted on applying his own oath, dragging Shearman along on a New Hampshire vacation to supervise the technicalities. Tilton had the burden of proof, of course, but his

---

[31] [David Dudley Field], *Law Reform Tracts No. 1: The Administration of the Code* (1852), 17; *see* Field, *Practice of the Courts*, 11.

[32] On physical adultery as a material element, see Laura Hanft Kotobkin, *Criminal Conversations: Sentimentality and Nineteenth-century Legal Stories of Adultery* (Columbia University Press, 1998). In December 1870, Elizabeth wrote out a confession confirming suspicions Theodore had expressed to her. Beecher cajoled an ailing Elizabeth to write a retraction, and Theodore pressed her to write a retraction of the retraction the same night. Tilton destroyed the confession in 1872 after executing what came to be known as the Tripartite Agreement between himself, Beecher, and Henry Bowen, editor of *The Independent*. The agreement was meant to settle all claims and extinguish rumors that Bowen had threatened to make public. See Fox, *Trials of Intimacy*, 133–78.

[33] The conventional source for the Beecher trial transcript is the three-volume set published by the McDivitt, Campbell & Co. Law Publishers, *Theodore Tilton vs. Henry Ward Beecher, Action for Crim. Con. Tried in the City of Brooklyn* (McDivitt, Campbell & Co., 1875). Shearman's law clerk Austin Abbott published a two-volume account which omits the daily commentary of the official version but includes transcripts of the preliminary arguments omitted in the official version. Austin Abbott, *Official Report of the Trial of Henry Ward Beecher* (George W. Smith, 1875). The complaint is available at 1 Abbott 1–2 and 1 McDivitt 3.

circumstantial case would be built out of evidence of Beecher's sense of guilt, shame, or impropriety expressed during those six long years.[34] What might Tilton's lawyers dredge up? Beecher's lawyers had a few months to find out.

The most straightforward means of discovering Tilton's case would have been to ask him in a deposition. But Shearman ruled out the strategy from the start. New York still retained the half measures of Field's transitional code, so a deposition of Tilton would have been "in lieu" of his live testimony at trial. Beecher's lawyers had no interest in reading a cold deposition transcript to an exhausted jury. "Every lawyer knows how ineffective a cross-examination is when not conducted in the actual presence of the jury," Shearman complained at a preliminary hearing.[35] Shearman also thought he saw a way to keep Tilton silent through the whole trial, but that strategy would only work if a deposition were avoided. New York's evolving law of marital privilege forbid testifying "against" one's spouse, but it was not clear if accusing a nonparty spouse of adultery counted. The argument eventually consumed two full days at trial, and Tilton ultimately prevailed. But Shearman worried the argument would be forfeited from the start if he deposed Tilton, since deposing an adverse party gave the party a right of rebuttal on the stand, a surefire way to give Tilton "an opportunity of putting his own testimony before the jury."[36]

In short, the code made Tilton speak both too much and too little for Shearman's purposes. On the one hand, it allowed Tilton's rebuttal testimony when Shearman sought to keep Tilton from speaking to the jury at all. On the other, the defense could compel Tilton to speak only in the form of a dry transcript that denied the forensic opportunity to make Tilton sweat under the gaze of the jury. If Tilton were to reach the stand, Shearman wanted to ensure a vigorous, live examination met him there. The law of the code did not offer a satisfactory way forward. But as a devoted member of Beecher's church, a congregation that often skirted the official law in the days of antislavery activism, Shearman knew other procedures might offer him redress.[37]

[34] On the strategy of the general denial, see Application for a Bill of Particulars, § 5, 1 Abbott 42. Shearman's efforts to verify the complaint, which required three attempts before it was successfully completed, are described at 1 Abbott 29–30.

[35] See *Code of Procedure of the State of New York, as Amended to 1870* (John Townshend, ed., 1870), 607–10, §§ 389–91. 1 Abbott 45.

[36] 1 Abbott 45. New York modified its marital privilege law in 1867, making husbands and wives generally competent and compellable to be witnesses, with the exception that spouses could not testify against their partners who were *parties* to an action for criminal conversation. 1867 N.Y. Laws 2:2221. By the express provision of the statute, Elizabeth could not testify as the wife of the plaintiff party Theodore. Since it was Henry, and not Elizabeth, who was the defendant party, nothing in the statute prevented Theodore from testifying about his wife's adultery. Shearman's legal team sought to exclude Theodore's testimony nevertheless on grounds of equity and fairness, along with a (weak) argument that the common law would have barred the testimony and remained operative despite the 1867 statute. See Mr. Abbott's Brief on the Incompetency of Husbands and Wives to Testify For or Against Each Other, Papers of Thomas G. Shearman.

[37] On Beecher's fame as an antislavery activist, including the surreptitious export of rifles to Free Staters in Kansas (famously under the false label of "Bibles" on the crates), see Debby Applegate, *The Most Famous Man in America: The Biography of Henry Ward Beecher* (Doubleday, 2006), 276–82. For a suggestion that nineteenth-century evangelical culture constituted an alternative legality to the law and police power of the states, see Christopher L. Tomlins, *Law, Labor, and Ideology in the Early American Republic* (Cambridge University Press, 1993), 25.

As clerk of the Plymouth Church, Shearman instigated church disciplinary proceedings after Tilton had threatened but not yet filed litigation. Tilton could have completely escaped church jurisdiction by resigning his membership, and indeed, his first response pleaded that a four-year absence from the church made his affiliation defunct. Beecher, still hoping the rumors might be laid to rest without the ordeal of a trial, exclaimed that God himself had inspired Tilton's maneuver.[38] Apparently other forces inspired the church's response. A committee of examiners informed Tilton that they would strike him from the rolls, not for his prolonged absence but for slandering the church's pastor. As expected, Tilton could not resist the bait. He wrote the Committee that he wished to "waive my non-membership" and appear to answer precisely one question: "Have you, Theodore Tilton, ever spoken against Henry Ward Beecher falsely?"[39]

Tilton appeared at the church the same night he sent his letter, but it took months for the Committee to prepare for Tilton's formal examination now that its former clerk, Shearman, had decided to appear as counsel for Beecher. When the day of the examination at last arrived, Tilton offered a detailed statement accusing Beecher of adultery and including fulsome quotations of letters between the parties, their associates, and Elizabeth. To conduct the questioning, the Committee retained U.S. Attorney Benjamin F. Tracy, who would later join Beecher's defense team. Tracy's church examination of Tilton was almost a dress rehearsal for the civil trial, prefiguring Tilton's testimony on the stand and the attacks Beecher's counsel would make. Tilton acknowledged under oath to the church committee that he had previously given many contradictory assessments of Beecher's character over the years, that he had affiliated with free-love advocates and held unorthodox views on marriage and divorce, and that he had developed political and professional rivalries with Beecher.[40]

In one respect, however, the church inquiry could not accomplish what a civil suit could: the church committee could not persuade Tilton to surrender the original letters quoted in his statement. Tilton argued that some of those documents, including an (unspecific) apology from Henry, were too valuable to release even temporarily, given the potential for litigation. Tilton also seemed nervous about how Beecher's lawyers might distort the written record, bluntly accusing the Committee: "You are six gentlemen determined, if possible, not to find the facts, but to vindicate Mr. Beecher." Adding Beecher's two retained lawyers to that number, Tilton grimly concluded, "There are eight of you . . ., and I am alone."[41]

---

[38] Charles F. Marshall, *A True History of the Brooklyn Scandal* (National Publishing Co., 1874), 32. 1 McDivitt 143.

[39] Marshall, *A True History*, 32–33; 1 McDivitt 47. On Shearman's actions as clerk of the Plymouth Church in 1873, see Marshall, *True History*, 33, 44, 48–54, 58–60. It appears that while Henry and Theodore were hoping to suppress investigation of the scandal through the church examination committee, Shearman was intent on pursuing the investigation up to the point he could declare Beecher exonerated.

[40] Tilton's full statement to the Committee is reproduced in Marshall, *A True History*, 112–29. The cross-examination is given in *ibid.*, 130–77. The Committee members are briefly described in *ibid.*, 106–8. While Tracy conducted some cross-examination of Tilton's witnesses at the trial, the cross-examination of Tilton himself was handled by William M. Evarts, reputed to be the greatest of New York's trial lawyers at the time. See 1 McDivitt 453ff.

[41] Marshall, *A True History*, 148–49, 177. After another month of negotiation, Tilton permitted a member of the Committee to view some of the original letters in the custody of a third party. It is not clear how much time was permitted for the examination. The allowance was made on August 11, 1874, one week before Tilton filed his civil action. *Ibid.*, 250–51.

Tilton was not alone for long. After the church examination, Tilton hired a former judge, Samuel D. Morris, as his chief legal adviser. Eventually, four more lawyers joined the team, but it was Morris who, upon filing the civil complaint, advised Tilton to also take to the offensive in the press. Under Morris's review, Tilton published in the September 1874 *Daily Graphic* twenty-five columns of fine print explaining his side of the case—all in addition to the transcript of Tilton's church examination, which had leaked to the *Argus* earlier that summer.[42] Tilton also shocked the literary world by publishing a purported decade of correspondence between himself and Elizabeth, taking up another thirty-two columns of print in the *Chicago Tribune*. (Morris advised the distant publication would be more tasteful than a Brooklyn rag.) Newspapers across the nation enviously congratulated the *Tribune* on its scoop and predicted that the letters would join those of Abelard and Héloïse in the canon of star-crossed epistles. Not to be outdone, New York's *Daily Graphic* used innovative technology to replicate some of Tilton's correspondence exactly, perhaps the first time in history that private letters were mass reproduced by modern photocopy technology[43] (see Figure 8.2).

Newspapers had obvious incentives to publish sordid details about the Brooklyn Scandal, but it is less clear what Morris expected his client to gain since almost all of Tilton's material could have been withheld until the moment it was sprung upon Beecher at trial. Perhaps the best clue is an anxiety that Shearman expressed during preliminary arguments, that the Brooklyn court might impanel a "stupid juryman, such as we, unfortunately, have sometimes." Shearman feared that conniving lawyers might lead such a person toward a terribly unjust syllogism: "I concede there is no evidence that these parties ever met in Brooklyn; there is no evidence that they ever met in New York; but I don't think any man could ever have written these letters unless he was guilty of something, and I am going to find him guilty of something."[44] Criminal conversation was a rare allegation, and as far as the lawyers could determine, Beecher's case was the first since the new code had taken effect in 1848. It was therefore difficult to predict the precise scope of jury instructions, including the jurors' leeway to rely on circumstantial evidence and the guilty tone of various letters. If Tilton's press releases could solidify a broad social sense that anyone who wrote such letters was guilty, so much the better for him once deliberations in the jury room began. As Figure 8.3 illustrates, certain letters had become so notorious they had acquired commonly accepted names, and the efforts of Beecher's counsel only drew further attention to the suspicions they raised. One newspaper at any rate

---

[42] *Daily Argus* (Brooklyn, N.Y.), July 21, 1874; *Daily Graphic* (New York, N.Y.), Sept. 18, 1874 & Extra Supplement. For Morris's advice, see 1 Abbott 26, and for Tilton's testimony to the same effect, 1 McDivitt 485–86, 505.

[43] "The Tilton Letters," *Chicago Tribune*, Aug. 13, 1874; "The Chicago Tribune's Enterprise," *Chicago Tribune*, Aug. 17, 1874; "Letters which Speak for Themselves," *Daily Argus* (Albany, N.Y.), Aug. 17, 1874; *Daily Graphic* (New York, N.Y.), Sept. 3, 1874. In a follow-up article, the *Graphic* bragged that it used processes "no other daily journal in this country has the facility to produce." *Daily Graphic*, Sept. 11, 1874. On the "Leggotype" technology developed by the *Graphic*, see "Reproduction photomécanique et photographie d'amateur au Canada: quelques notes sur le rapport entre l'histoire d'une technique et le développement d'une pratique culturelle," 91 *Nouvelles de l'estampe* (1987), 22–25.

[44] 1 Abbott 125.

Figure 8.2 Tilton worked with the *Daily Graphic* to print facsimiles of the letters between him, his wife, and Henry Ward Beecher. The *Daily Graphic* had developed its innovative photocopying technology just the year before.

Daily Graphic, September 18, 1874, 565.

AN APPROPRIATE HAT FOR MR. BEECHER.
NOT A CARDINAL'S—BUT A FOOL'S CAP.

Figure 8.3 The Beecher-Tilton correspondence became so well-known that particular letters could be referenced by nicknames. In this parody image, the efforts of Beecher's legal counsel to explain away the letters only draw further attention to the most embarrassing passages. Thomas Shearman is depicted at the top, at the end of a rope held by General Benjamin Tracy. William M. Evarts stands on the ladder to the lower right.
Joseph Keppler, "An Appropriate Hat for Mr. Beecher," *Frank Leslie's Budget of Fun*, April 1875, cover.

congratulated Tilton and Morris for a "superb" presentation "to the supreme court of the people."[45]

Tilton's gambit meant that Shearman, though he lacked the original letters, could sift an exceptional number of documents before the trial began. Nonetheless, Shearman still felt uneasy about his want of information. No matter how many news columns were published, there was always some chance that Tilton was holding something back for trial. Indeed, Tilton's publications frequently hinted that the darkest and dirtiest secrets had yet to be aired.[46]

---

[45] On the rarity of the charge and the lack of guiding precedent, see Appellant's Brief for a Bill of Particulars, 5, Papers of Thomas G. Shearman. The only recent case of criminal conversation the Beecher team was able to find had terminated early in the proceedings when the plaintiff could not prove a valid marriage had been performed in the first place. See Mr. Shearman's Brief on the Competency of Plaintiff as a Witness, 5 (discussing Dann v. Kingdom, 1 Thomp. & Cook 492 (1873)), Papers of Thomas G. Shearman. *Daily Graphic*, Sept. 18, 1874.
[46] See, e.g., Marshall, *A True History*, 127–28. In a newspaper publication that became known as Tilton's Last Statement, Tilton emphasized that his "whole case" had not yet been presented, and he continued

To make the defense more secure, Shearman moved to deploy a peculiar common law device used to force information: the bill of particulars. Most commonly sought in actions concerning debt, a bill of particulars ordered the complaining party to supply an additional document, usually a sworn affidavit, providing more specific details about the claim than the complaint had given. Since common law pleadings were often general and fictitious, a bill of particulars might be the defendant's one shot at learning about the plaintiff's case before trial. If a complaint alleged generally that a breaching defendant had not complied with the conditions precedent to performing on a contract, the bill of particulars forced the plaintiff to state which conditions had been breached and how. If the complaint generally alleged nonpayment for goods, the bill of particulars forced the plaintiff to itemize the unpaid accounts. To ensure a plaintiff was fully forthcoming with the facts in his possession, the bill of particulars contained an order limiting the plaintiff at trial to proving only the allegations offered in his affidavit. As one authority summarized it, the bill of particulars thus performed a "double office": it forced the preliminary disclosure of information, but then it also confined the trial to only the information so disclosed.[47]

It was the second function of the bill of particulars that most attracted Shearman. True, a bill of particulars might tell Shearman something of Tilton's case he would not know from the many newspaper publications and church examinations, but his aim was not so much to learn more about Elizabeth and Henry but to confine the record to what had already been made public. Tilton's complaint mentioned only two specific dates—October 10 and 17, 1868. The church examination revealed that Theodore's only evidence of adultery on those dates was Elizabeth's retracted confession which had not been preserved in writing and which the defense could paint as fabricated to allay Theodore's aggression against Elizabeth at the time.[48] If the trial could be confined to Theodore's evidence on those two dates, Shearman might make quick work of the case against his pastor.

The trouble for Shearman was best summarized in his own treatise on the matter. "As a general rule," Shearman had written in 1865, "a bill of particulars will not be ordered in an action for a *tort*."[49] Torts, or personal injuries, were usually specified sufficiently in the complaint itself. The code's drafting history accorded with this understanding. Originally, the code permitted courts to order a bill of particulars only in actions for account, that is, to itemize receipts and nonpayments. A later amendment proposed by Field permitted a court discretion "in any case" to award a bill of particulars but with the understanding that the discretion would not be exercised when the complaint was definite enough.[50] Where did that leave criminal

---

to withhold information as to "the times, the places, the frequency, together with other particulars which I feel a repugnance to name" because he could not "forbear to mention [them] again." *Daily Graphic*, Sept. 18, 1874.

[47] See David Graham, *A Treatise on the Practice of the Supreme Court of the State of New York* (Gould & Banks, 2d ed., 1836), 434; 1 Abbott 134.

[48] See 1 McDivitt 3; Marshall, *A True History*, 112–29.

[49] John L. Tillinghast & Thomas G. Shearman, *Practice, Pleadings, and Forms in Civil Actions in the Courts of Record in the State of New York* (Lewis Brothers, 2d rev. ed., 1865), 1:48.

[50] Compare 1849 N.Y. Laws 648 § 158 with 1851 N.Y. Laws 888–89 § 158; *Code of Procedure of the State of New York, as Amended to 1870*, 242 § 158.

conversation? On the one hand, adultery was a highly specific claim. It distinguished the charge from all other kinds of personal injuries and informed the defendant what kind of case he was to meet. On the other hand, adultery was not like a wrongful death suit or other kinds of uniquely disfiguring tort claims. Adultery was a repeatable act, and if it had been repeated, the plaintiff might choose to concentrate on one or another incident or shift grounds or dole out proofs as he liked at trial. That made a plaintiff in criminal conversation look more like the opportunistic creditor who ought to "itemize" his accounts upfront. Indeed, the propriety of a bill of particulars in a criminal conversation case became one of the thorniest legal issues of the Beecher trial. Shearman's motion occupied the Brooklyn court and the lawyers' arguments for over two months at the end of 1874 and involved three rounds of appeals, including to New York's highest tribunal. In the end, the power and discretion to award a bill of particulars was the only precedential law established by the Beecher-Tilton affair.[51]

In the opening round, Shearman, disclaimed any attempt to narrow the trial, focusing instead on the defendant's want of information. "We do not want to narrow the issue: we want to take in the whole issue, any issue that the plaintiff is prepared to make: we only want reasonable notice of it," he asserted at multiple points. Each side rested its arguments on the belief the other side's witnesses would act unethically. In an affidavit resisting the motion, Tilton charged that "Beecher and his interested champions in Plymouth Church have plentiful and opulent means at their disposal to purchase and procure false evidence in the coming trial." Preannouncing the date and times to which Tilton's witnesses would testify would only elicit alibis manufactured for the occasion. Shearman argued the chicanery would run the other direction. Witnesses with a grudge against the famously partisan abolitionist preacher might conjure up easily disproven episodes that would nevertheless surprise Beecher on the stand. With "no time to get those friends" who could prove an alibi, the jury might mistake Beecher's shock over a lie for guilt about the truth.[52]

Whatever the dangers of coached witnesses, the trial court was more interested in the remedies offered by the code. If indeed Sherman's motive was not to constrain the evidence Tilton would offer at trial, why move for a bill of particulars instead of using the code's procedures for making pleadings themselves more definite? The foremost expositor of Field's pleading standards, Shearman had a ready answer. Tilton's specification of adultery on two enumerated dates was more than sufficient as a matter of fact pleading, notwithstanding the additional general allegations of "diverse" other transgressions. In Shearman's theory, a bill of particulars was continued by the code because it performed a different function from pleading: it adduced the detailed evidence that was actually forbidden in a properly pleaded complaint, a complaint that ought to confine itself to "ultimate facts"—like adultery—without detailing the evidence of those facts. Relying on this distinction, Shearman had purposefully waited to move for a bill of particulars until Tilton declared himself ready for trial. The point was not to reform the initial pleadings, Shearman explained, but "to give us the benefit

---

[51] See Tilton v. Beecher, 48 How. Pr. 175, 59 N.Y. 176 (1874).
[52] 1 Abbott 9, 14, 17.

of his efforts in searching for evidence, and to tell us now the dates and places he is prepared to prove in this case."[53]

The trial court was unpersuaded. To Shearman's chagrin, the court quoted his own treatise on the point that a bill of particulars was generally unavailable in tort suits. If a motion to reform the pleadings was inappropriate, as Shearman protested, then the only remedy available was to depose Tilton.[54] An appeal to the general term of the court (a panel of two other trial judges) was equally unavailing for Shearman. Tilton's counsel cited post-code authorities that refused to read the code's reforms as establishing a party's "right to have an inquisitorial examination of his adversary's evidence." One declared that "the law has always considered sacred the rights of both parties to keep secret their preparations and means of attack and defense" and confined the parties in a divorce proceeding to the traditional equitable rules of discovery, which barred one party from examining evidence that only the other party could introduce at trial.[55] To these citations, the Brooklyn court added its own authorities, including an Irish case report: "It is said, Oh, it is a great hardship to the defendant to go to trial without knowing the precise times and places on which the plaintiff means to rely. But that is a hardship to which plaintiffs and defendants have been subject for hundreds of years—for as long as we have records of law." Unmoved by Shearman's protestations about surprise, the court concluded that "the parties can have a perfectly fair trial of the issues in the ordinary way."[56]

One could say that old habits were dying hard in Brooklyn, that chancery's rules for discovery were hanging on decades after chancery had been abolished. But the fissure Shearman had opened ran deeper than that. After all, the bill of particulars was equally as ancient as discovery devices at chancery. Granting the motion would not necessarily have been any less traditional than denying it. What troubled the court was not the unconventional devices Shearman was using, but the idea of the trial that lay behind them. For the Brooklyn court, a trial fundamentally remained an event at which the parties learned about their own cases in public along with the judge and jury. In keeping with the quest for truth through oath-bound examinations, surprise was endemic to trial because surprise was endemic to the enterprise of discovering truth. Shearman's vision, on the other hand, had too much of a theatrical cast to it, a vision in which all-knowing narrator lawyers prepared a performance for the unwitting fact-finders. In Shearman's vision, the bill of particulars aided the narrator in crafting the story by revealing the hidden facts. But the Brooklyn judges denied Shearman—and the other lawyers—that role. In the court's view, a bill of particulars aided the trial narrative only in the same ways pleading at common law had done: not by revealing the plot points but by narrowing them. In the same way common law

[53] *Ibid.*, 21, 31, 42–43. For the code procedure to make pleadings more definite, see *Code of Procedure of the State of New York, as Amended to 1870*, 246 § 160. A motion to make pleadings more definite was premised on "the allegations of a pleading" being "so indefinite or uncertain that the precise nature of the charge or defense is not apparent."

[54] 1 Abbott 31.

[55] *Ibid.*, 47 (quoting Hoyt v. American Exchange Bank, 1 Duer 652 (N.Y. Sup. Ct. Gen. Term, 1853)); 1 Abbott 23 (quoting Strong v. Strong, 1 Abb. Pr. N.S. 233 (N.Y. Sup. Ct., 1865)).

[56] 1 Abbott 55–56 (quoting Early v. Smith, 12 Irish Com. Law R., App. 35 (Q.B. 1861) (Lefroy, C.J., dissenting)).

pleading had prized narrowing a dispute to a single triable issue, the bill of particular's chief function was to limit the arguments that could be made and the things parties could say at trial. A modern lawyer might see the bill of particulars as forcing information at the cost of constraint. Jurists at the time saw it in reverse: the bill of particulars achieved constraint, but at the cost of preliminary disclosure.[57]

Having lost twice in the trial court, Shearman and his co-counsel sensed that their vision of well-informed adversarial counsel would not gain traction. Beginning with an appeal to the Court of Appeals, New York's highest tribunal, the defense lawyers shifted their arguments to emphasize the constraining power of the bill of particulars and their peculiar need to reign in Theodore Tilton.

The problem, as now formulated by Beecher's counsel, was that Theodore (once) and Henry (still) belonged to a world of hyper-Christian discourse that was likely to mislead a truth-seeker unversed in its theology. However much critics might accuse Henry's "religion of gush" for going soft on sin and perdition, Shearman knew better. On matters of romantic affection and marital fidelity, the sentimentalist evangelicals could hold just as exacting standards as their hardline Calvinist forebears. Above all, they took seriously Christ's admonition—quoted often during the trial—that to "look upon a woman with lust" was equivalent to adultery. Indeed, as Shearman pressed in his later arguments for a bill of particulars, Theodore had published an essay in 1870 arguing that "adultery of the soul" was even more pernicious than adultery of the body. Tilton's advocacy of a more liberal divorce law flowed from this conviction that spiritual adultery terminated a union as effectively as the physical adultery, even though New York law recognized only the latter as a legal ground for divorce.[58]

But none of this, Shearman contended, was sufficiently "tangible to bring in a court of justice." Henry Beecher could be tried for adultery of the soul only in the world to come. In the here and now, Tilton would have to prove "a sublunary act, and we object to proof of adultery which is said to have taken place not on the earth." Taken to its extreme, Shearman's bill of particulars might have excluded all circumstantial evidence as proof only of a spiritual and not physical affair. "When we come into court shall we be prevented from proving frequent gifts," Tilton's counsel asked in alarm, or "visits by the defendant to the plaintiff's wife in the absence of the plaintiff?" Certainly not, was the rhetorical answer. Yet who could list in advance all the tedious details like these that witness testimony might elicit? On that basis, Tilton's counsel insisted that adultery simply could not be itemized like debts for the sale of goods. Under the code, "a cause of action for *crim. con.* is one, entire and indivisible, and is not susceptible of severance or separation into parts or particulars."[59]

The court of appeals, by a divided vote, sent the parties back to argue before the trial judges. Impressed by the array of divorce actions that allowed bills of particulars when adultery was alleged, the court decided that criminal conversation was indeed

---

[57] On the modern construction of trial narratives, see Robert P. Burns, "The Distinctiveness of Trial Narrative," in Antony Duff et al., eds., *The Truth on Trial: Truth and Due Process* (Hart, 2005). For a mid-twentieth-century discussion of the vanishing role of surprise in common law trials, see Alexander Holtzoff, "The Elimination of Surprise in Federal Practice," 7 *Vanderbilt Law Review* 576 (1953).

[58] See Fox, *Trials of Intimacy*, 2–4, 115–16; Matt: 5:28; *The Independent* (Brooklyn, N.Y.), Dec. 1, 1870.

[59] 1 Abbott 46, 78, 122, 125.

an action in which a bill of particulars might be appropriate at the trial judge's discretion. That ruling said no more than what the code did already. The court did not opine on how the trial court should exercise its discretion, leaving the parties back where they started.[60]

What to do about the circumstantial evidence continued to bedevil the trial court. Shearman's co-counsel was emphatic that "there is no such thing as a unanimous opinion of the jury that adultery has been committed without any opinion of the jury that it has ever been committed any particular time or place." Supposing the court agreed, that entitled Beecher to know whatever times and places Tilton would attempt to prove at trial, but what limiting effect would such an order have on the circumstantial evidence? The judge assigned to the rehearing tried to please both parties. He awarded the bill of particulars so that the plaintiff "designates the day [of alleged adultery] with such reasonable approximation as that the defendant is fairly apprised of the charge," but made clear that at the trial Tilton could produce evidence of "alleged confessions" in which "no particular time or place shall have been referred to."[61] Most of Tilton's evidence did not consist of "confessions," however, so the status of the rest of the circumstantial evidence remained unclear. This time Tilton appealed to the general term.

Before the final round of argument, Tilton in exasperation filed an affidavit explaining that he had already made all of his evidence public, that he had no precise dates to allege other than the two in the complaint, and that he had no further evidence for those dates than Elizabeth's retracted confession and the witnesses (including Tilton and Beecher themselves) who had heard it. He could say no more in response to a bill of particulars, since "as to the times and places where some of the acts of intercourse were committed, the plaintiff is now ignorant, and will remain so until this court, by aid of its process, compels . . . unwilling witnesses to disclose the same on the trial."[62] By his own admission, Tilton himself was in the dark, and would only learn if he really had a case once the trial got underway.

Shearman gloated in victory. Through many statements and editorials, Tilton had "wanted to make the public believe that he had [left] something dark and mysterious and dreadful behind, so shocking and so frightful that he dared not utter it." But in the end Tilton had no more real idea of his wife's behavior than did an ordinary subscriber to the *Chicago Tribune*. To Shearman, that made the call to tie Tilton's hands an easy one. "A man may be justified in coming into court with an action upon contract, with a claim for the price of a few groceries, or for the amount of a butcher's bill, without being quite certain that he has the witnesses to prove the precise and specific facts," Shearman lectured, but a charge like this? "A charge that either brands with infamy his own wife and another man, or brands with a thousand-fold infamy his own brow for having the audacity and the wickedness to make a false charge of this kind"— such a charge Shearman contended should limit Tilton to the proofs he had gathered before trial. To recklessly make the charge and then learn whether it was true in court would be a ruinous policy.[63]

---

[60] See *Ibid.*, 80–86.
[61] *Ibid.*, 94, 107–9.
[62] *Ibid.*, 48, 90–91.
[63] *Ibid.*, 99.

The court, however, thought Tilton's affidavit undermined Shearman's position. Now that Shearman knew Tilton was holding nothing back, there was no information for a bill of particulars to disclose. Any surprise at trial was a surprise that would strike both plaintiff and defendant alike. After all the affidavits in and out of court and the flurry of news publications, one judge on the panel opined that "in few cases could a defendant be as free from a chance of being taken by surprise." If he were, the ordinary "ordeal to which unknown witnesses may be subjected on the trial" would be cure enough. Another judge concurred that since Beecher already had the advantage of disclosure, there was no further need to hamper Tilton with the constraint on his evidence.[64] In the end, Shearman got his information, but not the cabining effects of the bill of particulars. The final decision on pretrial disclosures came down December 29. The court began impaneling the jury the next week.[65]

V

Practically every account of the Beecher Trial emphasizes the extraordinary length of the trial: 112 days from seating the first juror to hearing the jury's final words. Left unmentioned is that the trial ran so long because the trial days were so short. The jury sat to hear arguments and evidence only on weekdays from 11 o'clock in the morning until 1 in the afternoon, and then again from 2 to 4 p.m., after a lunch adjournment. When the court suggested adding a Saturday session, or simply extending the morning and afternoon sessions by half an hour, counsel on both sides emphatically protested. Speaking for Beecher's counsel, the renowned trial orator William M. Evarts explained that counsel depended on the "fragments of the day" before and after the sessions to prepare for, produce, and respond to evidence as it entered the record.[66]

Production of previously unseen evidence was a near daily occurrence. The trial transcript is littered with the mundane negotiations of counsel to find and produce documents as witnesses mentioned them, usually with indications that opposing counsel had not seen the documents before trial, even if they were aware of their existence. Occasionally lawyers had to send for documents that had not been brought to court. Shearman and Evarts refused to produce documents from Plymouth Church when the plaintiff had only requested them from Beecher, coyly replying that "we have never thought Plymouth Church or the Christian religion was defendant here." On another occasion, they protested they had insufficient notice to search Beecher's papers for a requested letter. "I think an hour and a half is time enough to send to Mr. Beecher's house," retorted Tilton's counsel. The lawyers stipulated to reading a copy in the meantime.[67]

Indeed, the transcript itself became key to these negotiations. Jury trials were not commonly recorded at the time, but a cause célèbre like the Brooklyn Scandal drew

---

[64] *Ibid.,* 135–36.
[65] *Ibid.,* 138ff.
[66] 1 McDivitt 385.
[67] *Ibid.,* 103, 326–27, 328.

Figure 8.4 Thomas Shearman reads the Tilton correspondence into the official court record.
Frank Leslie's Illustrated Magazine, April 3, 1875, 56.

a crowd of shorthand journalists and clerks. One reporter for the *New-York Tribune* became the "official" reporter for the court, turning in rush transcripts to the judge and counsel at the end of each day's sessions. As Tilton's counsel was adamant that the documents in his possession could not leave his custody and could only be examined in open court, the lawyers spent entire days reading letters into the record. Out-of-court hours—those "fragments of the day" Evarts had referred to—could then be spent examining the transcript copy and searching for ways to undermine the witness at the next session. Tilton's counsel used even the business of reading documents as an occasion to appeal to the jury, the *Tribune* reporter noting that the lawyer "threw into the reading of them much sympathy and fervor." Beecher's counsel seemed to have only the transcript in mind, the reporter elsewhere noting "there was nothing all day but the monotonous reading of Mr. Shearman"[68] (see Figure 8.4).

With so much information to sift in the fragments of the day, specialized research-ers and indexers became critical personnel. Shearman had hired reputable trial law-yers like Evarts and Tracy to be the face of the defense in court, but the decision that may have saved the trial was hiring Austin Abbott to be the internal research engine of

[68] *Ibid.*, 436, 484.

the team. Younger brother to a law reporter and older brother to Beecher's successor at Plymouth, Abbott was then at the start of a prolific career as a case reporter and treatise author.[69] Abbott excelled at the work Field had hoped to make obsolete with codification: the hunt through case reports for precedent and persuasive authority. In internal memos and briefs, Abbott assured the Beecher team that no reported case of criminal conversation in New York was available to guide them. Instead the lawyers would have to draw analogies to divorce suits grounded on adultery charges, for which Abbott supplied numerous authorities going back decades in New York, England, and several other US jurisdictions.[70]

In later memos, Abbott turned his investigative method from the case law to the facts, closely scrutinizing, for instance, the church examination transcript to guess at Tilton's trial strategy.[71] Indeed, the investigation of the factual record could be just as wide-ranging as the search for helpful case authorities. One of Elizabeth's published letters to Henry used the odd locution "nest-hiding," a reference, it turned out, to an obscure passage in Henry's 1868 novel, *Norwood* (a book incidentally about a beatific woman pursued by two rivalrous suitors). Whatever surprises Tilton may have hoped to spring at the trial, the revelation of the coded reference was not among them. The Beecher team was ready with the page cite and an innocuous explanation. Likely it had fallen to Abbott's lot to sift the 550-page novel for such clues.[72]

The inglorious work at last produced a genuine surprise at trial and gave the Beecher team its big break. Careful scrutiny of the transcript compared to the *Chicago Tribune* and other publications of the Tilton correspondence revealed that Tilton had in fact extensively edited the letters before publication. Most of the edits were innocent enough, but Tilton had given the impression he had been operating as a scrivener, not an editor, in conveying the correspondence to the publisher. And some of the editorial decisions appeared significant. In one letter, Elizabeth apologized for her impurity, for which "I can nor will no denial take." But Theodore had removed the next two lines: "Hereafter I will guard my temper. You shall have a soul-pure wife

[69] See, e.g., Benjamin Vaughan Abbott & Austin Abbott, *A Collection of Forms of Practice and Pleading* (Baker, Voorhis, 1867); Austin Abbott, *The Legal Remembrancer: Containing Concise Statements of the Law as It Now Is* (Baker, Voorhis & Co., 1871); Benjamin Vaughan Abbott & Austin Abbott, *A Treatise Upon the United States Courts, and Their Practice* (Diossy & Co., 1869).

[70] See Mr. Abbott's Brief on the Incompetency of Husbands and Wives to Testify for or Against Each Other; Mr. Abbott's Brief on the Nature of the Action; Mr. Abbott's Brief on Evidence as to Character; Mr. Abbott's Brief on the Limits of the Issue as to the Fact of Adultery; Mr. Abbott's Brief on Competency of Declarations of Husband and Wife, in General; Mr. Abbott's Brief on the Competency of Evidence of the Demeanor of the Parties and the Wife; Mr. Abbott's Brief on the Competency of Evidence of Confessions of Adultery, in General; Mr. Abbott's Brief on the Right to Give in Evidence the Whole Admission, and to Explain It; Mr. Abbott's Brief on Admissions "In Confidence" and Letters "Without Prejudice"; Mr. Abbott's Brief on the Cogency Requisite in Evidence to Establish Adultery; Mr. Abbott's Brief on the Weight of Confessions as Evidence; Mr. Abbott's Brief on the Competency of Extrinsic Evidence of Intent, Papers of Thomas G. Shearman.

[71] Mr. Abbott's Brief on the Competency, in this Action, of Letters and Declarations; Mr. Abbott's Brief on what Facts are Material; Mr. Abbott's Brief on the Competency of the Alleged Confessions of the Defendant or the Wife; Mr. Abbott's Brief on the Incompetency of Secondary Evidence of Destroyed Written Confession; Mr. Abbott's Brief on the Competency of the Wife's Retraction; Mr. Abbott's Brief on Circumstantial Evidence of Adultery; Mr. Abbott's Brief on Connivance, Condonation, Recrimination and Compromise as a Bar to the Action (manuscript), Papers of Thomas G. Shearman.

[72] Henry Ward Beecher, *Norwood: Or, Village Life in New England* (Fords, Howard & Hulbert, 1867), 82. See Fox, *Trials of Intimacy*, 138–39.

by and by."[73] The restored text at trial showed a letter that seemed to hint at sexual indiscretion was really about Elizabeth's short temper. Even the official reporter (who sometimes drew complaints from both sides for editorializing in the transcript) noted when the "uninteresting" reading of the letters was punctuated by "a discovery which caused some comment" by comparing Tilton's published version of the letter to "an original copy of the letter itself." A modern commentator estimates that Tilton's selective publication did the most to discredit his testimony—then and now.[74]

In the end, the want of information could not be sated, despite the thousands of pages of transcripts, publications, and gossip repeated in and out of court.[75] On July 1, the 111th day of the proceedings, the jury foreman announced that his peers could not come to an agreement. After stressing the "embarrassment" and "humiliation" of an inconclusive verdict in a case of such public interest, the presiding judge implored the foreman to ask any questions of law the court might clear up for the jury. But to no avail. "It is a question of fact," the foreman replied, "a question of veracity of witnesses on which we do not agree, your Honor, and I would say I think there is not a possibility of agreement in this jury." The judge returned the jury to its deliberations anyway but relented the next day, discharging the jury without a verdict.[76] Evarts telegrammed Beecher "my hearty congratulations." Knowing a lack of verification was not quite the same thing as an exoneration, Evarts nevertheless instructed Henry to "regard the result as a complete triumph of truth."[77]

VI

The sharp constraints of the New York Code pinched the lawyers at multiple points in the 1875 trial of Henry Ward Beecher. The plaintiff Tilton could not be asked about his allegations without forfeiting the power to cross-examine him on the stand. No other witness could be interviewed on the record in advance without a court agreeing that ill health or permanent relocation was likely to absent the witness from the trial. Document production could not be compelled until trial, when the custodian was called to the witness stand. If attorneys wanted more than the terse—and incomplete—statement of facts found in the opening pleadings, they had to resort to the soft coercion and social pressures of private associations or public journalism.

But the New York Code regulated only New York. Increasingly, as other code states adopted versions of what Field regarded to be the final and complete draft of his code,

---

[73] See Fox, *Trials of Intimacy*, 222, for the letter regarding Elizabeth's temper. For a full comparison of the letters as published by Tilton and as printed in the court record, see *ibid.*, ch. 8.

[74] 1 McDivitt 484; Fox, *Trials of Intimacy*, 222.

[75] In addition to Marshall's *True History of the Brooklyn Scandal* prepared before the trial, McDivitt's three-volume transcript and Abbott's two-volume transcript, newspapers like the *New York Times* published single-volume reviews of the evidence afterward. See, e.g., *The Beecher Trial: A Review of the Evidence* (New York Times, 1875).

[76] 3 McDivitt 1040–42. It was later reported that the jury had taken fifty-two ballots before announcing its deadlock. "At the outset, they had been eight to four in favor of Beecher, and at the end they stood nine to three for him." Robert Shaplen, "The Beecher-Tilton Affair," *The New Yorker*, June 4, 1954.

[77] William M. Evarts telegram to Henry Ward Beecher, July 3, 1875, Box 10, Folder 406, Beecher Family Papers, Yale University.

a new set of practices emerged to force information before trial. Over the course of a decade, at least four midwestern jurisdictions—Kansas, Nebraska, Missouri, and Ohio—all came to the same conclusion that the code, fairly read, permitted lawyers to explore their adversaries' evidence before trial and even to incarcerate reluctant witnesses, all without court supervision.[78] While New York retained a conventional model of court-supervised examinations that tolerated surprise at trial well into the twentieth century, the midwestern practice supplied a blueprint for what would become a distinctive and foundational American practice: lawyer-driven discovery.

A case out of Ohio was typical of the midwestern approach. In *Shaw v. Ohio Edison Installation Company*, the future president and chief justice William Howard Taft compared different versions of the Field Code to arrive at the surprising conclusion that Ohio's code permitted far-reaching, lawyer-driven discovery without the interference of judicial officers like himself. In states that dropped the early code's language about deposing a party "in lieu" of calling the party at trial, the pretrial deposition of a party was straightforward: The code allowed it, unreservedly, in all cases and circumstances. But *Shaw*, like many of the midwestern cases, involved the attempted deposition of a mere witness, not a party to the suit. A plaintiff suing an electric company subpoenaed a third party, George Altenberg, to appear before a notary public and have his deposition taken. Altenberg appeared at the appointed hour and handed over a written affidavit, but he refused to be sworn or to submit himself to the lawyers' questioning. Using a special procedure, the notary petitioned Taft, the presiding superior court judge, to ask if the notary had the power to jail Altenberg for contempt.[79]

Taft began his code comparisons with the conditional deposition (*de bene esse*). The original Field Code had continued the chancery and common law practice of New York by permitting the live, adversarial deposition of a witness only if the witness was likely to be absent for the trial due to illness, relocation, or imminent death. The codes that traveled around the nation dutifully copied the provision, but with a significant variant: Some codes, like New York's, made clear that a judicial officer had to first decide that it was likely the witness would be unavailable before the deposition would be authorized. But as Taft noted, "no such discretion is given the courts of this state." The courts were not mentioned in Ohio's article. Instead, "notices upon opposing counsel and a subpoena for the witness are the only two preliminaries to a deposition before a notary." Nor was there an occasion to insert a judicial check on lawyers deposing witnesses who were quite likely to be available for trial. Probability of appearance, Taft observed, was a matter of degree. Technically, "it can never be proven that there is no possibility of loss of evidence," so a conditional deposition was always a guess at whether a possibility had become a probability. Since the code did

---

[78] See, e.g., *In re* Abeles, 12 Kan. 451 (1874); *In re* Davis, 38 Kan. 408 (1898); *Ex parte* Munford, 57 Mo. 603 (1874); *Ex parte* Krieger, 7 Mo. App. 367 (1879); Dogge v. State, 21 Neb. 272 (1887); Shaw v. Ohio Edison Co., 9 O. Dec. Rep. 809 (1887).

[79] *Shaw*, 9 O. Dec. Rep. at 809–10. As Taft noted, the Ohio Code required notaries to commit recalcitrant witnesses to jail for contempt, from whence the witness could seek court review. *Revised Statutes and Acts of a General Nature of the State of Ohio in Force January 1, 1880*, 1281 § 5252. An uncodified practice had developed, drawing on the chancery tradition, whereby notaries could certify questions to the court before taking action. See Bradshaw v. Bradshaw, 1 Russell & Mylne 358; State *ex rel.* Lanning v. Lonsdale, 48 Wis. 348, 370 (1880).

not authorize judges to make that guess, inserting themselves into the process "savors of judicial legislation, and ought not to be followed," Taft concluded.[80]

Since the code "relieve[s] the court from any responsibility" over depositions, that necessarily meant that "under the statute the party was the whole judge of the necessity for taking such [a] deposition." A witness who refused the deposition could be held in contempt and imprisoned by a notary's order at the instigation of the party. Taft was sanguine about the possibility "that a party will go fishing for evidence" in such a privatized system of investigation. If the deposition turned out to be needless, "then the party taking it must pay the costs," a sufficient deterrent, Taft thought, to groundless depositions. But as long as there was some relevance to the deposition, "the earlier a witness is committed to a statement the better for the sake of truth." Since "witnesses do not belong to one party more than to another," Taft argued, "what they know relevant to the issue should be equally available to both sides"—and to the court. Taft thus reconciled the midwestern codes' wildcat discovery provisions with the original justification of all of Field's reforms: on balance and despite the likelihood of abuse, more truth would filter in earlier to the trial.[81]

The preeminent historian of law and society J. Willard Hurst once observed that toward the end of the nineteenth century, the United States developed new "uses of the bar." Chief among these new uses, Hurst argued, was that lawyers had become "master[s] of fact." By the 1890s, "the complex of facts of the economy in particular offered both the setting and the pressure for the lawyer to take on a new role—as a specialist in incisive, accurate, facts appraisal of snarled or complicated situations."[82] Indeed, many of the midwestern discovery cases featured a corporate defendant, a primary actor in the new economy that either resisted or tested the boundaries of what the code could offer to its new masters of fact. Field's home state of New York doggedly retained the older view that factual investigation was a public function to be handled by public officials. Although New York's constitution had abolished the office of master in chancery, New York's code and the judges who administered it insisted that the courts remain the gateway to factual discovery, and well into the twentieth century judges decreed that "examinations are not intended to enable a party to discovery what his opponent's testimony will be, so that he may obtain witnesses to contradict it." The public trial remained the appropriate forum for learning about a case, and court, lawyers, and witnesses alike would learn about the case along with the public.[83]

---

[80] *Shaw*, 9 O. Dec. Rep. at 810–11. The New York code provided only that interested witnesses were not barred from testifying. *Code of Procedure of the State of New York, as Amended to 1870*, 612–13, § 398. Into the 1870s, pretrial examination of witnesses was still controlled by the Revised Statutes of 1829, which required parties to apply to a judge for leave to take a conditional deposition. See *ibid.*, 622–23, note (e). Ohio's code, like others of the Midwest, required only that parties apply to a clerk of court to issue a subpoena to witnesses and the officer tasked with overseeing the examination, usually a notary. *Revised Statutes of Ohio*, 1280 § 5246. Subsequent sections provided that a deposition could only be *used* at trial when the witness was unavailable, but the deposition could be *taken* without restriction "any time after service upon the defendant." *Ibid.*, 1282 §§ 5265–66. See also *Compiled Statutes of the State of Nebraska to 1881* (1887), 534 § 7, 785 §§ 366, 372–73; *Compiled Laws of the State of Kansas to 1868* (1879), 647, §§ 340, 346–47.

[81] *Shaw*, 9 O. Dec. Rep. at 811–12.

[82] James Willard Hurst, *The Growth of American Law: The Law Makers* (Little, Brown, 1950), 339–40.

[83] Sheehan v. The A. & B. Turnpike Co., 8 N.Y.S. 14 (1889). See also Beach v. Mayor, 4 Abb. N.C. 236 (1878); Chapin v. Thompson, 16 Hun 53 (1878); Knight v. Morgenroth, 87 N.Y.S. 693 (1904). Law reformers in the state bar association continued to press the legislature for discovery reform, to little avail. See, e.g.,

Outside New York, the Final Draft of the code and its transformation of privately retained lawyers into the new masters of fact became one of the code's enduring legacies. Early in the twentieth century, the discovery practices authorized by Judge Taft attracted the attention of a Michigan law professor, Edson R. Sunderland. Michigan was one of the few western states to reject the New York code, but Sunderland admired midwestern discovery rules because he believed "much of the delay in the preparation of a case, most the lost effort in the course of the trial, and a large part of the uncertainty in the outcome, result from the want of information on the part of litigants and their counsel" prior to trial. Sunderland tasked a graduate student at Michigan, George Ragland, to gather data on midwestern discovery practice. Ragland's four-hundred-page *Discovery Before Trial* became an intellectual foundation for Sunderland's discovery regime under the Federal Rules of Civil Procedure of 1938, which closely followed the midwestern codes and eventually displaced the court-centered model in New York.[84]

Describing the virtues of midwestern discovery, Ragland blended old common law fears about the oracular judge with new technological imagery that the codifiers had made familiar. The benefit of lawyer-controlled discovery, Ragland thought, was that "the work of the judge is simplified.... A considerable part of the pre-trial machinery for the formulation of the terms of the controversy becomes extra-judicial in practical operation." Like most machinery, discovery could produce efficiencies for the practitioner, "eliminat[ing]" a "great many cases" without trial and "expedit[ing]" trial for cases that remained. But Ragland's reforms, like most procedural issues, concerned much more than simple efficiency. The new codes' lawyer-driven discovery were claimed to restore judges to their properly limited role. The codes empowered judges to edit the pleadings by forcing their amendment, even as far as changing the prayer for relief. Out-of-court discovery gave lawyers a countervailing power of mastery over the factual record, control over "clarity in the definition of the issues" before any judge could seriously frame or distort the parties' case.[85]

Sunderland used another mechanistic metaphor for similar purposes: "Discovery procedure serves much the same function in the field of law as the X-ray in the field of medicine and surgery." Both Ragland and Sunderland expected that discovery's "extension" would eliminate surprise at trial, and litigation would "largely cease to be a game of chance."[86] Instead of the public adjustment of disputes and discernment of the issues in open court, discovery gave lawyers an investigative machine that could be operated from private offices, just like a doctors' x-ray device. The triumph of

---

Report of the New York State Bar Association (1899), 22:191; *Report of the Board of Statutory Consolidation of the State of New York on a Plan for the Simplification of the Civil Practice in the Courts of the State* (J.B. Lyon Company, 1912), 152–69.

[84] Edson R. Sunderland, Foreword, iii. See Subrin, "Fishing Expeditions Allowed," 702–10, 713–17. On Sunderland's decision to incorporate the lawyer-driven discovery regimes of the Midwest into the 1938 Federal Rules of Civil Procedure, see especially Ezra Siller, "The Origins of the Oral Deposition in the Federal Rules: Who's in Charge?" 10 *Seton Hall Circuit Review* 43 (2013).

[85] Ragland, *Discovery Before Trial*, 266.

[86] Edson R. Sunderland, "Improving the Administration of Civil Justice," 167 *Annals of the American Academy of Political and Social Science* 60 (1933), 74–75. Cf. Ragland, *Discovery Before Trial*, 251.

Sunderland's lawyerly investigator against the common law's public adjustor required decades of rule changes and found only halting success in New York's homeland of codification. Until the twentieth century, New York judges retained many former chancery powers that other states readily gave away to the new lawyerly masters of fact. Indeed, despite its storied abolition in 1846, the Court of Chancery still had a hold on the minds and practices of New York lawyers, as Field and Shearman would discover.

9

The Nature of Things

Law and Equity

I

The most well-known photograph of David Dudley Field is Matthew Brady's, likely taken around the time that Field traveled to Brussels to promote a two-volume draft of his international code in the 1870s (see Figure 9.1). Brady's portrait casts Field as an elder statesman of the bar, wearing the fine clothes and accessories fitting for an elite lawyer of international repute. This portrait was at least the fourth time Field had sat in Brady's studio. Brady had made an early daguerreotype of Field around the time of the original procedure code, and on other occasions had photographed Field with his brother Cyrus and other board members of the transatlantic cable project.[1] The 1870s image was clearly meant to capture Field at the culmination of his career, America's premier lawgiver and leader of the bar.

But at nearly the same time, quite a different image of Field was in circulation. The New York political cartoonist Thomas Nast despised Field. No other lawyer became the target of Nast's satirical art as often as Field. Balding on top but boasting uncommonly thick mutton chops for a civilian, Field's visage was easily parodied and instantly recognizable. Throughout the 1870s, Nast depicted (the usually unnamed) Field binding Justice in procedural red tape or standing guard as a lion over his clients' wealth.[2] (See, for instance, the cover image for this volume.) In Nast's final illustration of Field in early 1878, the Devil himself visits the brooding lawyer's office, seeking to retain Field's famous services (see Figure 9.2).

Nast saw Field not as an eminent reformer and codifier but rather as the chief lieutenant of a legal corps who exploited technicalities to exonerate and protect the corrupt leaders of an especially corrupt age. Field first earned the disdain of Nast and other municipal reformers in the late 1860s when he and his law partner Thomas G. Shearman became lead counsel to the notorious robber barons Jim Fisk and Jay Gould.[3] Field then defended the head of New York's Tammany Hall machine, William "Boss" Tweed, against both civil and criminal prosecutions brought by Samuel Tilden

---

[1] A Brady photograph of the six Field brothers is available at the Library of Congress Prints and Photographs Division, LC-USZ62–139570. The Field portraits connected to the Atlantic cable project are in the Matthew B. Brady Studio Portrait Photograph Collection, Series I, New York Historical Society. For the daguerreotype, see Figure 2.1 in this volume.

[2] See Renée Lettow Lerner, "Thomas Nast's Crusading Legal Cartoons," 2011 *Green Bag Almanac* 2d 59 (2011).

[3] On Field's corporate clients and career, see Daun Van Ee, *David Dudley Field and the Reconstruction of the Law* (Garland Press, 1986). See also George Martin, *Causes and Conflicts: The Centennial History of the Association of the Bar of New York* (Fordham University Press, 1997), 3–15.

Law's Machinery. Kellen R. Funk, Oxford University Press. © Kellen R. Funk 2025. DOI: 10.1093/9780197543962.003.0010

Figure 9.1 Portrait of David Dudley Field II by Matthew Brady, taken around 1875.
Library of Congress Prints and Photographs Division, Brady-Handy Collection, Film Reproduction No.
LC-DIG-cwpbh-05048.

and Charles O'Conor, making himself an even more frequent target of Nast's pen.
Tilden deeply disappointed Nast by retaining Field in turn for the disputed presidential election of 1876 (which is why Nast listed Tilden in the rogues' gallery of Field's
clients).

Nast's assessment of Field was largely shared by the railroad reformer Charles
Francis Adams Jr. After the Civil War, American railroads became massive financial assets, offering their owners and managers abundant opportunities for profit
and plunder. Although Fisk and Gould liked to call their acquisitions "raids," they
excelled in using lawyers to keep their investments within arguably legal bounds—
clandestinely buying up shares or the power to vote their proxies, trading stock on
inside information (not yet regulated or forbidden), and extending themselves personal loans which, on paper, would be paid back to the railroad corporation.[4] Before
retaining Field in 1869, Fisk and Gould had wrested control of the Erie Railroad from
Cornelius Vanderbilt in what Charles Francis Adams dubbed the "Erie War."[5]

---

[4] On the securitization and personal profits in nineteenth-century railroad ownership and management,
see Richard White, *Railroaded: The Transcontinentals and the Making of Modern America* (Norton, 2011).
[5] Charles Francis Adams & Henry Adams, *Chapters of Erie* (J.R. Osgood & Co., 1871); John S. Gordon,
*The Scarlet Woman of Wall Street: Jay Gould, Jim Fisk, Cornelius Vanderbilt, the Erie Railroad Wars, and the
Birth of Wall Street* (Weidenfeld & Nicolson, 1988).

Figure 9.2 Nast depicted Field as the literal devil's advocate in a drawing from 1877. The rogues' gallery over Field's shoulder highlights his notorious representations of robber barons Jim Fisk and Jay Gould, Tammany Hall machine leader William "Boss" Tweed, and Field's mercenary turn as counsel to his political rival Samuel Tilden in the disputed election of 1876.
Thomas Nast, "They Do Each Other Honor," *Harper's Weekly*, February 24, 1877, 152.

Of particular interest to Adams was "an Erie raid," which unfolded after Vanderbilt had withdrawn. Seeking access to Pennsylvania's coal mines, Fisk and Gould commenced their distinctive style of raid against the Albany & Susquehanna (A&S) Railroad, a 150-mile spur through western New York. Its president, Joseph Ramsey, proved more recalcitrant than Vanderbilt and, with headquarters in Albany, had his own skillful legal counsel. Each side continually won injunctions against the other over the summer of 1869. Field secured decrees from a New York City judge enjoining the issuance of new stock and the voting of recently transferred stock. Ramsey's lawyers secured a decree from an Albany judge enjoining the enforcement of the New York City injunction. Months of injunctions and counter-injunctions followed until the New York City judge granted Field's request to declare the A&S in receivership: The entire line and all its assets were transferred to temporary managers pending the next corporate election. But then the court in Albany decreed its own receivership in favor of Ramsey and managed to issue process one hour earlier than New York City.[6]

---

[6] Adams & Adams, *Chapters of Erie*, 135–91; Lerner, "Thomas Nast's Crusading Legal Cartoons," 65–68.

The maneuvering came to a head at the annual corporate election in Albany on September 7, 1869. Per the bylaws, shareholder voting could not begin until noon, and the poll had to remain open for an hour. Field and Shearman waited literally until the eleventh hour to spring their trap. Their reliable New York City judge had ordered the arrest of Ramsey and the other officers. At 11:45, Shearman proceeded to the officers' boardroom with the sheriff while Field transferred the Erie party's proxies to a band of fifty Irish "roughs" brought to town (and plied with drink) for the occasion, and together they proceeded to the meeting room for the vote. The Erie-favored directors won handily.[7]

The tale was all that a muckraker could want, and Adams relished telling it, but how to explain it? Here in a land of liberty, fresh from a war of emancipation—"this, be it remembered, was ... in New York, and not in Constantinople," Adams drolly reminded his readers—judges of the lowest trial courts were issuing secret decrees of imprisonment, seizing and redistributing property, and undermining one another's decrees. And as far as lawyers then and later could determine, none of it ran afoul of the code. As Adams saw it, the problem therefore arose from the code itself, under which "local judges ... are clothed with certain ... powers in actions commenced before them, which run throughout the State." Adams relished the ironic name of these "certain powers" that prospered injustice: "Equity."[8]

Like Field himself, equitable jurisprudence could at times appear stately and dignified, at other times as the diabolic assistant of the robber barons. This multifaceted quality makes it difficult to tell the story of equity in the Field Code. We can start by paying close attention to what lawyers meant by invoking "equity" in the mid-to-late nineteenth century. Then, as now, jurists pointed to various features of the old English chancery system as the essence of equity, and depending on which feature received the focus, the Field Code could be said to abolish, transform, or significantly enhance equitable powers.

II

Historians of nineteenth-century American law have been hasty in their treatment of equity. Ignoring the cautious arguments of colonial legal historians that "Americans objected to chancery courts rather than to equity law," some scholars have treated the gradual disappearance of chancery courts as if equity was disfavored, discarded, and "moribund" in America until coming to life again in the twentieth century. Influential jurisdictions like Massachusetts and Pennsylvania essentially did without courts of chancery, it is noted. New York and Virginia abolished theirs around mid-century, and new states in the West never created them. Not until late in the century did federal

---

[7] Adams & Adams, *Chapters of Erie*, 174–81; George Ticknor Curtis, *An Inquiry into the Albany & Susquehanna Railroad Litigations of 1869 and Mr. David Dudley Field's Connection Therewith* (D. Appleton, 1871); Albert Stickney, "The Truth of a 'Great Lawsuit,'" 14 *Galaxy* 576 (1872); Francis C. Barlow, *Facts for Mr. David Dudley Field* (Weed, Parsons & Co., 1871).

[8] Adams & Adams, *Chapter of Erie*, 22, 175.

judges seem to rediscover the equitable injunction, which they deployed against striking laborers.[9]

The problem is that many of these accounts tend to reduce the sprawling and sophisticated system of chancery to one or another small subset of its functions and then eulogize the demise of "equity." Thus Roscoe Pound and his admirers who drafted the 1938 Federal Rules of Civil Procedure, interested as they were in judicial discretion and pretrial investigation powers, thought they were reviving a long-dormant equity in their twentieth-century reforms. More recently, scholars have made "inquisitorial" devices like written, juryless process an essential feature of equity, while some have emphasized equity's flexible moral maxims ("those seeking equity must come with clean hands") over the "rigid" decrees of legislatures or common law courts.[10]

In this respect, modern commentary differs little from that of the nineteenth century. What counts as equity in the United States has often been in the eye of the beholder. The law-and-literaturist Gary Watt offers a helpful prescription here. Instead of reducing equity to one or another practice—or even a combination of notable practices—Watt proposes that equity is best understood as four "clusters" of language involving maxims, remedies, doctrines, and property.[11] Regarding the Field Code, it is the language of remedy that is of most concern, for it was Field's purpose to reduce equity entirely to the language of remedy.

One key feature of equitable remedies was that they supplemented the law ("followed the law," in Joseph Story's favorite maxim) by operating personally on a party, according to conscience, to keep that party from using the law as a tool of injustice. Watt offers a paradigm example of the very old case of an unrecorded land transaction with a credulous buyer. By the strict letter of the Statute of Frauds (1677), transactions in land not made in writing were not binding.[12] But from the seventeenth century onward, the court of chancery would not allow an unscrupulous seller to use that technical requirement "unconscionably" in order to renege against a good-faith buyer and keep the income. It is important to note how chancery would do that: the court did not "set aside" the normal rule, nor even, in theory, did it make an exception to the rule in a particular case. Instead, the court enjoined the seller personally from raising the Statute of Frauds as a defense to the buyer's suit to perform the transaction.[13]

---

[9] Stanley N. Katz, "The Politics of Law in Colonial America: Controversies over Chancery Courts and Equity Law in the Eighteenth Century," in Donald Fleming & Bernard Bailyn, eds., *Perspectives in American History* (Little, Brown, 1971), 5:257–84, 265; see also Daniel J. Hulsebosch, *Constituting Empire: New York and the Transformation of Constitutionalism in the Atlantic World, 1664–1830* (University of North Carolina Press, 2008), 60. For the "moribund" view of equity, see Peter Charles Hoffer, *The Law's Conscience: Equitable Constitutionalism in America* (University of North Carolina Press, 1990), 147; Stephen N. Subrin, "David Dudley Field and the Field Code: A Historical Analysis of an Earlier Procedural Vision," 6 *Law & History Review* 311 (1988).

[10] See Stephen N. Subrin, "How Equity Conquered Common Law: The Federal Rules of Civil Procedure in Historical Perspective," 135 *University of Pennsylvania Law Review* 909 (1987); Hoffer, *The Law's Conscience*, 91. Amalia D. Kessler, "Our Inquisitorial Tradition: Equity Procedure, Due Process, and the Search for an Alternative to the Adversarial," 90 *Cornell Law Review* 1181 (2005); Morton J. Horwitz, *The Transformation of American Law: 1780–1860* (Harvard University Press, 1979), 266.

[11] Gary Watt, *Equity Stirring: The Story of Justice Beyond Law* (Hart, 2009), 89–90.

[12] An Act for Prevention of Frauds and Perjuries, 29 Chas. 2 c. 3 (1677); Watt, *Equity Stirring*, 34.

[13] *Ibid.* For a collection of equitable dealings with the Statute of Frauds, see Roy Moreland, "Statute of Frauds and Part Performance," 78 *University of Pennsylvania Law Review* 51 (1929).

The law remained the law, fully in effect even in the case at bar. The only coercion was, in essence, a restraint on pleading. Could the seller plead the statute, he would win. But at chancery, he simply could not plead it. It was as if equity could remove the aces from a deck of cards at the blackjack table. The rules of the game are still the rules. The player might still win. But certain strategic moves are now closed off, not by rule, but because chancery has put them practically out of reach. The question then is how chancellors knew when to intervene in these ways "as shall be agreeable to equity and good conscience."[14]

As with the traditional proscriptions of oath-taking, it was not always clear in equitable jurisprudence whether the conscience equity acted upon was the arbiter's or the litigant's. Dennis Klinck warns modern readers not to give the language of conscience too much of a subjective and individualistic (i.e., Protestant) reading.[15] Conscience might guide a chancellor's rulings, but it also spurred a party to state the facts truly on oath in discovery or to obey the chancellor's injunction. After the Protestant Reformation, the equation of conscience with personal—and therefore a possibly arbitrary—belief made the chancellor's reliance on conscience problematic for critics of oracular law. By the eighteenth century, Klinck argues, conscience had ceased to hold independent analytic power in equitable jurisprudence. Conscience, that is, could only be understood in the precedential case law of the court of chancery. Traditional remedies granted in chancery were axiomatically in keeping with conscience. Novel twists on those remedies were not.[16]

For many ordinary lawyers in the mid-nineteenth-century United States, the description of equity as a set of procedures, remedies, and precedents summed up their views on the system. The workaday practitioner understood from experience which remedies could be pleaded at law and which required him to don the title of "solicitor" and file in chancery.[17] In turn, that experience kept lawyers mindful both that equity offered some space to explore alternative remedies where the common law proved inadequate and also that this space could not be reached except as an extraordinary recourse after the common law failed. As the legal historian Frederick Pollock wrote at the end of the century, equity kept alive the hope that there might be no right (or more precisely, no wrong) without a remedy.[18]

[14] See, e.g., Oliver Barbour, *A Treatise on the Practice of the Court of Chancery* (Gould, Banks & Co., 1843), 37.

[15] Dennis R. Klinck, *Conscience, Equity and the Court of Chancery in Early Modern England* (Ashgate, 2010), 5. See also Meg Lota Brown, *Donne and the Politics of Conscience in Early Modern England* (Brill, 1995), 25–36; Michael G. Baylor, *Action and Person: Conscience in Late Scholasticism and the Young Luther* (Brill, 1977), 201–02.

[16] Klinck, *Conscience, Equity and the Court of Chancery in Early Modern England*, 270–73. On conscience in early English equity, see Timothy S. Haskett, "The Medieval English Court of Chancery," 14 *Law & History Review* 245 (1996); J. L. Barton, "Equity in the Medieval Common Law," in R. A. Newman, ed., *Equity in the World's Legal Systems* (Établissements Émile Bruylant, 1973), 139–55; Helmut Coing, "English Equity and the *Denunciatio Evangelica* of the Canon Law," 71 *Law Quarterly Review* 223 (1955). Mike MacNair argues that conscience traditionally meant only "private knowledge of facts," but this meaning was significantly obscured by the nineteenth-century practice. Mike MacNair, "Equity and Conscience," 27 *Oxford Journal of Legal Studies* 659 (2007).

[17] For a guide to the early treatise literature, see chapter 2.

[18] Frederick Pollock, "The Continuity of the Common Law," 11 *Harvard Law Review* 423 (1898), 424–25.

In addition to these workaday practitioners, an impressive number of lawyers—especially among those who would become America's leading corporate counsel—devoted significant effort to thinking philosophically and systematically about their dual system of jurisprudence. Mostly, they never published their conclusions in books or pamphlets, and rarely did their views on jurisprudential abstractions enter their courtroom arguments. They did, however, speak up at the numerous constitutional conventions held around mid-century and in legislative reports each time the code was introduced or revised in a jurisdiction. One of the earliest and most influential of these occasions, New York's 1846 constitutional convention, featured the arguments and themes that would be debated across the country. Through the month of August 1846, twenty of the state's leading attorneys spoke one after the other, each describing in detail an ideal judicial system and the role of law and equity within that system.[19]

Legal history was a favorite starting point among lawyers debating law and equity, and practitioners showed an impressive facility with the history of Roman, Greek, and English law. Most agreed on the general outlines but disputed history's lessons. Many accounts began with Aristotle's distinction between Law, which was necessarily universal in its nature, and *Epieikeia*, "a correction of law, where by reason of its universality, it is deficient." Roman praetors were said to have introduced laws of *Æquitas* "for the sake of helping out, supplementing, and correcting the Civil Law." As for the English tradition, the story ran that after the writs had become fixed in number and form, the chancellor began making new writs returnable to his own court, establishing jurisdiction over extraordinary remedies. As the early chancellors were high church officials holding the title "keeper of the king's conscience," their jurisprudence emphasized the ability to rule according to discretion to do justice between the parties when the law, by its ordinary processes and general rules, was deficient. During the reign of Elizabeth I, it was settled that chancery could enjoin the enforcement of a common law judgment, but chancery would not interfere where common law could adequately address a case.[20]

As New Yorkers looked at the judicial systems of other states, they noted that those without courts of chancery—the favored examples were Massachusetts and Pennsylvania—either incorporated or mimicked equity jurisprudence and devices over time. Pennsylvania may not have had a "court of chancery," but from the colonial period onward, it maintained an Orphans Court in which equity powers and procedures pertaining to guardianship were administered. Unwilling to grant judges the equitable power to imprison for civil contempt, state lawmakers approximated

---

[19] See S. Croswell & R. Sutton, eds., *Debates and Proceedings in the New-York State Convention* (Albany Argus, 1846); William G. Bishop & William H. Attree, eds., *Report of the Debates and Proceedings of the Convention for the Revision of the Constitution of the State of New York* (Evening Atlas, 1846). For debates as the code spread, see *Report of the Commissioners Appointed to Prepare a Code of Practice for the Commonwealth of Kentucky* (1850); *Revision of 1860 Containing All the Statutes of a General Nature of the State of Iowa* (1860); H. Fowler & A. H. Brown, eds., *Report of the Debates and Proceedings of the Convention for the Revision of the Constitution of the State of Indiana* (1850).

[20] Bishop & Attree, *Report of the Debates*, 600–02; *Report of the Code Commissioners to the Eighth General Assembly of the State of Iowa* (1859), 440–43. For the sources of the New Yorkers' arguments, see especially Anthony Laussat Jr., *An Essay on Equity in Pennsylvania* (1826), 13–17; William Whewell, *The Elements of Morality* (John Parker, 1845), 329–32. For a twenty-first-century account of seventeenth-century equity, see David Ibbetson, "The Earl of Oxford's Case (1615)," in Charles Mitchell and Paul Mitchell, eds., *Landmark Cases in Equity* (Hart, 2012), 1–32.

chancery's injunctive powers to compel performance with "conditional judgments": juries returned catastrophically high damages awards, but execution was conditioned on the defendant's failure to perform what the court determined—following equity jurisprudence—they should do.[21] From these examples, New York lawyers agreed that equity would continue and might even prosper in a reformed system.[22] The question was in what form, a question that provoked weeks of rancorous debates.

III

The opponents of fusing law and equity in a single institution of uniform procedures—call them "separatists" for ease of reference—were fundamentally convinced that, as the lawyer George Simmons put it, the "division of remedies into legal and equitable, is founded on a natural distinction." In Simmons's taxonomy, capital-e Equity was synonymous with justice itself. It encompassed all of morality, from the "voluntary" precepts of religion to obligations "established by the State. *This [latter] part is the law,*" Simmons explained. Written law was equity calcified, a subset of justice whose principles had been articulated by judges and legislators. But even the best of human wisdom was fallible and incomplete; its expressions of justice aimed at universality but were insufficiently nuanced and failed to account for all the accidents and contingencies of life. A third subset of equity, then (in addition to morality and positive law) was the technical, little-e equity administered in chancery, the discretionary search for as-yet unexpressed or half-expressed principles of justice that could correct the occasional mishaps caused by human pretensions to universalize short-sighted legal principles.[23]

By reserving discretion to these extraordinary cases, Simmons believed the rule of law was maintained without granting too much arbitrary power to the courts. He concluded that human wisdom could "only divide the great mass of such cases into classes of actions, to be followed by the ordinary courts, and then constitute an extraordinary tribunal to take charge of the residue." Simmons, like other separatists, readily granted that the development of distinct institutions of law and equity was a historical accident, but he argued that the institutional separation pointed to a conceptual separation that was real, founded "in the nature of things" and thus impervious to historical contingency. As long as general laws used classifications to efficiently organize the great mass of human actions into categories of judgment, an extraordinary jurisdiction would have to intervene when the general categorizations failed.[24]

According to New York City lawyer Lorenzo Shepard, the fusionists' mistake was their belief that all wrongs could be "reduced to the same class, and be comprehensible

---

[21] See Laussat, *An Essay on Equity in Pennsylvania*, 56–57, 105–8. On equity in Massachusetts, see Phyllis Maloney Johnson, No Adequate Remedy at Law: Equity in Massachusetts 1692–1877, Yale Law School Student Legal History Papers, Paper 2 (2012), available at http://digitalcommons.law.yale.edu/student_l egal_history_papers/2.

[22] A confidence that is at odds with the conventional accounts of equity's demise. See, e.g., Subrin, "David Dudley Field and the Field Code"; Kessler, *Inventing American Exceptionalism*, 144–50; Horwitz, *Transformation of American Law*, 265–66.

[23] Bishop & Attree, *Report of the Debates*, 664, 667 (Simmons). See also J. T. Humphry, "Lecture at the Incorporated Law Society" 51 *Legal Observer* 67 (1856); Whewell, *Elements of Morality*, 316–27.

[24] Bishop & Attree, *Report of the Debates*, 666 (Simmons). See also Humphry, "Lecture," 68–69.

in the same general remedies." Abstracting a menu of remedies and making them available for all cases ignored how "wrongs are infinitely diversified in their natures and infinitely diversified in their remedies." Without the traditional confines created by the jurisdictional distinction between law and equity, the only alternatives Shepard saw were for courts to expand their injunctive powers—an act of tyranny—or for the legislature to enumerate every possible case in which the device would be permitted—a hopelessly tedious task that would inevitably remain incomplete.[25]

These remarks on the infinite diversity of wrongs and the difficult classifications of law show that what was at stake for the separatists at the twilight of the rule of writs was the fundamental legitimacy of the legal order. Equity and the rule of law required that like cases should be treated alike, but even this principle involved a manifest legal fiction, for no two cases in human experience were completely alike. It was the artifice of the lawmaker to discern commonalities between cases and invest them with legal significance, usually by applying a particular remedy to a certain set of commonly perceived harms.[26] Abolishing the classification and making all remedies available to every case would not "simplify" procedure but make it enormously more unwieldy, one separatist concluded, "as each case would rest upon its own particular circumstances and [become] its own form." Every case, that is, would become an equity case, but separatists argued that it was "dangerous to convert [New York'] standing army of judges into so many chancellors, with all the arbitrary power of that court." Equitable discretion was tolerable only because there were so many definite categories of legal cases to which it could not apply. It had taken centuries to enumerate the categories of remedies that worked for the run of cases and excluded equitable discretion. "To unite law and equity would be to retrograde for three centuries," another separatist warned.[27]

"Retrograde" was an epithet usually hurled at the separatists, but lawyers like Simmons and Shepard insisted they were at the leading edge of legal modernization. Like craftsmen seeking to return to feudal labor practices, it was the fusionists who, Shepard argued, were "at variance with a principle that has done more for the development of human industry, both physical and mental, than any other. I allude to the division of labor." The division of labor, hailed as the infallible principle of economic modernization, ensured that "the tendency of society is to separate the courts of law and equity, and so to secure more expert and competent judges, more prompt and perfect remedies," developments Simmons perceived in all modernizing jurisdictions. By giving the run of cases to common law courts but reserving equity to a highly skilled chancery bench, separatist jurisdictions were simply following the best practices of industrial science.[28]

Behind the division-of-labor ideal lay the suspicion that the jury posed a problem for the fusionists. Separatists lauded the value of the jury as long as it was confined to actions at common law, but, said Shepard, "it may be accounted among our

[25] Bishop & Attree, *Report of the Debates*, 622, 624 (Shepard).

[26] For a succinct discussion on this point, see Beverly Tucker, *Principles of Pleading* (Little, Brown, 1846), 1–4.

[27] Bishop & Attree, *Report of the Debates*, 591 (Marvin), 491, 668 (Simmons); Croswell & Sutton, *Debates and Proceedings*, 446 (Marvin).

[28] Bishop & Attree, *Report of the Debates*, 622 (Shepard), 663, 662 (Simmons). See also *ibid.*, 572 (Jordan).

misfortunes that [there] are causes to which it cannot be applied."[29] The fusionists thus faced a dilemma: to achieve fusion truly, they would either have to abandon the jury—an important safeguard of democratic liberty, at least within its sphere—or make all cases triable by jury—reducing New York's sophisticated business law to amateurism. Separatists recognized that in many instances, equity's supposedly extraordinary intervention had become routinized and bound to precedent as tightly as any common law form of action, but this did not mean the court could be abolished and its cases transferred to law. It was rather an indication of how successfully the division of labor and the absence of the jury had fitted New York law for modern commerce. "The exceeding complication of many subjects of equity jurisdiction, though it may be regretted," Shepard reasoned, "is one of the necessary incidents to high civilization—to extended commerce, and to the vast and involved circle of the transactions of men."[30]

If separatists did not convince fusionists with the ontological claim that, as Shepard put it, the distinction of law and equity was a "difference resting not solely in the will of the Legislature—nor in any great degree dependent on or controlled by it, but existing in the unalterable nature of things themselves," the separatists did win over a few lawyers with the argument that at the very least, fusion could not be accomplished merely through the abstraction of procedure from substance, with only the former undergoing reformation. As Simmons argued, "the very *forms* of proceedings stick so close to the *substance*—the practice of courts is so adhesive to their doctrines" that fusion would prove impracticable if attempted. Sympathetic fusionists like Charles Kirkland and Ira Harris agreed that fusion could be achieved only gradually and would involve many substantive changes. Merely redrafting the rules of pleading and expanding available remedies would not result in fusion, for "the present modes are incorporated and interwoven with all our habits of business, and I may say, almost with all our legal notions and ideas."[31] To these lawyers, traditional practices ran deep through the legal order and would not disappear within a generation—and certainly not within a single legislative session.

In sum, separatists claimed that at least a notional distinction between law and equity fundamentally inhered "in the nature of things." As long as the law traded in general classifications, an extraordinary jurisdiction would have to vest in some arbiter to declare that a particular case was inadequately remedied by the general classifications and required something more specifically tailored to the circumstances. Separatists maintained that institutionally separating ordinary from extraordinary jurisprudence could enhance expertise in both and allow for tailored procedures— factually detailed pleadings when the contextual circumstances mattered, conclusory statements presented to a jury when they did not. In none of these statements did the delegates treat these procedures—whether "inquisitorial" examinations, fact pleading, or the absence of the jury—as the essence of equity. If equity had an essence, it was its ability to work outside or beyond the common law classifications to provide an adequate remedy in a particular case.

[29] *Ibid.*, 621 (Shepard). See also Croswell & Sutton, *Debates and Proceedings*, 446–49 (Jordan).

[30] Bishop & Attree, *Report of the Debates*, 621 (Shepard). See also *Report of the Commissioners* (Kentucky, 1850), vi.

[31] Bishop & Attree, *Report of the Debates*, 621 (Shepard), 664 (Simmons); see also *ibid.*, 590 (Stetson), 575 (Kirkland), 639–41 (Harris).

Strikingly absent from separatist arguments was a robust defense of equity as a system of conscience. Simmons offered the classic defense of equity as a system of "discretion and good conscience" over against the common law system of "strict law." But he clarified that it was not "just as if the rules of equity jurisprudence were the dictates of the personal conscience and personal discretion of the judge." The equitable conscience was the objective conscience of the law, an idea as old as Lord Coke's tenure in the seventeenth century. Simmons meant that the law expressed clear and objective principles that guided jurists on when to abate the strict enforcement of any particular proceeding.[32] Simmons warned his co-delegates that if a formal and regularized mechanism for taking account of the law's conscience were not maintained, conscience would not disappear but would break through "*irregularly* and at random." Once "abolish equity jurisdiction in civil cases, and it will be exercised by courts and juries *without* law or rule, under the seductive influences of particular hard cases." Simmons maintained that states that had not developed courts of chancery ran an informal system of equity in precisely this way, relying on unpredictable spurts of remedial legislation or the oracular judge or jury to get around strict enforcement of the law, but in only a half-principled and certainly unarticulated way.[33] Simmons urged his colleagues not to put New York on the same path.

IV

To committed fusionists, the history of legal development in England and America proved only that the distinction between law and equity "has no foundation in the nature of things," as Field put it. "Its existence is accidental, and continues till now only because we have been the slaves of habit." Unlike his more moderate colleagues, Field was confident these old habits of thought could be transformed if lawyers better understood that names like "equity" and legal forms of action were not "real existences" but "rather ancient formulas, scholastic in their structure and origin, whose vitality has long since departed."[34]

This strong form of nominalism commonly appeared in fusionist arguments. The "natural" distinction between law and equity was "the erroneous conclusion of minds warped and contracted by long continued habits and prejudices, and by the 'set forms of speech' to which they have invariably been accustomed," argued Charles Kirkland at the New York convention. After the delegates agreed to create "one supreme court, having general jurisdiction in law and equity," the New York City corporate attorney Charles O'Conor regretted that the phrase "law and equity" entered the constitution at all, fearing that "as long as we spoke of law and equity as distinct things in our constitution, . . . the legislature would not feel at liberty to unite and blend them into one." Arphaxad Loomis, the future co-drafter of the Field Code, agreed. "Law and equity" seemed to have talismanic power to his colleagues, but "the difference was more in

[32] *Ibid.*, 664 (Simmons) (citing Whewell, *The Elements of Morality*).
[33] *Ibid.*, 663–64.
[34] [David Dudley Field], "The Convention," *New York Evening Post*, Aug. 13, 1846.

words than in reality. . . . There might as well be any other hieroglyphical symbol by which to proceed as to retain those under which the practice was now conducted."[35]

To support their point, fusionists spent entire days at the convention arguing that equity had become indistinguishable from law in its precedent-bound jurisprudence. The separatists' fears about arbitrary discretion dated back to the early seventeenth century, when John Selden famously joked that equitable "conscience" could be as variable as the size of "a Chancellor's foot." But, O'Conor argued, after two centuries of building precedents, "there was not at present any such thing recognized in juris-prudence, as the will or arbitrement of a good and conscientious man finding some measure of justice between neighbors. . . . The maxim that our rights were to be meas-ured by the length of the chancellor's foot was exploded long ago." The New York City lawyer Henry Nicoll agreed that "conscience" no longer informed the work of chan-cery at all, and "the court had long since ceased to be a tribunal of mere discretion. It administered justice in obedience to positive rules and in strict conformity to its own established precedents."[36]

Fusionists declared equity's "extraordinary" jurisdiction and its power to "supply the deficiencies" of the law were likewise empty phrases. The elderly Jacksonian lawyer Michael Hoffman insisted that "for more than a hundred years no court of eq-uity has claimed or exercised the power to modify or soften the rigor of the law—or grant relief on mere grounds of moral right, or conscience, that was not given it by fixed rules of law." On this point, the fusionists boasted the support of so eminent a jurist as William Blackstone, who had written that both systems "are now equally arti-ficial systems, founded on the same principles of justice and positive law, but varied by different usages in the forms and modes of their proceeding."[37]

Blackstone's distinction between principles of justice and modes of proceeding in-spired the fusionists to argue that procedural fusion could be accomplished without disturbing any substantive law. "The difference between law and equity, and the only difference," O'Conor claimed, "was in the form of pleading and the remedies." Following that argument, Nicoll encouraged the legislature to "amalgamate" the sys-tems, "altering no rule of law or equity—but simplifying the forms of bringing causes into court." Again and again, delegates drew contrasts between "form," "mode," and "proceedings" on the one hand and "substance" on the other. "The difference between 'law' and 'equity' is a difference in the *remedies* and *substantially* in nothing more," Kirkland summarized.[38]

Concerning those remedies, equity judges could decree money damages as per common law, but they also administered various other injunctive and declarative

---

[35] Bishop & Attree, *Report of the Debates*, 576 (Kirkland); Croswell & Sutton, *Debates and Proceedings*, 440 (O'Conor); Bishop & Attree, *Report of the Debates*, 590 (Loomis). See also *Report of the Code Commissioners* (Iowa, 1859), 440.

[36] Frederick Pollock, ed., *Table Talk of John Selden* (Quaritch, 1927), 43. Croswell & Sutton, *Debates and Proceedings*, 443 (O'Conor); Bishop & Attree, *Report of the Debates*, 601 (Nicoll). See also *ibid.*, 576 (Kirkland), 638 (Loomis). On the regularization of equity in the late seventeenth century to which the fusionists alluded, see Dennis R. Klinck, "Lord Nottingham's 'Certain Measures,'" 28 *Law & History Review* 711 (2010).

[37] Bishop & Attree, *Report of the Debates*, 679 (Hoffman); 3 *Blackstone's Commentaries* 434.

[38] Croswell & Sutton, *Debates and Proceedings*, 443 (O'Conor), 464 (Nicoll); Bishop & Attree, *Report of the Debates*, 576 (Kirkland).

remedies backed by their power to imprison parties held in contempt. No case in equity required pleading the forms of action; rather, bills in chancery consisted of (often quite detailed) factual statements, usually verified under oath.[39] Fusionists commonly understood that uniting law and equity basically involved extending equitable remedies and proceedings—perhaps with some alterations to diminish verbose pleadings—to all cases. O'Conor's view "was that the forms of pleading used in chancery, reduced and cut down to the extent they might be, were the true forms by which civil justice might be administered in all cases."[40]

This view of equity's straightforward proceedings gave the fusionists a rebuttal to the separationist's division-of-labor argument. As in any trade, the division of labor spurred progress only when it created "efficiency," a term favored by the fusionists. When two courts performed similar functions and the same case often had to seek remedies in both courts, law and equity did not sharpen expertise but created needless redundancies. "Why may not the judge have the power to administer to the party, what in his case the law determines to be a proper and necessary remedy," asked Hoffman. "Why should he be obliged, if he wants one remedy, to go to one court, and if he wants another to go into another?"[41]

Enough lawyers wished to see jury trial preserved that fusionists adjusted their plans to accommodate a possible expansion of jury trial into formerly equitable proceedings, generally optimistic that the factual complexities of equity were perhaps no worse than certain cases at common law. Even if equity proved too complicated for a jury trial, Hoffman argued fusion might have a salutary effect on equitable jurisprudence if judges and lawyers had to make equitable jurisprudence clear enough that it could be presented to a jury in the course of a few hours.[42]

In all these points, Field was the consummate fusionist. Perhaps no colleague exceeded Field's legal nominalism and legislative positivism. To Field, the supposed distinctions of equity were "little more than a play upon words"; "law and equity ought to mean precisely the same thing." In the past century, "it would not at any time have been thought proper or safe for the Courts to disregard an established precedent," and "in almost every instance where an improvement has been made in the laws, it has come from the Legislature." The only reason New York had separate court systems, "if reason it may be called, was purely historical," which was to say, accidental. As positive law had kept the courts distinct, so positive law could unite them and eliminate the distinction forever.[43]

[39] See Barbour, *Practice of the Court of Chancery*, 1:115–19.

[40] On equitable remedies, see generally *ibid.*; David Graham, *A Treatise on the Organization and Jurisdiction of the Courts of Law and Equity in the State of New York* (Halsted and Voorhies, 1839). Bishop & Attree, *Report of the Debates*, 562 (O'Conor). See also *ibid.*, 648 (Morris).

[41] Bishop & Attree, *Report of the Debates*, 676 (Hoffman); see also *Report of the Code Commissioners* (Iowa, 1859), 444. On efficiency, see especially Bishop & Attree, *Report of the Debates*, 643–46 (Harris); *First Report* (New York, 1848), 7, 75, 137; *Opinions of Lord Brougham, on Politics, Theology, Law, Science, Education, Literature* (H. Colburn, 1841), 227.

[42] Bishop & Attree, *Report of the Debates*, 616 (Brown), 678 (Hoffman), 600–01 (Nicoll).

[43] David Dudley Field, "Legal System of New York" (1866) in A. P. Sprague, ed., *Speeches, Arguments, and Miscellaneous Papers of David Dudley Field* (D. Appleton, 1884), 1:338, 340; David Dudley Field, "Law and Equity," 18 *Albany Law Journal* 509 (1878), 510–11; David Dudley Field & Alexander Bradford, *The Civil Code of New York Reported Complete* (1865), xxvii.

Field insisted that the distinction between law and equity "grows out of legal procedure; it does not spring from distinct, inseparable rights; it does not inhere in the nature of things." The only difference between law and equity was the remedy each court could decree; there was no such thing as a "legal right" distinct from an "equitable right." Lawyers commonly spoke that way, "but only because there are legal remedies and equitable remedies. Once abolish the distinction between the latter, and the distinction between the former perishes with it." By defining rights as "substantial" and remedies as "procedural," Field thought he saw a way through the legitimacy problems raised by the separatists. The latter worried that in a fused system, every case would become a long recitation of facts submitted to the unbound conscience of a judge. But Field argued that the rule of law was secured not by stringently defining remedies and their availability but by positively defining rights. The written law enumerated the rights of social actors. When those rights were violated, pleading need only show the fact of violation without contorting itself to fit a particular remedy. Instead of a cabined set of remedies, comprehensive legislation—a substantive code if the legislation were properly organized—would protect against judicial arbitrariness. If no positive right had been violated, a judge had no discretion to grant a remedy; if a right had been violated, then *any* remedy that vindicated the right would be appropriate. Field was not particularly concerned that judges would decree the "wrong" remedy. Professional experience would guide lawyers and judges toward appropriate remedies, and the appellate process would correct any windfall awards. Thus, as with his theory of pleading generally, Field once again relied on lawyers' ingrained habits of thought to dodge a conceptual difficulty of his prescribed remedial system.[44]

In sum, Field and his fellow fusionists believed the distinction between law and equity could be quickly and cleanly replaced by distinguishing between substantive right and procedural enforcement. They denied that chancery offered a unique approach to vindicating rights, certainly not one that was more concerned with doing justice according to conscience. Chancery's precedential jurisprudence convinced them that equity's methods of defining substantive rights and rendering judgments upon them were indistinguishable from those of the common law. "If equity be designed to supply the defects of law," Field reasoned, "it is as easy to incorporate the supplement into the body of the law itself as to keep it forever a distinct system."[45]

V

After New York abolished its court of chancery, Field and the other commissioners crafted the code ostensibly to provide "a uniform course of proceeding, in all cases,

---

[44] Field, "Legal System of New York," 340; Field, "Law and Equity," 510–11; *First Report* (New York, 1848), 74–75. Sam Bray and Paul Miller have argued that classical equity did not use "causes of action" as an organizing principle. Samuel L. Bray & Paul B. Miller, "Getting into Equity," 97 *Notre Dame Law Review* 1763 (2022). One might say that Field and the fusionists were not so much seeking to alter this aspect of equity, as that they themselves did not recognize it. By their era, equity's operation upon causes of action seemed as natural to them as the common law's.

[45] Field, "The Convention."

legal and equitable."[46] Acting on his belief that fusion was a problem only of procedure, Field sought to solve it in the code of procedure. "The distinction between actions at law and suits in equity [is] abolished," read the opening section to Part II, "Of Civil Actions." Complaints had to contain "a statement of the facts constituting the cause of action" and a demand for relief, but no matter what remedy a plaintiff requested, the court could grant "any relief consistent with the case." Judges were empowered to order sheriffs to arrest defendants, seize their property, or, if it appeared the plaintiff might suffer irreparable injury, enjoin a defendant's actions. New York now had only one court of general jurisdiction, so these powers were conferred on the thirty-three district court judges across the state. Under the code, every trial judge became a chancellor.[47]

Overall, the commissioners insisted that "the basis" for code procedure "was substantially that upon which courts of equity were originally founded." Looking back in 1878, Field observed that some states had adopted the code with "an express provision that, when the legal and equitable rules clash with each other, the latter shall prevail. Such a provision may be expedient, from abundant caution, but I conceive it nevertheless to be unnecessary," Field figured, "because it is implied in the blending of the procedure." Field's co-commissioner Arphaxad Loomis concurred; in his view, the code had produced a "system [that] approaches and assimilates more nearly with the equity forms than with those of the common law" by granting a plaintiff "any relief the facts warranted."[48]

The fusion of law and equity was a joint project across the common law world in the nineteenth century.[49] In general, one might say that Field Code sought to accomplish fusion largely through equity's diffusion.[50] Under the code, every trial judge became a chancellor, every case a potential application of equitable remedies. Most states that adopted the code abolished their separate chancery courts (or started out with the code and thus never established such courts). Codifiers directed judges to

[46] David Dudley Field, *What Shall Be Done with the Practice of the Courts: Shall It Be Wholly Reformed?* (1847), 7.
[47] 1848 N.Y. Laws 510 § 62; 522 § 120, 540 § 231; 527–35 tit. 7.
[48] *Second Report* (New York, 1849), 7; Field, "Law and Equity," 510; Arphaxad Loomis, *Historic Sketch of the New York System of Law Reform in Practice and Pleadings* (1879), 25–26. For decades, proceduralists took the commissioners at their word, see Roscoe Pound, "David Dudley Field: An Appraisal," in Alison Reppy, ed., *David Dudley Field: Centenary Essays* (New York University Press, 1949), 14, but modern accounts now reject the idea that the code sought to extend equitable practices to all cases. "Equity conquered common law" for the first time in the Federal Rules, argues Stephen Subrin, but the Field Code "leaned as much, or more, toward the view of common law procedure as to equity." Subrin, "How Equity Conquered Common Law," 909; Subrin, "Field and the Field Code," 337–38. I have sketched a refutation of Subrin's thesis in significant technical detail elsewhere. Kellen Funk, "Equity Without Chancery: The Fusion of Law and Equity in the Field Code of Civil Procedure, New York 1846–76," 36 *Journal of Legal History* 126 (2015). Suffice it to say here that Subrin's account suffers from relying exclusively on the first partial report of the code in 1848 and ignores the commissioners' Final Report as well as much of their contemporary writings. The point is worth noting as much of the literature declaring American equity "moribund" until the twentieth century relies on Subrin's conclusion that, as one account puts it, "the drafters of the [Field Code] had no use for equity." Hoffer, *The Law's Conscience*, 91.
[49] See especially P. G. Turner, John Goldberg & Henry Smith, eds., *Equity and Law: Fusion and Fission* (Cambridge University Press, 2019).
[50] See Funk, "Equity Without Chancery"; Kessler, *Inventing American Exceptionalism*, ch. 3; Patricia I. McMahon, "Field, Fusion and the 1850s: How an American Law Reformer Influenced the Judicature Act of 1875," in P. G. Turner, ed., *Equity and Administration* (Cambridge University Press, 2018), 424–62.

assess pleadings by the former standards of chancery rather than the conclusory statements of the common law writs, and they directed practitioners to plead equitable and common law actions and defenses together without signaling a distinction.[51]

None of this is to say that the code did make every case an equity case, or that traditional structures of common law practice suddenly disappeared. In the early years of the code, Field and other fusionists dashed off pamphlets and law review articles criticizing judicial decisions that distinguished between law and equity or forced "common law" litigants to follow the old forms of action.[52] Among New York's trial judges, Alexander Smith Johnson received the praise of fusionists for disregarding the distinction and allowing nontraditional joinders and remedies. Henry Selden, on the court of appeals, received their condemnation. It was "plain," Selden wrote, that the state constitution's grant of jurisdiction "in 'law and equity,' has not only recognized the distinction between them, but placed that distinction beyond the power of the legislature to abolish." Lawrence Friedman has written of these judges that "it was as if upper courts tried, not cases, but printed formulae, and tried them according to warped and unreal distinctions."[53]

Such criticisms overlook how much the code itself seemed to require a separatist jurisprudence. This was partly due to the commissioners' haste to produce multiple drafts of the code in the late 1840s. Many of the proceedings surrounding complicated equitable remedies, such as the partition of property (and related actions for account, dower, and waste), were defined and regulated by the 1829 Revised Statutes. Rather than go through these proceedings individually and recodify or reform them in the spring of 1848, the commissioners left the Revised Statutes in force as to many formerly equitable remedies. In their final draft in 1850, they largely recopied the Revised Statutes, explaining it as a matter of path dependence that had developed over the previous two years. The commissioners insisted that "the form of civil actions under the code, is in its nature adapted to almost every case requiring the interposition of judicial authority." Nevertheless, they retained special procedures for "actions

---

[51] Even jurisdictions that did not adopt the Field reforms vested equity powers in many more judges than England's lone chancellor (before 1813) and vice chancellors (after 1841). See Michael Lobban, "Preparing for Fusion: Reforming the Nineteenth-century Court of Chancery," 22 *Law & History Review* 389, 565 (2004). Most southern states employed two to four chancellors early on, before granting equity jurisdiction to county or district courts in the 1820s and 1830s. Federal district judges received a uniform equity code from the Supreme Court in 1822. Most code jurisdictions and an increasing number of reform states allowed the joinder of legal and equitable claims and encouraged the use of equitable practices—temporary injunctions and bench trial—in all litigation. Charles M. Hepburn, *The Historical Development of Code Pleading in America and England* (W.H. Anderson & Co., 1897); Kristin Collins, "A Considerable Surgical Operation": Article III, Equity, and Judge-Made Law in the Federal Courts," 60 *Duke Law Journal* 249 (2010); Laussat, *Essay on Equity*, 153–57.

[52] See [David Dudley Field], *Law Reform Tracts No. 1: The Administration of the Code* (1852); "Progress of Union of Law and Equity," 5 *United States Monthly Law Magazine* 1 (1852); John Norton Pomeroy, *Remedies and Remedial Rights by the Civil Action, According to the Reformed American Procedure* (Little, Brown, 1875); J. N., "The Codification of the Law," 3 *Albany Law Journal* 101, 121 (1871). And in a somewhat later era, Charles E. Clark, "The Union of Law and Equity," 25 *Columbia Law Review* 1 (1925); Charles W. Joiner & Ray A. Geddes, "Union of Law and Equity: A Prerequisite to Procedural Revision," 55 *Michigan Law Review* 1059 (1957).

[53] Clark, "The Union of Law and Equity," 4 (citing Marquat v. Marquat, 12 N.Y. 336 (1855) and New York Ice Co. v. North Western Insurance Co., 23 N.Y. 357 (1861)); Reubens v. Joel, 13 N.Y. 488, 497 (1859) (Selden, J.). Lawrence M. Friedman, *A History of American Law* (Simon & Schuster, 2d ed., 1985), 400.

in particular cases"—formerly equitable and regulated by statute—for the "advantage of following the beaten track already enlightened by the judicial consideration to which the code has been subjected."[54]

Another barrier to fusion by diffusion was the constitutional requirement to preserve the right to jury trial "in all cases in which it has been heretofore used." Although that prevented the commissioners from making the equitable bench trial the only mode of trial under the code, they could have accomplished fusion either by mandating jury trial in every case or, theoretically, leaving the mode of trial to the choice of plaintiffs, who could insist on the constitutional right of a jury trial if they wanted to. Instead, the commissioners gave the parties the option to waive or claim the right to a jury but also set default rules that differed based on the remedy sought. Actions seeking the recovery of real property or money damages defaulted to a jury trial, while "all other cases" defaulted to a bench trial. With these differing modes of trial came different procedures regarding timing and summonses, a distinction between legal and equitable traditions in all but name.[55]

A final barrier proved to be the codification of debtor protection laws, which had been the impetus for fusion reforms in the 1830s. Common law courts could not order the arrest of fraudulent debtors to execute their decrees of money damages. Chancery could, but only after going through the procedures of examination to establish that a defendant was fraudulently concealing assets. The Field Code made parties competent to be examined on oath at trial, thus extending equity's power to ferret out fraud in ordinary contract cases if the need arose. But in order to safeguard New York's act to abolish imprisonment for debt, the code abolished *capias* procedures (which treated the initiation of a civil suit the same as a criminal suit—with the arrest of the defendant until bail was granted), and it enumerated claims in which a party could be arrested at the outset or during the progress of a suit (*mesne* process).[56] In effect and by explicit decree, defendants could not be arrested in contract claims. Thus, throughout the code, both initially and as finalized by the commissioners, rights to certain remedies and modes of proceeding depended on the form of the complaint, which depended on the remedy sought, which in turn depended on the traditions distinguishing legal from equitable relief.

After judges and treatise writers reasoned that such rules preserved a distinction between law and equity and bound certain remedies to the form of the pleadings, Field responded with a hypothetical: Imagine there used to be separate courts for men and women, with different proceedings. Those who could not see that the code accomplished fusion were arguing that there was something "in the nature of things" that prevented a fusion of men and women's proceedings using "uniform pleadings, a uniform manner of taking testimony, trial by jury in every case in which a man was the suitor, and the reexamination of a verdict only after the manner practiced in men's courts."[57] The analogy may have been apt but not very instructive because the

---

[54] *Final Report* (New York, 1850), 378, note to tit. 11.
[55] N.Y. Const. of 1846, art. I, § 2; 1848 N.Y. Laws 547 §154, 536 §203; *Final Report* (New York, 1850), 227–33, 318–19.
[56] *Final Report* (New York, 1850), 451–53, § 1071 & note.
[57] Field, "Law and Equity," 510–11. See also Henry Whittaker, *Practice and Pleading Under the Code, Original and Amended, with Appendix of Forms* (E.O. Jenkins, 2d ed., 1854), 1:56 ("Although . . . the

language of this hypothetical formula preserved the old conceptual distinctions and even differentiated proceedings, as the separatists had pointed out.

Rather than distinguish between cases for money damages and "all other cases," the code states of Kentucky, Iowa, Oregon, Tennessee, and Arkansas explicitly preserved an institutional distinction between law and equity. Because these states—like most others—scheduled different court sessions for jury trial and bench trial, they referred cases to either the "law" or "equity" calendar and forbad the joinder of legal and equitable claims so as not to disrupt the schedule. Even New York continued this scheduling practice, while judges spoke in their decisions of sitting "in equity" or "at law." "They tend to keep up a distinction that no longer exists," Field lamented of his home state in 1878, "and go far to confuse and mislead."[58] Field did not say how much his own legal practice had contributed to the hardening distinction between law and equity, not least in the A&S litigation.

VI

Jay Gould's raid on the A&S Railroad—which New Yorkers would refer to afterward as "the Great Lawsuit"—was fairly straightforward compared to the many complicated financial schemes executed during his career.[59] In the summer of 1869, as the newly installed president of the Erie Railroad, Gould sought to purchase the A&S, ostensibly to connect the two lines. To do so, Gould needed to win over a majority of the board because the A&S's president, Joseph Ramsey, was by all accounts genuinely fearful Gould would plunder the corporation without adding value to the line, so he adamantly opposed the sale.

Gould's opening moves raised no legal (or equitable) complaints. Per the A&S charter, the towns along the line each received a share of stock that they were free to vote or transfer as their governing bodies wished. Gould began purchasing stock from towns eager to see their holdings go at par value (or to receive Gould's finder's fee). Gould used straw purchasers so as not to tip off Ramsey prematurely, but by the end of July it became clear that Ramsey and the directors loyal to him would be in the minority by September's annual board meeting. Though most observers of the

preamble [of the Code] seems to contemplate the abolition of all distinction between legal and equitable remedies also, that abolition is, to some extent, and must always continue to be, impracticable.").

[58] Field, "Law and Equity," 510–11.
[59] Besides the litigation documents, only a couple of which were printed, the main sources for the A&S fight are Albert Stickney, "The Truth of a 'Great Lawsuit,'" 14 *Galaxy* 576 (1872), and Francis C. Barlow, *Facts for Mr. David Dudley Field* (1871), two partisans for Ramsey and fierce critics of Field's; George Ticknor Curtis, *An Inquiry into the Albany & Susquehanna Railroad Litigations* (1871), a staunch (and well compensated) defender of Gould and Field; and *Charges of the Bar Association of New York Against Hon. George G. Barnard and Hon. Albert Cardozo and Hon. John H. McCunn* (1872), an ethics hearing prompted by the newly formed Association of the Bar of the City of New York. Of the three, Curtis clearly wrote with the (often unpublished, sometimes lost) litigation documents in hand, and he provided a more detailed account of those documents as to date, time, party, and legal theory. With cautious regard for Curtis's clear incentives to paint Field in the best light, the following account relies largely on Curtis for its chronology.

coming duel judged Ramsey's motives pure, Ramsey was the first to grasp the sword of litigation.[60]

The suing started in Oneonta, a tiny town about halfway between Albany and the Pennsylvania border. A Ramsey loyalist petitioned for an injunction in the nearest supreme court to restrain the town from selling its stock. The code permitted an injunction to be imposed *ex parte*—without hearing from the other side—"upon its appearing satisfactorily to the court . . . that sufficient grounds exist therefor." The code did not state what grounds were sufficient for an *ex parte* injunction; in eight pages of small type, New York's annotated 1868 code listed all the reported cases in which such injunctions had been granted and refused so that practitioners could consult the case law and try to make analogies in their own cause.[61] The Oneonta petition claimed that town leaders were planning to accept payment for less than par value in contravention of their public trust. Judge J. M. Parker granted the *ex parte* injunction on August 2 but dissolved it on August 5 when a Gould-allied director appeared and offered proof that Gould was paying full par value for the stock.[62]

Between the August 2 and August 5 Oneonta proceedings, Field and Shearman got to work, filing three separate lawsuits in New York City. One, on behalf of an A&S investor, targeted three thousand shares of stock that had reverted to the A&S and that the suit claimed Ramsey had reissued to his allies without receiving payment. (New York did not criminalize the issuance of watered stock until 1912, but in civil suits, investors or directors could seek to restore value lost in such transactions.) The petition requested that the reissuance be declared void but also that a neutral party be appointed to "receive" and hold the stock until it was stricken from the firm's books. On behalf of a director, a second suit sought an *ex parte* injunction ordering Oneonta's town stock transferred to Gould's purchaser. Importantly, the writ ran against the corporation's bookkeeper to record the sale, not against the town, which was already under Judge Parker's injunction not to sell. New York City Judge George Barnard instantly granted that injunction. On behalf of the same director, the third suit once again targeted the three thousand shares of reissued stock but sought a different remedy from the investor suit. This time, Field and Shearman asked that Ramsey be removed as director for his malfeasance and that the corporation be enjoined from issuing further stock except at a public sale. Barnard granted that injunction the same day as well, on August 4.[63]

Having dislodged the first stone, Ramsey was also busying himself with an avalanche of legal filings at precisely the same time. On August 5—it is unclear whether it was before he was served with notice of Judge Barnard's injunction suspending his authority—Ramsey filed suit in Albany in his own name, attempting to have Gould-allied directors removed from office. Ramsey's *ex parte* affidavit alleged a conspiracy among the directors to transfer possession of the A&S to the Erie Railroad for private ends rather than for the good of the company. Judge Rufus Peckham of Albany granted the injunction on the spot.[64]

---

[60] Curtis, *An Inquiry into the Albany & Susquehanna Railroad Litigations*, 5–8.
[61] 1868 N.Y. Code of Civ. Proc. 398–406, notes to §§ 219–220.
[62] Curtis, *An Inquiry into the Albany & Susquehanna Railroad Litigations*, 8–9.
[63] *Ibid.*, 11–18.
[64] *Ibid.*, 10–11. Peckham (Sr.) was the father of Rufus Peckham of *Lochner v. New York* fame.

Ramsey then attempted to shore up his position in the coming elections. To do so, he mortgaged the A&S for bonds, which he then loaned to allied purchasers. The purchasers used the money to buy 9,500 shares of stock that the board—now bereft of Gould directors—issued. Remarkably, Ramsey was engaging in the very behavior he had accused Gould of conspiring to commit, using corporation assets to funnel money into private hands so those hands could acquire more of the corporation's assets. To prevent further stock sales from upsetting the new balance of power, Ramsey had the corporation's books transferred offsite—journalists inclined to sensationalism claimed he hid them in an Albany graveyard.[65]

All of these Ramsey activities transpired on August 5. On August 6, the dueling litigants filed two more suits—one in Albany, one in New York—seeking the same relief: that the entirety of the A&S rail system be taken from the control of its board and president and transferred to a receiver pending the next corporate election. Barnard granted the New York receivership the same day, appointing Gould's close associate Jim Fisk as one of the "neutral" receivers. Judge Peckham in Albany, unaware of the New York filings, also granted a receivership and, being already on the spot, installed a Ramsey ally named Robert H. Pruyn as the receiver.[66]

Crucially for Field and Shearman, the next day, August 7, was a Saturday. When their clerk, John W. Sterling, arrived in Albany to serve the receivership papers on the corporation's headquarters, he found Pruyn already claiming to act as receiver. But time was on Gould's side. An obscure section of the code provided that in New York County only, orders took effect immediately upon being signed by a judge. In all other counties, judicial orders took effect only within business hours.[67] Sterling telegraphed Shearman, who sought a "writ of assistance" from Barnard, received the signature, and telegraphed the writ back to Sterling the same day. Among many A&S legends from the litigation, the telegraphed writ was probably its most famous episode among professionals. Apparently, it was the first time a lawyer had been so audacious as to attempt to serve process through this new technology. The writ itself was uncommon. A writ of assistance authorized the use of necessary force to counter resistance to an equitable receivership. By professional accounts, it had hardly, if ever, been issued in New York, and Shearman may have only known about it because he had spent the previous decade scrutinizing practice treatises while preparing his treatise on code pleading.[68]

The grant of a writ of assistance did not yet bring the parties to blows. Pruyn filed suit to enjoin the sheriff from acting on Shearman's writ on the theory that the writ was void for improper service. On Monday, Pruyn's injunction was granted. Rather than test the validity of the writ, Field raced to Albany and sent an emergency telegraph to Governor John Hoffman at West Point. Hoffman dispatched the militia before the dueling receivers could rally their mobs to fight for control of the railroad.[69]

---

[65] *Ibid.*, 10–11.

[66] *Ibid.*, 24–30.

[67] 1868 N.Y. Code of Civ. Proc. §§ 24, 401.

[68] Curtis, *An Inquiry into the Albany & Susquehanna Railroad Litigations*, 30–34. On Shearman's treatise-writing, see chapter 5.

[69] Curtis, *An Inquiry into the Albany & Susquehanna Railroad Litigations*, 38–44.

Having lost temporary control of most A&S assets to the militia, all efforts now focused on the September 7 board meeting. Judge Barnard ordered the three thousand reissued shares into a receivership, appointing Field's former law clerk, W. J. A. Fuller, as receiver. Like the writ of assistance, the use of receivership for shares of stock under section 244 of the code was—as the 1868 annotated code again shows—basically unprecedented. Receivers were commonly appointed to oversee estates, not a single slice of intangible property that was unlikely to be "materially injured or impaired," in the words of the code. Barnard also ordered an injunction in a suit by Gould to prevent the 9,500 shares of self-dealt stock from being voted at the meeting. Nevertheless, the day before the meeting, an Albany judge ordered that no stock be voted *unless* the 9,500 shares were also voted.[70]

That same day, September 6, Field and Shearman worked out their final preparations for the meeting. They faced two problems: they needed access to the corporate books to record the stock Gould had purchased since the books were withdrawn in early August, and they needed to prevent Ramsey from voting the proxies of his 9,500 shares of watered stock. They believed section 179 of the code could address both problems at once. That section abolished imprisonment in civil cases except for the fraudulent debtor—that is, one who concealed personal property that rightfully belonged to the plaintiff. Field drew up a pleading framing the corporation's books as just such property and seeking the arrest of Ramsey and his closest allies who had aided in the concealment. Judge Barnard signed the order the same day, as had become his custom, but Field and Shearman waited to serve it on the Albany sheriff until 11:45 the next day, fifteen minutes before the meeting began.[71]

As incredible as it may seem, this account has significantly simplified the A&S litigation. Ramsey's allies alone secured at least six more injunctions concerning the shareholders' meeting. The purpose of summarizing this dizzying array of injunctions, receiverships, and more exotic equitable remedies is to make three points. First, the litigation illustrates vividly (more than a treatise could) how fully equity—especially in its provisional remedies—did not inhere in articulable principles of substantive law but in chancery's traditional power to change the game without changing the rules. No party sought, and no judge granted, relief directly contrary to what another court had ordered (setting aside the simultaneously granted receiverships, when one court could not have known what another was ordering elsewhere). One judge ordered a town not to sell stock, another ordered a bookkeeper to record the transaction as if it had already happened. One judge ordered shares not to vote, another ordered the remaining shares not to vote without the first group. One judge ordered a writ of force, another—in desperation—enjoined the sheriff from executing writs. In all these cases, the first judgment remained technically undisturbed, the rulings intact, but the game could not be played out—the aces had been removed.

Second, these equitable maneuverings show how, as George Simmons had argued at the convention, "the very *forms* of proceedings stick so close to the *substance*" that they could not be pulled apart without serious damage to the fabric of legality.[72]

---

[70] *Ibid.*, 44–47.

[71] *Ibid.*, 63–64.

[72] Bishop & Attree, *Report of the Debates*, 664 (Simmons). And the damage from the A&S litigation would indeed be serious. See chapter 10.

After attempting to reduce equity to a list of procedures and remedies on a page, Field showed how greatly those remedies had depended on traditional structures of uncodified thought to keep them within practical bounds, especially the bounds of conscience. By requiring "sufficient grounds" for an equitable remedy, Field's code was not alluding to substantive rules to be codified elsewhere because there was no substance to codify. In the 1860s, there were no "elements" of an injunction as there were of a breach-of-contract claim. The grounds were sufficient or insufficient only in the judge's mind, hopefully illuminated by hundreds of cases deemed sufficient for an injunction, and by hundreds of cases deemed insufficient. Codifiers scoffed at the notion that conscience had any part left to play in modern equity, or that the law could have a conscience. Their own litigations demonstrated otherwise, showing how greatly their system depended on a habituated sense of propriety. But instead of the conscience of the law, their code had substituted the conscience of (the probably bribed[73]) Judge Barnard.

Finally, the litigations illustrate what Douglas Laycock called "the death of the irreparable injury rule." Laycock proposed that in a post-fusion system, the traditional requirement that equity intervene only if common law damages are shown to be inadequate ("irreparable injury") has functionally disappeared. It is always found automatically satisfied if, indeed, the question arises at all. Laycock suggested we accept the bargain of the codifiers. Every case is now an equity case, no case is extraordinary, and litigants may seek whatever relief they desire.[74] The A&S litigation suggests that Laycock may have been right, but only up to a point. Once again, the ambiguities of "procedure" and "substance" produced a slippage. Was the traditional requirement to show the inadequacy of damages a substantive rule of equity, an "element" of showing entitlement to relief? Or was it merely a pleading requirement, a talismanic phrase one uttered when invoking equity's jurisdiction that could accordingly be abandoned once all cases fell within equity's jurisdiction? By leaving the rule out of their reformed code of procedure, the commissioners implicitly opted for the second answer.

And yet the irreparable injury rule did not die with fusion. Rather, its traditional effects became all the more deeply entrenched. That is perhaps why negligent manufacturers pay tort victims money damages instead of entering into receivership. It is also why Field and Shearman could arrest Ramsey by plausibly arguing their claim sounded not in contract *ab initio* but in the law of fraud, a former preserve of equity. The irreparable injury rule may no longer be invoked. Still, to this day, the "adequacy" of money damages remains hardwired into practice, even for victims who lose life or limb. In contrast, the "extraordinary" decrees of equity remain available to corporate litigants, even when only lost profits are on the line.[75] The forms of proceedings have stuck close to the substance.

---

[73] See *Charges of the Bar Association of New York Against Hon. George G. Barnard* (ultimately impeaching Barnard for bribery).

[74] Douglas Laycock, "The Death of the Irreparable Injury Rule," 103 *Harvard Law Review* 687 (1990); Douglas Laycock, "The Triumph of Equity," 56 *Law & Contemporary Problems* 53 (1993).

[75] This asymmetry has become especially vibrant in federal equity, where the "corporate" litigants are increasingly state governments. See Kellen Funk, "Equity's Federalism," 97 *Notre Dame Law Review* 2057 (2022).

VII

Field and Shearman's deployment of equity in what could have been the culminating battle of the Erie War had been nearly flawless. Through their strategic combination of injunctions, receiverships, and arrests for attachment, they cobbled together a shareholder majority at the September 7 meeting while their Albany rivals were arrested. But whether through lack of nerve or simple miscalculation, the sheriff did not remove President Ramsey from the building but merely detained him in the boardroom. It took Ramsey only half an hour to draw up the proper bond paperwork and secure bail—$25,000 apiece for him and his allied directors. (Ramsey's arrest in the same room where a young J. P. Morgan was present proved fortunate.) The liberated directors then held their own meeting within the bylaws' conditions and elected their own slate of directors before one o'clock. After all the *ex parte* injunctions and receiverships, an actual trial would finally determine who controlled the A&S.[76]

After the trial the following January, Judge Darwin Smith of Rochester employed yet another power of equity to cut through the knot of injunctions and receiverships: the power to declare acts of fraud void. Smith found that Gould's Erie party had been engaged in a fraudulent conspiracy from the beginning. Barnard's first injunction had been decreed in a "suit instituted for a fraudulent purpose," and all the receiverships of track and stocks since then had been procured "in aid of fraudulent purposes." Thus, "in equity" these acts were void, the votes of Erie-received stock were void, and the Ramsey directors were duly elected and remained rightfully in possession of the railroad. "As the case was on the equity side of the court," Charles Francis Adams commented approvingly, "there was no intervention of a jury, no chance of an inability to agree on a verdict."[77] The mess that equitable remedies had created, equitable precepts had cleared away. The Albany party swept the field, as Thomas Nast exulted with a depiction of the "smash-up" of the Erie Ring (see Figure 9.3).

As with the "sufficient grounds" needed for an injunction, no list of substantive elements defined "fraud" for purposes of equitable remedies. But acting to restrain fraudulent parties from taking advantage of the strictness of the writ system had been one of chancery's oldest functions, one closely identified with the equitable conscience. Had he looked, George Simmons might have seen his prophecy of equitable conscience—no longer part of the formal regularized law—breaking through informally and irregularly in the law's uncodified gaps.[78] Smith's opinion used the phrases "I think" or "seems to me" over twenty times, reflecting both the fact that fraud was ultimately a matter of discretion for the judge to decide and that Smith had to rely on his own conscience to make the decision. Smith concluded by remarking on his "deep sense of oppression, from the weight of the great responsibility involved in [the case's] decision." But he found "relief . . . from the fact that my decision is not necessarily conclusive upon the parties, if I have erred in judgment or opinion, the error is not irrevisable."[79] Other consciences would eventually weigh the matter.

---

[76] See Adams & Adams, *Chapters of Erie*, 181–85.
[77] *Ibid.*, 188 (quoting People v. Albany & Susquehanna Railroad Co., 1 Lans. 308, 337–38 (1870)).
[78] Bishop & Attree, *Report of the Debates*, 663–664 (Simmons).
[79] People v. Albany & Susquehanna Railroad Co., 1 Lans. at 347–48.

JUSTICE ON THE RAIL—ERIE RAILROAD (RING) SMASH UP.

Figure 9.3 From top to bottom: Judge George Barnard, David Dudley Field, Jay Gould.
Thomas Nast, "Justice on the Rail—Erie Railroad (Ring) Smash Up," *Harper's Weekly*, March 30, 1872, 248.

Fortunately for Gould, Smith was correct about those other consciences. As Erie's lead counsel, Field appealed Judge Smith's decision, and the absence of a jury became the basis for his remarkable appeal. The foundation of Field's argument was the 1860 case *Hartt v. Harvey*. Fusionists usually did not regard *Hartt* important enough to include on their lists of offensive cases, but its reasoning followed Selden's jurisprudence on the natural distinction between law and equity: "Although the distinction between actions at law and in equity is abolished," its key section read, "yet the inherent distinction between legal and equitable jurisdiction and relief exists, and it is not in the power of constitutions or legal enactments to abolish it." The decision claimed that even the code recognized this truth "in prescribing different modes of trial for the two classes of action." Accordingly, the *Hartt* court held that in a suit to remove a corporate officer based on fraudulent voting, equitable remedies were inappropriate, and the plaintiff should have sought a common law writ of *quo warranto*. Well before its abolition, the New York court of chancery had strongly established the precedent that chancellors would not become deeply involved in corporate elections. As long as duly installed inspectors collected and counted the votes, equity would not allow the losers to rerun an election through litigation. Common law courts could remove officers who lacked a proper basis for holding office, but the *quo warranto* writ carried the procedural requirements that the "people of New York" be joined as litigants (effectively a public interest requirement) and the claim of official authority be subjected to jury trial. When the plaintiff in *Hartt* sought under the code to remove two directors without joinder of the people or jury trial, the court dismissed the complaint.[80]

As much as *Hartt* must have offended Field's vision of reform, the precedent was invaluable to his appeal. "As a court of equity," Field argued, Judge Smith's court "could not entertain jurisdiction . . . respecting the title to the office of directors." It was a settled principle that "equity cannot interfere in the government of corporations," and since "the action was one in the nature of *quo warranto*," the "defendants had the right of trial by jury." Justice Johnson—the same who was lauded by fusionists for his sympathetic views—approved Field's arguments. "Elections to office" were never "matters of equitable consideration. They depended only on legal inquiries and legal principles," Johnson ruled. That the case was "eminently proper for jury trial is obvious," and thus, the court vacated the more important judgments of Judge Smith and ordered a new trial.[81]

One could, of course, treat these cases only as an instance of Field's mercenary lawyering, his ability to set aside his personal philosophy of law to use every precedent that advantaged his clients.[82] But the *Hartt* line of cases totally belied the fusionists' claims that there were no "substantial" distinctions between law and equity that would be affected by a merger of the courts. So much of New York's corporation jurisprudence had arisen out of church disputes that its chancery court had long established precedents that equity would not invade corporate ballot boxes and remove officers (the disputed election in *Hartt* itself was in a church, not a business enterprise).[83] By sending corporate litigants to seek their remedy at law, the chancellors preserved the legitimacy of their functions by creating a rule that was indistinguishably substantive *and* procedural. Equitable discretion was too invasive for corporate elections, but a jury drawn from the community—in a case with a sufficiently high public interest—might arrive at a remedy that was both just and socially approvable. In Field's ideal jurisprudence, either Gould or Ramsey had the right to the corporate office, and a judge

---

[80] Hartt v. Harvey, 32 N.Y. 55 (1860), 66.

[81] People v. Albany & Susquehanna Railroad Co., 57 N.Y. 161 (1874), 164–65 (presentation of Field), 171–72, 176 (Johnson, J.). The Albany party successfully outmaneuvered Fisk and Gould once again, by leasing the road while the appeal was pending to the Delaware & Raritan Canal Company, a megacorporation with sufficient wealth and legal counsel to withstand further litigation by the Erie party. Field's successful appeal vacated punitive damages Judge Smith had assessed. Contented with that outcome, Fisk and Gould turned their attention to other ventures. See Adams & Adams, *Chapters of Erie*, 190–91.

[82] See Michael Schudson, "Public, Private, and Professional Lives: The Correspondence of David Dudley Field and Samuel Bowles," 21 *American Journal of Legal History* 194 (1977).

[83] On New York chancery's reluctance to enter into church disputes, see Robertson v. Bullions, 11 N.Y. 243 (1854).

sitting without a jury could vindicate that right—which is precisely what happened when Judge Smith ruled against Field. Field's appeal, however, drew on the logic that procedure itself created rights—the right to a jury trial, to a corporate office, to vindication of the public's interest—but as they had for centuries, these rights depended upon which remedy a litigant sought, which in turn dictated the procedures that had to be followed.

VIII

Writing to the *Albany Law Review* in 1878, Field succinctly, if unwittingly, highlighted the ambiguities of law and equity in the United States. "Fusion of law and equity is an expression common in England, though little used in this country," he explained. "We express the same general idea by the phrase, union of legal and equitable remedies." Indeed, American commentators since the time of Joseph Story had discussed the "union" of law and equity in ways resonant with the more famous Union formed by America's federated constitutional system. But while the Constitution's "more perfect Union" left its component states distinct and intact, fusionists like Field insisted that "the perfect union of law and equity" required, "to express differently the same idea, . . . the complete obliteration of every distinction between them."[84]

Although the project to fuse law and equity and sunder rights from remedies remained incomplete, its attempt in the Field Code powerfully influenced the development of American law. When Massachusetts native Walter Ashburner produced his *Principles of Equity* in 1902, he insisted that "the two streams of jurisdiction, though they run in the same channel, run side by side and do not mingle their waters." Ashburner's views became influential around the world, especially in Australia, where jurists insisted Americans were pursuing a "fusion fallacy." Nevertheless, Ashburner had little influence in his native country. In the United States, trans-substantive procedure became the dominant paradigm, law- or equity-specific procedures the oft-overlooked anomalies.[85]

As diffuse as equity became, several jurisdictions remained committedly separatist. Illinois, Delaware, and New Jersey maintained separate courts of chancery and left common law procedures relatively unaltered until the mid-twentieth century. By the late 1870s, fusionists liked to joke that Illinois and New Jersey were "the Yellowstone Park of common law pleading."[86] But despite their "retrograde" procedures, Illinois and New Jersey prospered commercially. That the leading edge of finance and corporate capitalism—futures trading in Illinois, general incorporation in New Jersey—could originate and flourish in these Yellowstone Parks indicated that modern

---

[84] Field, "Law and Equity," 509.

[85] Walter Ashburner, *Principles of Equity* (Butterworth Law Publishers, 1902), 23; M. Tilbury, "Fallacy or Furphy?: Fusion in a Judicature World," 26 *University of New South Wales Law Journal* 357 (2003). See Robert M. Cover, "For James Wm. Moore: Some Reflections on a Reading of the Rules," 84 *Yale Law Journal* 718 (1975). On the agendas of normal science and perceived anomalies within a closed scientific discipline, see Thomas S. Kuhn, *The Structure of Scientific Revolutions* (Chicago University Press, 3d ed., 1996 [1962]).

[86] See, for instance, "Current Topics," 32 *Albany Law Journal* 161 (1885); Charles E. Clark, "The New Illinois Civil Practice Act," 1 *University of Chicago Law Review* 209 (1933).

capitalism might find sufficient "certainty" and "efficiency" in the forms of action as it could under fact pleading. Charles O'Conor (one of Field's opponents in the coming Tweed litigation) admitted as much during the 1846 convention. Although O'Conor favored fusion and codification at the time, he conceded that the forms of action and the law-equity distinction were "tolerably understood by the profession generally," who could use the devices "to bring in such a verdict as worked out the ends of justice."[87] By the 1870s, O'Conor had abandoned the drive toward fusion, and with his fellow elite lawyers had started to grope for ways to calm the public's outrage over the Great Lawsuit and the wreckage Field and his fusion had wrought.

---

[87] Croswell & Sutton, *Debates and Proceedings*, 441 (O'Conor).

10

How Shall the Lawyers Be Paid

Fees and Costs

I

A labyrinth of paperwork wound from gold rush California to the witness stand of a New York courtroom in 1865, where sat the famed explorer and first Republican presidential candidate John C. Frémont. In odd ways, the litigation was centrally about Frémont and yet not about him at all. A fractured Republican Party had briefly considered unseating Lincoln to replace him with Frémont in 1864, which was partly what brought Frémont to the center of New York political squabbles as the Civil War was winding down.[1] But in the suit that brought Frémont to the stand, he was only a minor witness, called in primarily to discuss David Dudley Field's retainer fees.

Field had been an early champion of Frémont in the Republican Party and had eagerly joined Horace Greeley of the New York *Tribune* in supporting Frémont's 1864 bid. Their bitter opponents, going back to the days of the Democratic-Whig rivalry, were William Seward and his journalist lieutenant, Thurlow Weed. After Weed accused George Opdyke, a former mayor of New York City, of corruptly making "more money . . . than any fifty sharpers, Jew or Gentile, in the City of New York," Field sued, hoping to use a wide-ranging $50,000 libel suit to air his many grievances against Weed.[2]

One of the libel claims concerned an allegation that Opdyke had embezzled from Frémont's campaign. But once on the stand, most of Frémont's examination concerned the striking revelation that Frémont had paid Field a retainer of $200,000 before his 1856 presidential run, a staggering sum for a single legal representation at the time. As the defense counsel had hoped, Field could not help but take the bait, stretching out the examination on a tertiary point in order to justify his fee and, by implication, his integrity as a lawyer conducting a high-stakes litigation. Field walked Frémont back through a bewildering away of transactions structured to offload a mining interest that had gone bad before the presidential run. Field's fee, Frémont acknowledged, was paid in stock with a par value of $200,000 but whose market value was uncertain. Frémont had no objection "at all" when it was negotiated and had told Field at the time that he "richly deserve[d] it."[3] In sum, the two had contracted freely, and privately.

---

[1] See Sven Beckert, *Monied Metropolis: New York City and the Consolidation of the American Bourgeoisie, 1850–1896* (Harvard University Press, 2001), 126; T. Harry Williams, *Lincoln and the Radicals* (Wisconsin University Press, 1965), 326–29; Allan Nevins, *Frémont: Pathmarker of the West* (Longmans, Green & Co., 1955), 573–79.

[2] On Field's connections to Opdyke and his management of the libel case, see Daun Van Ee, *David Dudley Field and the Reconstruction of the Law* (Garland Press, 1986), 138–61.

[3] *The Great Libel Case, Opdyke Against Weed: A Full Report of the Speeches of Counsel* (1865), 8, 63–64.

Turning from Frémont to the gallery, Field taunted his opposing counsel. "My friend [Edwards] Pierrepont need not waste his thoughts" on such a high fee, Field snarled, "for nobody will ever make him such an offer, and he would not earn so much were he to live a hundred years." As for William M. Evarts, the future architect of the modern federal court system, Field invited him to "sit down with me and compare the fees he has received from the public treasury" for representing the government numerous times. "I will promise to make no public inquiry into the amount he has received, and we will both cry quits and be even."[4] Defending himself publicly a few years after the Albany & Susquehanna litigation, Field deployed the same tactics: insulting his fellow lawyers as unskilled and therefore envious of the high fees he could command, or else threatening to reveal his skillful opponents' own dubious compensation schemes.

Field was not the only lawyer who found it difficult to discuss his fees apart from his professional ethics. His code regulated both, with far-reaching consequences. Fees, however, must be understood in their relation to legal "costs"—by no means a mere synonym in the nineteenth century. Costs were the legal expenses, including fees, chargeable to the loser in a litigation. Before the code, New York strictly regulated the costs that victorious lawyers had to be paid by their adversaries. It was unclear whether the limits on costs imposed any restrictions on fees that lawyers could negotiate with their clients, but lawyers at the time commonly spoke as if the limits were the same. They loudly complained that theirs was the only craft burdened by legislative price-fixing.

Cost-shifting, including making the loser of a litigation pay the victor's attorney fees, is typical in Western legal systems, so much so that the prevalent practice of the United States in requiring each party to bear its own litigation costs today is seen as a distinctive feature of American legality, commonly dubbed "the American rule."[5] As the Supreme Court explained in its first invocation of the term, "the rule here has long been that attorney's fees are not ordinarily recoverable in the absence of a statute or enforceable contract," on the premise that "litigation is at best uncertain and one should not be penalized for merely defending or prosecuting a lawsuit, and that the poor might be unjustly discouraged from instituting actions to vindicate their rights if the penalty for losing included the fees of their opponents' counsel."[6]

The leading account on the history of the American rule by John Leubsdorf echoes the court's formulation. "In a sense, the American rule has no history," he writes. "As far back as one can trace, courts in this country have allowed winning litigants to recover their litigation costs from losers only to the extent prescribed by the legislature."[7] These formulations can be misleading, however, because rarely has there been

---

[4] *Ibid.*, 148–49.

[5] See Robert V. Percival & Geoffrey P. Miller, "The Role of Attorney Fee Shifting in Public Interest Litigation," 47 *Law & Contemporary Problems* 233 (1984); Thomas D. Rowe, Jr., "The Legal Theory of Attorney Fee Shifting: A Critical Overview," 1982 *Duke Law Journal* 651 (1982).

[6] Fleischmann Distilling Corp. v. Maier Brewing Co., 386 U.S. 714, 717–18 (1967). For the Supreme Court's modern explication of the rule, see Alyeska Pipeline Service Co. v. Wilderness Society, 421 U.S. 240, 247–71 (1975).

[7] John Leubsdorf, "Toward a History of the American Rule on Attorney Fee Recovery," 47 *Law & Contemporary Problems* 9 (1984), 9.

an "absence" of cost-shifting statutes in American history. Most US jurisdictions for most of the nineteenth century had comprehensive cost-shifting regulations, and for the majority of those jurisdictions, those regulations were in (or were superseded by) the Field Code. Although the code deregulated lawyer fees, it preserved the traditional logic and practices of cost-shifting, largely expanding the equitable practice of having lawyers petition the court for costs after each victorious motion or phase of litigation. That is, "loser pays" was a common feature of American litigation all through the nineteenth century, a feature affected but not abolished by the code's reformed regulations of attorney fees.

From a popular lawyer joke at the time, we can get a sense of how pervasive cost-shifting was, even during the supposed heyday of the American rule. A lawyer was called on to pray at a community picnic. "Not being experienced in such duty, he rose and attempted the Lord's prayer, and succeeded very well until he came to the passage 'Give us this day our daily bread,' when, from the force of habit, he immediately added, 'with costs.'" Cost-shifting was, almost until the time the Supreme Court declared it to be a foreign practice, the reflexive vocabulary of the American lawyer.[8]

What lawyers at the time called "the American rule" was not the regulation of cost-shifting but, actually, the Field Code's proclamation that lawyers were entitled to contract for and enforce their fee agreements instead of adhering to the English and civilian traditions of accepting fees as a mere gratuity.[9] In time, one American rule gave rise to the other as Field's system of unregulated fees put increasing strain on the code's justification for cost-shifting. Rather than deterring meritless or unscrupulous litigation practices through cost-shifting, Field and other elite lawyers turned increasingly to local bar associations to police attorney ethics. Lawyers could charge what clients were willing to pay, clients would pay only their own costs, and professional associations would oversee the fairness of it all. As Field's own experience with a bar association would show, however, attorney ethics under the code's free market system were regulated with a light touch indeed.

II

Despite the central importance of lawyer compensation to the structure of legal practice and professionalism, legal historians know surprisingly few details about how lawyers were paid in the nineteenth-century United States, beyond close studies of the legal careers of a few exceptional figures such as John Adams and Daniel Webster.[10]

[8] The earliest instance of the joke I have found is the *Bellows Falls Times* (Bellows Falls, Vt.), Nov. 13, 1868. The joke circulated widely in 1869 but continued to run around the code states as late as the 1890s. See, for instance, *Yorkville Enquirer* (Yorkville, S.C.), Oct. 31, 1896. See also New York Civil Practice Act (1921), §§ 1432 *et seq.* (detailing the rules for cost shifting, which was required in nearly every kind of action).

[9] See, for instance, H. Gordon McCouch, "Pierce v. Kyle: Agreement for Compensation Between Attorney and Client," 40 *American Law Register & Review* 751 (1892), 752.

[10] L. Kinvin Wroth & Hiller B. Zobel, eds., *Legal Papers of John Adams* (Harvard University Press, 1965), lxix–lxxii; Alfred Konefsky & Andrew King, eds., *The Papers of Daniel Webster: Legal Papers* (University Press of New England, 1982), 246–49. See also Justin Simard, "The Birth of a Legal Economy: Lawyers and the Development of American Commerce," 64 *Buffalo Law Review* 1059 (2016), 1108–11 (excavating some of the compensation practices of the elite Manhattan attorney Daniel Lord).

We can discern some patterns from contemporary case law—for instance, that the American colonies and states of the Early Republic did not enforce English rules against champerty (essentially, a payment by a lawyer to a client to instigate litigation) and therefore permitted a variety of contingency fee arrangements from early on in their history.[11] But although cases appear in every jurisdiction of lawyers suing former clients, undoubtedly, the choice to do so was not taken lightly, and lawyers appear to have been especially careful to keep from inviting negative precedents that would affect their fundamental ability to earn a living through the law.

Two dangers confronted a lawyer suing to collect a promised fee. The first was that the action might be disallowed entirely. Summarizing a civil tradition running back to republican Rome, Blackstone's *Commentaries* had asserted that "a counsel can maintain no action for his fees, which are given ... not as a salary or hire, but as a mere gratuity, which a counselor cannot demand without doing wrong to his reputation."[12] In 1790s England, Lord Kenyon emphasized in a series of opinions the rule that medical and legal professionals practiced for gratuitous honoraria, not compensation to which they had any colorable right in the law of property or contract.[13] Although a few states early after the Revolution repudiated the gratuitous fee rule by statute, New York was not one of them, and courts there would not confront the question of a lawyer's entitlement to compensation until the surprisingly late date of 1840.[14]

The second danger, particularly in New York, was that courts might recognize an entitlement to fees but then limit those fees to the amounts prescribed by statute. At the time, it was by no means clear whether "fees and costs" meant the same thing in the law. Generally speaking, "costs" were the charges that were shifted by the court from the loser to the winner of a litigation at its conclusion. These charges included actual costs, such as those for paper goods, and fees paid to clerks and to the winner's lawyer. That is, what made a charge a "cost"—even if it was nominally a "fee"—was that a loser at trial could be forced to pay it. Lawyers called these "taxable" charges.[15] Not all states provided for taxable costs and most certainly did not provide the depth and detail of regulation that New York gave to the subject. It was clear enough that New York's many limits on the charges per "folio" of attorney work product were meant to limit taxable costs imposed on an adversary, but were they also limits on what lawyers could receive from their own clients?

That was one popular interpretation in 1830s New York, even as lawyers attempted to find ways to charge beyond what the low limits of the Revised Statutes arguably allowed. Theodore Sedgwick chronicled both views in his explosive tract, *How Shall the Lawyers Be Paid?*, one of the clearer windows into how lawyer compensation may have worked in nineteenth-century New York. Sedgwick wrote that clients typically

[11] Peter Karsten, "Enabling the Poor to Have Their Day in Court: The Sanctioning of Contingency Fee Contracts, a History to 1940," 47 *DePaul Law Review* 231 (1998), 234–40.

[12] 3 *Blackstone's Commentaries* 28.

[13] See Chorley v. Bolcot, 4 T.R. 317 (1791); Turner v. Phillips, 1 Peake's N.P.C. 123 (1791); Fell v. Brown, 1 Peake's 96 (1791). See also Lipscome v. Holmes, 2 Camp. N.P. 441 (1810).

[14] At least, no New York court had confronted the question in a case subsequently reported on the record. See Stevens & Cagger v. Adams, 23 Wend. 57 (N.Y. Sup. Ct. 1840) (discussed below and collecting cases from other states that had abolished the English rule of gratuitous fees).

[15] See generally Walker Marshall, *A Practical Treatise on the Law of Costs in Suits and Proceedings in All the Courts of Common Law* (London, 2d ed., 1862).

conflated costs with fees. When clients discovered the amount of costs shifted at the end of the trial, "they make this same tariff the rule of compensation between the attorney and his client." If attorneys tried to charge more, some clients held "out all the terrors of the law," by which Sedgwick meant the threat that lawyers would have to litigate for their fees and possibly lose if the courts ruled their fees a gratuity. Other terrors could have been in store, as the Revised Statutes made it a misdemeanor for public officers to charge more than the fees "provided for by law."[16]

Nevertheless, Sedgwick acknowledged, lawyers did charge more than the folio fees made taxable by the Revised Statutes. These were called "counsel fees" in a technical attempt to evade the statute should the courts ever decide that prescribed costs were indeed the limits on what "attorneys" could charge their clients. The idea was that a "counselor" who advised on the law was a different sort of professional and provided a different service from an "attorney" who appeared in court, standing in their client's place. Just as America had not generally followed the English separation of barristers from solicitors, attorneys and counselors were often the same person in the same cases, but at least arguably the client was paying two different fees to two different professionals. Unlike the prescribed attorney fees in the Revised Statutes, which were low amounts tagged to the number of folios in a filing (generally 25 cents a folio at common law and 28 cents a folio in chancery), counsel fees could be charged by the task or for a total representation and could range up to hundreds of dollars. In time, counsel fees, too, were covered by statute. The Revised Statutes provided that counsel fees could be taxed to the other side, including a retaining fee between three and four dollars.[17] Sedgwick recognized that lawyers opened themselves to claims of extortion if they insisted on counsel fees over and above the statutory rates, "but in point of fact," he concluded, "no lawyer can or will work, and no client expects that he can or will work, without them."[18]

Sedgwick's admission about counsel fees is interesting because it undercut the two most prominent points in his tract: his depiction of lawyers as degraded artisans and his argument that fees had to be reformed to give lawyers the proper incentives in their craft practices. Sedgwick complained that "no other workman," such as the "physician, the sculptor, [or] the tailor ... is paid according to statute ... without any reference to the individual qualification of talent, industry or integrity" of his craftsmanship.[19] But of course, thanks to counsel fees, eminent lawyers could expect their compensation to rise with their talent and industry.

Sedgwick was on somewhat firmer ground in claiming that, counsel fees notwithstanding, lawyers had an incentive to "make all our papers prolix, and to create useless labor and expense" by litigating technical points of pleading that, if won, shifted costs their way independently of the ultimate merits of the suit. Counsel fees were flat

---

[16] Theodore Sedgwick, *How Shall the Lawyers Be Paid?* (1840), 5–6. *Revised Statutes of the State of New York* (1829), 2:518 § 7.

[17] *Revised Statutes of the State of New York* (1829), 2:621–32.

[18] Sedgwick, *How Shall the Lawyers Be Paid?*, 9–10. Daniel Lord reaped up to $15,000 a year in counsel fees, certainly well beyond the taxable rates of the Revised Statutes. See Simard, "The Birth of a Legal Economy," 1108–11.

[19] Sedgwick, *How Shall the Lawyers Be Paid?*, 7.

rates that clients usually agreed to before a representation began; they would be paid regardless. A lawyer could thus increase his compensation by inflating the page count of filings and then winning, if not the case, at least "interlocutory" motions arguing the finer points of pleading and practice. But in Sedgwick's telling, lawyers faced not a mere incentive but an "inevitable tendency," an "eternal and irresistible temptation of pecuniary interest."[20]

Instead of recognizing how counsel fees could mitigate the incentives to over-file, Sedgwick spoke as if the lawyers' practice was economically determined by the Revised Statutes. "There is no justice in condemning the conduct of the individual," he concluded. "It is the system that must be reprobated . . . for the sake of justice." Perhaps that was because Sedgwick was just such an "individual" who would stand condemned otherwise. As he admitted about pleading an unpaid debt, "Here I can tell the story in two lines, yet if I were to narrate it to a court, I should think it very unprofessional to put it in less than twelve hundred words, or thereabouts" which he claimed he and all other lawyers naturally had to do.[21]

Despite his complaint that lawyers were the only craftsmen to have their fees regulated by statute, Sedgwick's solution was to leave those regulations in place. It was a "rule of inherent justice" that losers in litigation had to pay the winner's costs, so public law had to ensure that only the true "expenses of the controversy" shifted, not necessarily the luxurious expenses of employing "counsel of . . . extraordinary ability." Sedgwick moreover believed that taxable costs might become the sole compensation of counselors—as clients were continually insisting—as long as the rates were raised to sufficiently compensate those who engaged in such "a toilsome, an honorable and an expensive science." Sedgwick suggested that fees should attach not to the folio of work product but to the amount of money demanded as a remedy, or a monetized equivalent of an equitable remedy, with interlocutory costs abolished and a penalty applied to those who dragged out delays. Doing so would ensure that "time is paid for instead of the services, and time represents with sufficient accuracy the services that are performed" by a lawyer.[22]

Sedgwick's brief tract set out a number of themes that became central to the Field Code reforms. As late as 1840, the relationship between lawyer fees and taxable costs remained uncertain in New York. Although lawyers had found a way to charge fees above the taxable rates in the Revised Statutes, it was uncertain whether courts would enforce the collection of such fees. Lawyers like Sedgwick commonly spoke as if the fee regulations were their only certain source of income, and Sedgwick cast lawyers as virtually powerless to act contrary to financial incentives, an idea that would have a long history in debates about professional ethics. By turning from fees based on page counts to an early form of the billable hour, Sedgwick showed how difficult it could be to measure and monetize the value of a lawyer's services with precision.

---

[20] Ibid., 7, 19.
[21] Ibid., 19. See also ibid., 7 ("There are checks upon this it is true, but they are inoperative compared to the sleepless interest of the pleader or practitioner.").
[22] Ibid., 10–11, 17.

III

At almost the same time Sedgwick was penning his tract, a New York court was finally confronting the question of whether lawyer fees were mere gratuities as a matter of state practice. Stevens & Cagger, a prominent firm known for its appellate practice, argued two appeals for a Mr. Adams in the New York Court for the Correction of Errors, New York's highest court of appeal at the time.[23] Adams agreed to pay $300 for Samuel Stevens to conduct the oral arguments. Stevens structured the transaction as a counsel fee: another lawyer acted as "attorney" and filed the actual appellate pleading, while Stevens conducted oral argument as "counsel." But when it came time to collect, Adams insisted on paying only the taxable cost of an oral argument under the Revised Statutes—a mere $3.75.[24]

The case was so perfectly structured to favor the lawyers that one wonders if it was not manufactured for that purpose. For one, the fact that there was an express agreement removed the thorny problem of how courts should value a lawyer's service if lawyers could indeed collect more than the taxable amount. The stark disparity—almost literally a hundredfold—between the agreed amount and the actual payment surely could not have endeared Adams as a defendant before the court. Perhaps most importantly, the fact that the case concerned an appellate argument helped get past what New York's highest court noted were "the plain words of a statute." The Revised Statutes prescribed fees for services rendered by "the officers" of a court. The last section of the Revised Statutes' fee regulations then provided that "no judge, justice, sheriff, or other officer whatsoever, . . . shall take or receive any other or greater fee or reward" than those declared in the preceding regulations. Although the Revised Statutes did not expressly define officers to include lawyers, Adams's counsel pointed out that many other statutes and cases had declared lawyers to be officers of the court. Both the trial court and the Court for the Correction of Errors recoiled from that reading, however. One escape hatch was the recognition that the Revised Statutes limited the taxable costs in an appeal "only to one counsel on each side, who shall have been actually employed and rendered the service charged." Many appellate lawyers worked in two-lawyer teams, as Stevens & Cagger did, so clearly, the trial court reasoned, the statute was designed to keep such firms from taxing double costs, not from keeping one advocate from being compensated entirely.[25]

From there, the court found a number of other reasons New York's fee regulations could not be treated as a limit on counsel fees. The trial court noted that the Revised Statutes not only prohibited officers from collecting higher than their prescribed fees, it actually criminalized the act, deeming it a misdemeanor. Given the prevalence of counsel fees, the court was sure the statute was not intended to criminalize the vast majority of the practicing bar. Further, the court reasoned that the limitations, directed as they were to sheriffs and "other" officers, "applies only to such officers as

---

[23] On the firm's prominence, see George Rogers Howell, *History of the County of Albany, N.Y., From 1609 to 1886* (W. W. Munsell & Co., 1886), 1:146–47.

[24] Stevens & Cagger v. Adams, 23 Wend. 57 (N.Y. Sup. Ct. 1840), 59.

[25] *Revised Statutes of the State of New York*, 2:650 §§ 4, 5, 7. Stevens & Cagger v. Adams, 26 Wend. 451 (N.Y. Court for the Correction of Errors 1841), 461 (Senator Gulian C. Verplanck, concurring); Adams, 23 Wend. at 57–58, 61–62.

are compellable on the requisition of parties to render the services appertaining to their offices, but has no application to counsel." The logic of that decision accords with the work of Nicholas Parrillo on the nineteenth-century shift from a fee- and bounty-based regulatory culture to one of salaried judges and bureaucrats.[26] Parrillo found one key stage of that development in changing notions about whom public officers served, and how they should serve. By mid-century, most states were moving away from a fee system that encouraged public officers to treat their clientele as a "customer class" and render extraordinary services for bonus fees and profits. Instead, officers were increasingly expected to expend their best efforts serving all of the public at once. Fee caps became a way not just to limit an officer's total compensation from ballooning to unseemly proportions but also to destroy any incentive for officers to cultivate a clientele and provide extraordinary services for extraordinary pay.[27]

The restrictiveness of New York's Revised Statutes seems to map onto these newly developed views about public service quite well, but as the *Adams* court recognized, the prescription of lawyer fees fit uneasily into this emerging world of public servants. The problem was that in the craft logic of practice, some lawyers would naturally exhibit, as Sedgwick argued, more "talent, industry or integrity" than others and would see their services in higher demand. Were the eminent leaders of the bar to be paid the same as neophytes? Could a lawyer who won a high-stakes case with technical sophistication and skill really receive no monetary reward for the effort? Here, the *Adams* court noted that the Revised Statutes were stricter than previous New York fee statutes in that the Revised Statutes prohibited "taking" or "receiving" a higher fee. Earlier laws had required that lawyers not "exact, demand, or ask" any greater fee. Under a strict reading of the Revised Statutes, even the English and European idea of fees as gratuities was out of bounds.[28] Ultimately that reading was too implausible for the court. The principle was too deeply ingrained that lawyers of disparate skill ought to have their superior craftsmanship specially remunerated.

Once past the difficulty of taking the statute literally, neither the trial court nor the court of appeal had much trouble deciding against the civilian rule of fees as gratuities and in favor of enforcing lawyers' contractual rights to their compensation. "The reward of the Roman advocates was influence with the people, from which grew political distinction and power," Stevens argued. But "with us, the reverse is the case . . . The relation between the counselor and his client is created by contract, and like all other contracts may be enforced in a court of law." Chancellor Reuben Walworth made the chain of reasoning even more explicit in the decision of the high court. "The [Roman] distinctions of patron and client . . . ceased in this state when slavery was abolished," he declared in the Court for the Correction of Errors. In the American Republic, no "business or profession . . . is so much more honorable than the business of other members of the community." Professional honoraria belonged to a world of status, where lower classes served the higher as slaves. But a republic of free and

---

[26] Adams, 23 Wend. at 59; Nicholas R. Parrillo, *Against the Profit Motive: The Salary Revolution in American Government, 1780–1940* (Yale University Press, 2013).

[27] Parrillo, *Against the Profit Motive*, 93–101.

[28] Sedgwick, *How Shall the Lawyers Be Paid?*, 7. See, for instance, *Laws of the State of New York* (Kent & Radcliffe 1802), 2:66.

equal men, according to Walworth's reasoning, was a world of contract.[29] Walworth affirmed that Stevens & Cagger could collect on their contract; no jurist on the court (comprising the entire state senate at the time) dissented.

The *Adams* case resolved that New York lawyers had the right to sue for their contractual fees, even when those fees vastly exceeded the prescribed rates of the Revised Statutes, which were now defined away as merely the taxable costs of litigation. The decision received an unsurprising amount of acclaim among the bar, but it left open the question of how to value a lawyer's services in the absence of the kind of express agreement Stevens had with Adams. The case that would decide that question was litigated on the very eve of the Field Code, in the spring of 1848, just before the code took effect in July. The case was something of the reverse of *Adams*. James T. Brady was the lead lawyer for the City of New York, called the "corporation counsel."[30] By 1848, the corporation counsel was a salaried position, at $2,000 annually, but Brady prosecuted a number of successful suits for the city in chancery that resulted in $8,511 of costs recovered to the city as victor. Brady brought an action essentially to add the taxed costs to his personal compensation, more than quadrupling his salary. Since his contract with the city did not mention taxable costs and did not explicitly limit his compensation to his salary, there was no express agreement as there had been in *Adams*.[31] Whereas Stevens had sought to escape the low statutory rates of common law appeals, Brady was seeking to reap a windfall from the high statutory rates of chancery.

The New York City judge and case reporter Lewis Sandford ruled that Brady was entitled to the costs. He interpreted Brady's salary to be his "counsel fee" only, so Sandford laid down the rule that lawyers who actually engaged in litigation as attorneys (or solicitors in chancery) were presumed to be owed *at least* the taxed costs that resulted.[32] Sandford relied on a recent assembly committee report, which reasoned that "custom and the decisions of the courts" had established that "the counsel is entitled to all, over the amount allowed by the fee bill, that competent witnesses may swear his services are worth." Competent witnesses were "lawyers, of course, just as a farmer, mechanic, or laborer, would in all cases be the best judge of the time, labor and value of any piece of work." In all, the committee figured, the value of a lawyer's services were to be proved case by case in court—by the client if it was argued the value was less than the taxable costs, by the lawyer if it was argued to be more. Responding to a petition to "equalize" lawyer fees by requiring all practitioners to collect no more than the prescribed rates, the committee refused to create "any legislation compelling the profession of law to submit to restrictions not placed upon any other class of

---

[29] Adams, 23 Wend. at 57; 26 Went. at 452. For an early formulation of the status-to-contract idea, see Henry Maine, *Ancient Law, Its Connection with the Early History of Society, and Its Relation to Modern Ideas* (1861), 170. On a recent assessment of Maine's thesis, see Katharina Isabel Schmidt, "Henry Maine's 'Modern Law': From Status to Contract and Back Again?" 65 *American Journal of Comparative Law* 145 (2017).

[30] The term reflected New York City's legal origins as a municipal corporation. See Hendrik Hartog, *Public Property and Private Power: The Corporation of the City of New York in American Law, 1730–1870* (Cornell University Press, 1989).

[31] Brady v. The City of New York, 1 Sand. 568 (N.Y. Super. Ct. 1848).

[32] Sandford was not terribly distressed at the windfall, which he blamed on the city's litigiousness and poorly drafted contracts. *Brady*, 1 Sand. at 592.

society," and to leave lawyers to "the great principles of supply and demand, and of the free moral and intellectual capacity of man, to regulate and control his ordinary business operations."[33]

Thus, by the time of the Field Code, New York lawyers had won an unequivocal right to their compensation, but unless they secured an express agreement from their clients or put on proof at trial, their services were presumed to be valued at the amount prescribed by the Revised Statutes as taxable costs, a presumption some clients and legislators were trying to make a hard and fast rule as late as 1845. Lawyers were still public officers of the court for many purposes, but new conceptual separations of public office from private gain had not attached to them as it had to sheriffs and other servants of judicial process. And despite both the law on the books and the law in practice declaring their freedom from the prescribed rates of the Revised Statutes, lawyers continued to present themselves as the only craft profession in the Republic that had its rates set by legislation.

IV

Of all the reforms undertaken by the 1848 code, fee reform received some of the lengthiest and certainly the most passionate commentary in the commissioner's report. The report effaced the steady work of the courts in the 1840s to secure lawyers' contractual rights to their compensation. Instead, one could easily come away from reading the First Report with the impression that the Field Code was the first time in world history that lawyers gained rights to their fees and freedom from legislative regulation. If the code was not so revolutionary in effect, it was at least unabashed in articulating the logic of its rules: "We cannot perceive the right of the state, to interfere between citizens, and fix the compensation which one of them shall receive from the other, for his skill or labor. . . . It is not [government's] province, to make bargains for the people or to regulate prices."[34]

Accordingly, the code welcomed lawyers to a world of free contract. Section 258 abolished "all statutes establishing or regulating the costs or fees of attorneys, solicitors and counsel in civil actions," as well as "all existing [court-created] rules and provisions of law, restricting or controlling the right of a party to agree with an attorney . . . for his compensation." It declared that "hereafter the measure of such compensation shall be left to the agreement, express or implied, of the parties."[35]

The report agreed with Sedgwick that the unreformed system "encourages the multiplication of processes, and . . . is not proportioned to the real labor performed." The commissioners' main objection was to the Revised Statute's many pages of tabulated folio fees. "One case requires little thought; and almost takes care of itself," the report explained. "Another requires a vast amount of study, careful preparation, and great

---

[33] *Journal of the Assembly of the State of New York* (1845), 837; Report of the Select Committee on Lawyer's Fees and Costs in Courts of Law, in *Documents of the Assembly of the State of New York*, 68th Sess., No. 227 (1845), 66:1–9.

[34] *First Report* (New York, 1848), 204–05.

[35] 1848 N.Y. Laws 544 § 258.

learning. These cannot be measured by any table of fees."[36] As Sedgwick had argued, it was chiefly the lawyer's time that was his product, not his paper filings.

However, the commissioners did not follow Sedgwick's recommendation to abolish interlocutory appeals or costs or to penalize parties who delayed a suit by raising objections to form and practice. Instead, they believed the code had already eliminated those tactics by instituting fact pleading. The commissioners expected that under their system, technical objections would be few and readily resolved because of the comprehensive clarity of their code; and by holding parties to plead just the facts, verified by oath, they expected judges could cut to the essence of a claim without getting held up by form or "sham defenses." Fee reform was to fit hand in glove with pleading reform. By eliminating fees based on the folio of work product, any incentive to inflate pleadings with fictions and redundancies for the sake of compensation would be removed, and lawyers could make the best use of their valuable time by quickly and succinctly stating only the necessary and relevant facts.[37]

As in the tracts and reports from earlier in the 1840s, the commissioners' report emphasized the equality of the legal profession with other crafts and professions, despite the fact that lawyers already had the freedom to charge what their clients were willing to pay. The state "may prescribe the salary of the clergyman, or the fee of the physician, with as much reason as the compensation of the attorney," they wrote—which was to say, without reason at all. They reiterated the republican dictum that equality under contract was "the only just rule."[38]

The *Adams* court had to wrestle with the question of whether lawyers were public officers for purposes of the Revised Statutes' fee regulations; having abolished the Revised Statutes, the practice commission went further and declared lawyers to be members of a privatized profession. After comparing lawyers to physicians and clergy, the report anticipated the objection "that the attorney is an officer, admitted by the courts, and therefore, in a position different from the others." But it answered simply "that he is not a public officer, chosen to perform public duties." The lawyer, in this account, was "a private agent" admitted to the court "for private purposes, and on behalf of private persons."[39]

The First Report's account of the lawyer as a purely private actor, engaged in the "freedom of industry" alike with any other citizen, stood in some tension with the 1850 Final Report's recommendations for bar admissions. By extending the domain of "procedure" over attorney admissions, the commissioners faced an awkward choice. Compromises with and between the anti-lawyers had left the 1846 constitution ambiguous. It provided that "any male citizen, of the age of twenty-one years, of good moral character, and who possesses the requisite qualifications of learning and ability, shall be entitled to admission to practice in all the courts of this state," but it placed the clause in the same section that regulated the judiciary's appointment powers, implicitly leaving it to the courts to decide who would be admitted to the bar.[40] When a later

---

[36] *First Report* (New York, 1848), 205–06.
[37] *First Report* (New York, 1848), 70–73; See also *Final Report* (New York, 1850), 2:274–75; *Report of the Commissioners Appointed to Prepare a Code of Practice for the Commonwealth of Kentucky* (1850), ii.
[38] *First Report* (New York, 1848), 205–06.
[39] *Ibid.*, 205.
[40] *Ibid.*; N.Y. Const. of 1846, art. 6 § 8. On the anti-lawyers, see chapter 3.

legislature passed a bill permitting anyone to appear as "a special attorney" on behalf of any litigant, the courts struck the provision down as unconstitutional. The commissioners stated that they did not want to insert themselves into the constitutional debate and were "not expressing an opinion of our own," yet they codified the rule that only the courts could admit attorneys to the bar.[41]

Further, the Final Report gave an extensive policy justification for maintaining the prerogative of courts to control access to the bar. Because "the profession of a lawyer is essential to society," the report argued, "its character and honor are public interests." To show why, the commissioners sketched a straight line from the character of the bar to the health of the republic. Because "the judicial department is recruited from the legal profession," the "character of the judges" necessarily reflected "the character of the lawyers. Made at the bar; their moral characters there take their complexion. To degrade the bar therefore leads directly and inevitably to the degradation of the bench." Therefore, "anywhere a corrupt legal profession is to be found it is found in the midst of a corrupt and corrupting people." So despite the First Report's declaration of "the right of the citizen to engage, at will, in any honest calling" and to "receive such reward as he can agree for it," the Final Report came down on the side of regulated barriers to the bar.[42]

In defending this choice, the commissioners took special exception to an idea recently propounded by the leading English legal reformer Lord Henry Brougham, who had declared that "an advocate, in the discharge of his duty, knows but one person in all the world, and that person is his client. To save that client by all means and expedients, and at all hazards and costs to other persons ... is his first and only duty." Brougham privileged the lawyer's private duty to his client above his public duties to the state, arguing that "in performing this duty [a lawyer] must not regard the alarm, the torments, the destruction which he may bring upon others ... though it should be his unhappy fate to involve his country in confusion."[43] Such a view, the New York commissioners wrote, "betrays not only an unsound heart, but an unsound understanding." A lawyer's duty "as a moral being requires him to advise justice," the report explained, and "his position as a legal adviser does not exempt him from the moral duties which bind other men." A lawyer, that is, was in some ultimate sense a public officer, making public scrutiny and regulation of his profession necessary.[44]

To hold all these views together, Field departed from Sedgwick on the determinative power of compensation. Sedgwick had written of economic incentives as "irresistible" to the lawyer. He therefore advocated their continued public regulation as long as the incentives were realigned away from technicality and overfiling. Although Field shared many of Sedgwick's concerns, he did not share the language of incentives. Field regretted that the Revised Statutes compensated "mere drudgery," but that is how he spoke of it: as inadequate compensation rather than as a meaningful incentive. Field proposed that lawyers could make any amount of compensation for which

---

[41] See *Final Report* (New York, 1850), 202; Devries v. McKoan, 1 Code Rep. 6 (N.Y. Sup. Ct. 1848).

[42] *Final Report* (New York, 1850), 206.

[43] *The Trial at Large of Her Majesty, Caroline Amelia Elizabeth, Queen of Great Britain; in the House of Lords, on Charges of Adulterous Intercourse* (1821), 2:3.

[44] *Final Report* (New York, 1850), 207–08.

they contracted, and doing so need not impugn their professional integrity. A paid advocate could, he surmised, "in civil cases present defenses recognized and provided by law, although he may himself disapprove of the principle and policy of the law. But here the advocate should stop." The "law and all its machinery" were means to the end of justice, and no lawyer "in his zeal for the means" could forget the ends.[45]

V

Critics then and now revisited Field's words in light of the Erie Wars. Field's advocacy for Gould seemed to follow precisely the outline Brougham had drawn up, using every means for the private advantage of the client while "involv[ing] his country in confusion." Field's Final Report had declared that "to assent to the bad scheme of an unjust client, is to become equally guilty with him, and the two are as much conspirators to effect a wrong, as if they had originally concocted a plan of iniquity with the view of sharing in the plunder." What then of Judge Darwin Smith's findings that Gould and his "associates" had engaged in a pervasive conspiracy to fraudulently wrest control of the Albany & Susquehanna for private gain? After Darwin's decision but before Field's successful appeal, the New York Times rebuked Field without naming him. Gould should have found a lawyer at the "Tombs bar," meaning the disreputable low-class lawyers who hung around the Manhattan jail. Instead, he opened his pocketbook to "a leading jurist and law-reformer of the State . . . and, instead of being shown the door, found no difficulty in employing him in his worst cases." The paper went on to describe Jim Fisk's visit to Henry Ward Beecher's Sunday school to pluck Field's partner Thomas G. Shearman from the pew.[46]

Field ignored the Times, a long-time political antagonist of his. But when Samuel Bowles, editor of the Springfield Republican, reprinted and commented on some of the New York material, Field lashed out. "What gives you, sitting in private and writing anonymously, authority to render 'judgment' upon me," Field wrote to Bowles at the end of 1870. Field then invoked the two central ideals of his code: public facts and private practitioners. "I am not disputing your right, as a collector of news, to publish any facts concerning anybody," Field wrote, "but you certainly have no greater right to publish your opinions respecting the character or conduct of a private person, than you would have to publish them to his face in a private company." Bowles countered that although a lawyer might be responsible to private clients, he also "takes a responsibility to the public, on which it may arraign, dispute and judge him." An exchange of twenty letters followed between Field, Bowles, and Field's son Dudley, now a junior partner in Field's firm.[47]

[45] Ibid., 207–08. It is also possible, though unlikely, that different commissioners wrote different commentaries on attorney compensation and bar admissions. An editor of Field's collected writings claimed Field's authorship only of the paean to professional duties, A. P. Sprague, ed., Speeches, Arguments, and Miscellaneous Papers of David Dudley Field (D. Appleton, 1884), 1:296–302, but given the public criticism of Field's fees at the time his writings were being collected (see below), one should not make too much of the exclusion of the privatization passages from Field's collected works.

[46] Final Report (New York, 1850), 207. New York Times, Dec. 5, 1870.

[47] David Dudley Field & Samuel Bowles, The Lawyer and His Clients (1871), 5, 15, on file with the New-York Historical Society. The contours of the debate are covered in Michael Schudson, "Public, Private,

The lengthy correspondence never strayed far from the opening point: what did it mean for Bowles, or any member of the public, to "judge" Field's actions as a lawyer? From where did that authority arise, and what standards applied in such a judgment? Conversely, what gave Field the power to dodge public inquiry into his practices, and how could a lawyer really hold himself aloof from a fraudulent conspiracy joined by his chief clients? Field did not mind taking up the latter question. Suppose his clients were bad men; what then? Should only "saints . . . have a monopoly of lawsuits"? Here Field picked up the old Whig language of "the independence of the bar." If Gould was wicked, so much more did he need skilled counsel to protect what rights he legitimately had in a democratic society. "I speak for [my clients] in the courts of the country, stand between them and popular clamor, just as I would stand between them and power, if they were menaced by power of any kind, monarchical or republican," Field huffed. On this account, the lawyer checked arbitrary power—of both king and mob—by adhering to professional standards that the public, as outsiders, could not judge.[48]

In a final editorial, Bowles recognized that Field was attempting to make the lawyer's moral code coterminous with practical expertise. As long as the lawyer's techniques were within the letter of the law, Field would be immune to public scrutiny. That argument might be sound, Bowles argued, if the law were an exact science, in accord with divine law in every way, but not "if human imperfection is to be recognized in law and lawyers." Nevertheless, Bowles conceded the ground to Field's technical argument. Disclaiming any knowledge of New York law or legal practice, Bowles admitted that as far as he knew, "You have sinned against no statute; I will not undertake to say, even, that you have violated any prescript of the code professional." That was all Field needed to claim victory. Whoever may have swayed public sympathies, Field was adamant that a knowledge of craft was necessary to understand what Field had done, much less to judge it. Bowles, by admitting his ignorance of craft, had divested himself of jurisdiction to judge.[49]

Recognizing Field's maneuver, New York City lawyer Francis Barlow, known among the bar as General Barlow for his decorated Civil War service, took up Field's offer to condemn him for his manipulation and abuse of technical procedures. In a series of long letter-articles to the *Tribune*, Barlow recounted the Albany & Susquehanna raid day by day, highlighting the unusual and dubious procedures Field and Shearman had deployed, including the service of summons by telegraph; the last-minute arrest of Ramsey; and the many *ex parte* orders obtained from Judge George Barnard, including one obtained by rushing Barnard back to New York at midnight from his mother's home in Poughkeepsie. Barlow especially sought to demonstrate Field's orchestration of Ramsey's arrest, noting that Gould had paid Field $10,000 to be onsite in Albany the day of the shareholder's meeting.[50]

and Professional Lives: The Correspondence of David Dudley Field and Samuel Bowles," 21 *American Journal of Legal History* 191 (1977).

[48] Field & Bowles, *The Lawyer and His Client*, 6, 8–9.
[49] *Springfield Republican* (Springfield, Ill.), Jan. 30, 1871; Field & Bowles, *The Lawyer and His Client*, 10.
[50] Francis C. Barlow, *Facts for Mr. David Dudley Field* (1871), 12. For the details of these maneuvers, see chapter 9.

Called upon to justify himself on the actual technicalities involved in his representation, Field drowned out Barlow's essays with his counterresponse. Field not only published massive editorials himself, he also commissioned another lawyer, George Ticknor Curtis, to write a volume-length account of the A&S litigation that highlighted the nefarious tactics of the Ramsey side and sympathetically explained and exonerated Field's conduct. Though Curtis presented his account as that of a neutral observer, Field's brother Cyrus reimbursed him $3,500 for his efforts.[51] As Field gathered other letters from colleagues attesting to his integrity and professionalism, critics responded that the letters were no doubt "worth what was paid for them." Field specifically denied receiving any special fee for appearing in Albany at the disputed election, which he explained as a matter of pure happenstance. In response, Barlow produced the receipt from the Erie Railroad's accounts.[52]

But just as Bowles had done, Barlow made a tactical blunder at the close of his correspondence with Field. Barlow first appealed to the reading public to see "whether Mr. Field has made a fair, candid and responsive answer to the charges which I have brought against him." Then perhaps concerned that the morality of Field's practices was being buried under technical arguments, Barlow closed with the promise to "take care that his conduct is investigated before a body of men who cannot be deceived by small tricks and petty evasions." Field leaped at the offer, interpreting it as a pledge to take the matter before the nascent Association of the Bar of the City of New York (ABCNY). "After all, the professional tribunal is the true one" that should judge him, Field wrote. It had been founded "for the mutual advantage of its members, and as well to protect them from unfounded attacks as to maintain the purity and dignity of the profession."[53] Whether or not Field was winning on the merits, he was certainly winning on procedure. Once again he shifted jurisdiction, this time from the court of public opinion to a private bar association.

The ABCNY had been founded in early 1870, during the midst of the Field-Bowles correspondence. Its leaders were a mix of municipal reformers as well as lawyers who had directly participated in the A&S litigation on one side or the other. Although they founded the association in direct response to the public outcry over Field's lawyering, its most recent historian notes that "it seems incredible, but the first three [official] histories of the Association . . . never mention Field by name." Bar associations were nothing new by the late nineteenth century, but many early bar associations had gone defunct around mid-century. The New York City association became the first of many modern bar associations, and, like New York's code, it provided a model that others could emulate.[54]

---

[51] George Ticknor Curtis, *An Inquiry into the Albany & Susquehanna Railroad Litigations of 1869 and Mr. David Dudley Field's Connection Therewith* (1871). Curtis reported only that he was "requested by an intimate friend of Mr. David Dudley Field, to examine the proceedings." *Ibid.*, 2. Thomas Shearman recorded Cyrus Field as the source of the payment in his memoirs, noting that Field & Shearman eventually reimbursed Cyrus. Shearman also noted that Jeremiah S. Black "wrote one or two telling articles in our favor," leaving it unclear whether Black, too, was commissioned to write in Field's defense. Memoirs of Thomas G. Shearman, 1:188, Papers of Thomas G. Shearman, Shearman & Sterling Law Library.

[52] *New York Herald*, Dec. 11, 1872; Barlow, *Facts for Mr. David Dudley Field*, 41–42, 54–55.

[53] Barlow, *Facts for Mr. David Dudley Field*, 68–69.

[54] George Martin, *Causes and Conflicts: The Centennial History of the Association of the Bar of the City of New York* (Fordham University Press, 1997), vi; John A. Matzko, "'The Best Men of the Bar': The Founding

The founding documents and speeches of the ABCNY were shot through with appeals to public interest and public service, both implicit and explicit rebukes of Field's privatized ideal of the lawyer. The call to organize the association, circulating in the papers in December 1869, advertised that the association would "sustain the profession in its proper position in the community, and thereby enable it, in many ways, to promote the interests of the public." Refusing to be cowed by his colleagues and former associates, Field made sure to be one of the earliest subscribers to the call. At the first meeting, George Templeton Strong counted two hundred lawyers. "The decent part of the profession was well represented . . ., and among them was the virtuous D. D. Field," he wryly commented. With Field in the room, his opponent from the Opdyke litigation William M. Evarts used the opening discussion to ensure all understood that Field's censurable activities made the association necessary:

> Why, Mr. Chairman, you and I can remember perfectly well (and we are not very old
> men), when, for a lawyer to come out from the chambers of a Judge with an *ex parte*
> writ that he could not defend before the public, before the profession and before the
> Court, would have occasioned the same sentiment toward him as if he came out with
> a stolen pocket-book.[55]

It was clear enough to Evarts that Field could not defend his injunctions to the public. Now he would have to defend them to the profession.

More implicit barbs came from Samuel Tilden, then in the midst of his multipronged political and legal offensives against Boss Tweed. Tilden's remarks opposed the public-mindedness of the bar to private fee-seeking. In the midst of breaking up municipal "rings" of all sorts, Tilden declared that he did "not desire to see the Bar combined, except for two objects. The one is to elevate itself . . .; the other object is for the common and public good." But "if the Bar is to become merely a method of making money, making it in the most convenient way possible, but making it at all hazards, then the Bar is degraded." Tilden closed by linking his concern for public-mindedness over fees in a peculiar fusion with New York imperialism. If New York was to remain "the commercial and monetary capital of this continent," it had to "establish an elevated character for its Bar, and a reputation throughout the whole country for its purity in the administration of justice." Tilden then reiterated that the commercial wealth of the state depended on its bar not pursuing its fees at all costs.[56] To gain the world for New York, its lawyers had to keep their souls.

Field maneuvered as expertly in the bar association as he had in the courts. Within the first year of the organization, he gave the "committee on amendment of the law" its first assignment by referring to them proposed code amendments that restricted the equitable appointment of receivers. The association crafted the amendments into

---

of the American Bar Association," in Gerard Gawalt, ed., *The New High Priests: Lawyers in Post-Civil War America* (Greenwood Press, 1984), 76, 79.

[55] *Report of Proceedings of the Bar Association of the City of New York* (1870), 28, Papers of the Association of the Bar of the City of New York. *Diary of George Templeton Strong*, ed. Allan Nevins (Macmillan, 1952), 4:273; .

[56] *Report of Proceedings of the Bar Association of the City of New York*, 20–21.

a bill and sent it to the legislature, where no action was taken. Field not only got to retain his title as the great law reformer, but he also scored the implicit point that his actions had been legally sanctioned at the time and, given the legislature's indifference, were legal still. Field was also active in amending the association's bylaws to establish a grievance committee to hear members' professional complaints about one another. Crucially, the bylaws provided that any proceedings would remain private until the committee ordered publication.[57]

Sometime after Barlow pledged to have Field investigated by the profession, the grievance committee instituted proceedings on Field's litigation practices but never issued a report. By September 1872, some of the members had organized a special committee to investigate lawyers implicated by the recent state impeachment proceedings against Judge Barnard. Field, of course, was one such lawyer, given all the *ex parte* orders granted by Barnard in the A&S litigation. But as with the grievance committee, the special committee delayed reporting, continually asking for more time.[58]

Finally, Field professed to have had enough, and during a December meeting of the association, he gave one of the most remarkable speeches of his career. "I mean to meet this now and here," he declared, demanding that the association print the original records from the grievance committee, "every word [of which] was taken in shorthand and remains of record." Once again, Field's main complaint was that his private practices were being submitted to public judgment. Despite the duly conducted secret investigation of the grievance committee, "these raiders have chosen to make their charges publicly before the whole body in a way to have them reported and published to the world without giving the member assailed an opportunity to defend himself." Field reminded his colleagues their professional duties were "judicial in their character." Judgment on Field's career was pending, but the "raiders" were seeking to stir up "public opinion" to influence it.[59]

Field then unleashed his scorn on those he considered to be the chief "raiders," Barlow above all. Field claimed that the grievance committee would not publish its records because Field had revealed "evidence of disreputable practices by most of [his opponents] and a clue to further evidence." He then named some of them. Barlow he charged with public embezzlement while attorney general. Joshua Van Cott, he claimed, had forged a bond with his dead brother's signature, and down the list Field went. But more terrible in Field's eyes than the lawyers' corruption was their practical incompetence. Field went on at length detailing Barlow's blunders in a particular suit before the Marine Court. He concluded that all his opponents "have so little knowledge or experience of difficult lawsuits that they do not know whether an order is right or wrong." Given their lack of technical sophistication, how could they possibly judge Field's actions? "I might as well talk to a child as to [Barlow] about a course of action in a difficult case," Field sneered. "Would you have me justify my action to such a man—so incompetent, so ignorant?"[60]

---

[57] Martin, *Causes and Conflicts*, 56–58; *Charter and Constitution of the Association of the Bar of the City of New York* (1873), 16.
[58] Martin, *Causes and Conflicts*, 57–60, 91–92.
[59] *New York Herald*, Dec. 11, 1872.
[60] *Ibid.*

If the Chicago journalist could not judge Field's professional conduct, nor could the New York Attorney General, nor could the gathered bar of New York City, who could? Field landed on the only practical answer left available: the courts. Litigations from the A&S and Erie suits were still playing out. Let them run their course, Field reasoned. "Must we have two suits of practitioners—one for the courts and another for this association?" In time, judges would pronounce on the litigation tactics of the lawyers, as Judge Smith had done in the A&S suit. And in time those opinions would be reviewed. (Smith had been reversed on Field's technical jury argument by the time of the grievance proceedings before the association.)[61] Implicitly, Field was once again arguing what he had urged from the first with Bowles: whatever was found legal by the courts was moral as a matter of practice.

The association undertook no further proceedings on Field, and he was never censured. In the next decade, Field was elevated to the presidency of the American Bar Association. The "public conscience" Samuel Bowles had argued for had been transfigured into a professional conscience of the organized bar. But in reality, the professional conscience was little different from the private conscience that had exonerated Field all along. A historian of the city bar association notes that all records from the grievance proceedings and from the special committee have gone missing from the archives.[62] Perhaps Field did indeed introduce evidence about his unscrupulous colleagues. A project to privatize the bar that began with the deregulation of fees ended in the utterly private proceedings of a bar association founded with the express purpose of furthering the public interest. Whatever the association's professional judgment of Field and his accusers, it remains private to this day.

VI

While Field expected the abolition of fee limitations to work a revolution in the bar, his views on taxable costs were quite traditional. The code made it "a general rule" that "the losing party, ought . . . to pay for the expense of the litigation." The reason was the conventional one. "He has caused a loss to his adversary unjustly, and should indemnify him for it." As with many departments of practice under the original code, the paradigm given was of debt collection. "The debtor who refuses to pay, ought to make the creditor whole," the report reasoned, not just for the unpaid debt but for the legal hassles of trying to collect it. Both the reasoning and the example were featured in Theodore Sedgwick's tract a decade earlier, which had declared, "It is intolerable that a person should without the payment of a just demand, drive the plaintiff to bring suit, . . . keep him at bay for years, and at last when he is finally compelled to discharge the demand, be released on mere payment" of the debt. Justice demanded that the defendant, and by extension any losing litigant, make good "the onerous expenses which his folly or injustice has occasioned."[63]

[61] *Ibid.* Regarding the sequence of the A&S litigation, see chapter 9.
[62] Martin, *Causes and Conflicts*, 91, 100 n.5.
[63] *First Report* (New York, 1848), 206–7. Sedgwick, *How Shall the Lawyers Be Paid?*, 10.

On this ground, the code disagreed that critics of the loser-pays rule were future-oriented progressives. By the 1840s, a host of lawyers and laymen alike had criticized cost-shifting rules and especially the theory that cost-shifting corrected the "injustice" of a litigant filing or defending a suit ultimately adjudged to be without merit. In practice, critics charged, suits were concluded on technical points of procedure so often that characterizing one litigant as virtuous and the other as unjust was a mistake. "If a promissory note was mis-recited by a word, a non-suit was the result," complained Field's co-commissioner Arphaxad Loomis. Could it really be said the loser of the suit was an unjust actor, inflicting needless harm on his adversary? No, critics answered. Losing a suit was more a misfortune than an act of malice. Like the rain falling on the just and unjust, one account observed, lawyers "take fees from both plaintiff and defendant in collecting debts" without any real regard for fault. Taxable costs were more a measure of "skill in law jugglery," than the justice of the cause.[64] For these reasons, a number of states abandoned or severely scaled back English cost-shifting rules, most prominently Massachusetts and Pennsylvania. And some, like Iowa, declined to import the code's cost-shifting provisions.[65]

Nevertheless, Field insisted on cost-shifting. The leading account on cost-shifting in America generally credits the Field Code for launching states toward the "American rule" where each party bore its own litigation costs, including attorney's fees, but it calls the code itself a "paradox" and "incoheren[t]" for permitting free contract between clients and their attorneys but then imposing nominal charges on litigants who had no contract to compensate the other side's attorney.[66] Yet jurists at the time recognized that "free contract" could coexist with fee shifting. Field adopted the conventional logic that the winner deserved—had earned—compensation from the loser because his code was supposed to make it so. By eliminating "fiction and evasion" in the pleadings, Field argued the code system would finally bring about the world the treatises had for so long described in theory, where to proceed on a losing claim was tantamount to acting in bad faith.[67]

Keeping a system of cost-shifting required commissioners to face again the question of how to value a lawyer's services. They agreed that clients' freedom to contract with their lawyers did not include the freedom to stick their opponents with the total bill, but they did not proceed to offer a valuation. Instead, the one task they left to the legislature in reporting the code was to fill in the blanks for the costs that would follow

---

[64] Arphaxad Loomis, *Historic Sketch of the New York System of Law Reform in Practice and Pleadings* (1879), 6; John W. Pitts, *Eleven Numbers Against Lawyer Legislation and Fees at the Bar* (1843), 29, 53. See also Hiram P. Hastings, *An Essay on Constitutional Reform* (1846), 26; Michael Hoffman, "Letter on Reforms Necessary in the Body of Law, in the Written Pleadings, and in the Practice of the Courts" (Mar. 21, 1846), in Thomas Prentice Kettle, ed., *Constitutional Reform in a Series of Articles Contributed to the Democratic Review* (1846), 68.

[65] Sedgwick, who agreed with Field's traditional views of cost-shifting, said of Massachusetts and Pennsylvania that they left righteous suitors "to pay for having had the pleasure of a law suit." Sedgwick, *How Shall the Lawyers Be Paid?*, 10. *Report of the Code Commissioners to the Eighth General Assembly of the State of Iowa* (1859), 381, note to § 845.

[66] Leubsdorf, "Towards a History of the American Rule on Attorney Fee Recovery," 17–21.

[67] 1848 N.Y. Laws 544 § 258. *First Report* (New York, 1848), 206–07; A Letter from D. D. Field, Esq. of New York, on Law Reform, to Representative John O'Sullivan in *Documents of the Assembly of the State of New York*, 65th Sess., No. 81 (1842), 5:56; David Dudley Field, *What Shall Be Done with the Practice of the Courts? Shall It Be Wholly Reformed?* (1847), 33–37.

each phase of litigation, offering only the lame advice that any amount selected would be too little to compensate for the lawyer's time in some cases, and too much in others. The 1848 legislature decided seven dollars would be awarded for litigation that terminated before trial, twenty dollars after trial, and fifty dollars after appeal. The commissioners reasoned that their phased system approximated the costs "generally upon the difficulty of the case, and the amount at risk." It also served to encourage litigation to settle rather than continue, unlike the system that rewarded the multiplication of filings.[68]

The other major question was how to shift costs. Judicial discretion over awarding costs had been about the only distinction between the Revised Statutes' provisions for costs at common law, where shifting happened automatically at the end of a litigation, and in equity, where lawyers had to petition for costs and courts had the discretion to grant or deny the petition. Once again, the commissioners punted. Costs shifted automatically in cases involving claims for money damages or the recovery of real property; costs shifted in all other cases at the discretion of the court. Cost-shifting thus became yet another ground on which the commissioners inadvertently preserved the traditional distinction between law and equity.[69]

The Field Code did not spawn the "American rule" in 1848, but over time, the commissioners' attempt to preserve cost-shifting did indeed fall victim to their abolition of regulated lawyer fees in three ways. First, the Field Code made clear that taxable costs were untethered from the value of a lawyer's services. In the theory propounded by the code reports, taxable costs were based on penalizing an unjust actor for prolonging litigation, not on an approximation of the value of services rendered. Before the code, New York judges had articulated a legal standard that made the taxable costs the presumed value of the attorney's fee on an implied contract until the parties proved otherwise. After the code, the presumption disappeared, and lawyers had to prove their implied contracts by deposing their brethren to testify about the market rates of their services.[70]

Second, critics persisted to believe that a loser of a litigation was, as one Wisconsin assemblyman put it, an "unfortunate victim." The 1852 Wisconsin legislature was considering New York's code. An assembly committee advised against the code's cost-shifting provisions, or having any cost-shifting at all. It argued that, given the imperfections of human justice, most losing litigants were more likely to be "a defeated though honest party" rather than users of "chicane and trickery." It likened fee bills to the indiscriminate destruction of a natural disaster, and it encouraged tribunals "to be lenient in general, even towards the unsuccessful party; for such is the [courts'] imperfection, that could a change of venue be taken to the court of Heaven, who knows how many of their decisions would be reversed."[71]

---

[68] 1848 N.Y. Laws 545 § 262; *First Report* (New York, 1848), 205–7; Field, Letter to Representative John O'Sullivan, 56.

[69] *Revised Statutes of the State of New York*, ch. 10, tit. 1, §§ 2, 3; 1848 N.Y. Laws 544–45 §§ 259–61.

[70] Brady v. The City of New York, 1 Sand. at 568. See Benjamin Vaughan Abbott and Austin Abbott, *Digest of New York Statutes and Reports* (1884), 387–89.

[71] Report of the Committee Relating to Fees to Be Allowed the Party Recovering Judgment, in *Journal of the Assembly of the State of Wisconsin* (1852), 344–52. See also Fleischmann Distilling Corp., 386 U.S. at 718.

Even the Field commentary from 1850 recognized that not all losing litigants were knowingly inflicting injustice on their opponents. In the same commentary disputing Lord Brougham's ideal of the zealous advocate, Field wrote that, even in a codified system, "the law, moreover, is not so clear and precise, but that it may be mistaken or perverted. A strong mind at the bar, and a weak one on the bench, lead often to erroneous judgments. . . . Before ordinary tribunals, more depends on the advocate than is generally imagined."[72] Field's rebuke of Brougham not only undercut his reasons for cost-shifting, it also showed why the view of a losing litigant as misfortunate rather than malicious could not but be amplified under Field's fee system. If so much depended not on merit but on counsel, and if magnates like Gould and the corporations they controlled could pay exorbitant rates for the "best" counsel, what was the point of penalizing losers? Of course, the haves were going to come out ahead.[73] Such was the logic that underlay much of the uproar when Field agreed to represent William "Boss" Tweed after his corruption prosecutions. Few articulated any legal objection to Field's argument—Tweed had been sentenced to eleven years in prison under a statute that provided for a maximum penalty of only one year. What both lawyers and laymen alike found galling was that Tweed, freshly convicted of embezzling $6 million from the city, could nevertheless pay high rates to a lawyer who would inevitably find some technical defect with the prosecution.[74] By deregulating compensation, the Field Code only solidified the objection that litigation came down to who could afford the best lawyer, undercutting the reason to shift those costs to the loser.

Lastly, the Field Code spurred momentum to alternative fee arrangements. As Peter Karsten has shown, contingency fees were widely used in early American practice, but lawyers employing that fee structure often ran a risk of seeing their fees ultimately disapproved by courts wishing to hold them to English champerty rules. By abolishing all former statutes and court rules regulating attorneys' fees, the Field Code and its imitators unmistakeably endorsed the contingency fee and other arrangements that permitted lawyers to bring claims on behalf of those who could not pay upfront.[75] Courts thereafter might set aside contingency fees that were "unconscionable" in their rate or manner of negotiation, but the principle itself had to be allowed under a code that had wiped the slate clean of former regulations. "Many a poor man with a just claim would find himself unable to prosecute his rights, could he make no arrangement to pay his advocate out of the proceeds of his suit," a judge explained in the early code state of Missouri.[76]

By the 1920s, academic commentators cited the prevalence of suits by poor litigants under contingency fees and other arrangements as a further reason that cost-shifting would be inappropriate in the general run of cases. Here, the "misfortune" of losing a litigation coincided with the larger misfortune of poverty and all its constraints

---

[72] *Final Report* (New York, 1850), 207–8.

[73] Marc Galanter, "Why the 'Haves' Come Out Ahead: Speculations on the Limits of Legal Change," 9 *Law & Society Review* 95 (1974).

[74] See Renée Lettow Lerner, "Thomas Nast's Crusading Legal Cartoons," 2001 *Green Bag Almanac 2d* 59 (2001), 63–75; Kenneth D. Ackerman, *Boss Tweed: The Rise and Fall of the Corrupt Pol Who Conceived the Soul of Modern New York*, (Carroll & Graf Pub., 2005), 239–71; Martin, *Causes and Conflicts*, 104–19.

[75] Karsten, "Enabling the Poor to Have Their Day in Court," 234–42.

[76] Duke v. Harper, 2 Mo. App. 1, 10–11 (1876).

on pursuing rights claims in the courts.[77] The gradual elimination of cost-shifting ensured that lawyers could offer their services pro bono without running the risk of a disastrous cost award should they prove unsuccessful. Thus, an attorney like Louis Brandeis, in the heyday of his litigations as "the People's Lawyer," could explain his pro bono representations as a "luxury cost" of time rather than money. "Some men buy diamonds and rare works of art; others delight in automobiles and yachts," Brandeis famously pronounced. "My luxury is to invest my surplus effort . . . to the pleasure of taking up a problem and solving, or helping to solve, it for the people without receiving any compensation."[78] That, too, was a fee arrangement made possible by the code.

VII

By eliminating the restrictions placed on lawyers' fees, the code made possible both David Dudley Field's adventures in corporate lawyering as well as Louis Brandeis's public service for no fee at all. That, of course, does not make the value of the code's policies a historical wash. Robert W. Gordon has frequently argued that the lionization of figures like Brandeis is one of the American legal profession's central problems. By celebrating the occasional public-minded attorney, lawyers and legal historians normalize the far higher percentage of the profession that confined itself to private gain.[79] By acknowledging that the Field Code made both paths possible, we should not lose sight of which path its own author ultimately chose.

Field's argument that the procedural judgment of the courts set the outer boundaries on professional ethics became something of a de facto rule. Field's partner, Thomas Shearman, invoked it shortly after proceedings wound down in the bar association. When a new slate of directors finally ousted Gould from the presidency of the Erie Railroad, the new head counsel, Samuel L. M. Barlow (no relation to Francis), dismissed Shearman. Sherman's "only subsisting obligation" was that he "not act against the Company, in matters in which [he had] special knowledge."[80] As Gould's personal counsel, Shearman protested that he would go on representing Gould against his former client, the Erie Railroad. He assured Barlow that he had "consulted some professional friends, entirely disinterested, all of whom agree with my view of duties," but he also offered to submit the question to a presiding appellate or trial court judge "and to abide by the decision of either Judge."[81]

---

[77] See Arthur L. Goodhart, "Costs," 38 *Yale Law Journal* 849 (1929).

[78] Quoted in Melvin Urofsky, *A Mind of One Piece: Brandeis and American Reform* (Charles Scribner's Sons, 1971), 36.

[79] See, for instance, Robert W. Gordon, "Law and Lawyers in the Age of Enterprise," in Gerald Geison, ed., *Professions and Professional Ideology in America* (University of North Carolina Press, 1983), 70–110; Robert W. Gordon, "'The Ideal and the Actual in the Law': Fantasies and Practices of New York City Lawyers, 1880–1910," in Gawalt, *The New High Priests*, 51–74; Robert W. Gordon, "The Independence of Lawyers," 68 *Boston University Law Review* 1 (1988); Robert W. Gordon, "The Lawyer Citizen: A Myth with Some Basis in Reality," 50 *William & Mary Law Review* 1169 (2009).

[80] Samuel L. M. Barlow, *Correspondence with Thomas G. Shearman* (1872), on file with the St. Louis Mercantile Library at the University of Missouri–St. Louis.

[81] *Ibid*, 3, 6–7.

Barlow wrote back with a tone both amused and annoyed by turns. "I, too, have consulted disinterested professional friends, who agree with me," he opened. Barlow refused to submit to any judge "a hypothetical case, which might not, probably would not, contain the facts necessary for their proper determination." Instead, he appealed to Shearman's fee, reminding him that he and Field had collectively taken "out of the funds of the company over $300,000, and apart from any strict rule of professional etiquette, this fact alone would in the judgment of the company be a sufficient reason why you should take no part" in further litigation.[82]

"The amount of fees received by me cannot possibly affect the questions under consideration," Shearman shot back, arguing that in all the time he spent on the railroad's affairs, he had never "received more than a fair and just compensation." Once Barlow had turned down the offer of submitting a "hypothetical" case, Shearman followed Field's rule and threatened to meet him in a real one.[83] Shearman did indeed continue as Gould's chief counsel in subsequent litigation against Erie, a further episode in Gould's career as colorful as any other.[84] Because Gould ultimately settled with the Erie, in-court appearances were few, and Barlow had no chance to lodge an objection to Shearman's representation. (Shearman tried to provoke Barlow into seeking an *ex parte* injunction, but Barlow seems not to have taken the bait.[85]) Now considered a textbook violation of professional canons, Shearman's representation against his former client was essentially sanctioned by silence—silence of the court procedurally and silence of the bar professionally. Deregulation in its many forms had become an American rule.

[82] *Ibid.*, 6–8.

[83] *Ibid.*, 7, 10–11.

[84] In short, Gould had embezzled some $12 million from the Erie Railroad. To pay it back, he colluded with the new president of the railroad to announce their amicable settlement but then publicly broke off relations several times, each time buying Erie stock as it dropped and selling it as it rose. See Trumbull White, *The Wizard of Wall Street and His Wealth, or The Deeds of Jay Gould* (John C. Yorston & Co., 1892), 79–87; *Proceedings of the Special Committee on Railroads (Hepburn Commission)*, 5 vols. (Evening Post, 1879). For evidence of Shearman's continuing representation of Gould, see *New York Tribune*, Nov. 25, 1872; *New York Herald*, Dec. 6, 1872; *New York Herald*, Dec. 20, 1872; *New York Herald*, Dec. 21, 1872.

[85] Barlow, *Correspondence with Thomas G. Shearman*, 10–11.

Conclusion

Even if, in all present events, men did act justly and legislate justly, still
there would remain traces of the ancient order of things.
—William Whewell, *The Elements of Morality* (1845)

I

"In the law schools the study of procedure in the past has been pushed into a corner
as dull, uninteresting, and unimportant," acknowledged Charles E. Clark, dean of the
Yale Law School and chief codifier of federal procedure in 1938. Clark spoke from
experience in observing that students showed little interest in the development of
practice, a study that could only guarantee they would learn about obsolete devices irrelevant to their future careers. But as much as Clark considered himself an apostle of
legal modernity, he thought his students' boredom with procedural history a serious
mistake. "It is most necessary for the understanding of what has gone on in the past,"
he concluded, "not to speak of the social need of knowing what effective law administration is." Clark felt so confident in the modern reforms he advocated in part because
he believed history vindicated their effectiveness.[1]

An older generation of legal historians certainly did not think procedure boring,
but neither did they share Clark's optimism that the study of procedure's history
would extol the genius of modern legal practice with its emphasis on substantive
rights and procedural remedies. The nineteenth-century English legal historian
Frederic Maitland posited that the fundamental contradiction navigated by legal
practices is that any human system of justice must commit at the outset to tolerating
harms that lie without a remedy. Time is too short; the facts are too complicated and
abundant for every case—perhaps even for any case—to be judged aright. So, how
did people abide this contradiction in the past? Where did they, and where must we,
let the gaps lie in a system of justice? For a startling number of cases, as Maitland
recognized, the answer to those questions could not be found in a substantive rule
of rights but in the procedures that culled the facts and the time into a manageable
if artificial problem that was then capable of resolution. It "may seem true enough
to us," Maitland lectured at the end of his career, "that in order of logic Right comes
before Remedy. There ought to be a remedy for every wrong." But legal history was
not logic. Political struggle and compromise gradually legitimated certain forms of
proceeding in the public courts. From then on, Maitland concluded, "the forms of

[1] Charles E. Clark, "The Handmaid of Justice," 23 *Washington University Law Quarterly* 297 (1938), 304.

Law's Machinery. Kellen R. Funk, Oxford University Press. © Kellen R. Funk 2025. DOI: 10.1093/9780197543962.003.0012

action are given; the causes of action must be deduced therefrom." Rights that could not be made to fit the compromised and limited forms of vindication available were, in a practical sense, no rights at all.[2]

The preeminent historian of law and society in the United States, J. Willard Hurst, thought something similar. Although Hurst and Maitland wrote well before the historical turn toward cultural anthropology, both had a keenly developed sense, anticipating future literature, that practice was not reducible to abstract propositions on a page but inhered in embodied rituals and performances. Because practice is embodied, it is subject to real constraints, above all the constraint that human life is not infinite. As Hurst put it, "something that modern enthusiasts . . . tend to overlook" is that "people are limited. They don't have endless stocks of energy to spend on anything. This is part of history."[3] That is especially so where inherited practices have already navigated and addressed, if uneasily and temporarily, where to spend the time and resources available to a system of public justice.

The historians' assessments echoed those of code skeptics from the mid-nineteenth century. In a survey of legislative and equitable theory, the English polymath William Whewell warned law reformers in the 1840s that "the influence of the past Facts of History upon Law, though constantly wearing out, can never be quite obliterated." Even if through sudden, perfect insight, "men did act justly and legislate justly, still there would remain traces of the ancient order of things."[4] On that reasoning, lawyers in the anglophile state of Maryland became one of the rare codification commissions that did not attempt to borrow Field's text, opting instead for a few rules that encouraged reforms toward factual pleadings without specifying details of oath-taking, examination, and trial. They explained that the old system's defects were "not inherent in the system, but result from the same cause as the defects in all other human inventions—the inability of man to make anything perfect."[5]

If that sounds almost theological, perhaps it is.[6] Since the third century, church historians have been fond of affirming the maxim that "the rule of prayer is the rule of faith." Among other things, the maxim helps to remind them that Christianity, like most religions, is first embodied in practices before it is articulated in doctrine— beliefs begin as a matter of worship before they become a matter of creeds. Ultimately, the maxim affirms that practice is, quite apart from formal theology, both a source of

[2] See F. W. Maitland, *Equity and the Forms of Action at Common Law: Two Courses of Lectures*, ed. A. H. Chaytor & W. J. Whittaker (Cambridge University Press, 1910), 300, 304–05; Frederick Pollock & Frederic W. Maitland, *The History of English Law Before the Time of Edward I* (Cambridge University Press, 2d ed., 1898), 561–62.

[3] Hendrik Hartog, "Snakes in Ireland: A Conversation with Willard Hurst," 12 *Law & History Review* 370, 375 (1994).

[4] William Whewell, *The Elements of Morality* (1845), 1:326–27.

[5] *The First Report of the Commissioners to Revise the Rules of Practice and Pleadings* (Maryland, 1855), 91–92.

[6] Hurst credited the writings of Reinhold Niebuhr for inspiring and structuring his thoughts about human limitations within legal history. See Hartog, "Snakes in Ireland," 375–76. My account has a sympathetic affinity, less with Niebuhr than with the source of Niebuhr's theology in Augustine. See Oliver O'Donovan, *The Ways of Judgment* (Eerdmans, 2008); Charles T. Mathewes, *A Theology of Public Life* (Cambridge University Press, 2008). The problem of limitations as framed here also owes much to R.A. Markus, *Saeculum: History and Society in the Theology of St. Augustine* (Cambridge University Press, 1988).

knowledge and a way of knowing. What is religious belief? Look at how the religious pray, and what they pray for.[7]

So, too, in Anglo-American legality, law as a system of substantive rules followed well behind law as a set of practices whose logic became articulable only partially and gradually. What is procedure? It is both something to know about the law and a way of knowing law. The legal term "pleading" itself originated in religious supplication, and across the Anglo-American legal tradition, a primary component of pleading was the "prayer for relief."[8] In procedure, the rule of prayer is literally the rule of law. What is the law? Look at how the lawyers pray, and what they pray for.

With unrelenting faith in positivism, the word without the practice, the codifiers of procedure frequently overlooked this crucial dimension to knowing—and changing—the law. Like theology students sneering at the people in the pews, the codifiers genuinely believed that procedure could easily be cabined off and subordinated to a legal theory of rights and correlative duties, and practitioners would fall in line.[9] But the entanglement of procedure with practice and of practice with the actual workings of the law made procedure at once more capacious than the codifiers expected and exceedingly difficult to change on the ground. In the Anglo-American tradition of practice, pleadings inhered so closely to remedies that both became defined as procedural in the codes. Yet remedies hewed so closely to substantive rules that procedure expanded far beyond the boundaries within which the codifiers' political arguments promised it would stay confined. At the same time, the prayers of the lawyers could not remain formless. Over the run of cases, categories of remedies seemed to elicit certain kinds of prayers naturally. So, the forms of action and the distinction between law and equity lived on in the lawyer's prayers, even as they were abolished from the law books. Ultimately, the law books were not the only, or even the primary, way of knowing the law.

II

Much of this study has been devoted to showing how surprisingly little legal practice in the United States changed in the century after the Field Code. Early modern, even medieval, structures of thought and habit continued to tether civil remedies to writ-based reasoning, Euro-American Christian theology, and a conceptual distinction between generalized law and case-specific equity. These structures persisted in

[7] On the maxim in the history of Christian doctrine, see Jaroslav Pelikan, *The Christian Tradition, Vol. 3: The Growth of Medieval Theology (600–1300)* (Chicago University Press, 1978), 66–80.
[8] The Federal Rules followed the Field Code in exchanging "prayer" for "demand." See 1848 N.Y. Laws 521, § 120; Fed. Rule of Civ. Proc. 8 (1938). But the habitual expression continues in use in the case reports, as any Westlaw search can show, and it was often used by the New York code commissioners in their commentary. See, for instance, *Final Report* (New York, 1850), 2:8–9.
[9] For two contending theories of how legal rights could operate apart from the procedures that vindicated them, see John Norton Pomeroy, *Remedies and Remedial Rights by the Civil Action, According to the Reformed American Procedure* (Little, Brown, 1876); and Wesley Hohfeld, "Some Fundamental Legal Conceptions as Applied in Judicial Reasoning," 23 *Yale Law Journal* 16 (1913). Clark expressed himself partial to Hohfeld's account. Charles E. Clark, "The Code Cause of Action," 33 *Yale Law Journal* 817, 828 (1924).

the face of the code's explicit abolitions not simply as a matter of resistance from the profession. Rather, they inhered in the code's foundational assumptions, as a matter of background practical logic. Even the code's more enduring changes—to pretrial discovery, lawyers' fees, and cost-shifting—all sprang unexpectedly from the codifiers' adherence to traditional dogmas about needless "fishing expeditions" for evidence and the justice of losers paying for a litigation. And when the codifiers sought to elevate their system to a uniform practice in the national courts, they continued to carry these latent habits and modes of thought with them.

But in time—and in the law schools—code practice eventually became the bedrock of subterranean habits and modes of thought. Students now learn about Charles Clark's standards for "notice pleading" against the background of nineteenth-century "fact pleading" rather than of the common law writs. Code pleading is the original fact, the before-time, while the writs recede from view. Fusion of law and equity is spoken of as accomplished fact, the only debate being whether it was accomplished in the Federal Rules or before them, a debate that has to assume the codifiers' definitions of equity as mere procedure and remedy even to be legible. Most significantly, the pedagogy of code procedure has shrunk the domain of "pleading" so that scholars today conceive of it only as a narrow subdepartment of "procedure" rather than the all-encompassing structure of legality nineteenth-century pleading contained.[10]

As with the accounts of Hurst, Maitland, and Whewell, there is an undercurrent of tragedy to the legal modernization wrought by the codifiers. Even if the machinery of procedure could not totally remake the garden of legal practice in the industrial image the codifiers preferred, still their major innovations managed to shift much of what had been under public control in legal practice—the investigation of facts and their deployment in civil remedies, the regulation of lawyers' compensation and ethics, the very framing of disputes and their possible resolutions—into the hands of private parties and their mercenary legal counselors. While this movement sharpened the legal tools at the disposal of civil rights crusaders like Albion Tourgée and Louis Brandeis, the diminishment of equity and the abolition of chancery ensured that no public body remained to educate or police the law's conscience. Tourgée and Brandeis stand out precisely because of the individual choices they made with their careers, no real thanks to the legal system in which they trained.

As many of the code's innovations and heterodoxies became an assumed part of the fabric of legality itself, they became endowed with a much weightier pedigree that obscured their novelty. This is not just another way of saying the substance-procedure distinction is overblown. That critique has been a project of academic proceduralists since at least the 1960s when the Supreme Court began a more rigorous and often futile policing of the substance-procedure divide.[11] But much of that critical literature

---

[10] See, e.g., Kevin M. Clermont, "Three Myths about Twombly-Iqbal," 45 *Wake Forest Law Review* 1340 (2010); Stephen N. Subrin, "How Equity Conquered Common Law: The Federal Rules of Civil Procedure in Historical Perspective," 135 *University of Pennsylvania Law Review* 909 (1987); Mary Brigid McManamon, "The History of the Civil Procedure Course: A Study in Evolving Pedagogy," 30 *Arizona State Law Journal* 827 (1998).

[11] The critical commentary largely arose after Hanna v. Plumer, 380 U.S. 460 (1965). As John Hart Ely recalled, "We were all brought up on sophisticated talk about the fluidity of the line between substance and procedure." John Hart Ely, "The Irrepressible Myth of Erie," 87 *Harvard Law Review* 693 (1974). See also

supposes an origin of the substance-procedure distinction in the deep past of classical legal thought established, if not by the time of Bentham and Blackstone, then at least around the time of the American Revolution.[12] The Field Code's history reveals that the substance-procedure distinction was a far more recent creation, less a hoary ancient myth being exploded by the critics than a recently completed project of the critics' own law professors. The substance-procedure divide was largely the creation of political arguments in the 1840s, whose reach expanded during Reconstruction, but which gained almost no purchase in actual legal practice until several decades after the promulgation of the Field Code and no widespread purchase in the law schools until after the promulgation of Clark's code in 1938.

This history as presented thus agrees with the recent work of Amalia Kessler in arguing for the novelty of the substance-procedure divide and for the prominence of the Field Code in this history. But whereas Kessler describes adversarialism as the essential feature of American procedural culture, this study has avoided picking one element of procedure as essential. It has, instead, followed the advice of ritual theorists to "circumambulate" around legal practice and ritual to map it from multiple vantage points, exploring arguments from the authors of the codes of procedure, attending to the complaints from both professional and lay receivers of the codes, and reconstructing—to whatever limited degree—the practices and practical logics that took shape under the codes.[13]

What these materials show is that from 1828 to 1938, procedure's most enduring feature was its surprising (given the law's discursive obsession with precision) ability to evade precise definition. It was, to some, the "adjective," the "machinery," the "handmaid" of the law: a tool to apply substantive rules without drawing attention to itself. To others, procedure was indeed form, but the very form of justice itself, methods of vindicating rights that were inseparable from vindication per se. Procedure as machinery became the dominant paradigm of the period, providing an effective political argument for severing procedure from "the law" that had to be respected and preserved in its observance from time immemorial. Machinery could be improved and experimented on, tinkered with, but only by the expert machinists. Thus procedure as machinery was politically double-edged. It was both safe *for* democracy—it could be legislated in an age that distrusted legislation—but it also had to be saved *from* democracy, entrusted to expert lawyers to keep the overall mechanism running.

Jay Tidmarsh, "Procedure, Substance, and *Erie*," 64 *Vanderbilt Law Review* 877 (2011) (reviewing the post-Ely literature).

[12] See, e.g., William E. Nelson, *Americanization of the Common Law: The Impact of Legal Change on Massachusetts Society, 1760–1830* (Georgia University Press, rev. ed., 1994), 69–88; Charles Donahue Jr., "'The Hypostasis of a Prophecy': Legal Realism and Legal History," in Matthew Dyson & David Ibbetson, eds., *Law and Legal Process: Substantive Law and Procedure in English Legal History* (Cambridge University Press, 2013), 12–16.

[13] Amalia D. Kessler, *Inventing American Exceptionalism: The Origins of Adversarial Legal Culture, 1800–1877* (Yale University Press, 2017), 10–12. Ronald L. Grimes, *The Craft of Ritual Studies* (Oxford University Press, 2014), 73–75.

The eventual institutionalization of procedure inthe law schools highlights the centrality of lawyers and their practices in establishing the field's metes and bounds. From the time that Christopher Columbus Langdell introduced sequenced courses in American legal education, law schools have usually required students to take procedure as a first-year course. This requirement stands in stark contrast to English and continental legal education, where procedure is either omitted from the curriculum entirely or held off until postgraduate apprenticeships.[14] In part, this requirement demonstrates the continuing constitutive power of procedure in American legal thought, but it also shows the prominence of the lawyer-as-litigator paradigm that arose in the years after trial lawyers promulgated the code that redefined American legal practice. The code imagined its primary audience to be the practitioners using it rather than the judges administering it. So, too, did the earliest civil procedure courses. Langdell defined civil procedure in his inaugural course as comprising five topics: "1) getting the defendant into court, 2) pleading, 3) trial, 4) judgment, and 5) execution of the court's decision," a sequence geared to teaching students litigation tactics well after most elite law practice had become law-office lawyering.[15]

In 1938, the year the Federal Rules went into force, Charles Clark expressed regret at how intensely the procedure curriculum focused on litigators navigating a single case. In his view, procedure pedagogy needed to incorporate more of the history of procedure as a system with many component parts that might interact in unexpected ways. As in his codification efforts generally, Clark was turning his pedagogy to focus on judges. Clark worried that too many judges, trained to think like litigators with their horizons limited to the case before them, were making "expedient" rules against technicality, creating disastrously more technical practices elsewhere in the system.[16]

Although Clark directed his efforts toward the judiciary, his insistence that legal history held one key to "the social need of knowing what effective law administration is" helps to illuminate one final consequence of the lawyers' code that governed American practice from 1848 to 1938. Sean Farhang and others have argued that an exceptional feature of the United States is that what other countries regulate through robust administrative regimes, the United States shunts off into private litigation for enforcement. America has become a "litigation state" that governs more through private litigation than through public bureaucracy. Farhang begins with the Civil Rights Act of 1964 as the "foundation" of his story.[17] What the history of the Field Code suggests is that this foundation is far broader, far deeper, and for that reason far more intractable, running back to the time that Americans put litigators in charge of writing

---

[14] See Robert Stevens, *Law School: Legal Education in America from the 1850s to the 1980s* (University of North Carolina Press, 1983), 41.

[15] On law's constituting consciousness, see Robert W. Gordon, "Critical Legal Histories," 36 *Stanford Law Review* 57 (1984); Susanna L. Blumenthal, "Of Mandarins, Legal Consciousness, and the Cultural Turn in US Legal History," 37 *Law & Social Inquiry* 167 (2012). On the turn toward office lawyering, see John H. Langbein et al., *History of the Common Law: The Development of Anglo-American Legal Institutions* (Aspen, 2009), 1021–28.

[16] Clark, "Handmaid of Justice," 304.

[17] Sean Farhang, *The Litigation State: Public Regulation and Private Lawsuits in the U.S.* (Princeton University Press, 2010). See also Martha Minow, "Public and Private Partnerships: Accounting for the New Religion," 116 *Harvard Law Review* 1229 (2003); Trevor W. Morrison, "Private Attorneys General and the First Amendment," 103 *Michigan Law Review* 589 (2005).

the rules of litigation. By the time of the 1964 Act, more than a century of structured habits of thought made it seem possible and even desirable for Congress to turn to the "Litigation State" as the best way to vindicate civil rights. The long reign of the lawyers' code gave the United States a deep tradition of relying on litigators as a primary mode of civil governance, a tradition that itself would not be easily effaced, even with the changing of the codes.

Index

For the benefit of digital users, indexed terms that span two pages (e.g., 52–53) may, on occasion, appear on only one of those pages.

Note: Figures are indicated by an italic *f* following the page number.

www.ingramcontent.com/pod-product-compliance
Lightning Source LLC
Chambersburg PA
CBHW071325150126
38291CB00004BB/49